English Language as Hydra

LINGUISTIC DIVERSITY AND LANGUAGE RIGHTS

Series Editor: Dr Tove Skutnabb-Kangas, *Åbo Akademi University, Finland*

Consulting Advisory Board:
François Grin, *Université de Genève, Switzerland*
Kathleen Heugh, *University of South Australia, Adelaide*
Miklós Kontra, *Linguistics Institute, Hungarian Academy of Sciences, Budapest*
Robert Phillipson, *Copenhagen Business School, Denmark*

The series seeks to promote multilingualism as a resource, the maintenance of linguistic diversity, and development of and respect for linguistic human rights worldwide through the dissemination of theoretical and empirical research. The series encourages interdisciplinary approaches to language policy, drawing on sociolinguistics, education, sociology, economics, human rights law, political science, as well as anthropology, psychology, and applied language studies.

Full details of all the books in this series and of all our other publications can be found on http://www.multilingual-matters.com, or by writing to Multilingual Matters, St Nicholas House, 31-34 High Street, Bristol BS1 2AW, UK.

English Language as Hydra

Its Impacts on Non-English Language Cultures

Edited by

Vaughan Rapatahana and Pauline Bunce

MULTILINGUAL MATTERS
Bristol • Buffalo • Toronto

Library of Congress Cataloging in Publication Data
A catalog record for this book is available from the Library of Congress.
English Language as Hydra: Its Impacts on Non-English Language Cultures/Edited by
Vaughan Rapatahana and Pauline Bunce.
Linguistic Diversity and Language Rights: 9
Includes bibliographical references and index.
1. Languages in contact--Pacific Area. 2. Pacific area--Languages. 3. English language--
Foreign coutries. 4. English language--Influence on foreign languages. 5. English
language--Political aspects. 6. English language--Social aspects. I. Rapatahana, Vaughan.
II. Bunce, Pauline.
P130.52.P16E54 2012
306.44–dc23 2012009135

British Library Cataloguing in Publication Data
A catalogue entry for this book is available from the British Library.

ISBN-13: 978-1-84769-750-9 (hbk)
ISBN-13: 978-1-84769-749-3 (pbk)

Multilingual Matters
UK: St Nicholas House, 31-34 High Street, Bristol BS1 2AW, UK.
USA: UTP, 2250 Military Road, Tonawanda, NY 14150, USA.
Canada: UTP, 5201 Dufferin Street, North York, Ontario M3H 5T8, Canada.

The policy of Multilingual Matters/Channel View Publications is to use papers that are
natural, renewable and recyclable products, made from wood grown in sustainable
forests. In the manufacturing process of our books, and to further support our policy,
preference is given to printers that have FSC and PEFC Chain of Custody certification.
The FSC and/or PEFC logos will appear on those books where full certification has been
granted to the printer concerned.

Typeset by The Charlesworth Group.

Contents

Contributors

Lalaine F. Yanilla Aquino

Associate Professor, Department of English and Comparative Literature, College of Arts and Letters, University of the Philippines, Diliman, Quezon City, Philippines.

I am Lalaine F. Yanilla Aquino, a Filipino and a Professor of English Studies. I have lived in the Philippines all my life, and I am a product of the Bilingual Education Policy (BEP), in which English is one of the two media of instruction. My first language is Tagalog – the language of my father, who is from Tayabas, Quezon. I can comprehend a little Aklanon – the language of my mother, who is from Aklan and a little Kapampangan – the language of my husband, who is from Pampanga. At home, my husband and I use Filipino in conversing with our children, who are all studying now still under the BEP. My very own linguistic history and experience is a good example of the multilingual country that is the Philippines. Though I have nothing against English being used as a medium of instruction in Philippine schools, I strongly believe that Filipino children have the right to learn the basic concepts and skills (and literacy, as well) *initially* in their mother tongue. The Philippine government owes it to the Filipino people to give its support, in terms of providing instructional materials, teacher training and other necessary infrastructures, as a recognition of this right.

Xavier Barker

Member of the Nauru Language Committee, ex-Director (Acting), University of the South Pacific campus, Republic of Nauru.

My name is Xavier Barker. I am both an Australian and a Nauruan, who has been educated in Australia and the Pacific. I am currently studying Language Endangerment at Monash University in Melbourne. The shift to English began with my English-teaching father and it has been completed in my children's generation, who do not know any Nauruan. As both a member of the most recent manifestation of the Nauru Language Committee and as a Campus Coordinator of the University of the South Pacific in Nauru, I have not advocated removing English from Nauruan schools, but I have strongly encouraged the maintenance of Nauruan, alongside the learning of English as a second language. It is important, whilst forging a unique identity for Nauru, which recognizes our past, that we remain pragmatic enough to recognize that English is the most widely spoken Pacific language.

Jeanie Bell

Lecturer, Centre for Australian Languages and Linguistics, Batchelor Institute for Indigenous Tertiary Education, Northern Territory, Australia.

My first language is English, and I identify as a member of the Jagera and Dulingbara clan groups of south-east Queensland, Australia. I use words from a range of Aboriginal languages mixed in with English on a daily basis. I also regularly speak a variety of Aboriginal English. As an adult, I have studied and learnt, from recorded documentation, my heritage language Badjala from Gari (Fraser Island), and while I technically know this language and its grammar, I only use it in limited situations.

Pauline Bunce

English Teacher, Perth, Western Australia; Former teacher-in-charge, secondary classes, Cocos (Keeling) Islands.

My name is Pauline, and I am an out-of-touch Australian with British roots. While Australia is undoubtedly my home, there are often times when I do not necessarily feel 'at home' in the country. I have lived more than half of my life outside mainstream Australian society, in various parts of Asia and in Asian parts of Australia. As a Malay speaker, there are times when I feel almost Asian, and there are other times when I struggle to be fully Australian. I'm now teaching English to adolescent new arrivals and refugees in an Australian school. It isn't always easy to live in intersecting worlds, but I wouldn't want it any other way.

Tamati Cairns

Kaumatua, Te iwi o Tuhoe, Aotearoa-New Zealand

My parents, Erina Rotarangi nee Cairns (Tuhoe) and Karaihe Rotarangi (Ngati Raukawa), gave birth to their fourth of 15 siblings (that's me) in Mokai, known as Te Pae o Raukawa, on the floor of my grandmother Teiria and grandfather Rotarangi Hamilton's lounge. Mokai is approximately 30 kilometres north-west of Taupo. By virtue of a decision made by my Grandmother Teiria, I was given to my *Koroua* and *Kuia* and raised in the small Māori community of Ruatahuna, in the heart of the Te Urewera homeland. Ruatahuna is surrounded by an aged native forest, known today as the Urewera National Park, and is a valley that supports a small farming and hunting community. Ruatahuna is referred to as the heartland of the Tuhoe people, *te Kohanga o Tuhoe*.

The adoption had been via Māori custom and tradition, *Matua Whangai*, and also what appears to be a pragmatic solution to a *whanau* birth explosion. There must have been other reasons that only the *Kuia* and the *Koroua* and the wisdom of 'Old' would know, and the foresight of such a decision, for whatever the reason. I shall be forever in their debt, having been blessed with the fluency of *te Reo Māori me oona tikanga* and the privilege of growing up in such a special place, Ruatahuna.

Eugene Chen Eoyang

Professor Emeritus of Comparative Literature and of East Asian Languages and Cultures, Indiana University, USA; Chair Professor Emeritus of English, Humanities and Translation and former Director of General Education, Lingnan University, Hong Kong.

My name is Eugene Chen Eoyang, and I learned English at an English Grammar School as a Chinese refugee in Karachi (India, as it was then) under the Raj. At the age of seven, my mother brought us to America, where I quickly converted my English-accented English to something like Brooklynese. Appalled by this decline in the 'quality' of my English, my father put me in another school, where the teaching (and the accent) was better. I graduated from Harvard with a degree in English and earned an MA in English Literature at Columbia University. After a six-year stint in publishing (Doubleday), I pursued a PhD in comparative literature at Indiana University, where I taught, on and off, for 33 years. In 1996, I moved to Hong Kong, where I taught in the English Department at Lingnam University for 12 years (serving as head from 2006–2007) – with the exception of three semesters' leave, when I returned to teach at Indiana University. From 2000–2008, I also directed the General Education Programme at Lingnan. I think my Dad (who died in 1987) might have been pleased that I was admitted in 2001 as a fellow of the British Royal Society for the encouragement of the arts, merchandise and commerce.

Noor Azam Haji-Othman

Director of the Language Centre, Universiti Brunei Darussalam, Brunei Darussalam.

My name is Noor Azam from Brunei, a former British protectorate on the north-east coast of Borneo Island. I am of mixed heritage, with a Dusun father and Tutong mother, whose traditional languages I speak, in addition to Malay and English. I was born and bred in Tutong District, a harmonious blend of ethnic cultures, faiths and languages, all of which can be heard overlapping each other around a coffee table in town. I have always spoken English as far as I can remember, it being a widespread language in Brunei both outside and in the schools. At 17, I left for studies in the UK, returning for good only after about 14 years. Ironically, it took a British university, French language courses and an inspiring German professor to make me realise the immense significance of going back to my roots and conducting research on the traditional languages and cultures of Brunei.

Sandra Land

Lecturer, Centre for Adult Education, University of KwaZulu-Natal, Republic of South Africa.

My name is Sandra, and I am a white South African. I am confident that I am South African, but beyond that I fall into doubt – am I an African? I think I might be, but my black African compatriots tend to laugh at me if I say so, even though I can make the statement fluently in isiZulu. Although three of my grandparents were British, I do not think I am British, and British officials assure me emphatically that my ancestry gives me no claim to British nationality. Rejected then by both Africa and Europe, I am, continentally speaking, an outcast, a vagrant relic of colonialism, but, as someone who undoubtedly benefited by being born on the privileged side of apartheid, perhaps a worthy heir to the rejection inflicted on so many by successive governments of my twisted, torn, beloved country.

Anne-Marie de Mejía

Associate Professor, Centre for Research and Teacher Education, Universidad de los Andes, Bogota, Colombia.

I was born and grew up in London. However, I always suspected that I would one day live 'abroad'. Since I was young, I had always heard about the importance of our French ancestors, and although I had a very English upbringing, I increasingly wanted to explore other parts of the world, very different to the UK. Through a series of circumstances, I ended up in Colombia, where I live and work and feel very much at home, having now spent more of my adult life here than in the UK. My children, on the other hand, though largely brought up in Colombia, have travelled in the other direction – to the UK.

Muhammad Haji Salleh

Malaysia's National Laureate, Professor School of Humanities and Senior Fellow, Centre for Policy Research and International Studies, Universiti Sains Malaysia, Penanag.

Though I was born in Malaysia and began to speak Malay early, the progress of my schooling was a gradual emptying of the Malay and replacing it with the colonial language. For a long time, I was alienated from the tongue of Malaysia and functioned reasonably well in English. However, after being culturally and linguistically lost in Europe, the US and Asia for more than three decades, I have returned to my mother tongue, to write in it, and I made a conscious decision to stop writing poetry (my main and most intimate genre) in English. Now I am in the process of digging into the epistemology of the language and culture. Recently, I have written on the poetics of Malay literature. Otherwise, I teach, write essays and translate. I now have some 50 books of poems, essays, theoretical explorations, translation, etc.

Ngũgĩ wa Thiong'o

Distinguished Professor, Comparative Literature and English, University of California, Irvine, USA.

Call me Ngũgĩ wa Thiong'o (pronounced 'Googey wa Theeongo'), in short, Ngũgĩ. In my recent memoir of childhood, *Dreams in a Time of War*, I have talked about growing up in Limuru Kenya, where I was born in 1938. I went to school during the years of the Mau Mau armed struggle against British colonial settler rule. Kenya's independence was in 1963. I speak three languages – Gĩkũyũ, Kiswahili and English. Currently, I am Distinguished Professor of English and Comparative literature at the University of California. I write my fiction, drama and poetry in Gĩkũyũ only. I have published a small journalistic piece in Kiswahili. I write my academic books in English. I believe in translations as a way of making languages and cultures give and take from each other equally.

Robyn Ober

Researcher, Batchelor Institute for Indigenous Tertiary Education, Northern Territory, Australia.

I identify as a Murri (Aboriginal) woman, with connections to the Djirribal/Mamu rainforest people in North Queensland, through my mother, and the KuKu Yalandji, through my father. I do not speak my heritage languages, because of past government policies and historical events which had a huge impact on Indigenous Australian languages. I speak a dialect of Australian English known as Aboriginal English or Murri English, which is a distinct North Queensland dialect. This is my first language, but, of course, I also speak and code-switch to Standard Australian English as the need arises. I am very interested in the history and emergence of Aboriginal English as a contemporary Indigenous language in Australia.

Arjuna Parakrama

Former Professor and Chair of English, Peradeniya University, Sri Lanka.

Among academics, I'm often seen disapprovingly as an activist, and among activists, I'm invariably treated with some suspicion as an academic, both fraught relationships generating productive unease. Not fitting in seems to be my fate and forte. This analysis of language and power stems from my broader lifework (un-)learning from multiple marginalised communities and my doomed attempts at understanding the nature of subaltern resistance to dominant discourse. I love teaching and that's about

xii English Language as Hydra

the only thing I seem to do, in whatever job I find myself. When I'm convinced that I'm of no more use to anybody, I'm going to spend my days birdwatching and writing poetry. I'm almost there now.

Joseph Sung-Yul Park

Assistant Professor, Department of English Language and Literature, National University of Singapore, Singapore.

I am a Korean-American who was born in the US, but grew up in Seoul, South Korea. As I reveal in my chapter, even though I identify myself as Korean, there are many aspects of my life that make me feel unsure of my sense of belonging. This is particularly so as I have spent a large part of my adult life outside of Korea, including the USA, Macau and Singapore. As I grow older, I feel less certain about where 'home' might be for me. But that has also given me ample opportunities to think about the questions of belonging and identity.

Alastair Pennycook

Professor of Language Studies, University of Technology, Sydney, Australia.

I have been working for many years in language education in many parts of the world, and for much of that time, I have been struggling to make sense of English, the role it has played historically, its contemporary role in relation to globalization, the damage it does, the hope it brings. Now that I have the privilege of a senior academic position and the chance to travel even more widely around the world, listening to teachers, looking at linguistic landscapes, talking to people from so many different backgrounds, I continue to ask these questions around English, endlessly exploring the ways it is understood, taken up, rejected and discarded and trying to work out its shifting relation to other languages. I remain puzzled and troubled.

Robert Phillipson

Professor, Department of International Language Studies and Computational Linguistics, Copenhagen Business School, Denmark.

After a conventional middle-class British upbringing, I worked for the British Council in English teaching in post-colonial Algeria and communist Yugoslavia. Strong influences in my exile have been living in more socially just Scandinavia, work at a university stressing multi-disciplinarity, critical scholarship from Africa and India and writing with my radical wife, Tove Skutnabb-Kangas. I continue to be appalled by the hypocrisy of the West in educational language policy. I attempt to undermine linguistic imperialism, to strengthen linguistic diversity locally, in the EU system and through collaboration with inspiring scholars from many parts of the world.

Vaughan Rapatahana

Native English-speaking Teacher, Hong Kong.

Former head of English departments in Aotearoa-New Zealand, Republic of Nauru, Brunei Darussalam, P.R. China.

Vaughan Rapatahana feels his viewpoint is well covered in the Genesis of this Book and the Introduction, respectively.

Rani Samant Rubdy

Associate Professor, English Language and Literature, National Institute of Education, Nanyang Technological University, Singapore.

As an Indian who grew up to an awareness of the many rich subcultures that co-exist within what may be called the Indian culture, I have come to regard linguistic diversity as a natural and indistinguishable part of cultural diversity. And so I see the imposition of any uniform or common language on a multilingual country, such as India or Singapore, as wholly unsuitable to (indeed, as violating) their very spirit and ethos. The basic problem is that having gained independence, we have striven to be no more than imitators of the West in shaping our social, political and cultural ideologies (biases, really), instead of recognizing the complexity and uniqueness of our situation and evolving our own solutions. This we have yet to do. A good beginning would be to stop thinking of our linguistic situation as a problem and start building on its strengths.

Graham Hingangaroa Smith

Distinguished Professor. Vice Chancellor/Chief Executive Officer, *Te Whare Wānanga o Awanuiārangi*: indigenous-university, Whakatane, Aotearoa-New Zealand.

My name is Hingangaroa Smith. I am an indigenous Māori from Aotearoa, New Zealand. My Tribal backgrounds are Ngāti Apa, Te Aitanga-a-Hauiti and Ngāti Kahungunu. I work in alternative and conventional education settings to transform high and disproportionate levels of educational under-development. I believe that the social and economic transformation that is necessary by Māori can only be built on a prior or simultaneous education revolution. Furthermore, successful education for Māori must embrace their desire to still 'be Māori' and to maintain their Māori language, knowledge and cultural integrity.

Acknowledgements

We wish to sincerely thank the following people for their invaluable advice and support: all of our interviewees and our tireless contributors; the Cocos Malay people of the Cocos (Keeling) Islands; Dr Patrick Armstrong; Dr Alastair Pennycook; Dr Robert Phillipson; Dr Tove Skutnabb-Kangas and Bill Purves.

As the English language Hydra has reared its ugly heads in a great many other locations, we also acknowledge those contributors whose chapters we were unable to squeeze into the present collection: those from China, Scotland, France, Ethiopia, Japan, Malaysia and the United Arab Emirates. Thank you for your support.

Series Editor's Note

Tove Skutnabb-Kangas

A feel for this book comes immediately upon reading the editors' statements on its genesis. When an 'outsider' (Pauline) – turned almost an 'insider' – and an almost 'insider' (Vaughan) – turned almost 'outsider' – meet, and they recognise a common analysis – disgust and rage – and possibilities for change-agency, the resulting combination can be extremely powerful. Admittedly, the economic/class situation of both Vaughan and Pauline makes them true outsiders, in relation to most of the world's colonised people/s, regardless of the degree of physical or mental means used in past and present colonialisms. But it is also a fact that a fairly secure economic situation is mostly a prerequisite for writing and editing books. That said, however, very few well-paid TESOL-ers ever turn radical or even critical. Here, it has happened, and this is also why the book's relevance reaches far beyond the countries it describes.

Linguistic capital is convertible to other types of capital and resources, including formal education and life chances. Capability deprivation (in Economics' Nobel laureate Amartya Sen's sense) leads to poverty. Knowledge of the English language is today made to seem an important part of linguistic capital for most people in the world. If the subtractive performing of what is supposed to be teaching English actually leads to linguistic capital dispossession and, thus, capability deprivation, it may, together with the lack of mother-tongue-medium multilingual education that often accompanies it, be part of a linguistic and/or cultural genocide and a crime against humanity.

The editors and authors of this important book (that *had* to be written, as the editors acknowledge) make a valiant and, to a large extent, successful effort to capture the Hydra's heads. They describe the glorification of (competence in) English and the stigmatisation of (people speaking/signing) many other languages and (their) competences in them (sometimes even when one knows English in addition to them). They also expose the rationalisations of the relationship between them, where the knowledge of English and the ways it is taught are always presented as something beneficial to the learners. 'We' are 'helping' 'them', supporting them in acquiring new resources, even when this invalidates the very resources they do have: their own languages, cultures, knowledge and world views.

Using Ngũgĩ's metaphor of languages as bridges (also see Mohanty, 2009), we surely do need two-way bridges, where information can flow equally and easily in both directions. We do not need one-way bridges, where the teaching of English is meant to form a no-return bridge, to transfer people away from their own backgrounds, languages and cultures. It takes multidisciplinary efforts, courage, passion and action – based on thorough analysis – to fight this Hydra successfully. Historically, English is the most powerful language Hydra to evolve to date, and a replacement will not appear in either my or the editors' lifetimes. Is there any chance of taming it, I wonder?

References

Mohanty, A.K. (2009) Multilingual education – A Bridge Too Far? In A.K. Mohanty, M. Panda, R. Phillipson and T. Skutnabb-Kangas (eds) *Multilingual Education for Social Justice: Globalising the Local* (pp. 5–19). New Delhi: Orient Blackswan.
Sen, A. (1985) *Commodities and Capabilities*. Amsterdam: North Holland.

The Genesis of this Book

Vaughan Rapatahana and Pauline Bunce

English Language as Hydra was originally going to be titled, *English Language as Thief*, because that was how I felt about this language during and after several stints spent as a teacher of English as a 'second' language ('foreign', surely) in several locations, including my own homeland, Aotearoa-New Zealand. It was here that I turned my back on *Pakeha* (Caucasian, qua English language) education in 1983 and submitted my resignation from that system via a letter quoting Ivan Illich to the *New Zealand Post-Primary Teachers' Journal.*

I chose the notion of *Thief* because I increasingly felt that I was 'teaching' middle-class, *Pakeha*-derived and *Pakeha*-obsessed themes and protocols to largely non-Caucasian students whose first languages had never been English. Not only was I party to stealing their dollars, but also their time, their good humour, their very *Weltanschauung*. Generally, they expressed no real interest in acquiring the English language, but they had been given no choice by their parents or school administrations – themselves trapped in the zeitgeist of Englishism. All around my students there blared English-language computers, television screens, movies, music and posters. English was 'forever in their face', swirling around them.

Quintessentially, however, I was also a thief. Below the surface-level lip service, many indigenous and autochthonous people were pissed off by the presence of people such as myself. We were re-colonialists.

In my role as a fully qualified, 'native-speaking' teacher of English, I have partaken in generously funded long-term stays in the Republic of Nauru, Brunei Darussalam, the Peoples' Republic of China, Hong Kong and the United Arab Emirates. I have lived in superior accommodation, generously paid for under the terms of the respective contracts, on ample and above national average (often tax-free) salaries with attached gratuities, with funded medical insurance schemes, return airfares, interest-free car loans and regular holidays. I was, somehow, ranked as being economically 'more worthy' than over 90% of the local populations, only because I was a NET – an apparently native-speaking English teacher.

In New Zealand, however, I always felt inauthentic, unless I was teaching in Māori-empowered schooling systems, where the English language was at least parried by the *patu* (club) of *Te Reo Māori* (the Māori language). This is why, after teaching overseas, that I only ever taught again in Māori language schools in my homeland, and why I also knew that this book had to be written.

The lustrous position of the native-speaking English teacher in so many traditionally non-English communities continues unabated today. In fact, such highly privileged teaching schemes are a complete scandal, thinly wallpapered over by the commercial agents of Englishism and showing few signs of retreat. If anything, the industry's tentacular grasp is more so today, as the TOEFL and IELTS language tests grow up as 'Siamese Twins' – a term so manifestly orientalist that it makes me wince.

A further irony is that English is *not* my main language, but because of an accident of birthplace, it has served to privilege me and so many of my peers, mainly, but not exclusively, Caucasian. We have become richer with absolutely no guarantee whatsoever that the students we 'teach' will ever attain our level of English language empowerment. I wonder if, in fact, they were ever 'meant' to. Such is the unspoken 'Hydra in the room'. This book had to be written.

Vaughan Rapatahana,
Hong Kong

I have come to the *Hydra* project from the other side of the 'divide'. I was not a teacher of English in my home country – Australia – but midway into my career as a Geography teacher, I chanced to enter the privileged world of second-language English teaching, and it has taken me across the world ever since. For a very long time, however, I resisted the 'siren calls' of teaching in 'international schools' – the overseas private schools of the expatriate world. I told myself that, if I were going to teach English overseas, it was going to be 'local schools and local kids' for me. And so it was for a long time, but the untold privileges of doing so just kept flowing onto my plate, largely uninvited.

When I started out, I had no language qualifications, other than being a high school Geography teacher who happened to speak English. That, plus a sense of adventure, was all I needed to gain a teaching position in the Australian territory of the Cocos (Keeling) Islands and to later become the teacher in charge of the islands' three-teacher secondary school. A teaching licence was all I needed to instruct my islander students in English, Geography, Social Studies, Mathematics, Health and Physical Education, Technical Drawing, Typing and Business Communication, Art, Home Economics, Vocational Education, Media Studies and later on, primary and secondary Malay Language and Culture. In my spare time, I wrote a book about the islands and undertook two correspondence courses in ESL teaching. Too easy for an English speaker!

My profound ignorance was certainly blissful for a while, however, the more Malay I learned, the more I read about languages and language learning, the more I entered a completely new world. I became aware of myself as a learner of a second language – the new world that was opening up to me via my new-found language skills – and the parallel challenges and experiences that my students must also have been experiencing in their new-found language of English. How could I have been so naive? I was onto something far more powerful than any drug. I was gradually learning to listen to all the unrecorded stories about the islands' turbulent history and the valiant struggles of the island people against the colonial copra-plantation system that had ruled their lives for six or seven generations. Other stories told of a First World War confrontation with a German warship and Japanese bombing raids in World War II. I also watched as the United Nations implored Australia to 'normalise' the islands.

I realized that the tiny Cocos atoll was a complete microcosm of the wider, colonial world. This was my first experience of live-action, fully fledged colonialism. We were living in a time machine, surely, because it was 1982. After seeking permission to spend a night in the Malay village, I watched as the plantation owner took his barefoot, early morning walk – dagger-in-belt. I saw the fawning behaviour of the islanders when he spoke to them. I drew breath when I first saw the scale of his island mansion, hidden behind a wall, at a discrete distance from the islanders' prefabricated concrete houses with their kerosene lamps and water-wells. That night, I was also completely enraptured by the performance of a *bangsawan* – a traditional Malay dramatic performance. Somehow, the islanders had held onto many, many aspects of their Javanese past, and I was captivated. I was truly in a time machine, and yet I was in 20th century Australia.

What was I doing there, teaching English and opening up the inevitable flood-gates of Westernization? Was this just 'the way of the world'? If it was, couldn't the islanders, somehow, have it both ways? Couldn't they be free of the plantation system, but also free to choose what they wanted for their future in their own time? I soon learned that this wasn't my business. Such matters were the prerogative of teams of monolingual clerks and bureau managers in Canberra and my blissfully unenlightened teaching colleagues.

I began to read more and more about the debilitating effects of English-only education on indigenous peoples. I was inspired by Jim Cummins and Tove Skutnabb-Kangas' collection entitled, *Minority Education: From Shame to Struggle* (1988). Most of my colleagues thought that I was crazy to 'worry' about what we were doing there. I have been worried ever since.

I met and worked with Vaughan in Brunei Darussalam. In him, I found another teacher-skeptic. When we met up again in Hong Kong, and Vaughan suggested the current project, I leapt at the chance to work on this collection with him. We stayed with the notion of English as *Thief* for quite some time, but as we began to read some of our early contributions, we saw a multiplicity of (mostly negative) other personas. The notion of a *Hydra* emerged.

Selamat berjuang.

Pauline Bunce,
Perth, Western Australia

Foreword

In classical Greek mythology, if one of the Hydra monster's nine heads was cut off, two new ones grew in its place and one of these was considered invincible. Vaughan Rapatahana and Pauline Bunce have captured the spirit of the Hydra's multiple heads by ascribing the diverse functions of the English language to a set of categories that serve as vivid section headings in this book. How invincible English will be in the long term is an open question, but the contributors to this collection – severally and in impressive chorus – firmly denounce some of the monstrous misuses to which the English language is put. Many of them also exemplify that change is possible.

The statement on the genesis of the book explains how a New Zealander of Māori origin and an Australian of European heritage have become increasingly concerned – indeed, appalled – at the way the English language is being promoted and taught in contexts in which they have been directly involved for decades. It is refreshing to encounter such honesty, professional humility and determination to document what is happening in a wide range of countries. They invited colleagues with similar concerns in a substantial number of Asian and Pacific countries, Africa, and Latin America to spell out what is happening and to justify why the Hydra monster image faithfully captures an alarming set of professional crimes.

The depth and detail of the descriptions make for compelling reading. The book is a wake-up call to those responsible for the global promotion of English, on both the supply side (Australia, UK, South Africa, USA etc.; governments, universities, language professionals) and the demand side (those governments that ignorantly recruit 'native speaker' teachers of English, e.g. Korea, Malaysia, Hong Kong, etc.), as though the mere chance of birthright is an educational *deus ex machina.*

There are plenty of books on the multilingual realities in most of the countries described in this volume. However, the extensive literature on English and English teaching worldwide tends to be monopolized by Western researchers. Many of them are triumphalist, celebrating the global 'success' of English, whereas far fewer are critical and stress the injustices of imperial dominance, post-colonial privilege and the continued marginalisation of what are seen as 'lesser' languages. This book gives voice to 'les damnés de la terre' – the accursed of the world – to cite Frantz Fanon, the highly influential theorist of colonial liberation (1963).

What makes the book distinctive and original is the unifying Hydra theme, its exploration in chapters that are imbued with a passion to reflectively diagnose the damage that the monster is doing. However, it is important to stress that none of the contributors is crudely 'anti-English'. They rightly assume that one cannot, indeed, one should not do away with the monster, but there is a genuine need to subdue and control it so that its negative practices and pernicious effects can be limited. Some chapters also provide examples of enlightened educational and social policies that can lead to a constructive *modus vivendi* with the beast.

That alternatives are possible and exist comes through in the opening text by the famous Kenyan novelist, Ngũgĩ wa Thiong'o. He describes how English need not function in a monstrous way, provided good conditions are in force for the strengthening of linguistic and cultural diversity. The alternative for post-colonial countries is to remain steeped in mental slavery. This is a condition that Gandhi warned Indians against in 1909. In 1943, when power was slipping away from the British Empire and towards an American one, Winston Churchill presciently foresaw that the empires of the future would no longer be territorial, but 'empires of the mind'. It is this form of empire that this book challenges and seeks to end. Ngũgĩ refers to some of his own creative and theoretical writing. I can warmly recommend his *Wizard of the Crow* – a long, hilarious and profound novel about corruption in 'aid' bodies (the 'Global Bank') and in the government of an African former colony. The English Hydra in this work of fiction is a monster with close affinities to the ways in which English serves the interests of post-colonial elites as a language of inclusion for the few and of exclusion for the many.

The two chapters on the English language as bully (in the Republic of Nauru and on the Cocos [Keeling] Islands) report on the various ways in which different Australian authorities have treated local languages and cultures in recent decades. Their bigoted, ignorant and patronising ethnocentricity is a re-run of earlier colonial arrogance. Little seems to have changed in language policy since the colonial period, as denounced, for instance, by creative writers such as Ngũgĩ and Shirley Lim. Lim (1996) writes that, until 1969, 'the educational structure in Malaya was British colonial', the exam system was 'violently oppressive to our childhood' and that 'we had grown up in a compulsory language system, but, as if to strip us of all language, we were constantly reminded that this language did not belong to us. Depriving us of Chinese or Malay or Hindi, British teachers reminded us nonetheless that English was only on loan, a borrowed tongue which we could only garble' (1996: 103, 126, 180). Tope Omoniyi from Nigeria (2003: 23) calls the continued role of French and English in former colonies a 'rape on democracy'.

Little seems to have changed. The contributions to this book document what it is like to be at the receiving end of neocolonial 'aid', such as English causing Nauruans to suffer from a 'linguistic battered-wife syndrome' as a deliberate result of explicitly linguicidal policies. Such policies are less admissible in Europe (where some minority languages, such as Welsh in the

UK and Basque in Spain, now thrive), but Australians of European ancestry evidently feel that they can get away with it with Aboriginal people and in various Islander communities. Similarly, in the Philippines, children are still punished – financially – for using their mother tongue in school, a form of abuse that was common in Wales and in many African colonies several decades ago, but no longer.

The Nauruans, Australian Aboriginal and Islander peoples could even consider charging various agencies of the Australian government with committing crimes against humanity at the International Court of Justice. A strong case has been made for this being legally tenable (Skutnabb-Kangas & Dunbar, 2010). A study of the shocking opportunism of Australian 'aid' schemes to strengthen English learning in Asian countries (Widin, 2010) describes in detail how unethical and deeply immoral the schemes are, since, in reality, they serve Australian interests and definitely not those of the recipients.

The Hong Kong chapter digs deeply into the causal factors behind an Asian territory (like several others) importing native speakers of English as teachers. This is an extremely insightful analysis of how the 'English language Governess became a Chinese person with a British accent', unloved, but respected and, apparently, immoveable. The study exemplifies how orientalism and linguistic imperialism have been recreated and renewed, with a very poor return on the investment in such teachers, but one that serves to maintain a fundamentally racist structure within the English-teaching profession, with very detrimental effects on local teachers and learners. The governess serves her commercial masters well and her protégés in the education system badly. Unlike what one might have thought, governesses and colonial language hierarchies are alive and kicking and ruthlessly so.

The South African portrait is mostly at the societal level, though with one admirable example of personal agonies, too. It is a compelling description of the allure of English and its anchoring in an economy that serves the interests of only a fraction of the population. It makes admirable use of Bourdieu's insights into the workings of language and power and shows that change in the direction of African languages will be an uphill road.

The Korean coverage reveals how demanding the existential struggle is for an individual with a hybrid identity, in a society which is neurotically anxious about developing competence in English. It beautifully illustrates the psychological dimension of linguistic and cultural border-crossing. Like several other chapters, this reveals the racist underpinning of beliefs in the superiority of the USA/UK/Australia and English, vis-à-vis other cultures and languages. The deeply embedded racism of the international English Language Teaching (ELT) business is increasingly being explored by scholars who, not surprisingly, are themselves Afro-American (Romney, 2010) or from Pakistan (Mahboob, 2010), Japan (Kubota, 2009) or Hong Kong (Lin,

2006). The Korean chapter also exemplifies how native speaker competence is a relational concept, and that the subjective internalisation by Koreans of the status of privileged norms for English has dire emotional consequences. There is fascinating reflection here on how far the 'border Hydra' can ever be definitively crossed.

The chapter on Aotearoa (New Zealand) is a panoramic analysis of English as, in effect, a nemesis for the Māori language and culture throughout history, although vigorous attempts are being made to maintain the vitality of Māori. This provides grounds for hope that this Hydra is being, at least partially, contained. The analysis of Australian language policy for its Indigenous people is rather less optimistic. The concluding Coda of the volume, by a distinguished Malaysian poet, traces a trajectory from English dominance to significant promotion of a national language, to the championing of the rights of all languages.

The Sri Lankan chapter demolishes myths about standards and native speaker competence by showing persuasively how all language analysis needs to be firmly rooted in local multilingual social contexts, which are intrinsically hierarchical and stratificational. Elegant propositions show that much Western scholarship is biased and false – shockingly so, since the injustice involved, choreographed by corrupt Sri Lankan elites in league with Western interests, is buried in learned positivistic cant.

The Philippine and Brunei chapters document the complexity of managing diversity in multilingual countries, with English in an ambivalent 'auntie' role. They document dual or multiple Hydra heads, with English figuring strongly in elite formation or in the export of skills and invariably with controversy about the quality and relevance of instruction in English.

The Singapore chapter builds on the sizeable volume of research into language issues in the country and concludes that a 'partnership' with the Hydra in Singapore has been criminally effective in eliminating mother tongues and in stigmatising local variants of English. Ways forward are suggested that would reduce the grasp of a British English norm, enable a larger proportion of the population to prosper and strengthen linguistic diversity and vitality, instead of smothering it.

The analysis of the expansion of English in Latin America, especially Colombia, demonstrates that the marketing of the language – by local elites and international bodies, such as the British Council – may have useful instrumental effects for some, but it diverts attention away from the needs of the indigenous peoples and fraudulently assumes that an expansion of English is in the interests of all.

Freedom of expression, including academic freedom, is recognized as a central ingredient of societies that respect human rights and attempt to build democratic polities. British and American bodies concerned with English are actively attempting to extend the role and influence of English globally. The US teachers' association – Teachers of English to Speakers of Other Languages (TESOL) – announced on 19 September 2011 that it has been renamed as TESOL International Association. It clearly has global ambitions, and it is convinced that its expertise is universally relevant, as 'it reaches out to new groups and individuals around the globe'. The same is true of the language testing bodies in the USA (TOEFL) and the UK (Cambridge), which both aim to increase their influence and earnings worldwide. Thus, Cambridge ESOL has six departments. Its 'Business Development Group' alone has 'around 100 staff involved in sales and marketing activity. They include UK-based staff in support and strategy roles and staff overseas distributed across 25 offices in 19 countries'. Cambridge ESOL is part of Cambridge Assessment, which also conducts examinations domestically and 'internationally' for children from 5–19, reaching, literally, millions of children. Just as in colonial times, this entails learners being examined for their competence in a British cultural universe and language.

These activities are economically driven. The same is true of the activities of the British Council, which now earns two-thirds of its income from English teaching and testing, though some of its staff and academic consultants are increasingly critical of traditional 'aid' efforts (Coleman, 2011). On the other hand, the assumption that Anglo-American ELT expertise is universally relevant, or that the British know how to solve the educational problems of postcolonial states worldwide, is fundamentally false. I have challenged a recent survey of work of this nature (Phillipson, 2010) and also analysed how the arguments put forward for currently promoting English in India are a re-run of the British imperialist agenda of nearly two centuries ago (Phillipson, forthcoming).

The publishers and editors of scholarly journals play a decisive role in gatekeeping, in selecting what is or is not disseminated to a wider public. Critical scholars, myself included, experience censorship and various attempts to silence us, in order to prevent the publication of work that is unwelcome to those in power. But as friends have told me when my *Linguistic Imperialism* (Phillipson, 1992) was being criticised, it is better to be demonised than ignored. The facts presented in my book have never been disproven, but so far as I am aware, the ELT profession as a whole has not been decisively influenced by it, nor by its successor volume (Phillipson, 2009), even if it has had an impact on many individuals worldwide, including the editors of this collection.

Vaughan and Pauline's book presents a wealth of new factual evidence and analysis that is certain to ruffle many feathers. It deserves to have a more explosive impact. This book meets a real need, and its contents should be heeded by policy-makers in the countries it covers, as well as being read by all those involved in English language teaching circles. There really ought to be major concern about the reality of the English language as Hydra – the beast is certainly not mythical.

Robert Phillipson

References

Coleman, H. (ed.) (2011) *Dreams and Realities: Developing Countries and the English Language*. London: British Council.

Fanon, F. (1961) *Les Damnés de la Terre*. Paris: François Maspero.

Fanon, F. (1963) *The Wretched of the Earth* (C. Farrington, trans.). New York: Grove.

Kubota, R. and Lin, A. (eds) (2009) *Race, Culture, and Identities in Second Language Education. Exploring Critically Engaged Practice*. New York and Abingdon: Routledge.

Lim, S.G. (1996) *Among the White Moonfaces: Memoirs of an Asian American Woman*. Singapore: Times Editions – Marshall Cavendish.

Lin, A. (2006) Contexts of English-in-education policy and practice in postcolonial Hong Kong. *Asian Journal of English Language Teaching* 16, 25–44.

Mahboob, A. (ed.) (2010) *The NNEST Lens. Non-Native English Speakers in TESOL*. Newcastle upon Tyne: Cambridge Scholars.

Omoniyi, T. (2003) Language ideology and politics: A critical appraisal of French as a second language in Nigeria. In S. Makoni and U.H. Meinhof (eds) *Africa and Applied Linguistics, AILA Review* 16, 13–23.

Phillipson, R. (1992) *Linguistic Imperialism*. Oxford: Oxford University Press.

Phillipson, R. (2009) *Linguistic Imperialism Continued*. New York and London: Routledge. (Also published in New Delhi, India for seven South Asian countries by Orient Blackswan).

Phillipson, R. (2010) The politics and the personal in language education: The state of which art? A review article on *The Politics of Language Education. Individuals and Institutions,* (J.C. Alderson, ed.). In *Language and Education* 24 (2), 151–169.

Phillipson, R. (forthcoming) Macaulay alive and kicking: How linguistic imperialism continues. In A.G. Rao (ed.) *Foreign Languages in India: Towards a Glocal World*. Delhi: Orient Blackswan.

Romney, M. (2010) The colour of English. In A. Mahboob (ed.) (2010) *The NNEST Lens. Non-Native English Speakers in TESOL*. Newcastle-upon-Tyne: Cambridge Scholars.

Skutnabb-Kangas, T. and Dunbar, R. (2010) *Indigenous Children's Education as Linguistic Genocide and a Crime Against Humanity? A Global View*. Guovdageaidnu/Kautokeino: Galdu, Resource Centre for the Rights of Indigenous Peoples. Online at http://www.e-pages.dk/grusweb/55/

Widin, J. (2010) *Illegitimate Practices. Global English Language Education*. Bristol: Multilingual Matters.

Introduction: English Language as Thief

Vaughan Rapatahana

Several years ago, Hong Kong poet, Gigi Wong, wrote the following poem about having to learn English at school. Her academic success depended on this foreign language, even though she never spoke it outside her classroom. Her frustration is clear, as is her correlation of the language with fiscal empowerment. To her, English is so many discordant things –

English is...

English is a thief; it steals my life.
English can make my tongue twist into a knot.
English is a hard rock; we must break through it.

English is a symphony, so marvellous.
English is an art.
English is a slice of bread I eat every day.

English is a hunter; it kills many students.
English is very, very troublesome.
English is A for apple, B for boy and C for cat.

English is trying your best.
English is a never-ending game.
English is a bowl of herbal tea.

English is a very big cake; we must eat it bit by bit.
English is tests and quizzes.
English is money, people should have some.

Well said, Gigi! In a few simple lines, she has managed to capture the beguiling, but contradictory nature of the many-headed creature that is the English language and the multiple effects that it can have upon its learners. She has not called it a monster, not quite. She is far too polite. Unlike Gigi, however, the writers who have come together in this volume may not always be so well mannered.

Each one of our contributors has taken the symbolism of the monstrous Hydra – the mythical multi-headed beast from Greek mythology – and, head-by-head, they have applied this idea to the multiple roles that are played by the English language in a range of national contexts. In the original myth, the Hydra was a terrifying, beastly serpent from the swamp that terrorised a village by attacking its inhabitants and their animals. It defended itself with its deadly breath, its poisonous blood and an amazing capacity to be able to replace any of its severed heads with two more.

We must stress from the outset that we are not trying to anthropomorphise the English language itself. The language, per se, is not a culprit. It cannot be. Its resemblance to the mythical Hydra comes directly from the way that it has been used, promoted and declared to be essential. It is the people and the agencies that promote and demand its necessity that are the targets of our critique.

In *English Language as Hydra*, the reader will come face-to-face with a multi-faceted creature that does indeed have a wide range of personae, some more frightening than others. Such is the troublesome nature of this beast. Unlike the swamp dweller of ancient Argos, however, today's English language Hydra has managed to increase its geographical range to span the planet. English has adapted to a wide range of environments by developing different heads in different places and sometimes different heads in the same place. It has also developed its own symbiotic relationships with societies, businesses, governments and education systems.

What happened when this exotic creature entered each new sociolinguistic ecosystem? What reactions and accommodations have resulted from its intrusion? Has there been competition, conflict, extinction or mixing? Or have there been more subtle adjustments? What was the nature of its arrival? How did it work its way into each local setting: as an imposed foreign language or as a medium-of-instruction? Did it come hand-in-hand with expatriate teacher schemes in various TESL/TEFL/TEAL guises (Teaching English as a Second/Foreign/Additional Language)? Indeed, why is there such a strongly perceived need for the English language per se in so many communities? What problems and benefits has it brought?

The very task of delineating the various roles that the English language can and has played is a complex one. It is 'a terminological and ideological minefield' (Phillipson, 2010: 3). The multiple roles that can be played by the English language span the following range: *lingua franca*, international language, national language, additional language, post-colonial language, localized language and native language. The English language has also been described by a range of metaphorical labels, such as a killer language (Skutnabb-Kangas, 2003), a Trojan horse (Cooke, 1988), a Tyrannosaurus Rex (Swales, 1997), an octopus (Bunce, 2009), a cuckoo (Phillipson, 2006), an auntie (Dasgupta, 1993) and a chameleon (Phillipson, 2007; Eoyang, 2003a).

In this volume, we propose that Hydra is the most appropriate term to use. To us, this beast has multiple personalities – some distinct, some inter-related. We can also see 'cousin heads' emerging in the roles of localised English and techno-variants, such as rap lyrics and the language of telephone texting. Some of these heads may snap at the larger ones, some may poke out their tongues in defiance, some will be ignored, some suppressed and some may even be swallowed up by others.

In this book, a range of metaphorical identities of the Hydra will be examined in specific situations in different countries. We fully acknowledge Eoyang's (2003: 13) point that, 'ironies abound: English is at once demonized as the language of the imperialist, yet it is also the preferred language for anti-imperialist, postcolonial theory...'. The English language not only hermaphroditically propagates itself, it is also capable of backbiting itself. This is a wildly seething array of Hydra heads.

This book will focus on the use of so-called 'standard' or 'native-speaker' Anglo-American English language. This has been a significant, top-down linguistic imposition on, and within, the communities surveyed here. The supporters of such 'standard' varieties of English have set it up as a highly desirable international language. Many have deemed it necessary and neutral, and several have declared that a standardised version of it should be taught, whenever possible, by monolingual native speakers. It is this supremacist vision of the English language that we seek to dismantle here.

This particular vision of the English language drives the relentless worldwide demand for the language. Its charioteers can be teachers, textbook writers, academic journal editors, language testers, translators of indigenous languages into English, university bureaucrats, parents, educational administrators, politicians or virtually anyone who stands to benefit from its propagation. This book will examine its perfidious effects on those who are deemed not to possess it, as well as their reactions to this state of affairs. Our book has, in many ways, come about as a direct result of the widespread practice of importing significant numbers of native English-speaking teachers (NETs) and imposing them upon non-English-speaking communities.

Alastair Pennycook (2010: 121) reminds us that we also need to completely rethink what a language, per se, really is. He speaks of the vision, in this globalized age, to be rid of 20th century grand narratives, such as imperialism, *lingua francas*, etc. and '...to consider that languages may be undergoing such forms of transition as to require new ways of conceptualization in terms of local activities, resources or practices'. We also accept, as Pennycook and Phillipson have both pointed out, that the English language is contextualised by local conditions and practices: it is very much a process. However, we must remember that, for most people, there is, in fact, an 'objective' language – their own – which is all too often stifled and suppressed by the agencies of the behemoth that is English.

We feel that Pennycook is right about the need to concentrate on localized 'Englishes', but at the same time, this point has been lost by administrators, politicians and educators. We also feel that Phillipson is right about the hugely detrimental effects of 'standardized', neo-imperialistic Anglo-American English, but he is also overlooked by the very same people. Indeed, despite their apparent differences in approach to the English language, these two scholars have a great deal in common, possibly more than they realise. It is almost as if a time warp exists between the 21st century – where Pennycook and his ilk are coming from with their notions of localized *lingua franca* Englishes – and the ways in which 20th century notions of 'standardized' English are being maintained by national administrations. Oddly, both viewpoints currently exist side-by-side.

We also acknowledge that the English language is by no means the only linguistic Hydra roaming the planet, but it is probably the largest and most hungry of these beasts. This obdurate creature – with its many, and often conflicting, characteristics – sprouts heads that can appear to be polar opposites, while others may be conjoined with different languages, such as Spanish, French, Arabic, Malay and Mandarin. This is a vexing creature that cannot be beheaded by a single blow, because of its strongly persistent and stubborn qualities.

Some of the writers in this book are First Nation or indigenous people (as defined by the International Labour Organization Convention 169). The other writers are representatives of, and indigenous to, the societies under investigation or, at the very least, bilingual insiders who have spent a considerable amount of time in these communities. Most, if not all, are autochthonous to the areas they write about. So we cannot, and do not, claim that *English Language as Hydra* is exclusively written by indigenous writers, rather that each chapter is tightly focused on the effects of English language education on the traditional, non-English utilising community in each place.

The Collection

This international collection offers its readers a wide array of perspectives, localities, writing styles and passionate, personal involvement in dealing with the ever-evolving and rather healthy English language Hydra. The collection is book-ended by the reflective observations of two prominent literary figures and two well-known applied linguists. Malaysian Literary Laureate, Muhammad Haji Salleh, describes his own linguistic journey and Kenya's Nobel Literature Prize nominee, Ngũgĩ wa Thiong'o, calls for languages to act as bridges. These highly personal accounts are joined at either end of the collection by the analytical commentaries of Robert Phillipson and Alastair Pennycook, both of whom are world-renowned linguistic scholars. Here, they each provide us with their observations on the immense power that is being wielded around the world by the English language and its legions of language teachers. Make no mistake: such power is pervasive and omnipresent and insinuative, insidious and insidiously self-maintaining.

Our collection of case studies begins with some of the most brutal of the Hydra's heads – those that have held unfettered sway in the world's smallest places, such as the Republic of Nauru and the Australian Indian Ocean Territory of the Cocos (Keeling) Islands. In such places, the beast has operated like an overbearing playground bully. In indigenous Australia, the creature has become an ever-rolling juggernaut, crushing so much before it. In Aotearoa (New Zealand), English and Māori face off against one another on a very uneven playing field; the former continues to dominate, to act as nemesis for the latter.

The book's central chapters examine the more subtle, manipulative and beguiling roles of the English language that have played out in Sri Lanka, Hong Kong, the Philippines, Brunei Darussalam and South Africa. In these places, the language has worked its way into society, where it has woven a range of 'magic spells' on the local populations. A very personal account by a bilingual South Korean writer reveals the many ways in which languages can really 'mess with your mind'. Finally, in Singapore and South America, the English language sits awkwardly beside a number of other languages, with each feeling varying degrees of discomfort.

The Message

This collection aims to make the following points about the global domination of the English language.

(1) The spread of the English language is insidious, pervasive and self-perpetuating

We believe that the core problem involved in the teaching and using of the English language in historically non-English speaking countries and societies is that it has become a Trojan horse. Wherever it goes, it takes with it, via its inherent discourses and structures – in a seemingly beneficial fashion – a whole panoply of inherent controls, expectations, attitudes and beliefs that are often counter to those of the learners themselves (Cooke, 1988; Ljungdahl, 2003; Pennycook, 1998; Phillipson, 2009; Wierzbicka, 2006, 2010). At the same time, the language continues to promulgate its own unique importance as a vehicle for material and economic success. This is particularly so in this age of globalisation. The agents of the English language are highly skilled in portraying it as something vital and valuable, while they mask its Janus-face.

For indigenous peoples – the *Other* – the English language is a double-edged sword. Indigenous peoples are widely expected to learn English, often at their own expense and at the potential expense of their own languages, precisely because they *are* the Other. Such is the rampant strength of English language hegemony. The English language has been sold so effectively and has been established so well by its agencies, that it has become central to many education systems. Apparently, one must have it to 'do well in life'. In some of the situations that are covered in this book, those in power (often an educated-in-English elite) have reinforced this view of the language. They have also reinforced their own control by effectively disenfranchising – or attempting to disenfranchise – the local languages.

There is something seductive about English; somehow the language attracts people to it, because they are impressed by its perceived ability to offer them a better life. Indigenous languages can suffer immensely, especially if English is taught subtractively at their expense. Indeed, such languages may well disappear (Skutnabb-Kangas, 2009). Various forms of *linguistic imperialism* (Phillipson, 1992, 2008) and *linguicism* (Skutnabb-Kangas, 1989) are still very much alive.

The writing style that is acceptable for publication in English-language academic journals requires highly developed English-language skills and procedures that are frequently not available to many non-English speaking writers. Bourdieu (1984: 255) wryly observed that 'the dominant impose, by their very existence, a definition of excellence [which is] nothing more than their own way of existing'. Make no mistake, the spread and sustenance of the English language is all about power and, most specifically, about the power of money. As Robert Phillipson (2009:12) has observed, 'imperialism, including linguistic imperialism, has always been about profit'. We are well aware that even this book could be construed as an example of linguistic imperialism. It is, after all, designed to counter the hegemony of English language agencies, yet it is written in English, published in the United Kingdom, and it conforms rigorously to the strictly standardised and stringently enforced bibliographical and academic parameters. The irony here is massive. We wish to escape being cast in the role of 'subaltern' to such top-down 'master' parameters and to ensure that this book benefits the non-native users of English and promotes their own languages, yet we are compelled to this in the ways of the masters.

Tupas reminds us that 'English divides'. All those calls for a grasping of the language to ensure 'global competitiveness' emanate from the upper- and middle-classes. 'English has never been "class-free"', he states, 'despite attempts to picture it as an equalising language' (Tupas, 2008: 7).

(2) The English language can be powerful, destructive and inimical

Writing from a Māori perspective, Takirarangi Smith (2000: 53, 60) has emphasized the fundamental epistemological and ontological differences contained within, and by, language:

European/Western/Pakeha tools of analysis have meant that pre-colonial notions of reality have become submerged in the face of the English language... But [we need to remember that] there is also another world view which occurs in another spatial and temporal dimension, which is not that of European or Western notions of time and space.

Linguistic structures can determine our perceptual and, thus, our cognitive selves. This is well summed up in the following *whakatauki*, or proverb, from New Zealand Māori:

Ko taku reo, taku ohooho, ko taku reo taku mapihi mauria
My language, my awakening, my language is the window to my soul.

Different languages create different worlds. Ultimately, languages cannot be translated from one to another. One must always understand the cultural context in order to understand the meaning of a given word in a given language (Wittgenstein, 1953). Any systems superimposed by the English language could also be potential threats, because they are ontologically manipulative. According to Ngũgĩ wa Thiong'o (1986: 4), 'the choice of language and the use to which language is put is central to a people's definition of themselves in relation to their natural and social environment, indeed in relation to their entire universe'. If one is compelled to utilize a language which is not one's own, there is a potential for people to become alienated, to be forced to take on the values which are inherent in the oppressors' language. If not watched and taught carefully, it can kill the indigenous being, as several chapters in this book will attest. Young people can all too easily end up as 'linguistic half-castes' (Giridhraradas, 2010) in the process.

It is the view of these writers that it remains the nature of the adherents of the English-language beast to stalk, savage and steal indigenous cultures and languages. At worst, this can invade their *wairua* (a Māori term, which roughly translates to self-image, self-esteem, soul), and this is what we will convey in our book. Here, we designate the English language as a Thief.

(3) The process of English language domination is complex and contradictory

There is no simple algorithm whereby English hegemony can be described as merely a simplistic, top-down impositional process by quasi-colonial organisations. There is a whole slew of players and contexts involved. Robert Phillipson (2011: personal communication) notes the presence of many variables within linguistic imperialism, including 'the interlocking of push and pull factors, internal and external causes, structural dimensions (material resources) and beliefs (ideologies, attitudes)'. Considerable complexity also emanates from the various Englishes that can be found in the world today, sometimes competing within the same locale. Alastair Pennycook (1998: 165) stresses the complexity involved here: '...culture is not seen merely as a reflex of material conditions... and power operates in more complex ways than simply as something possessed by the "powerful"'.

(4) There are fight-backs against the domination of the English language

Our book also considers *resistance* to English language hegemony. There are contemporary situations in which there is a 'fight-back' against English-language dominion. These range from official policies – put into place by the proponents of other languages – *not* to utilize English (e.g. Francophone policies) to the legalized insistence on the teaching of indigenous languages (e.g. New Zealand Māori *kura kaupapa* or Māori philosophy/language schools) to the burgeoning of regionally reworked, local Englishes. Then again, of course, one can downright refuse to write and speak in the English language at all. Our indigenous writers wish to retain their ontological ownership in resisting what the English language brings to bear and in maintaining their own languages. Despite the recent trend to praise these 'fighting back' counters to so-called standardized English, the fact remains that much of the systematization and extolling of such regional calques stems from academics and does little for those actually supposed to be speaking and writing them. 'Unfreedom', rather than freedom, is the direct result of such academic constructs (Tupas, 2008).

(5) The English language is not acting alone in its cultural thieving

It is not only the English language – or the work of its agents – that is trampling on indigenous cultures and tongues. Other languages, such as Spanish, French, Malay and Mandarin, are also guilty, albeit with a smaller criminal record. Guilty, too, are all those languages that have been designated as official, national and standard.

––––––

So here we have the English language as a multiple-headed Hydra. It is a complex and contradictory beast of tremendous range and power. It has voracious feeding habits, and it tends to leave massive deposits wherever it roams. The current influence of the English language is spreading, not diminishing. One wonders how long the beast will continue to maraud and with such apparent freedom to do so. I will end our Introduction with a poem of my own. It is self-explanatory.

linguistic imperialism continued

who is this english?
who t e s s e l l a t e s himself,

titillatingly,

into sanctimonious pose,
when 'actually' –

whatever that clasp of syllable
might 'mean' –

he's an epigone gone waaaaaay wrong:
an imprimatur imposter
fly-dropping a c r o s s our every page
in kleptomanic *frenzy*;

a bogey-man dressed to kill,
insinuating the world/the word
he's here to serve us,

as
he gluts his stylish
stylus

through
us
all

for Robert Phillipson

References

Bourdieu, P. (1984) *Distinctions: A Social Critique of the Judgement of Taste*. London: Routledge and Kegan Paul.

Bunce, P. (2009) Private email communication re MacArthur, T. (2003) Reported in *Newsweek* July.

Cooke, D. (1988) Ties that constrict: English as a Trojan horse. In A. Cumming, A. Gagne and J. Dawson (eds) *Awareness: Proceedings of the 1987 TESL Ontario Conference* (11056–62). Toronto: TESL Ontario.

Dasgupta, P. (1993) *The Otherness of English: India's Auntie Tongue Syndrome*. New Delhi: Sage.

Eoyang, E.C. (2003) Teaching English as culture: Paradigm shifts in postcolonial discourse. *Diogenes* 50 (May), 3–16.

Eoyang, E.C. (2003a) English as a post-colonial tool: Anti-hegemonic subversions in a hegemonic language *English Today* 19 (4), 23–29.

Giridharadas, A. (2010) Language as a blunt tool of the digital age. *The New York Times,* 16 January. Online at http://www.nytimes.com/2010/01/16/world/americas/16iht-currents.html?pagewanted=all

International Labour Organization (1989) Convention 169. Available at http://www.ilo.org/indigenous/Conventions/no169/lang--en/index.htm

Ljungdahl, L. (2003) The English language and linguistic imperialism: The Trojan horse? *International Journal of Learning* 10, 1503–1511.

Ngũgĩ wa Thiong'o (1986) *Decolonising the Mind: The Politics of Language in African Literature.* London: Heinemann.

Pennycook, A. (1998) *English and the Discourses of Colonialism.* London and New York: Routledge.

Pennycook, A. (2010) English and globalization. In J. Maybin and J. Swann (eds) *The Routledge Companion to English Language Studies* (pp. 113–121). Abingdon: Routledge.

Phillipson, R. (1992) *Linguistic Imperialism.* Oxford: Oxford University Press.

Phillipson, R (2006) English, a cuckoo in the European higher education nest of languages. *European Journal of English Studies* 10 (1), 13–32.

Phillipson, R. (2007) English, no longer a foreign language in Europe? In J. Cummins and C. Davison (eds) *International Handbook of English Language Teaching* Vol. 1. New York: Springer.

Phillipson, R. (2009) *Linguistic Imperialism Continued.* Hyderabad: Orient Black Swan.

Phillipson, R. (2010) Americanisation and Englishisation as processes of global occupation: Coalition or coercion of the willing? Unpublished notes for a presentation at the DUO 1V Dialogue conference, Washington DC, June.

Phillipson, R. (2011) Private email correspondence.

Ramanathan, V. (2005) *The English-Vernacular Divide.* Clevedon: Multilingual Matters.

Skutnabb-Kangas, T. (2003) Linguistic diversity and biodiversity: The threat from killer languages. In C. Mair (ed.) *The Politics of English as a World Language: New Horizons in Postcolonial Cultural Studies.* Amsterdam: Rodopi.

Skutnabb-Kangas, T. (2009) Linguistic genocide: Tribal education in India. *Indian Folklife* April. Available at www.wiki.indianfolklore.org.

Skutnabb-Kangas, T. and Phillipson, R. (1989) 'Mother tongue': The theoretical and sociopolitical construction of a concept. In U. Ammon (ed.) *Status and Function of Languages and Language Varieties* (pp. 450–478). Berlin and New York: Walter de Gruyter and Co.

Smith, T. (2000) *Nga tini ahuatanga o whakapapa korero. Educational Philosophy and Theory* 32(1), 53–60.

Swales, J.M. (1997) English as *Tyrannosaurus Rex. World Englishes* 16 (3), 373–382.

Tupas, T.R.F. (2008) Postcolonial English language politics today: Reading Ramanathan's *The English Vernacular Divide. Kritika Kultura* 11, August, 5–26.

Wierzbicka, A. (2006) *English: Meaning and Culture.* Oxford: Oxford University Press.

Wierzbicka, A. (2010) *Experience, Evidence and Sense.* New York: Oxford University Press.

Wittgenstein, L. (1953) *Philosophical Investigations.* G.E.M. Anscombe, trans. Oxford: Basil Blackwell.

Wong, Gigi (c. 1998) *English is…* Formerly available on Asian Voices website, now defunct.

1 The Challenge – *Ndaraca ya Thiomi*: Languages as Bridges[1]

Ngũgĩ wa Thiong'o

Andũ amwe moigaga atĩ thiomi nyingĩ thĩinĩ wa bũrũri kana wa thĩ nĩ ta nyũmba ya mbamberi, atĩ ũiguwano gatagatĩinĩ ka mĩikarĩre na ka ndũrĩrĩ no ũrehirwo nĩ gũkorwo andũ makĩaria rũthiomi rũmwe tu. ũguo ti gwo ma. Kĩrĩa kĩagĩrĩire nĩ thiomi kwaranĩria, hatarĩ ũhoro wa imwe kũhinyĩrĩria iria ingĩ ... Thiomi ihane ta ndaraca cia kũnyitithania mĩikarĩre.

Some people argue that many languages in a country or in the world can make a house of Babel; they believe that understanding between cultures and among nations can only be brought about by speaking one language. I don't believe that to be the truth. What is important is for languages to be able to communicate without a few of them dominating others. Languages can become bridges.

A bridge assumes an existing gulf, almost impassable ordinarily, between two entities. A bridge enables crossings across the gulf. The nature of the gulf dictates the design and architecture of the bridge. A recognition and close assessment of the gulf is essential in determining the kind of bridge that is needed. In other words, do not spend your resources and energy building bridges where there are no gulfs to cross. A bridge enables a constant to-and-fro between two entities – in short, it enables crossings, transitions and even continuities. In other words, a bridge is not a one-way crossing, for exodus only. The image of the bridge, therefore, brings to the fore the intellectual and artistic wealth that could be an enormous commonwealth, if we built bridges to enable crossings.

The opposite of a bridge is a wall, a barrier, that which bars contact and exchange, or if there is contact and exchange, it is that of a horse and its rider. Remember that between the horse and the rider there is plenty of contact, exchange and even a flow of trust and affection. But the structural basis of their relationship is that of a dictator and the dictated. Uneven power relationships, even those enabling contact, can be barriers to mutually beneficial crossings, transitions and continuities between languages and cultures.

Unfortunately, relationships between languages have not always been characterized by the image of the bridge, but by that of the wall. This is the wall of the inequality of power. The inequality has its basis in economics and politics, but philosophically, its roots lie in the conception of a relationship between languages in terms of a hierarchy: a kind of linguistic feudalism and linguistic Darwinism.

Linguistic and cultural feudalism is the view, consciously or unconsciously held, that some languages – between and even within nations – are of a higher order than others; that they constitute an aristocracy, while others – in a descending order of being – occupy lesser positions, different degrees of minionage. This is because the dominant languages have become perceived, even by the dominated, as having all the magic power of knowledge and the production of ideas – culture itself – whereas the dominated languages are seen as having the opposite. They are seen as incapable of producing knowledge, good ideas and good art.

This perception has nothing to do with the inherent powers of languages. It has been brought about by a historical process. In my book, *Decolonising the Mind*, published in 1984, I told the story of my relationship to my mother tongue, Gĩkũyũ, and my language of education, English. English was also the official language of the colonial state. I told how we used to be punished when we were caught speaking an African language in the school compound. We were humiliated by being made to carry a piece we called 'Monitor' around our necks, literally stating that we were stupid. Thus, humiliation and negativity were attached to African languages in the learning process. A good performance in English, on the other hand, was greeted with acclaim. Two things were taking place in the cognitive process: a positive affirmation of English as a means of intellectual production and a criminalisation of African languages as means of knowledge production. With English, went pride; with African languages, shame. For a long time, I used to think that this was an African problem.

But some years ago, when I was researching my new book, *Something Torn and New*, I found out that what was done to Africans had already been done to the Welsh. In the 19th century, Welsh children caught speaking their mother tongue in the school compound were also humiliated by being made to carry something around their necks with the initials, 'W.N.' (Welsh Not). At the very least, my colonial story had been re-enacted in Wales.

Even earlier than Wales was the case of the relationship between the English and the Irish languages. English colonial settlement was first tried out in Ireland in the 16th century. But the English were finding it difficult to conquer the Irish or, rather, to tame them. In 1598, Edmund Spenser – a contemporary of Shakespeare and the celebrated author of *The Fairie Queene* and other poetic works – published *A View of Ireland at the Present Time*. Spenser was an English land-owner in Ireland and a neighbour to Walter Raleigh – the founder of the colony of Virginia. In his book, *A View of Ireland*, Spenser literally prescribes a cultural solution to the political and military problems posed by the Irish resistance. He argues that, if you change their names – strike out the Mc's and O's of their naming system – and then impose English, the Irish would soon forget the Irish nation. Language conquest would enable, indeed, complete political conquest. The solution to native resistance was thus seen as lying in the erasure of their memory through changing their language and naming systems.

Africans who were taken to the Americas by force by Raleigh and his descendants to become plantation slaves had their languages and their names literally banned, almost as if the colonists were reading from Spenser's manual. In the place of African names, they were given those of their owners. Even the drum language was banned by the act of banning the instrument itself. But the plantation master never lost his linguistic connection to Europe. The Spanish, French, Dutch and English plantation owners all remained connected to their own European languages.

We find similar practices in Asia. Japan banned the Korean language and imposed Japanese during the brief Japanese colonial era. We can say the same things relative to the indigenous peoples of Australia, New Zealand and North and South America. In the history of modern colonialism, all the colonial powers, at one time or other, have imposed their languages on the conquered peoples, thus ensuring that the entire system of production, dissemination and consumption of knowledge takes place through the colonial language alone. Even the very identity of the colonized is expressed in the language of conquest. In Africa, we talk of Francophone, Lusophone and Anglophone Africa – in other words, identities that are based on the languages of the colonial conquest.

The case for mental conquest through language was put best by Lord Thomas Macaulay, who argued – in his famous 1835 *Minute on Indian Education* – that English should be used to create a class, Indian in name, but otherwise imbued with an English mentality. This class, he argued, would help the British effectively govern the vast nation. They would more or less stand as a buffer zone between the governors and the governed.

The result of many years of an imperial relationship between Europe and the rest of the globe is a world of languages divided into a dominant few – largely from Europe – and a marginalized many, largely from Africa, Asia and the Americas. A handful of European languages constitutes an aristocracy. Today, four of the six official languages of the United Nations are European. They dominate in the production and dissemination of ideas; they dominate in publishing and distribution and in the consumption of knowledge; they control the flow of ideas. Intellectuals who come from the, supposedly, lesser languages find that, to be visible globally, they must produce and store ideas in Western European languages, mostly English. In the case of most intellectuals from Africa and Asia, this is how they become visible on the world stage, but simultaneously invisible in their own cultures and languages. Global visibility comes at the price of local or regional invisibility. And within a nation, national visibility comes at the price of regional and communal invisibility.

The consequences for Africa in terms of self-perception and pride, and the conveyance of knowledge, are enormous. A gulf is created between the intellectual elite and the people. The middle class generally becomes defined by its abilities in European languages; the masses, by their rootage in African languages. But since knowledge production and storage is largely in European languages, it also means an ever-deepening gulf between the abilities of the possessors of the two language systems to access each other's knowledge.

I was at a Pan-African conference in Dar es Salaam some years ago to discuss strategies and tactics for encouraging and deepening a reading culture in Africa. One speaker light-heartedly said that if you wanted to hide something from an African, put it in a book. This would be sad, tragic even, were it true. But I put it differently and said that if you wanted to hide knowledge from an African child, put it in English or French. Or if you wanted to hide the keys to the future, hide them in the dominant European languages. Tragically, this is what we do to our children every day in Africa, Asia and in the indigenous cultures of Australia, New Zealand, the Pacific and the Americas.

I remember when my mother used to send me on a journey alone to meet relatives. She would pack food and water for me and then would sit me down and tell me everything about the path before me to ensure that I would not get lost. She punctuated every instruction with the question: do you understand? Only then would she let me go. She was not doing something out of the ordinary. It would be a very irresponsible parent who would give instructions in words and languages that the child does not fully understand.

Nothing is more important than life's journey, and yet, we in Africa and other indigenous cultures send our children on the journey of life with instructions coded in the dominant European languages. The colonialist may have wanted us to go astray, but why would we, an independent Africa, want our children to get lost? Is it a case of the lost giving instructions on how to lose your way in life? The colonists may have even wanted to create a gulf of knowledge between the elite and the people. But why should we in Africa want to continue to deepen and widen the gulf?

I wish it were simply a case of linguistic feudalism, but the reality is that linguistic feudalism is being transformed into linguistic Darwinism. Linguistic Darwinism is the extreme product of the hierarchy of languages, where the growth of a dominant language is dependent on the death of other languages. Languages can grow, but only on the graveyard of others – an attitude that underlies all practices of monolingualism. In the most extreme form of monolingualism, linguistic Darwinism sees the growth of a national language as being dependent on the death of all the other languages. This is the assumption behind many national language policies: in order for the national language to be, other languages must die. There are many variations of this, for instance, when big regional languages are empowered at the expense of the smaller.

The death of any language is the loss of the knowledge contained in that language. The weakening of any language is the weakening of its knowledge-producing potential. It is a human loss. The saying, often cited, that 'the death of an old person is the death of a whole library' is probably true for all languages. Imagine the impoverishment of world culture if all the learning in, say, classical Greek and Latin, had died with the languages? Today, we can only imagine, but never really know, the quantity and quality of knowledge lost with the disappearance of so many languages on earth. Each language, no matter how small, contains the best knowledge of its immediate environment: the plants and their properties, for instance. Language is the primary computer with a natural hard drive.

African languages face the destiny of the dinosaurs: extinction. For the national, African and even the global good, the prevailing power relationships of languages and cultures have to be challenged and, hopefully, shaken up. This was the motivation behind my books, *Decolonizing the Mind* and *Re-Membering Africa*. What is the way out? My first prescription was that writers from marginalized cultures and languages had the duty and responsibility to make themselves visible in their languages. As I did not want to be saying, 'Do as I say, but not as I do', I made the decision – way back in 1978 – to break with English as the primary means of my writing, particularly in fiction and drama. I have no regrets. I still believe that writers and other intellectuals have the duty to challenge and shake up linguistic feudalism and linguistic Darwinism – that hierarchical view of languages – in theory and practice.

But later, I realized that, even though writers bore the primary duty of producing ideas in African languages, there was another equally important player. Writers do not write in order to decorate their home shelves with unpublished manuscripts. They want to be published, in order to reach the reader. But alas, there were no major publishers in African languages. So a lack of publishers in African languages led to a lack of writers in African languages and, therefore, fewer readers of African-language productions and, therefore, fewer publishers willing to risk money by venturing there, creating a vicious circle. The publisher, then, is an integral part of any meaningful challenge to linguistic feudalism and linguistic Darwinism. I have written several works in Gĩkũyũ. But this would have been impossible without the willingness of East African Educational Publishers to invest their resources and skills into the project.

The writer and the publisher need a third partner – the government. Many multilingual African states do not have a national language policy regarding their own African languages. Whatever we may say of colonial states, they – through literature bureaus – often came up with some sort of policies. Far from helping, some post-colonial governments have even shown active hostility towards African languages. Governments have to create an enabling environment in terms of policies and resources. We have only to look at Kiswahili in Tanzania today – the result of Nyerere's progressive linguistic foresight – continued by the succeeding Tanzanian governments. By Kiswahili having a home and a base, it is the one African language that is becoming an active player in the globe. There is, of course, the vexed question of Kiswahili suffocating other African languages, but this is a result of linguistic feudalism.

I could add other partners – booksellers, for instance. They have to be willing to stock books written in African languages. At present, there are very few bookshops that sell such books. Other partners are the award-givers and conference organizers. At present, many awards meant to help in the growth of African literature actually work against African literature. They give awards that stipulate English as the linguistic means of literary production. Conference organizers within, and outside, Africa recognize only those intellectuals and writers who work in English. In Africa, national, continental and global visibility has only gone to writers in English.

The three partners – government, writers and publishers – are the most primary. The working together of these three primary players would go a long way towards empowering knowledge in African languages and, hence, considerably reducing that gulf between African and European languages as producers of ideas.

A question frequently asked, after I talk about the necessity of using African languages as literary instruments, is that of the multiplicity of languages. The presence of many languages within nations can be a strength if the relationship between them is not based on notions of hierarchy, but rather on those of a network. In the vision of a network, there is not one centre, there are several centres equidistant from each other, but connected in a mutual give-and-take. Every language draws from another. Every language gives to another. All languages end up giving to, and taking from, each other, laying the groundwork for a complex independence and interdependence within and between cultures.

But how do they do that? Or rather, how would they do that? By building bridges between them, through translations. Translation is what enables that traffic of ideas between languages. In his book, *A Discourse on Colonialism*, the Martiniquan poet, Aimé Césaire (2000), once described culture contact and exchange as 'the oxygen of civilization'. Language networking through translation can only help in the generation of that oxygen within, and between, nations.

To the other players that I have mentioned, I would also add the translator. The translator is the maker of bridges between languages. Translations have played an important role in the history of ideas. The much-talked-about European renaissance would have been impossible without translations. Christianity and Islam – and their spread all over the world – have been enormously aided by the translations of the *Bible* and the *Qur'an*. Translations and translators can play an even bigger role in the African renaissance. In my book, *Something Torn and New*, I have talked of translations between African languages; translations from Europhonic African literature into African languages; the translations of diasporic works of Caribbean and African American writers into African languages in a vision I describe as Restoration; and finally, the translations of the finest traditions in world cultures into African languages. This bridge-building would have a big impact in the restoration of pride, initiatives and productivity to Africa.

Wherever we are, we have to debate and even share experiences in the kinds of bridge-building that will really create a literate African intellectual, who – rooted in his or her own base – is an integral and active member of the global intellectual community. 'Father, do not send me into the dark alone among strangers', says the persona in one of Sonia Sanchez's poems (2000). Parents have the responsibility to send their children out into the world equipped with the self-confidence that arises from a clear knowledge of their base. Let me put it this way – to know one's language, whatever that language is, and to add others to it is genuine empowerment. But to know all the other languages, while being ignorant of one's own, is mental slavery. I hope that Africa will choose empowerment.

Notes

(1) Based on an address given at the Garden City Literary Festival, Port Harcourt, Nigeria, September 23–26, 2009.

References

Cesaire, A. (2000) *Discourse on Colonialism.* Joan Pinkhom (transl). London and New York: Monthly Review Press.

Sanchez, S. (2000) *Poem at Thirty in Shake Loose My Skin: New and Selected Poems* (p. 4). Boston: Beacon Press.

2 English Language as Bully in the Republic of Nauru

Xavier Barker

Background

Only 21 square kilometres in area, the island of Nauru in the western Pacific Ocean is one of the world's smallest countries. It is low-lying, with a fertile coastal strip encircling a central, once phosphate-laden, plateau. The island has possibly been inhabited for 3000 years by Micronesian and Polynesian peoples. Originally, it seems that there were 12 clans or tribes on the island and, according to an early report on education on the island, there had also been a diversity of dialects (Groves, 1936). A British sea captain and whale hunter was the first European to visit this island in 1798, naming it 'Pleasant Island'. From around 1830, the Nauruan people had more frequent contact with whaling ships and traders. Gradually, sailors from these ships began to take up residence on the island, and cocoa plantations were established there. A highly destructive, 10-year conflict broke out on the island in 1878, which eventually led to it becoming part of the German Protectorate of the Marshall Islands and a focus of missionary interest in 1888 (Rensch, 1993).

Its phosphate reserves were discovered at the beginning of the 20th century, and this became the mainstay of its modern economy. In 1914, following the outbreak of World War I, Nauru was captured by Australian troops and given in trust by the League of Nations to Britain, Australia and New Zealand, which took over the rights to the phosphate production. During the Second World War, the island was occupied by Japan, and almost two-thirds of the population was exiled to the island of Truk (now in the Federated States of Micronesia). Hundreds of these exiles died from starvation and disease. Those who stayed behind worked as slave labour for the Japanese military, and many of them also died from starvation (Fraser & Nguyen, 2005; Nazzal-Batayneh, 2005).

Independence eventually came in 1968, despite some opposition from Australia, and in 1970, the new government purchased the rights to the phosphate business from Australia for AUD 21 million (Nazzal-Batayneh, 2005). This brought considerable wealth to Nauru, at one time giving its citizens one of the highest per capita incomes in the world. However, the country became increasingly reliant on phosphate returns, as imported goods and services began to replace the old subsistence economy. The revenue enabled the Government to provide an extensive welfare system, with free education, health care, electricity and water, along with some subsidised government housing. But continued phosphate mining on Nauru left behind a jagged, rocky wasteland, which, in turn, has brought about drier, micro-climatic changes. Since independence, the habitable land has decreased by two-thirds, and the population has quadrupled. No family has avoided the urbanization that followed (Fraser & Nguyen, 2005).

English as a Bully in the Wider Pacific Region

There are some 1400 languages spoken in the Pacific region, encompassing Australia, Polynesia, Micronesia and Melanesia. Excluding Australia and Aotearoa (New Zealand), the populations of Micronesia, Melanesia and Polynesia combined are about 9.2 million, giving each language in the Pacific an average of 6500 speakers. Even this very low average is somewhat distorted by ignoring the fact that Fijian, Fiji Hindi, Tongan, Tahitian, New Zealand Māori and Samoan actually account for about 1,250,000 speakers on their own (Lynch, 1998). It is also necessary to recognize that English is, by any measure, a Pacific language as well. The fact that it has metropolitan origins is irrelevant. Fiji Hindi, Hawai'ian Creole, Nauruan Pacific Pidgin (NPP) and Melanesian Pidgin all owe something to languages which have only recently been introduced into the Pacific, and yet, they are unquestionably – typologically and culturally – Pacific languages, rather than Indo-European.

It is vital that we understand the relative global scale of the languages and populations in the region. Here, one-quarter of the world's languages are being spoken by less than 0.1% of the world's population (*ibid.*). It is clear that a common language is necessary. In Melanesia, this role has been filled by Melanesian Pidgin, manifesting itself in the mutually intelligible Bislama, Tok Pisin and Pijin. However, Melanesians need to communicate, not only among themselves, but also with their neighbours in Micronesia and Polynesia, not to mention 'Meganesia' – Australia and Aotearoa. The only language common across all these geographies is English. Perhaps it is a fortuitous coincidence that English is also the language of wider communication in Australia, New Zealand and the United States. English is also the official language of the University of the South Pacific (USP), which serves 12 countries in the region, including Nauru. English proficiency is a requirement for the completion of any course of studies with the university – not surprising in a region that is home to a quarter of the world's languages. It is possible, however, to complete degrees in either of Fiji's two major languages – (Bauan) Fijian and Fiji Hindi.

While no official regional language has been declared, English appears to be the *de facto* official language of the Pacific Islands Forum – finding itself to be the linguistic common ground among the 16 member states. English is not only dominant in the region as the language of education and the language of government, but it is dominant in Nauru as well. Several pieces of legislation give it official status in a number of domains, while it appears to have become the *de facto* official language in government, the media and education, without any legal support.

The Socio-Economic Argument for English in the Pacific

It is not so much that English is the *common* language across the Pacific that raises suspicion. Phillipson (1992: 52) argues that English is just one arm of imperialism. It is one of 'six mutually interlocking types of imperialism: economic, political, military, communicative… cultural and social', in which linguistic imperialism is, itself, a sub-type of *cultural imperialism*. On Nauru, the idea that English necessarily leads to economic success is a self-perpetuating notion. An English-proficient oligarchy pushes the idea that in order to participate in a – largely imagined – global community, a proficiency in English is needed. Therefore, Pacific education systems are geared towards focusing on developing English skills, and experts are sought externally, or locals are trained, to perform the duty of teaching English. English has become an end in itself. The falsehood which permeates all of this is that participation in trade, diplomacy, academia, economics, commerce, law and education can *only* be performed in English.

There is a heavy element of pragmatism in Pacific education systems, which continues to promote the shift to English through submersion programmes. It is, as mentioned above, the language of instruction at the university in which Nauru is a stakeholder and the regional *lingua franca* on governmental and diplomatic levels. It is also an established Pacific language. While the acquisition of English can improve one's economic outlook on a regional scale, there are lessons to be learnt from the mass-shift towards English among the urbanized Māori population of 1950's New Zealand (see the Māori chapter in this volume). Language loss, with or without urbanization, has been repeated in every country in the region.

Colonization has changed both the place and the content of learning. It is true that accumulating a greater wealth of linguistic capital does indeed give the individual more power in the linguistic market – more information exists in and about English than Nauruan, more commerce is undertaken in English, more diplomacy, more trade, more technology is described and so on. But not all people will acquire English to the degree that they will be able to take part in that market, so this is a key failing of socio-economically driven development programmes. Failing to provide the same access to opportunity to those who do not possess the same linguistic capital as the elite means that too many will be largely unable to participate in the very social lives and economic lives which are allegedly being developed for their benefit. In other words, only through the successful acquisition of English will an indigenous Nauruan be able to fully participate in the society or the economy that drives educational policy. From an educational point of view, the danger of English-submersion is that Nauruan will ultimately be brushed aside in what will become a subtractive form of bilingualism (Skutnabb-Kangas, 2002).

Despite all this, however, it is still possible to conceive of *additive bilingualism* on Nauru, in which English can be acquired as an additional tool in the intellectual tool-kits of Nauruan children, while still encouraging the academic development of Nauruan. Indeed, bilingual education can both reverse language shift and encourage language diversity. Sadly, far too many Nauruans believe it is simply not possible to teach mathematics, science or geography in their own language, regardless of the fact that they know all too well that they still use Nauruan to explain concepts to their students.

Many Nauruans suffer from a kind of 'linguistic battered-wife syndrome'. They have been convinced by the teachings of English practitioners that their own language is somehow incapable of performing some tasks. It is infuriating to acknowledge that the idea that Nauruan is ill-equipped for *anything* is still being bandied about by Nauruans, unaware that to the English practitioners, the language they are speaking about is, in fact, a euphemism for the speakers of that language. It is a veiled way of declaring the indigenes unfit for modernity, in much the same way that 'developing' has become an accepted euphemism for 'savage'.

External Pressure

There is considerable external pressure on Nauru to shift its linguistic loyalty to English and, typically, education is the arm most often used to apply this pressure. The Australian Government's aid agency, AusAID, for example, offers the Australian Leadership Awards (ALA) and scholarships with which Nauruan leaders can complete Masters or Doctorate studies in Australian institutions. The ALA candidacy requires a certain IELTS score, in line with visa requirements. To date, however, no testing facility has been made available in Nauru, so Nauruans are precluded, by default, from applying for this scholarship. To address this, the Nauru campus of the University of the South Pacific (USP) wrote to AusAID to find out about securing funding to help bring IELTS examiners to Nauru to allow our students to gain eligibility for the ALA scholarship. The request was successful, and a provision was made in the manner of a small recurrent grant to fly an examiner from Australia to Nauru to examine Nauruans in subsidized examinations. While the outcome was good, an email copied to me in error betrayed AusAID's true intentions. The Programme Manager for Nauru with AusAID wrote: 'She's [sic] absolutely right – high level English skills are about Nauru's only hope for the future. What is [the Director] thinking in this regard¿¿¿' Another message quickly followed this email from the Programme Manager to apologize for it being sent to the wrong person, but not for misidentifying me as a woman.

The email, however, revealed more than just AusAID's dream of an English-speaking Pacific. AusAID's representative on Nauru could no longer make his claim that the Director of Education was a disinterested party. Ostensibly, he was a Nauruan public servant, but this email demonstrated at least some collusion between AusAID and the Director to sabotage the Ministry of Education's ambitions to develop a curriculum in a language that the children of Nauru could understand. Why should high-level English skills be Nauru's 'only hope for the future'¿

In 2004, the *Australian Rationalist* magazine published an opinion piece by this writer, in which I claimed that the series of Memoranda of Understanding made since 2001 were, in fact, veiled colonialism and that the price of aid under Prime Minister Howard's 'Pacific Solution' (to house asylum-seeking refugees on Nauru) was for Australian public servants to seize control of the island's government departments. It was clear now that this was what was happening, at least in education. If it was expert assistance being rendered by the Director of Education, Howard perhaps could have respected the Nauruans', the Republic's and the region's wish to develop vernacular curricula (PIFS, 2001). The AusAID Programme Manager's language does suggest that the Director of Education was in some sort of decision-making role. It is not otherwise clear why AusAID would not be more interested in the plans of the Minister or the Secretary of Education, than the thoughts of an alleged underling.

I had also written, at around about the same time, to the Director of Education to ask if he had access to any information on a language-in-education policy. He responded to tell me that:

> on the language policy, the Secretary has approached the Minister on that and he is asking for more information. The original proposal was made to the Minister last year and we are trying to find a copy of that. There is no endorsed policy on language in schools. The proposal is to have Years 1 and 2 in Nauruan, with Year 3 to 5 as transition and Years 5 onwards in English. Pearl and her committee have prepared the Nauruan dictionary and pronunciations, based on the Bible translations. Teachers will be trained so that there is commonality across all classes and schools. (personal communication, 2005)

Inadvertently, the Director of Education seems to have overlooked the fact that his addressee was actually a member of the Committee. The factual errors are clear. The intention was always to provide vernacular immersion from infant school (pre-school) through Grade 3, before introducing English as a subject-of-instruction in Grade 4. Most strikingly, his claim that the committee had prepared a Nauruan Dictionary was completely untrue. Not only had we not prepared one, we had not even discussed it.

Despite the obvious intention of the Ministry of Education (MOE) to pursue the development of vernacular education, the Director would later indicate to me that there was no intention for English to be taught as a second language. It would be the *only* language taught in schools (personal communication, 2005). Accordingly, the Director proceeded to make arrangements for a curriculum package to be imported from the Australian Capital Territory. Here was perhaps his most audacious move to interrupt the transmission and maintenance of Nauruan culture and language. At the same time as the MOE indicated its intention to develop a Nauruan curriculum, 'AusAID's inside man' was preparing to sweep it aside and introduce an English-only curriculum. AusAID's official representative on Nauru was asked about this move towards English-only education, but was assured that the Director worked for the MOE, not AusAID, so AusAID could not intervene.

The strong parallels to what is happening to other Australian-financed regions, in terms of a deliberate rejection of the indigenous language involved, are striking (see the chapter on the Cocos (Keeling) Islands, this volume).

Language Use in Nauru

To better understand the problems associated with trying to 'officialise' Nauruan, we need to look at the language situation outside education. Nauruan is marginalized in almost every social domain, while English continues to encroach on what was once 'Nauruan territory', including the government and the church. Where English has normally been either official *de jure* or *de facto*, its status has grown stronger. The island's media, for example, are now even more English-based than ever. The Nauruan Parliament permits both English and Nauruan to be spoken in the House (Mehra, 1990). It is quite a curiosity to hear a Nauruan parliamentary session. Submissions can made in English and debated in both Nauruan and English, with flawless code-switching and no real preference given to either language. In this way, it reflects language usage in countries such as Vanuatu and Fiji, which both have more than one official language. In the case of Vanuatu, there are systems in place to ensure language equity. Vanuatu's Constitution (Article 64) requires that the Ombudsman be tasked with reporting on 'observances of multilingualism'. Robert Early (1999), however, observes that the Constitution neither defines what multilingualism means, nor is there a clear distinction between language equity and language equality. It may serve Nauru – from a language-planning viewpoint – to have a clear policy on how citizens may expect to have equal access to information, when taking into consideration the numerous domains in which Nauruan shares the stage with English, which is by no means the second language for all Nauruans.

The media on Nauru are under no legal obligation to allocate equal power to the languages of Nauru. Television broadcasting was introduced to Nauru at a formal commissioning ceremony on 31 May, 1991. Regular transmissions were established the next day, and the Nauru Television Service (NTV) now operates 24 hours per day. The only locally produced programme is a popular, but irregular, half-hour news bulletin produced by NTV personnel and delivered in the Nauruan language. Basic policy for the Nauru Television Service was prepared for the Nauru Government by TVNZ, when they initially established the service. Although there have been some changes in practice, the basic policy has not been amended, and it still stands. Among the original objectives, the following are most pertinent (Bentley, 2002):

Programming objectives were considered and proposed as follows:

(1) Present a programme schedule that reflects and promotes cultural, educational, community and social interest in Nauru.
(2) Schedule a balance of programme types (news, current affairs, documentary, sports, adult and children's comedy, drama, health, education, etc).
(3) Provide viewers in Nauru with an improved global information base.
(4) Present a daily 5–10 minute local news programme.
(5) Televise major local sports and social events.
(6) Compile and present a weekly 15–30 minute current affairs/local interest programme, within 12 months of commissioning.
(7) Promote local television programme-making skills.

Of particular interest is that, while there is not a clear obligation to give Nauruan any sort of equity with English in television programming, there is still a duty to provide programming schedules which reflect and promote cultural, educational, community and social interest in Nauru. This requirement can only be read as a demand for locally produced programmes, presumably in Nauruan. Presently, the Nauru Media Bureau produces 30 minutes of news in a mix of English and Nauruan each night for Nauru TV. Radio Nauru announcers mostly speak Nauruan on air, but the general programming is dominated by English-language music, documentaries and news. A local newspaper is delivered electronically, and its content is in English as well. It is no easy task to produce an acceptable volume of media in Nauruan, but the Nauru Media Bureau must continue to pursue this goal.

Only by providing information in a widely understood language can they hope to improve the global information base. It is not a small issue that English-dominated media encourages the shift away from Nauruan by creating the unfair impression that Nauruan is not suited or not equipped to perform the task.

English has been decreed the official language in a number of Acts of Parliament. The Courts Act of 1972 ensures that English is given higher status than Nauruan in the courts of law. It is the declared language of the Supreme Court, and all Nauruan exhibits need to be translated into English (*Courts Act*, Section 47, Language of the Courts). The only other readily available Act of Parliament which specifically calls for English is the Banking Act of 1974, which declares that all accounts and records in any financial institution be kept in English (*Banking Act*, Section 13).

Neither of these Acts affords the Nauruan language the same power as English. This is strange in a country where only a handful of people grow up speaking English outside of the classroom. It is possible to demonstrate that English has indeed bullied its way into a position of prestige, but we have not, thus far, provided any motivation for this.

Pressure to Promote English

Now that we have a somewhat clearer picture of the language situation (both historical and contemporary), it is time to examine where the pressures to further promote English are coming from, both internally and externally.

Nauru has an estimated population of around 10,000 people, of whom 8000 are likely to identify as Nauruans. The remainder of the population is composed of Tuvaluans, I-Kiribati, Filipinos, Indians, Solomon Islanders, Fijians, Chinese, other Asians, other Pacific Islanders (OPIs) and Europeans (a term which Nauruans use generically to cover white people, regardless of their nationalities) (Sumbuk, 2008).

In such an environment, it might be expected that the dominant language would be Nauruan or that some other *lingua franca* might have developed during the long period of contact between these groups. Nauru's population, however, has been quite dynamic. The Chinese and European populations have been rather fluid groups of sojourners who have entered Nauru for short-term business matters or as contracted experts. Over the course of the last 100 years, a unique pidgin has developed to fill a *lingua franca* gap between the Chinese population and all the other communities and between Nauruans and the resident OPIs. This unique island pidgin has been studied by the linguist Jeff Siegel (1990), who called it Nauruan Pacific Pidgin (NPP). Although held in rather low esteem by its speakers, NPP is still a vital language, and it is unlikely to fall out of use, as long as non-indigenes live and work on Nauru.

Nauruan itself is a unique Micronesian language with some 9000 speakers. The Nauruans call their island *Naoero*, themselves – *Dei-Naoero*, and the name they give to their language is *Dorerin Naoero*. The relationship of Nauruan to other Micronesian languages and, indeed, to the Austronesian group has been questioned (Nathan, 1974), but Nauruan is, in many ways, typically Micronesian. This is mostly through its use of a complex noun-classifier system and a rich phoneme inventory. Lexical similarities also exist between Nauruan and the Micronesian languages, as well as with the other Austronesian languages. Just the same, there is no mutual intelligibility between Nauruan and any other language. While Nauruan is a Micronesian language, it has no close relationship with the Austronesian languages that are outside the Micronesian group. Although the use of Nauruan is largely restricted to Nauru itself, there are diasporic communities in the region in which Nauruan is the language of commonality, notably in Fiji, the Marshall Islands and in Australia, where several hundred Nauruans are spread across Melbourne, Sydney, Brisbane and Perth. Of all the expatriate communities, the Marshallese group is most likely to use Nauruan outside the home.

Nauruan has never been accorded any official status on Nauru. Since the introduction of formal education, metropolitan languages have been used as the media of instruction in the village schools. There were a few brief periods during which it is possible to ascertain that Nauruan was being used, however even in those periods, it seems that developing vernacular literacy was only ever considered with a view to later transferring those skills to English. While no official recognition has been given to the Nauruan language, recent public consultations have demonstrated strong and growing community support for both access to information in Nauruan and the 'officialisation' of the language (Nauru Cabinet, 2006; Nauru Constitutional Review Commission, NCRC, 2008). During community consultations for the NCRC and the National Strategic Development Strategy (Nauru Cabinet, 2006), it came to light that the Nauruans overwhelmingly felt that their language was greatly marginalized. English dominates the media, and any written information disseminated by the government is done in English, resulting in a largely uninformed population. This covertly encourages a shift towards English and Nauruan language suicide. Nauruan is, generally speaking, not taught formally at schools, and if it is taught at all, this is not the result of public policy. Nauruan does enjoy intergenerational transmission, but it is increasingly finding itself sharing the stage with English and NPP in previously Nauruan-only domains.

Nauruan, it would seem, is being attacked on all fronts by a relentless army of English practitioners: teachers, policy-makers, legislators, donors and missionaries. A balance must be found between the pragmatism of learning English as a second language in order to communicate with the billions of people in the world who are not able to speak Nauruan, and in maintaining and developing the Nauruan language as a sovereign resource to be inherited by future generations. The fact that English happens to be the *lingua franca* in the region only conspires to reinforce the illusion that English is a 'world language'. Native-like competency in English could only be claimed by the minutest percentage of Pacific Islanders, and many never learn it.

Melanesian Pidgin and French will, in time, be found to be just as guilty of language murder as English. The fact that Melanesian Pidgin is endemic to the Pacific will not absolve it of its crimes as another 'killer language'. It is clear that Nauruan is in danger of becoming extinct (Topping, 2003). For decades, Nauru's leaders have recognized the desire of the community at large to elevate the status of Nauruan. While efforts have been made to develop (and also to stifle, it must be said) vernacular education for a long time, new plans to develop a National Commission on Language are hugely encouraging.

Language and Education on Nauru

Since the arrival of Christian missionaries on Nauru over a hundred years ago, the Nauruan language has been written down in at least two competing orthographies. Aloys Kayser – an Alsatian priest and anthropologist – got the ball rolling in 1907 when he published his *Katechismus in Ekklesia Katholik*. Phillip Delaporte – a German-born American linguist and Protestant missionary – followed up with his *Kleines Taschenwörtebuch Deutsch-Nauru*. Most people consider Delaporte's 1918 *Bibel* to mark the birth of 'Nauruan literature', but by the time it was published, Kayser had already produced three prayer books in Nauruan (1908, 1915a and 1915b). In addition, another German, the anthroplogist Paul Hambruch, had also published a large, two-volume account of his findings on Nauru (1914), which included a brief German-Nauruan glossary of a few hundred words (his own third orthography). While the *Bibel* did not truly mark the 'birth of Nauruan literature', it did, perhaps, mark a high point, for it had taken 11 years to complete, and it enjoyed the full-time translation skills of chiefs Detudamo and Aroi during this time.

Karl Rensch (1993) describes how from 1910, Delaporte established a series of schools on Nauru, in which children were taught to read and write Nauruan. However, Hambruch (1914) reported that – unique among the German Pacific Territories – German was the language of instruction in Nauruan schools. Perhaps there was a failure here to distinguish between the German Administration's schools and those of the missions. Just the same, such muddling sets a fine tone for the conflicting reports that were yet to come.

The Australia-New Zealand-United Kingdom joint administration on Nauru (on whose collective behalf Australia governed) took control of the four schools already on Nauru in 1923 as part of their trustee mandate

(Chambers, 1994). Also introduced at this point was compulsory education and an 'English-based curriculum ... akin to contemporary Australian equivalents' (Chambers, 1994: 124). Albert Ellis – the prospector who first realized Nauru's natural wealth of phosphate resources – gave a firm indication in his book (1935) that an English-lexified pidgin was being used as a *lingua franca* between the Nauruans and the white administration, while Rensch also tells us that by 1921, NPP had become the language of wider communication. Wedgwood (1935–36) reports that English was being taught in all schools on Nauru by that stage. Indeed, the then-Director of Education, W.C. Groves, wrote in the 1949 *Yearbook for Education* that during his tenure on Nauru (from 1937–1938), Nauru's education system was 'a model for all the Pacific'. Groves reported that education began with full immersion in the vernacular, with English gradually being introduced to classes between Grades 3 and 6. He further reports that there was a positive attitude to primary education and that Nauruans regarded it as 'their own'. Groves was also important as a member of the 1938 Nauru Language Committee, which produced the only official document on Nauruan orthography (*Gazette,* no. unknown, 1938).

From that 'model system' to the period in the 1950s when my father was attending school, this bilingual approach appears to have remained in place. Most people of that generation can read and write well in both Nauruan and English. Many of that generation remember fondly being corrected on their Nauruan usage by the priests of the Mission du Sacré-Coeur who ran (and still do run, though no longer with Nauruan proficiency) the Catholic schools on the island.

There is a lack of detailed information, formal and informal, about what the education system was really like on Nauru during the 1960s and 1970s. Rapatahana (personal communication, 2010) provides assurances that 'there absolutely was vernacular instruction in the time [he] taught in Nauru, from 1979 on'. In fact, Rapatahana also verifies that during his time teaching on Nauru, there were some formal Nauruan lessons at Nauru Secondary School, as well some vernacular teaching in the primary schools. By 1987, the Nauruan government had sought the expertise of Barbara Moore, who was a Project Fellow with USP's Institute of Education. Her project was to explore the possibility of developing a Nauruan Language Programme for Schools. It was noted by Moore that there was 'great interest' in teaching Nauruan, but an equally great concern about the 'implications, where to start, the correct form, the methods to use', etc. (1987). What we can reliably say about education between the 1950s and 1987 is that, judging by Moore's account, vernacular education was no longer being systematically practised at any level. Dr Maria Gaiyabu, Nauru's Secretary for Education and a former teacher herself, confirmed this feeling of apprehension about this period in an email to me in 2009:

As far back as 1996, during David Westover's tenure as Secretary for Education, there was a language policy on immersion [in] Nauru Language at Infant level. It was endeavored to gradually build up to Primary and Secondary but curtailed by so many 'experts' and the lack of skilled and knowledgeable people to pursue its continuity.

Sadly, there is no records [sic] of the policy here. God knows what happened... As well, the hiccup at the time was conflicting interest between Nauru Language Bureau and the Curriculum Officer, Maggie Jacobs, on which spelling to use. The latter advocated the Bible version as authentic, being the only written translation. On the other hand, the schools were confused [about] which to follow as two forms of spelling were issued.

Moving into a New Century

At the start of the 21st century, it was clear that there was growing regional concern about the lack of vernacular curricula. In 2001, at a meeting between the Ministers for Education of the Pacific Islands Forum (PIFS), 'the relevance and lack of Pacific foundation of the curriculum' was recognized as being a causative element in the alienation and poor performance of students. The same Ministers 'acknowledged the value of using the indigenous language as the language of instruction in the early years of education' (PIFS, n.d.: 5). When the Ministers met again in 2004, they agreed to 'consider adopting national language policies as part of the education planning process' (PIFS, n.d.: 18).

In 2007, the then Minister for Education approved the formation of a Nauru Language Committee (NLC). Twelve people were selected to become members of the Committee, and three technical sub-committees were formed, namely, a teacher-training committee, a resource committee and a curriculum and policy committee. The NLC would be acknowledged by the Minister, but would have no mandate to implement any policy that might be formulated by the committee. The Committee came about as an initiative from the Education Department, which had identified a need to promote a 'national identity, encouraging participation in national life, dealing with globalisation, language and cultural issues' (Jeremiah, 2007). The Committee embarked on a mission 'to teach and preserve the traditional written Nauruan language' (ibid.). In its draft submission, it outlined nine objectives to be met in just three years:

- To implement a reading and writing Nauruan Language Programme into the Education Curriculum, via the Curriculum, Accreditation, Statistics and Examinations (CASE) Unit of the Education Department.

- To strengthen our children's vernacular and lay the foundations for the learning of a second language.
- To restore our children's national identity and pride by restoring their vernacular inheritance.
- To develop and train teachers who will be teaching the Nauruan Language Programme in both schools and in the community.
- To develop tutors who can continue to train teachers as the programme grows and ensure programme continuity.
- To compile and edit currently available vernacular resources for use in the classrooms.
- To create more resources in the vernacular.
- To widen the range of Nauruan Studies by eventually introducing classes on the History of Nauru and local Cultural Studies.
- To create a Steering Committee to manage and maintain the vernacular programme during its three-year pilot period (ibid.).

The plan was ambitious, but it did reflect broader support for the elevation of Nauruan's status in both education and society at large (Pacific Islands Forum Secretariat, PIFS, n.d.; NCRC, 2008). To date, I believe that only the first objective has grown teeth. The Pacific Regional Initiative for the Development of Education (PRIDE) Project, through the USP's Institute of Education, received a submission for funding for a project called the Nauru Language First Reader Programme. The programme was approved, perhaps rather hurriedly. In just eight weeks, the NLC had moved from having no standard orthography to having funding for a seven-month programme developing resources in the Nauruan language using an orthography that was certain to be met with great resistance from the third of the population who did not use it.

Ultimately, the Department of Education, through the Committee, promoted a strategy to 'develop a new Early Childhood Program based on Nauruan Language and Culture' (ibid.). In the Policy Sub-project, the strategy was to 'implement the language policy for education with special reference to the use of Nauruan language in schools' (ibid.). This sub-project was directed at programme (iii) of the second stage of the language programme, 'compiling a resource collection' (ibid.). In particular, the goal of this sub-project was to produce 20 Nauruan Language Readers for young children. I am greatly encouraged by the strong will of the local Education Department to undertake this work, but both myself and Professor Sumbuk of the University of Papua New Guinea have presented reports (Sumbuk, 2008; Barker, 2008) to the Minister of Education urging some calm. We both felt that a broader, more holistic approach was indeed necessary, and we asked the Minister to consider the establishment of a National Commission on language, with a view to establishing a wider policy. It was necessary to recognize that Nauruans would like to see their language declared as official and to be given access to information in their first language (NCRC, 2008).

Building Additive Bilingualism

An Australian researcher, who visited the island in 1936, stated that young Nauruans assumed that 'European customs are superior to Nauruan customs', simply by virtue of being European (Wedgewood, 1936: 361). She worried that the Nauruan of the time was a person with little sense of social responsibility, and she called for a way to link the past with present. She recognized that Nauruans should reap the benefits of a 'complex European civilization' in the process. There is a means to link the past with the present, although she did not spell it out at the time. The Nauruan language is the body into which the past and present have already been encoded. Almost 75 years have passed, and the argument is still the same. It was the primary force driving the establishment of the Nauru Language Committee, although alarms of language decay were tolling loudly from the mavens, as well. The benefits of European civilization are indeed more accessible in English. So, through a supportive bilingual maintenance programme, it is possible to bridge Nauru's past with her present.

In such a programme, the study of the vernacular as a subject would continue after transition to the second language as medium-of-instruction. This is a necessary transition to prepare Nauruans for the English environment of the University of the South Pacific. Currently, plans are in place to begin that transition from beyond Grade 3 to an English-as-a-subject and Nauruan-medium-of-instruction classroom. By the time Nauruans enter secondary school, they will transition to Nauruan-as-a-subject and an English-medium-of-instruction education – a modality which will continue through their tertiary education. Lotherington-Woloszyn (1993: 29) notes that many Pacific Islanders acquire second languages as a result of cross-cultural interaction, forced by the close proximity of so many language communities. She also notes, however, that too few children are, apparently, 'lucky enough to acquire a working knowledge of standard English' (ibid.) in that fashion. It is only through schooling that most Pacific Islanders will learn English.

The current Minister for Education (2010), the Hon. Roland Kun, is a strong advocate for the development of language rights on Nauru. He has sought advice quite widely – from linguists and educationists – to ensure that his direction is as informed as possible, as is his style of governance. He has recently proposed a raft of measures to develop language planning and maintenance programmes as part of a holistic approach to language issues, not simply matters as they pertain to education. It is with his direction that the Cabinet has recently agreed, in principle, to the establishment of a National Commission on language issues. It is the Minister's vision that the

Commission will design and implement language policy, using the Ministry of Education as the primary body for dissemination. Under the Minister's plan, Nauruan would be elevated to have official status alongside English. He is not so naïve as to think that language equality will be magically installed by this act, nor that Nauruan would be instantaneously held in the same esteem as English. Just the same, it is an important step in permitting Nauruans to begin thinking that their language is up to the task of performing all the functions that English does.

It takes some courage, on behalf of a government, to introduce measures such as the proposed Commission intends to do. The people elected to government are part of an English-educated oligarchy, who, in taking these steps, need to disinterest themselves from the process. To introduce policies – and practices, more importantly – through which Nauruans can participate fully in their society is an important step towards final decolonization. This will involve shifting from the typical Pacific rhetoric, in which governments ostensibly commit to preserving and maintaining their indigenous cultures and languages, while at the same time pressing public policy towards the world outside the region, to developing and improving English proficiency, literacy rates, attainment of formal education and into developing the English-language arts of the stage, screen, song and prose.

Minister Kun's proposals signal a certain will to resist Australian hegemony and the economic occupation described by Phillipson (2008). Developing linguistic human rights is also a possible outcome, should the plans come to full fruition. They will provide children with an education in a language that they understand, and they will make information accessible to every Nauruan as a noble aspiration. This is a far cry from the current situation, in which only those who have sufficient English-language skills are able to monitor their government. The plan, inasmuch as it will be manifest in a maintenance bilingual programme, will also satisfy the principle proposed by the PRIDE Project (PRIDE, 2004), in which English and vernacular languages are used equally, but separately, in the formal learning environment and in which the two languages are equally promoted. This principle is one of UNESCO's four pillars of learning as 'the right of indigenous peoples to their own interpretation of their history as well as the right to learn in their own language' (UIE, 1997a, cited in UNESCO, 2005: 141). (see also, Skutnabb-Kangas, 2002).

The new approach to the linguistic issues on Nauru is an encouraging sign of decolonization. World-class education is being developed, while support is still there for the maintenance of the indigenous languages. It is by maintaining Nauruan through education that the nation will be able to develop an army of skilled language-users who will be better prepared to participate in language planning projects, thus developing the language for modern use. Only an *additive bilingual programme* can be considered of value here. The Government of Nauru, in beginning to develop a vernacular language plan, has broken the tacit bond between our island and the West. For too long, we deferred to what was pushed, falsely, as a global language. Now we can promote indigenous culture and language as being 'equal' to English. Nauruan thinking will now become an undertaking in the language of our forefathers.

Conclusion

Nauruan can be considered an endangered language on several counts. The population of the speech community is small, and the physical environment here is hostile. But as Nauruan begins to emerge from a hostile political environment, the most alarming threat is the socio-economic circumstances that continue to pressure Nauruan out of existence.

In Nauru, English is a bully, which uses commonality to perpetuate its senior ranking long after this can be justified. It is the illegitimacy of the claims of superiority that allow one to draw parallels with other illegitimate claims, such as those of racists and sexists. English is the ultimate 'rankist'. Even so, the problem remains that 1400 languages, spread among 9 million people with common goals and aspirations – such as the University of the South Pacific and the Pacific Islands Forum – is a problem. There needs to be a constant check in place to ensure that indigenous languages and cultures are maintained, in spite of the use of English for some pragmatic matters.

While we Pacific Islanders can indeed keep checks on English to make sure she is performing an additional role to that of our vernacular languages, we must also resist the pressure from organizations such as AusAID, which continue to act as agents of English dominance. As with the schoolyard bully, so, too, with the linguistic bully – if the aggressive behaviour is not challenged, the behaviour becomes habitual (O'Moore & McGuire, 2001). Like the schoolyard bully, only by active disapproval can the power imbalance be redressed.

We do need English. Only 10,000 people – at the most – are available to share the knowledge that is encoded in Nauruan. It is a Pacific language, and it is spoken by many islanders in the region as a second language. As a Pacific language, it is the property of Pacific Islanders. It is a tool that we own and which should be available to us to use as we see fit. The elevation of vernacular languages – in both status and esteem – is the only way to reverse the current situation, where, somehow, the possessed – the Nauruan citizen – has been only playing as possessor of the English language.

Postscript by Vaughan Rapatahana

I went back to the Republic of Nauru in February, 2010, after first going there in 1979, as Head of English at Nauru Secondary School. Topside remains a bitter ironic symbol for the barren devastated landscape wrought there, ultimately, only serving to make non-Nauruan fields greener, more fertile, richer. The English-speaking colonial powers robbed one land to make their own plains flourish. As of now, it remains a signal symbol of rampant (neo-)colonialist greed, years after the event.

Topside, Nauru

like one-armed
drownings,
these
scarred
escutcheons

crash
through the quaky crust,
dusty,

in no clear
pattern

some
    stalk
        others

a few
                adrift,

even more
                          abandoned;

all eyeless.
doomed.

there is <u>nothing</u> else here

frigate birds stay away,

even the leaves have left

      g g
just ja ^ ^ ed
monoliths:
dead men.

expedition
over –

stone surrender
to the indefectible
sun

References

Barker, X. (2008) Report on the Nauru Language Committee. Unpublished manuscript, University of the South Pacific.

Bentley, J.E. (2002) Pacific Islands television survey report. Online document, accessed 30 June 2009. http://portal.unesco.org/ci/en/files/8153/11858921141bentley_report. pdf/bentley_report.pdf

Chambers, D. (1994) *Boss Hurst of Geelong and Nauru*. South Melbourne: Hyland House.

Cummins, J. (1994) 'The acquisition of English as a second language. In K. Spangenberg-Urbschat and R. Pritchard (eds) *Reading Instruction for ESL Students* (pp. 36–62). Newark, DE: International Reading Association.

Delaporte, P. (1907) *Kleines taschenwörterbuch Deutsch-Nauru*. Online dictionary, accessed 5 May 2010. http://www.trussel.com/kir/naudel.htm

Delaporte, P. (1918) *Bibel*, Bible Society of the South Pacific, trans. Suva, Fiji: Bible Society of the South Pacific.

Director of Education (2005) Personal communication.

Early, R. (1999) Double trouble, and three is a crowd: Languages in education and official languages in Vanuatu. *Journal of Multilingual and Multicultural Development* 20 (1), 13–33.

Ellis, A.F. (1935) *Ocean Island and Nauru*. London: Angus and Robertson.

Fraser, H. and Nguyen, M. (2005) Between a mined-out rock and a hard place. *Uniya: View on the Pacific Briefing Series*. Online document, accessed July 2005. http://www.uniya. org/research/view_nauru.html

Gaiyabu, M. (2009) Personal communication.

Gaunibwe, M. (2004) The selling of Nauru. *Australian Rationalist* 68 (Spring). Available at: http://www.rationalist.com.au

Government of Nauru (1972) *Courts Act 1972*. Yaren, Nauru: Nauru Government Press.

Government of Nauru (1974) *Banking Act 1974*. Yaren, Nauru: Nauru Government Press.

Government of Nauru (2006) *National Sustainable Development Strategy*. Yaren, Nauru: Nauru Government Press.

Government of Nauru (2008) *Report from the Nauru Constitutional Review Commissioner*. Yaren, Nauru: Nauru Government Press.

Government of Vanuatu (1980) *Constitution of the Republic of Vanuatu*. Online document, accessed 9 December 2009. http://www.vanuatu.gov.vu/government/library/ constitution.html

Groves, W.C. (1936) *Native Education and Culture-Contact in New Guinea: A Scientific Approach*. Melbourne: Oxford University Press.

Groves, W.C. (1949) Nauru: A pattern for the South Pacific. In *The Year Book for Education* (pages unknown). Paris: UNESCO.

Hambruch, P. (1914) *Nauru Ergebnisse der Sudsee Expedition, 1908–1910: II Ethnographie, B Mikronesien, Bd. I*. Hamburg: L. Friederichsen & Co.

Jeremiah, C. (2007) Nauru Language Program 2008–2010. Unpublished draft presented to the Nauru Language Committee.

Kayser, A. (1915a) *Buch it Detaro*. Nauru: Mission Katholik.

Kayser, A. (1915b) *Buch it Detaro*. Nauru: Mission Katholik.

Kayser, A. and Gründl, F. (1908) *Buch it Detaro*. Nauru: Mission Katholik.

Lotherington-Woloszyn, H. (1993) Is there an easy solution to bilingual education in the Pacific? *Directions: Journal of Educational Studies* 29(15, 2), 28–39.

Lynch, J. (1998) *Pacific Languages: An Introduction*. Honolulu: University of Hawai'i Press.

Mehra, N.N. (1990) *Practice and Procedure of the Parliament of Nauru*. Nauru: Parliament of Nauru.

Metge, J. (1976) *The Māori of New Zealand*. London and Boston: Routledge and Kegan Paul.

Moore, B. (1987) *Developing a Nauruan Language Programme for SchoolsUniversity of the South Pacific Institute of Education*. In G. Nathan Nauruan in the Austronesian language family. *Oceanic Linguistics* 12, 479–501.

Nazzal-Batayneh, M. (2005) Nauru: An environment destroyed and international law. Online article, accessed 6 October 2010. Available at http://www.lawanddevelopment.org/articles/nauru.html

O'Moore, M. and McGuire, L. (2001) *Bullying at School*. Dublin: Anti-Bullying Centre, Trinity College.

Pacific Islands Forum Secretariat (n.d.) Forum basic education action plan. Online document, accessed 18 April 2010. http://www.forumsec.org.fj/resources/uploads/attachments/documents/FEDMM%2005%20FBEAP%20and%20reviews.pdf

Pacific Regional Initiatives for the Delivery of Basic Education (PRIDE) (2004) Culture, literacy and livelihoods: Reconceptualising the reform of education. In *Oceania Literacy and Livelihoods: Learning for Life in a Changing World* (35: 45). Vancouver: Commonwealth of Learning.

Pacific Regional Initiatives for the Delivery of Basic Education (PRIDE) (2008) Nauru language first reader program 2008. Unpublished application for sub-project funding under the PRIDE Project.

Phillipson, R.H.L. (1992) *Linguistic Imperialism*. Oxford: Oxford University Press.

Phillipson, R.H.L. (2008) The linguistic imperialism of neoliberal empire. *Critical Inquiry in Language Studies* 5 (1), 1–43.

Rapatahana, V. (2010) Personal communication.

Rensch, K. (1993) Father Aloys Kayser and the recent history of the Nauruan language. In K. Rensch (ed.) *Nauru Grammar*. Yarralumla: Embassy of the Federal Republic of Germany.

Siegel, J. (1990) Pidgin English. *Journal of Pidgin and Creole Languages* 5 (2), 157–186.

Skutnabb-Kangas, T. (2002) Language policies and education: The role of education in destroying or supporting the world's linguistic diversity. Online article, accessed 4 October 2011. http://www.linguapax.org/congres/plenaries/skutnabb.html

Sumbuk, K. (2008) *Recommendations to Nauru Language Committee*. Unpublished paper, University of Papua New Guinea.

Topping, D.M. (2003) Saviors of languages: Who will be the real messiah? *Oceanic Linguistics* 42 (2), 522–527.

UNESCO (2005) *EFA Global Monitoring Report 2006*. Paris: UNESCO Publishing.

Wedgwood, C.H. (1935/1936) Report on research work in Nauru. *Oceania* 6, 359–394.

3 Out of Sight, Out of Mind... and Out of Line: Language Education in the Australian Indian Ocean Territory of the Cocos (Keeling) Islands

Pauline Bunce

Introduction

In a speech to the Asia Society Australasia in Singapore on 12 August, 2008, the former Australian Prime Minister, Mr Kevin Rudd, pledged to make Australia 'the most Asia-literate country in the collective West'. He said that all Australian businesses, academic institutions and government agencies needed to understand Asia. He called on all Australians to become more active in Asia, in particular, by learning Asian languages. To this end, he then allocated extensive funding to a National Asian Languages and Studies in Schools Program (NALSSP), which was to focus on the languages and cultures of China, Indonesia, Japan and Korea. The 'aspirational target' for this scheme is that, by 2020, at least 12% of Australian students will leave secondary school equipped with sufficient fluency in one of the target languages (Mandarin Chinese, Indonesian, Japanese or Korean) to be able to 'engage in trade and commerce in Asia and/or university study' (Department of Education, Employment and Workplace Relations, DEEWR, 2009: 2).

Funding has been made available for all state and territory schools in the country to support the teaching and learning of Asian languages and the study of Asia, including programmes that support the implementation of the *National Statement for Engaging Young Australians with Asia in Australian Schools* (Curriculum Corporation, 2006). Given these important regional goals and generous funding, it would only be logical to assume that those Australian schools which already have significant numbers of students from the Asian region would see themselves as having a head-start in pursuing such a vision. Just imagine a school in which 100% of pupils already spoke one of the target Asian languages. What would their school's language and literacy programmes look like?

At least one such school already exists. It is the Home Island primary campus of the Cocos (Keeling) Islands District High School, in an Indian Ocean Australian Territory, 2768 kilometers north-west of Perth, Western Australia. In this little school of approximately 70 students, all the children speak Cocos Malay – an island version of Indonesian (Ansaldo, 2009). Why is it, then, that this tiny school of all-Indonesian speakers is most often described by its teachers as '100% ESL' (English as a Second Language)? Surely this is 'deficit thinking' (Valencia, 1997). This defines these youngsters by what they do not yet know (Skutnabb-Kangas, 2000). Why did this school establish some kind of 'quarantined language block' for English-only use and impose its own school-wide 'Standard Australian English Charter' (*Annual Reports*, Cocos (Keeling) Islands District High School, 2007, 2008)?

While the education provided in the Home Island School and its sister campus on West Island is entirely funded by Australia's federal government, the teaching service is delivered under a contract with the state of Western Australia's Education Department. The federal Department of Regional Australia, Regional Development and Local Government may state on its website that a 'vigorous bilingual programme' is under way at the two schools, but the reality could not be further from such a claim, nor further away from the landmark *Education Policy Statement* that was signed by all three levels of government in 1989, in which the following statements appeared:

> The education policy to be followed at the schools will be determined by the Commonwealth.
>
> Instruction in Malay by a teacher in early years... English is to be introduced progressively until all subjects are taught in English by Year 7... Teaching will be in accordance with Malay cultural patterns... Modern approaches to the teaching of English as a Second Language and to Bilingual Education will be adopted... [In the secondary classes] the WA curriculum to be adapted to local needs, including Cocos Malay culture and Indonesian/Malaysian... Formal instruction in Indonesian/Malaysian will be offered. (*Education Policy Statement*, 1989)

The current educational practices in this Australian Territory are at odds with Commonwealth government thinking about the place of Asian languages in Australian schools and the fundamental principles of bilingual education. The islands' schools' practices could also be in direct contravention of the international assurances given by the Australian Government to the United Nations General Assembly in 1984. On the Cocos (Keeling) Islands, the practice of English-language teaching is nothing less than

'dominant-language-medium   assimilatory   submersion   education'
(Skutnabb-Kangas, 2009). Within this book's galaxy of Hydra heads, the
choice for Cocos is clear – in this remote Australian territory, English
language education is a bully.

The Absolute Importance of Mother-Tongue Education

Of course, the Australian Cocos Malay parents on Home Island want
the best for their children. They remember their own struggles with learning
English, and they are well aware that their hard-earned, current positions in
the various Cocos workplaces have a lot to do with their own facility in
Australia's national language. For three decades now, the English language
has been thoroughly promoted by mainlander, monolingual speakers as
offering 'all things to all people', while the local Cocos Malay language has
been denigrated (mostly by non-Malay speakers) as merely an 'oral dialect'
that is 'not good enough' or, somehow, 'lacking in sophistication'. This
attitude has worked against all calls for bilingual education in the territory.
Three decades of mainland school teachers and countless visiting government
officials have displayed a collective and appalling lack of knowledge regarding
language education and multilingualism. Yet all have felt qualified to 'know
what's best' for the islands' students, many of whom currently struggle to
complete a full secondary education.

During my recent visits to the islands, in 2009 and 2010, many of my
former students (the current parent group) despaired that their children
were not learning English as well as they had done in the 1980s, even though
the islands' schools are far better resourced now than many mainland
Australian schools. What the parents have forgotten is that they, themselves,
came late to school-English. Their cohort was much older than the current
crop of secondary students. The parent-group had spent their early years
fully immersed in their first language and culture and had gained an excellent,
naturally acquired cognitive development. By the time that I met them in
the rudimentary secondary school in 1982, they were absolutely ready and
highly motivated to transfer their well-established concepts and problem-
solving skills into another language. They had the ideas – all they really
needed was a lot of new vocabulary.

We now know that early dominant-language medium education for so-
called 'minority group' children can actually be detrimental to their cognitive,
linguistic and educational development. It can also contribute to the social
marginalization of their communities. In fact, a substantial body of research
has shown that the length of mother-tongue medium education is more
important than any other factor (including socio-economic status) in
predicting the success of indigenous and minority students, including their

success in the dominant language (Cummins, 2000; Skutnabb-Kangas, 2000; Tollefson & Tsui, 2003; Mohanty, 2006; Heugh, 2009; Skutnabb-Kangas et al., 2009).

To deny this reality, and to forcibly impose English in the mistaken belief that the Malay language is the children's worst enemy, is nothing short of 'linguistic imperialism' (Phillipson, 1992). While the wider Malay-Indonesian language is under no threat of extinction, its traditional Cocos variety is certainly coming under pressure from: (1) a muddle-headed, on-island snobbery that has emerged from decades of teacher-jibes against Cocos Malay; and (2) the recent and readily available models of standard and idiomatic Bahasa Indonesia and Bahasa Malaysia that are used on the internet and on satellite television.

Some Historical Background

The Cocos (Keeling) Islands are a Territory of the Commonwealth of Australia. The tiny coral atoll may appear to be little more than a speck on any map of the vast Indian Ocean, but its very location is highly strategic from a geopolitical standpoint. Along with its contentious neighbour to the north-west – the island of Diego Garcia in the Chagos Archipelago – which has long served as a huge US military base (Pilger, 2004; Vine, 2009; Fogle, 2011), Cocos is a vital piece of strategic territory in an ocean with a paucity of islands.

The Cocos (Keeling) Islands' schools are an Australian Commonwealth responsibility and are fully financed by the federal government under a Service Delivery Arrangement (SDA) between the federal-level Department of Regional Australia and the West Australian Education Authority. There are two schools on the islands – one with only primary classes and one with both primary and secondary classes. These schools have been combined into the two 'campuses' of the Cocos Islands District High School.

All the children who attend the Home Island School are Malay, speak Cocos Malay as their first language and follow the customs and culture of their island home. Their ancestors were brought to this remote atoll in the Indian Ocean as labourers for a copra plantation in 1826. Over subsequent decades, the labour force was reinforced by further groups of workers sourced from several islands of present-day Indonesia. A distinctive island culture and Malay dialect then developed within a feudal plantation society, ruled over by successive generations of a Scottish family. In 1955, the islands passed from British to Australian sovereignty. They were designated a 'non-self-governing territory' under the auspices of the United Nations, and all residents became Australian citizens. This was the islands' political status until 1984, when the Cocos Malay people voted for full integration with Australia in an Act of Self Determination (ASD), which was witnessed by a United Nations Visiting Mission.

A small school for mainland Australian children was established next to the airstrip on West Island in 1955, but it was 24 more years before anything comparable was provided for the Cocos Malay population on Home Island, in 1979. Despite Australia's trusteeship over the island territory, all matters of Cocos Malay education and welfare were left to the islands' former owner, Mr J.C. Clunies-Ross. During that time, he only operated a tiny, part-time school for a selected few of his workers' children, in which he taught a very restricted curriculum. It took two visits of United Nations Missions to the islands in 1973 and 1980 to shame the Australian government into providing wider access to schooling for Home Island's Malay children. Even then, the government funded a new school building on West Island before a proper school was built on Home Island on a new site, well outside the Clunies-Ross family compound.

Compulsory education for all children in the island territory was finally mandated in the 1980 Education Ordinance, making this Australian territory one of the last places in the world to put such legislation into place.

Even though the islands' educational services had been provided, in some fashion, by the state of Western Australia (WA) since 1955, there was no formal written agreement between the two levels of government with regard to education policy. The Commonwealth merely bought the 'WA package' and let the state authority choose its own teachers, conduct its own inspections and advise (or not) its island students on studies beyond the compulsory years.

I was privileged to teach the first-ever groups of secondary students on the islands in 1982–1983, albeit in the former airport control tower, which had been condemned and left abandoned for a number of years. I returned to the territory in 1987–1988 and taught in the newly built West Island School. During that time, all expatriate island personnel were limited to two-year contracts, for fear that people would become out-of-touch with mainland events and educational practices. Indeed, communications with the mainland were very limited. We relied on crackly radio-telephone contact and fortnightly chartered air services. In 1987, I was the first teacher to be offered a return-contract. No doubt, this was related to my on-going social work with the Cocos Malay community on the mainland and an invitation from the islands' leaders to write a commemorative book on the atoll's history, ecology and culture for Australia's bicentenary celebrations in 1988 (Bunce, 1988).

In 1983, in the lead-up to the UN-sponsored vote, an interesting 'test of wills' took place between the Commonwealth government and the WA Education Department over the islands' schools' language policies, teacher-appointment procedures and the curriculum content, given the pledges and promises that the Australian government was making to the United Nations. One of these was a naive assurance that the UN, its agencies and its international work would be directly incorporated into the schools' teaching programmes. Stubbornly, WA's Director of Schools at that time saw this request as 'outside interference' in the school's curriculum. I was teaching on the islands at the time and watched as this dispute was taken as a 'last straw' by the WA education authorities. Two senior education officials from WA made an overnight visit to the islands to personally confront on-island Commonwealth officials, regarding language policies and other perceived instances of 'interference' in matters of school administration. From then until today, the Cocos schools have continued to remain at the centre of an on-going State-Commonwealth educational 'tug o' war'.

Not to be outdone in the State-Commonwealth tussle at that time, the federal government sent an expert on second-language acquisition to the islands in October 1984, to test the islanders' English-language skills. His subsequent report was highly critical of the nature of language teaching in the islands' schools. His report (Ingram, 1984) created a huge furore on the islands, with some teachers driving around the West Island community with a mock coffin, labelled 'Cocos education' on a car roof. The report's strong and detailed recommendation that the Cocos Malay teaching aides be given opportunities to be up-graded to 'full-status teachers', in similar fashion to Aboriginal teaching assistants in the Northern Territory, remains unaddressed to this very day. Several of the aides had attended year-long teacher training programmes on the mainland in the 1970s and 1980s, and they had taught alongside mainland teachers for several years. But as there appears to be no official mechanism in the WA state system for the up-grading of 'indigenous aides', these highly experienced teachers continue to play second-fiddle to younger, monolingual, mainland teachers.

WA's simplistic over-reaction to the federal government's criticism was to severely curtail the teaching of Malay language and culture and to emphasise English at all costs. By 1986, there was no Malay content left in the secondary school and only incidental coverage in Home Island's primary school. A subsequent attempt by the Island Administration to reintroduce Malay language and culture to the high school, in line with their UN agreement, was strongly resisted. The classes, conducted by the islands' interpreter, were regularly and conspicuously undermined by excursions, assemblies, meetings and the like.

In 1987, the Commonwealth appointed a teacher-interpreter of Indonesian to the islands' schools. Unfortunately, the position was only part-time in any one school, and the incumbent was regarded in the staffroom as an 'admin spy'. A WA-sourced Indonesian teacher followed, and the resistance eased somewhat. The departure of the 'coffin bearers', my own re-appointment to the islands in 1987, and the presence of the Indonesian teacher meant that there were now two bilingual teaching staff from WA and some new teachers who were eager to learn Cocos Malay. Relations with the Commonwealth improved somewhat, until an incident at the end of 1988 drew the (then) all-Malay Cocos Council into the education arena.

In 1986 and 1987, a representative of the Cocos Council had been involved in teacher-selection interviews. Late in 1988, they learned that teacher selections for the following year had already been finalised and that they were not to be consulted. No one seemed interested in their bitter complaints. Just before my second exit from the islands at the end of 1988, the Council invited me to address them on the 'changes and differences I had seen between my two terms on Cocos' – 1982–83 and 1987–88. I decided to take a more indirect tack. I addressed and proceeded to explode a number of language-learning 'myths' that I knew had been presented to them by a procession of school principals and WA education officials. It was a deliberate consciousness-raising exercise, in which I was determined to boost their pride in being and speaking Malay. I suggested that they invite one of their former advisers back to the islands as an education consultant. This they did, and the stage was reset for some more high-energy State-Commonwealth discussions on education policy on the islands (Whittington, 1989).

In July 1989, representatives from the Commonwealth Department of Territories, the WA Ministry of Education, the Island Administration and the Cocos Council thrashed out the first-ever negotiated education policy statement for the territory (*Education Policy Statement*, 1989). A bilingual school plan for Home Island was approved by the Commonwealth Minister for Territories, but its implementation and staffing requirements were a real stretch for the WA Education Ministry. When one bilingual teaching couple's extended contract eventually expired and they left the islands, the plan stalled. Without strong commitment and bilingual leadership in the school, even the Home Island parents became worried about the apparent 'late start' to English-language learning, and the school reverted to its earlier, English-with-translation mode. The former WA status quo was thus reinstated in the 1990s.

As the 1984 United Nations' and ASD's 'spotlight' on the islands gradually faded, the Commonwealth government moved the Indian Ocean Territories portfolio from department to department and gradually let Cocos' matters slip from view. New service delivery agreements with various West Australian government departments were put into place in the 1990s, communications with the mainland improved, expatriate contracts were no longer restricted to two or three years and the appointment of teachers reverted to WA hands. Some of the 1984 'coffin bearing' teachers have since returned on a long-term basis, and the school itself is now empowered to interview and appoint its own teachers.

During a visit to the islands in 2004, I was approached by one of the Cocos Malay 'support teachers', who asked me to make some enquiries about school holiday arrangements when I returned to the mainland. This teacher was concerned that the most important traditional celebration on the islands' calendar had been 'downgraded' and that the mainland teachers had scheduled the year's holiday arrangements to suit themselves, rather than the community. I converted this enquiry and a few questions of my own into a sequence of Questions on Notice that were asked in the WA Legislative Assembly on 22 June, 2004 (Figure 3.1). The state department's response was that the schools were the federal government's responsibility.

Since then, all of my efforts to have these questions addressed by the Commonwealth government have failed. Today, the old State-Commonwealth

---

Cocos (Keeling) Islands, Education Programmes and School Holiday Arrangements

2022. Hon. Robin Chapple to the Parliamentary Secretary, representing the Minister for Education and Training. With regard to education on the Australian Territory of the Cocos (Keeling) Islands, I ask:

(1) If the Minister is aware of the 1989 agreement between the (then) Ministry of Education in WA, the (then) Commonwealth Department of Territories and the (then) Cocos (Keeling) Islands Council, regarding the central importance of the Cocos Malay language and culture in the territory's education programmes?

(2) If no to (1), why not?

(3) Will the Minister name all of the current West Australian teachers of Cocos Malay children who are fluent in either Cocos Malay, Indonesian or Bahasa Malaysia?

(4) Will the Minister name all of the current West Australian teachers of Cocos Malay children who have ESL (English as a Second Language) or LOTE (Languages Other Than English) qualifications?

(5) If no names can be provided for (3) and (4), why is that the case?

(6) Will the Minister explain why the most significant cultural and religious celebration of the year for the Cocos Malay people, 'Hari Raya', is no longer accorded a week-long school holiday?

(7) Will the Minister explain how and why the islands' teachers have been able to arrange a three-week long holiday for the schools in the middle of the year?

(8) Was there any community or Cocos Council consultation regarding the holiday arrangements mentioned in (6) and (7)?

(9) Has there been any community or Cocos Council consultation, regarding the recruitment and the continuation of teacher contracts on the islands?

(10) Will the Minister explain why there is no longer any formal Indonesian Language programme in the islands' secondary school classes?

(11) Will the Minister outline the WA Education Department's plans for upgrading the current Cocos Malay Teaching Assistants to full-teacher status?

(12) Will the Minister outline the WA Education Department's current vision for Bilingual Education for the Cocos (Keeling) Islands, given the 1989 agreement?

(13) Will the Minister outline the new policy and financial ramifications for Cocos schools, following the Commonwealth's decision to include Cocos Malay students in their Indigenous Language Speaking Students Programmes?

Hon GRAHAM GIFFARD replied:
(1)-(13) The responsibility for the provision of Education Services on Cocos (Keeling) Island [sic] rests with the Commonwealth Minister for the Indian Ocean Territories.

Figure 3.1 An excerpt from *Hansard*, WA Government Legislative Assembly, 22 June 2004

see-saw of responsibility continues to exist, with WA apparently being able to make all the educational decisions, without even having to be answerable to their own state parliament for the actions they take as service providers for the Commonwealth, and the Commonwealth Government apparently not being obliged to respond to Commonwealth matters raised in a state parliament. Even the detailed submissions that I have made to the Prime Minister (in 2009 and 2010) and two federal cabinet ministers (one delivered by hand) in 2010 have had little effect. In 2011, a long-delayed, brief reply from one federal ministry firmly declared that there were 'no problems' regarding language education in the territory.

The islands, their cultural heritage and their educational policies have truly become 'out of sight and out of mind', falling, as they do, into the cracks between State and Commonwealth jurisdictions. Even the Cocos Islands Council appears to have left the issue alone in recent years. This could reflect the fact that its younger councillors and administrative staff may be reluctant to challenge the authority of the islands' teachers on educational matters. The bullies win again.

Current Educational Concerns

My 2004 return visit to the atoll was sponsored by the Cocos (Keeling) Islands Council. I was a guest at the islands' 20th-anniversary celebrations of the UN-endorsed Act of Self Determination. I visited both campuses of the Cocos Islands District High School and was really impressed by their wealth of facilities. However, one really telling moment occurred when I spoke to the all-Malay Kindergarten Year One combined class on Home Island. I sat down on a tiny chair and began to describe my life amidst the skyscrapers of Hong Kong, where I was living at the time. I spoke in Cocos Malay. After a few moments, the Cocos support teacher stopped me and started to retell the children what I had been saying, also in Cocos Malay. The children, the interpreter and I immediately burst out laughing. That day, the interpretation would have to be from Malay to English for the non-plussed, non-Malay-speaking class teacher. The everyday role of the support teacher was so obviously that of a one-way interpreter from English-speaking adults to her Malay-speaking students. The three adults in the room that day were all very aware that we had made a rather Freudian slip and that we had inadvertently stepped into the forbidden zone of language-use protocols with a guest who was known to hold a very different perspective from that of the current school leadership.

In the Cocos Islands District High School's 2007 and 2008 *Annual Reports* (WA Department of Education), there is an entry for the K-1 class headed, 'Bilingual program', under which it states that 'all teacher instructions were translated'. Students learned vocabulary 'alongside Cocos Malay', had 'LOTE lessons with Nek [grand-parent]' and the room displays were all bilingual, using red letters for Malay and blue letters for English. This is not a 'bilingual programme' in anyone's language The classic definition of bilingual education requires that the educational system uses two languages as media of instruction, in subjects other than the languages themselves (Andersson & Boyer, 1978; Skutnabb-Kangas, 2000).

The original bilingual plan that I drew up for the school in 1989 – as part of a post-graduate diploma in Bilingual Education with the Northern Territory University (now Charles Darwin University) – had at least three or four years of early teaching in Cocos Malay, with the gradual introduction of English in the middle years. The students' mother tongue was to have been given full status, and students were to have progressed towards increasingly sophisticated literature and discourse in either Bahasa Indonesia or Bahasa Malaysia (both of which have vast resources available in print and electronic form). This plan was incorporated into the 1989 *Education Policy Statement*, agreed between the local, state and federal governments, mentioned above.

The continual re-allocation of the Indian Ocean Territories portfolio around different Commonwealth departments, the fading importance of promises made to the United Nations and a change in staffing practices in the WA Education Department has seen the islands' schools slip out of the national and international spotlights and revert to an 'isolated ESL situation' in the eyes of the WA Education Department. The schools are still a Commonwealth responsibility, however, and they are still fully financed by the Commonwealth. Today, the schools' wealth of educational resources, its teams of 'specialist teachers' and classroom aides, and its comfortable, up-to-date facilities far exceed those that can be found in many metropolitan, mainland schools. It would seem that the Commonwealth government is more than happy to merely 'sign off' on the funding for any WA-based scheme or entitlement, no questions asked.

In the Attorney-General's Department's online report on the islands (2005–2006), the school is described as 'distinctly unique [sic], attempting to recognise and value an isolated culture and language whilst attempting to integrate students into the wider Australian lifestyle and develop appropriate English language skills'. In the online reports of Commonwealth government agencies, the phrase 'vigorous bilingual program' is present in every case. By contrast, the word 'bilingual' is almost completely absent from WA's online sources on the islands' schools. When the term is used, it appears as an adjective for the support staff and in the phrase 'bilingual classrooms'. The WA state-based, online descriptions of the schools are peppered with the terms 'ESL' and 'literacy challenges' (unspecified, presumably meaning English). One wonders whether the Commonwealth really knows what it is getting for its money under this service-delivery arrangement.

Is there is any discussion at all on Cocos education between the two levels of government anymore? It was hugely disappointing to read the

Governor-General's reference to the islander students as 'ESL', in a speech that he delivered at West Island School in March 2007. It is clear that his speech was written for him by a WA hand, as a Commonwealth writer would surely have stressed their oft-repeated claim to the schools having a 'vigorous bilingual programme':

> What makes this school so special is that 85% of you study the curriculum in a second language, English. This is a wonderful achievement and shows the tremendous support and cooperation that exists between pupils and teachers. (Major-General Sir Michael Jeffery, Governor-General of Australia, West Island School, 2 March 2007)

The current absence of a Commonwealth administrative executive on the islands (the atoll is now administered from Christmas Island, some 900 kilometers away), the higher political profile of Christmas Island (with its infamous detention centre for asylum seekers), the long-term nature of teaching contracts in Cocos schools and the almost manic pursuit of (English-language) 'literacy targets' have combined to create all-round complacency regarding the linguistic rights of the Cocos Malay citizens of the territory. Yet, these rights were enshrined in the 1983–1984 agreements made by Australia to the Cocos people, in full sight of the United Nations.

From Colonial to Post-Colonial

Prior to the Act of Self Determination on 6 April 1984, Australia administered the territory of the Cocos (Keeling) Islands under the auspices of the United Nations Special Committee on Decolonisation. During the lead-up to the Act of Self Determination (ASD), many requests were made by the Cocos Malay people, and all manner of assurances were given to them by the Australian government.

Following high-level meetings with the Australian Prime Minister, Mr R.J. Hawke, the Minister for Foreign Affairs, Mr W. Hayden, and the Minister for Territories and Local Government, Mr T. Uren, the Cocos Malay leaders sent a letter to the Australian government on 21 September, 1983, in which they declared their readiness to undertake the ASD. In this historic document, the Cocos Council made the following statements:

> All the Cocos Malay People felt happy to hear the news that the government will continue to protect and safeguard our religion, our traditions and our culture. It is our intention that no outsider interfere in matters such as this.

> We wish the government, in cooperation with the Council, to continue its efforts in the field of education not only for our children but also for the adult population so that we can continue to progress.

We are frank with the government, we have opened up all our secrets. So we ask the government to open up its secrets to us, to open up all its plans for the future of Cocos, which is our homeland. (Department of Foreign Affairs and Trade, 1983 archives)

At the 39th session of the United Nations General Assembly on 7 November 1984, at which the UN Visiting Mission – which had observed the islands' ASD – presented its report, the representative of the Australian Department of Territories, Mr J. Enfield, assured the world's assembled UN representatives that, 'in welcoming the people of Cocos into the Australian community, the Australian Government would honour its commitments to them' (United Nations General Assembly, A/C.4/39/SR.15, 1984: 5). The Cocos Malay chairman of the Cocos Council, Mr Parson bin Yapat, then spoke to the General Assembly about the islands' history and the developments that had followed each of the previous United Nations Visiting Missions in 1973 and 1980. In his final sentence, he said, 'most importantly, the Australian Government had promised to help the Cocos Malay people to preserve their customs and practices, as part of the family of people which make up the Australian nation' (United Nations General Assembly, A/C.4/39/SR.15, 1984: 6). After the subsequent acceptance of the Visiting Mission's report, the Australian UN representative, Mr R. Woolcott, only reiterated his government's wish 'to welcome them as full and equal members of the Australian community, and it would not retreat from the obligations it had undertaken to preserve their religious beliefs and culture' (United Nations General Assembly, A/C.4/39/SR.15, 1984: 8).

Unfortunately, it is all too common in such international declarations for the word 'language' to be omitted and for the speaker to just assume that the catch-all phrases of 'customs and practices', 'religious beliefs and culture' and 'the protection of [their] customs and traditions' will suffice (R.J.F. Radrodo, Fiji, member of the UN Visiting Mission, United Nations General Assembly, A/C.4/39/SR.15, 1984: 7).

Since that time, the United Nations has endorsed the *Declaration on the Rights of Persons Belonging to National or Ethnic, Religious and Linguistic Minorities* (1992) and the landmark *Declaration on the Rights of Indigenous Peoples* (2007). Sadly, both of these are non-binding, and Australia was one of four original dissenters to the passage of the second. The Australian government reversed the latter decision in April 2009, however, calling it an important step in healing past injustices. It remains to be seen if this about-face on traditional rights will be extended to the Cocos Malay people.

The UN declaration on indigenous rights sets out the individual and collective rights of indigenous peoples, including their rights to culture, identity, *language*, employment, health, education and other issues. It emphasises the rights of indigenous peoples to maintain and strengthen their own institutions, cultures and traditions and to pursue their development in keeping with their own needs and aspirations. It also prohibits discrimination against indigenous peoples and promotes their full and effective participation in all matters that concern them, including their right to remain distinct and to pursue their own visions of economic and social development. The recognition of Cocos Malay as an official language in the island-territory would be an easy and respectful demonstration that the Australian government is taking this declaration seriously (Bunce, 2009), however, this has not occurred.

In practice, Australia does not have a particularly good record when it comes to language-maintenance policies and the linguistic rights of minority groups. On the Cocos (Keeling) Islands, the country is continuing to run what can only be called a 'subtractive' education system, in which the linguistic rights of the Cocos Malay people have long been dismissed and turned upside-down into an 'ESL challenge' for the largely monolingual West Australian teachers who work in the islands' schools.

The Cocos Teachers' 'ESL Challenge'

The 2007 and 2008 *Annual Reports* of the Cocos Islands District High School are public documents, and they were freely available on the website of the WA Department of Education and Training until quite recently (see Figure 3.2). Every class teacher and WA-appointed specialist had their own section in these reports. The only subject that was not reported on, in 2007, was LOTE (Languages Other Than English), for either the Home Island primary classes or the West Island secondary classes. This was rectified in the 2008 report, but the whole notion of LOTE has been gravely misrepresented, with Cocos Malay students being praised for being 'talented and gifted in this area' (*Annual Report*, 2008: 19). Of course, this is the case, as Malay is their *first* language. It is not an 'additional language'. It should be obvious that they would perform well beyond the levels expected of young students elsewhere who are learning foreign languages from scratch.

In the 2007 *Annual Report*, it is a complete shock to see one West Island and three Home Island teachers mention, by name, some 17 students who were perceived to be 'below-par' in literacy and numeracy rating and/or have special needs. As this document must have been through at least two levels of editing and vetting by school and departmental officers, this breach of individual privacy rights is unethical and shameful. Surely, the only names of children that can be published are those whose names have already been released in the public arena in connection with meritorious events. No such exemplary students are mentioned in the 2007 online report. The 2008 report has rectified the situation somewhat, but one teacher still refers to individual students by their initials and describes two of them as being

---

2007 Annual School Report

Home Island Primary Classes (all students are Cocos Malay)
Kindergarten/Pre-primary class: All teacher instructions were translated.
Year 3 and 4 class (4 students named for not meeting targets): Strategies are needed to promote 100%
English speaking in classrooms. Children should only need to revert to Cocos Malay through teacher
assistance when they need to clarify a concept or an idea.

West Island Secondary Classes (mostly Cocos Malay students)
Year 9-10 Society and Environment (2 students named): Literacy issues continue to cause problems with most
Home Island students. (Name)'s lack of progress is directly related to his lack of English proficiency. Lack of
vocabulary is a constant problem and hinders understanding of new topics and language of various texts. The
majority of students continue to demonstrate a lack of understanding of the wider issues outside Cocos.
Whole-school Literacy specialist: Continue to provide support to 'areas of greatest need' on Home Island,
making use of the quarantined Language Block. Ensure that spoken English is a priority in all classrooms.
Teachers should continue to accurately model Standard Australian English (SAE), and education assistants
should promote spoken English, wherever developmentally appropriate.

2008 Annual School Report

Home Island Primary Classes (all students are Cocos Malay)
Kindergarten/Pre-primary: Basic vocabulary for English learned alongside Cocos Malay. Bilingual Programme
– all teacher instructions were translated.
Year 3-4: Speaking and listening has continued to be an area of concern. The class requires continual
reminding to use Standard Australian English and the level of listening skills is below what is expected. The
children are skilled at locating information that requires simple recall of information, but are reluctant to make
predictions and give an answer that asks 'why'. They do not readily take risks and will write nothing if they
believe their response could be incorrect. SAE is still an area that requires continual reinforcement… the class
does continually need to be reminded of our commitment to learning and speaking in SAE.
Year 5-6: Firm boundaries were set on speaking English. Kids need to be immersed in SAE. All students being
ESL means that to learn the 'language of maths' on top of English takes a lot more time. A constant battle to
maintain expectation of only speaking English in class. Bribes worked for a while. Not sure as to the best way.
A suggestion is that when students step into a classroom, it is only an English Zone, and when they step out, it
is a Cocos Malay speaking zone.
LOTE specialist: All students achieved well beyond the appropriate levels expected of their own year levels
using LOTE outcome statements. A strategy of internet pen-pals with Indonesian students was not pursued,
due to a lack of knowledge of suitable pen-pal schools in Indonesia. Students are talented and gifted in this
area.

West Island Secondary Classes (mostly Cocos Malay students)
Year 7 Society and Environment: (9 students who did not meet targets identified by their initials, 2 described as
'lazy') Many of the resources in the S&E learning area need to be replaced. Items that relate to early explorers
of Australia, both maritime and overland, need to be purchased. As do resources that will assist in the teaching
of resources [sic] (mining – dvd for these students, as they have a limited worldview in their isolated nature)
[sic] and Aboriginal studies. Need to enhance student's [sic] worldviews.
Year 8-10 Science: An emphasis on English learning acquisition [sic]. Year 8-9: Not enough English spoken in
this group. Year 10: More emphasis placed on the Speaking English Charter.
Year 8-10 Society and Environment: Some are below (expected levels), due to literacy issues, such as reading
and understanding complex text, vocabulary development and a lack of wider world knowledge.
Whole-school Literacy specialist: The Standard Australian English Speaking Charter needs support. Ensure
that English continues to be a priority in all classrooms. Continue to provide support to areas of greatest need
on Home Island, making use of the quarantined Language Block. Ensure that all teachers are familiar with the
Bilingual Programme as outlined in the *Literacy Scope and Sequence 2008.*

Figure 3.2 Excerpts from the Cocos Islands District High School *Annual
Reports*, 2007 and 2008

'lazy'. When all classes have fewer than 20 students, and most have under
10, even initials will easily give away students' identities. This is a clear
breach of the children's fundamental human rights.

In both reports, the Cocos Malay students' bilingual and bi-scriptal
assets have been turned into their worst handicaps. Nowhere in these
reports is there any clearly demonstrated understanding of the pedagogical
foundations of 'bilingual education'. Instead, there is a strong preoccupation

with the 'literacy' requirements of the Australian national testing programme, known as NAPLAN (National Assessment Program in Literacy and
Numeracy). The school's 'Bilingual Policy' (referred to in Figure 3.2, in the
school's document, *Literacy Scope and Sequence*, 2008) has the following
statement as its very first bullet point, under the heading Kindergarten-
Pre-Primary: 'English to be the mode of communication for teachers. Class
room teachers to model correct use of Standard Australian English. Education
Assistant to translate when required'.

This is no 'vigorous bilingual program', as has been claimed by the Commonwealth. Nowhere is the children's first language properly acknowledged
or honoured in these reports. The 'Quarantine Block' mentioned in them
comprises two classrooms on one side of a covered play area at Home Island
School. These are the rooms in which the two oldest groups of primary
children are taught and the ones that fell foul of a media exposé in 2009 (see
below).

In both the 2007 and 2008 *Annual Reports*, the Home Island School's
kindergarten teacher expresses some exasperation in continually needing to
stress that the directionality of print in English and Malay is 'different from
the direction of print in Arabic'. This is certainly an important point in
helping her students to become bi-scriptal, but it should also indicate to her
that these young children are already 'print aware' and that they have
considerable understanding of letter-sound correspondence in another
alphabetic script. The Arabic letters that the children have learned can also
be used to write Malay, in a script that is called 'Jawi', that was used
extensively by their island ancestors. These students are not entering school
letter-blind or phonemically unaware. They have already learned about
consonants and vowels and the distinctive ways in which they are presented
and pronounced in the Arabic script. As correct Arabic pronunciation is
essential in learning Koranic recitation, it is not surprising that the students
are wary about taking risks and making mistakes in any new language.

What has happened to Malay-language instruction since the inter-
governmental promises of 1989? On Home Island, mother-tongue maintenance has been reduced to translation, parallel vocabulary work, 'LOTE
with Nek' and listening to visiting elders speak about aspects of the
islands' history, preferably in English (personal communication, 2010). On
West Island, Indonesian classes were taught on-and-off by the long-term,
expatriate Tourism Officer for some years. There was no mention of LOTE
in the secondary school's 2008 report, but it reappeared in 2009. This is a far
cry from the 1980s, when Indonesian classes followed a formal language
and literature curriculum that was designed and taught by Commonwealth-
appointed teachers.

The LOTE comment in the 2008 *Annual Report* (Figure 3.2) hides the
true nature of this reinstated programme. The young, newly appointed

ENGLISH ZONE!

Remember!

School Priority &Target 2.3
Ensure that the speaking, teaching and learning of English is a priority in all learning areas.

At Cocos Islands DHS every staff member will use, model and encourage Standard Australian English at every opportunity. Students are expected to speak English at every appropriate opportunity.

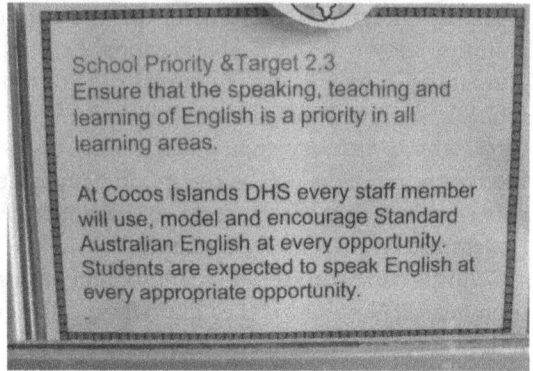

Figures 3.3 and 3.4 Brush your teeth and speak English! Two prominently displayed signs at children's head-height in the so-called 'Quarantine Block' of Home Island School (Photos: P. Bunce, 2009)

teacher of Indonesian at the time was not a native speaker, and her spoken language was, apparently, difficult for the islanders to understand. According to a number of parents, she was under strict instructions not to speak Indonesian with the children outside her language lessons. To further curtail her mother-tongue access to the students, she also had to teach lessons in Art, in English (personal communication, 2009). This Art-Indonesian combination has since reappeared in a WA government staffing advertisement for appointments to the school in 2012 (Department of Education, Western Australia, 2011).

A viable Malay/Indonesian Language programme for the school could be reinvigorated with some diplomatic effort on the part of the Commonwealth. Overseas 'semester-exchange options' for bilingual Indonesian or Malaysian university students could be arranged, to bring Malay-speaking youth into Australian schools and community life for a few months at a time. This would fit in well with the National Asian Languages and Studies in Schools Program (DEEWR, 2009). What wonderful role models they could be for Cocos youth who may feel disempowered by the restrictive, monolingual nature of island educational opportunities (Mohammed Isa Minkom, 2002).

On a visit to the islands in 2009, I was shown one of the school's 'speaking tickets' (Figure 3.5) by a former student of mine, who is now the parent of a primary-aged student. This ticket had been issued to her child by a classmate who was acting as one of the 'English Police Force', a role that was rotated around the class and one that entitled the young officers to wear old Australian Federal Police uniform shirts! This was a blatant breach of police security regulations, let alone a serious breach of the children's human rights. About a month after my visit, the scandal of the police

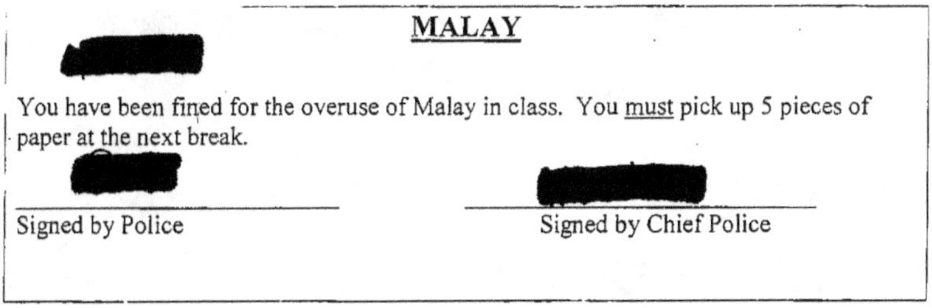

MALAY

You have been fined for the overuse of Malay in class. You must pick up 5 pieces of paper at the next break.

_____   _____
Signed by Police   Signed by Chief Police

Figure 3.5 A 'speaking ticket' issued by Home Island School
(Photo: P. Bunce, 2009)

shirts and a related episode in the Shire Council Offices, in which several administrative officers were similarly 'fined' for speaking Malay at work, became a front-page news story in the national newspaper, *The Australian* (Taylor, 2009).

To prohibit and punish children for speaking their own language is a breach of their human rights. Article 30 of the *United Nations Convention on the Rights of the Child* (United Nations, 1989) reads, as follows:

In those States in which ethnic, religious or linguistic minorities or persons of indigenous origin exist, a child belonging to such a minority or who is indigenous shall not be denied the right, in community with other members of his or her group, to enjoy his or her own culture, to profess and practise his or her own religion, or to use his or her own language.

In August 2009, I sent an online enquiry to the Australian Human Rights Commission regarding this matter, and their reply places the issue right in the middle of the 'classic' State-or-Commonwealth jurisdictional divide:

Under the Australian Human Rights Commission Act 1986 (the AHRCA), this Commission can investigate complaints of breaches of human rights only against the Commonwealth or one of its agencies... From the limited information provided, it is unclear if such a requirement has been imposed by the WA Department of Education and Training. If this is so, then it would not be possible to bring a complaint of a human rights breach against the Western Australian Department of Education under these provisions... In order to lodge a complaint under the RDA [Racial Discrimination Act of Western Australia], the person making the complaint needs to be 'aggrieved', meaning that they need to be from the racial or ethnic background which is being targeted. (AHRC email, personal communication, 6 August 2009)

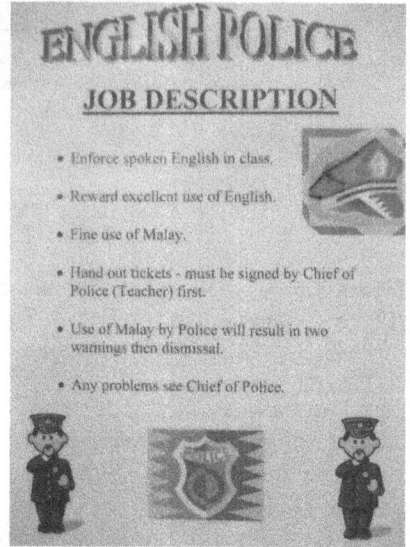

Figures 3.6 and 3.7 Classroom wall posters on 'English Law', Home Island School (Photos: P. Bunce, 2009)

At the same time that this issue was hitting the headlines on the mainland, there was also an ongoing, routine parliamentary inquiry under way, regarding the changing economic environment in the Indian Ocean Territories (Joint Standing Committee on the National Capital and External Territories, 2009–2010), the transcripts of which are all available online. One session was held on Home Island on Tuesday 29 September 2009, at which a representative from the school was called to give evidence. Among other things, this person was also questioned about the recent scandal of language bans at the school. The astonishing reply was an inaccurate representation of the situation that had been the case just one month beforehand. On page 38 of the committee's transcript, this person is reported to have said, 'We do not ban any speaking of the Cocos Malay language'.

The employment situation of the long-term Cocos Malay 'support teachers', or 'education assistants', is also quite scandalous. Several of them are eminently qualified to become full-time classroom teachers after upwards of 20 years' teaching experience and attendance at numerous training courses. Sadly, they appear doomed to forever play second-fiddle to a never-ending succession of naïve, younger, mainland teachers. What kind of role model is presented to the younger generation of Cocos Malay students when a grandparent of theirs continually works as an assistant to mainland teachers who are half their age and openly display a limited knowledge of the islands' language and customs?

Two Communities, Two Different Worlds

Since the early 1990s, the islands have had access to satellite television. An internet service became available around the year 2000. Today, most Cocos Malay households have at least one television and one internet-connected computer. During my stay in the community in 2004, it seemed that the televisions were set 'full time' onto Indonesian-language channels. Casual conversations were sprinkled with references to TV dramas and Indonesian popular culture. I even noticed small changes in the ways in which people addressed each other, notably the near disappearance of the endearment, 'Bik' (auntie) – the island term that was formerly used to address me.

The biggest change that I noticed in the community in 2004 was in the islanders' religious and cultural identity. Open and easy contact with the Malay-speaking world beyond the islands has put the community in far better touch with mainstream Islam. Significant numbers of families have performed the Haj to Mecca, religious education is well established, dress has become more conservative and people were demonstrating a new-found confidence in their religious knowledge and practices. The islanders' religious lives had become fully 'mainstream'. This was in clear contrast to the fragmented mix of traditional island practices and isolated elements of modern Islam that had characterized the community during the 1980s. With satellite communications, it has been possible for everyone to become religiously informed via television programmes and internet sources. I noticed a clear religious confidence among the young women, even those with young children who worked at home.

The palpable resurgence of Islam, a new-found global connectedness with the wider Malay-Indonesian-speaking world and the adoption of various aspects of global popular culture were clear indications to me of a viable, knowledgeable, adaptable community that was in touch with the wider world – all via the Malay-Indonesian language. Such is the power of global communications that a young Malay boy was able to tell me all about the 'social life' of bees – something that he had learned from an Indonesian science programme on satellite television.

These observations of everyday village life contrast markedly with the demeaning and patronising comments made in the *Annual School Reports* by some secondary teachers about the students' 'limited world view'. Perhaps they were referring to culturally specific knowledge of mainland Australian society and school topics, such as 'resource extraction' and 19th century explorers.

Clearly, the long-term and island-bound expatriate teachers do not fully realise the nature of the knowledge that their students are gaining in their after-school, mother-tongue world. Far from 'knowing little about the outside world', as two teachers remarked in the online school reports, they might be pleasantly surprised by the students' South-East Asian worldliness. While the teachers may believe that school-knowledge and the English language constitute the 'elixir of life', their adolescent students quite possibly see their school world as a little 'old fashioned', 'uncool' and out of touch with their daily reality. Almost half the islands' teaching staff have been on the islands for between five and 10 years. How aware are *they* of even the Australian mainland's 'digital generation', let alone the nature and influence of online and televised popular culture in South-East Asia?

In 2010, I saw electronic items such as iPhones, iPods, iPads and wireless laptop computers in abundance in Cocos Malay homes, and they were frequently in use on the inter-island ferry. It seemed that just about everyone under the age of 40 had a Facebook account. What was lacking was some form of adult guidance over the responsible use of such social media. In this respect, the Cocos youth are surely no different from their mainland counterparts. How many mainlander teens are knowledgeable about 19th century explorers and Australia's mineral resources? One wonders whether the teachers have ever considered their students' ability to access Malay-Indonesian websites to either assist in their learning of concepts or to provide text for online translation.

In my view, it is ironic that it is the *expatriate* community that I now see as the more 'globally isolated' of the two populations. While the islands' mainland teachers are enjoying their fishing, tennis and 'wellness days' on deserted islands, their students are busy learning more about their religion, making wider-world language connections and following the latest music trends in South-East Asia. There is no pressing need for 'penpals' (see LOTE section, 2008 *Annual Report*, Figure 3.2, above) as the students are already speaking with Indonesian and Malaysian youth via Skype. By contrast, their teachers have become professionally entangled in a confusing web of 'outcomes statements' and 'literacy targets' set by distant educational policy-makers.

By 2010, it would appear that most Cocos teachers had some access to the Australia-wide professional development programme known as 'ESL in the Mainstream', plus the WA-based, aggressively named 'Getting it Right' (GiR) remedial English literacy endeavour. Just the same, it would seem, from reading their online *Annual Reports*, that they do not fully understand how to adapt, nor how to apply these ideas to the unique situation that they face on the Cocos (Keeling) Islands. They just seem to be making use of the 'literacy' jargon of recent years to further drive home their English-at-all-costs regime.

They have become 'English bullies', who would, according to the 2008 *Annual Report*, soon be wearing some kind of staff uniform to signify their team-solidarity.

In 2010, the social relations between the two communities – the mainland government servants on West Island and the Cocos Malays on Home Island – had, in my view, reached their lowest ebb in two decades. Each community seemed to be merely putting up with the other's presence. The decline had begun with the 'English Law enforcement' episodes of 2009, and this was followed by an unlawful dismissal episode, the defacing of a sign with a religious insult and the exposure of salary under-payments by mainlander managers. This 'bad blood' has been perpetuated by the continued presence of some long-term mainland officers who display little interest in the Cocos Malay community.

With no Administrator living on the islands, and the massive political distractions of the detention centre on neighbouring Christmas Island, the affairs of the Territory of the Cocos (Keeling) Islands have been allowed to *anyut* (a Cocos Malay word, possibly of Javanese origin, meaning to drift away out to sea, usually referring to a boat that has been badly tied or poorly anchored). It would seem that there is no longer anyone either speaking to, or for, the Cocos Malay people. They have, literally, been rendered voiceless. In such a situation, when a place is 'out of sight and out of mind', the bullies can reign unimpeded.

Conclusion

A colonial mindset continues to characterise the islands' schools, in the sense that it is the expatriates who still decide what is 'good for' the local population. The irony of the situation is that it is the 'colonised' who have transformed themselves from an isolated, timeless, largely non-literate plantation labour force into an informed and increasingly confident community with strong cultural and linguistic ties to South-east Asia. The 'colonisers', by contrast, have hardly changed, in either name or outlook. Their continued power today rests solely on their monolingual command over English-language education.

With the Australian government's 2009 ratification of the United Nations' *Declaration on the Rights of Indigenous Peoples*, we can only hope that the anomalous and highly discriminatory situation of education on the Cocos (Keeling) Islands will again come to international notice and that the federal government will once more be shamed into doing a better job in their Indian Ocean Territory. International embarrassment has, historically, been the *only* mechanism strong enough to forge changes in government policies regarding this island territory. Until the Cocos Malay people themselves are granted the full authority to make their own decisions about matters that impact on their culture and language, their full human rights will continue to be 'out-of-sight and out-of-mind' on both the WA and Commonwealth governments' educational agendas.

References

Andersson, T. and Boyer, M. (1978) *Bilingual Schooling in the United States* (2nd edn.). Austin, TX: National Educational Laboratory Publishers, University of Texas.

Ansaldo, U. (2009) *Contact Languages: Ecology and Evolution in Asia*. Cambridge: Cambridge University Press.

Attorney General's Department (2005–2006) *Cocos Islands Governance and Administration*. Online document, accessed 28 December, 2007. http://www.ag.gov.au/www/agd/agd.nsf/Page/TerritoriesofAustralia_Cocos(Keeling)Islands_CocosIslandsGovernanceand-Administration

Bunce, P. (1988) *The Cocos (Keeling) Islands: Australian Atolls in the Indian Ocean*. Brisbane: Jacaranda Press.

Bunce, P. (2009) Cocos Islands: the view from Asia. *Crikey*, 7 September. Online at http://www.crikey.com.au/2009/09/07/cocos-islands-the-view-from-asia/

Cocos Islands District High School (2007) *Annual Report, 2007*. Online document, accessed 20 December, 2009. http://www2.eddept.wa.edu.au/schoolprofile/main_page.do (archived).

Cocos Islands District High School (2008) *Annual Report, 2008*. Online document, accessed 20 December, 2009. http://www2.eddept.wa.edu.au/schoolprofile/main_page.do (archived).

Cocos Islands District High School (2008) *Literacy Scope and Sequence – Bilingual Program*. Unpublished school document.

Cummins, J. (2000) *Language, Power and Pedagogy: Bilingual Children in the Crossfire*. Clevedon: Multilingual Matters.

Curriculum Corporation (2006) *National Statement for Engaging Young Australians with Asia in Australian Schools*. Canberra: Australian Government Publication.

Department of Education, Employment and Workplace Relations, DEEWR (2009) *National Asian Languages and Studies in Schools Program*. Canberra: Australian Government Publication.

Department of Education, Western Australia (2011) Teacher – LOTE – (Indonesian/Arts) – Cocos Islands District High School. Online job advertisement, accessed 17 September 2011. http://www.jobs.det.wa.edu.au

Department of Foreign Affairs and Trade (1983) *Translation of 'Letter Concerning ASD as transmitted by telex 21 September 1983'*. Unpublished archival document.

Department of Regional Australia, Regional Development and Local Government (2011) *Cocos (Keeling) Islands Governance and Administration*. Online document, accessed 14 October, 2011. http://www.regional.gov.au/territories/Cocos_Keeling/governanceadministration.aspx

Education Policy Statement (1989) Unpublished Australian Government document.

Fogle, B. (2011) Ben Fogle: My fight for the forgotten islanders. *Telegraph*, 12 February. Online at http://www.telegraph.co.uk/news/worldnews/africaandindianocean/mauritius/8320609/Ben-Fogle-My-fight-for-the-forgotten-islanders.html

Heugh, K. (2009) Literacy and bi/multilingual education in Africa: Recovering collective memory and knowledge. In T. Skutnabb-Kangas, R. Phillipson, A.K. Mohanty and M. Panda (eds) *Social Justice Through Multilingual Education* (pp. 95–113). Bristol: Multilingual Matters.

Ingram, D.E. (1984) *Observations on Language Education on the Cocos (Keeling) Islands: Report to the Administration*. Unpublished report to the Australian Government.

Jeffery, M. (2007) *Speech delivered at West Island School*. Online at http://www.gg.gov.au/governorgeneral/archived.php?year=2007

Joint Standing Committee on the National Capital and External Territories (2009–2010) *Inquiry into the Changing Economic Environment in the Indian Ocean Territories*. Online transcripts at http://www.aph.gov.au/house/committee/ncet/EconomicEnvironment/hearings.htm

Mohammad, Isa Minkom (2002) *The Cocos (Keeling) Islands Youth Support Centre*. Online document, accessed 28 December, 2007. http://www.thesource.gov.au/involve/NYR/pdf/2002_social_cohesion/social_reports/ mohammed_minkom.pdf

Mohanty, A.K. (2006) Multilingualism of the unequals and predicaments of education in India: Mother tongue or other tongue?. In O. Garcia, T. Skutnabb-Kangas, M. Torres-Guzman (eds) *Imagining Multilingual Schools. Languages in Education and Glocalisation* (pp. 262–283). Clevedon: Multilingual Matters.

Phillipson, R. (2009) *Linguistic Imperialism*. Oxford: Oxford University Press.

Pilger, J. (2004) Stealing a Nation. Online documentary film, accessed 17 September 2011. http://johnpilger.com/videos/stealing-a-nation

Skutnabb-Kangas, T. (2000) *Linguistic Genocide in Education – or Worldwide Diversity and Human Rights?* Mahwah, New Jersey and London: Lawrence Erlbaum Associates.

Skutnabb-Kangas, T. (2009) The stakes: Linguistic diversity, linguistic human rights and mother-tongue-based multilingual education or linguistic genocide, crimes against humanity and an even faster destruction of biodiversity and our planet. Keynote presentation at the Bamako International Forum on Multilingualism, Bamako, Mali, 19–21 January. Available at http://www.tove-skutnabb-kangas.org/

Skutnabb-Kangas, T., Phillipson, R., Mohanty, A.K. and Panda, M. (eds)(2009) *Social Justice Through Multilingual Education*. Bristol: Multilingual Matters.

Taylor, P. (2009) Crime in paradise lost in translation, *The Australian*, 17 August.

Tollefson, J.W. and Tsui, A.B.M. (eds) (2003) *Medium of Instruction Policies: Which Agenda? Whose Agenda?* Mahwah, NJ: Lawrence Erlbaum.

United Nations (1989) *Convention on the Rights of the Child*. NY: United Nations Publications.

United Nations (1992) *Declaration on the Rights of Persons Belonging to National or Ethnic, Religious and Linguistic Minorities*. NY: United Nations Publications.

United Nations (2007) *Declaration on the Rights of Indigenous Peoples*. NY: United Nations Publications.

United Nations General Assembly (1984) Thirty-ninth Session. *Summary Record of the 15th Meeting*. 7 November 1984. Record No. A/C.4/39/SR.15.

Valencia, R.R. (1997) *The Evolution of Deficit Thinking: Educational Thought and Practice*. London: Falmer Press.

Vine, D. (2009) *Island of Shame: The Secret History of the U.S. Military Base on Diego Garcia*. Princeton, NJ: Princeton University Press.

Western Australian Legislative Assembly (2004) Cocos (Keeling) Islands, Education Programs and School Holiday Arrangements. *The Hansard,* 22 June.

Whittington, R.J. (1989) Education in the Cocos (Keeling) Islands: Report to the Cocos (Keeling) Islands Council. Unpublished document.

4 English Language as Juggernaut – Aboriginal English and Indigenous Languages in Australia

Robyn Ober and Jeanie Bell

Overview

Aboriginal English, as a dialect of English, is now recognised as the first language of many Aboriginal Australians, and it is also used by small numbers of non-Indigenous Australians. This form of communication is rich, highly structured and a complex form of the English language, and it is widely appropriated in the social and cultural domains of Aboriginal people. This chapter will examine the communicative roles of Aboriginal English in Australia and the ongoing efforts of Aboriginal people who are determined to maintain and revitalize many of the 250 traditional languages that were once spoken across this country. It is important that English is not seen as 'merely an instrument for communication'. Robert Phillipson (2008: 5) makes the case that 'it is a value one identifies with for the social functions the language is seen as serving, its utility in the linguistic market'.

One example of how Aboriginal English has evolved over several decades is reflected in the poetry of Lionel Fogarty, a well known radical writer from South East Queensland:

> Nature, Jukambe might tell or lend
> Collectively my people now
> I don't see at grassland or hill creek tract
> Where Jukambe worked and played
> Yea my some communication, still many tribespeople
> Dialect young and old not sold.
> Yea, bunya pines brighten old Jukambe members
> Individual, too keep children Yoogum Yoogum...
> Jukambe is my people, cause white mans name taken place
> Relived, I am. In your spirit, Jukambe.

> (Fogarty, 1983: 48)

Alongside the widespread use of Aboriginal English, considerable numbers of Aboriginal people in Australia are also endeavouring to reclaim and revive the traditional languages of their ancestors. Some of these languages have been severely weakened and, in other cases, decimated since the arrival of the English language onto our land just over two centuries ago. While a small number of relatively isolated ancestral languages have managed to survive the linguistic (and literal) genocide of early colonisation, the speakers and custodians of all these languages – particularly the weaker ones – now have to educate themselves, their families and their communities about the additional effort needed to ensure the survival of these languages into the future.

Unfortunately, the majority of indigenous children in Australia are now required – both by policy and pressure – to use Standard Australian English (SAE) on entrance to primary school, and they are also expected to improve their competency in this language as they progress through the various government-run education systems in the country. This has not always been an achievable goal for many indigenous people, due to the huge disparities in the social and economic lifestyles of a large proportion of the Australian Aboriginal population. According to Eades (2008), Aboriginal people make up about 2–3% of the Australian population. But 'Australian Aboriginal people share with other Indigenous minorities around the world the legacies of colonial dispossession – with living conditions and indicators typical of people in third world countries... The linguistic impact of colonisation has also been drastic' (Eades, 2008: 1).

The English-language teaching 'juggernaut' has decimated a range of traditional lifestyles as it has moved across the country. In the past, in the days of settlement and land grabbing, this was unrelenting. In present times, a great many Aboriginal people are moving from the more remote communities to seek opportunities in the urban areas through education and employment. Over the past two centuries, many Aboriginal people have been forcibly removed and entangled in waves of urban drift from their traditional homelands. In many places, they continue to struggle for survival, both physically and mentally, on the fringes of emerging growth centres. In 2002, Bell wrote that

> ...because of the devastating effects of colonization on blackfellas in this Country – through disease, murder and other forms of attempted genocide over the past 200 years – our language and culture has taken on a different shape and form.... While it has not survived intact, but in varying degrees of healthiness, it has survived. Many of us are working with what remains in determined efforts to rebuild ourselves and our families and communities back to a point where we are no longer victims of a system that set out to destroy us as a race. (Bell, 2002: 43)

The language revitalization movement in Australia has grown considerably over the past 20 years. This has been encouraged by limited support from government funding, academic endeavours involving university-based linguists and active community-based language workers who are employed by Aboriginal Language Centres scattered around the country. At the same time, there is a growing awareness in those language communities which are involved in this revival of the realisation that any achievable success with such programmes can only come about with strong commitment and hard work on their part, combined with the mostly positive benefits that can be derived from collaborative partnerships with linguists and educators (Bell, 2010).

How the English Language Changed the Course of History for Aboriginal Australians

Historically, it was the Aboriginal people living close to the eastern coast of Australia who first started hearing and mimicking English in the second half of the 19th century. In coastal Queensland, as in other parts of Australia, such traditional Aboriginal people were commonly multilingual speakers of up to five or six traditional languages or dialects from around their region. However, by the first half of the 20th century, those Aboriginal people who regularly mixed with the colonisers from 'the home country' (England) developed a competence quite close to the more formal variety of English that was often referred to as the 'Queen's English'. It was not long before the government authorities of the time enforced various rules and regulations which prohibited Aboriginal people who were living on government reserves and church-run missions from speaking their traditional languages and practicing their culture.

Those Aboriginal people who had less interaction with the outside world continued to resist using English for as long as possible, even when it meant that they were only able to speak their traditional languages in secret locations. Inevitably though, throughout South-East Queensland and other parts of Australia, increasing exposure to the English language for the majority of Aboriginal people in the more settled parts of the country resulted in the emergence of a reduced form of English, which contained numerous words and grammatical features from the old languages. This early contact language was commonly referred to as 'pidgin English' across many parts of Australia. Mühlhäusler (1996: 7) observed that there was adequate evidence to show the 'underlying linguistic unity of most if not all varieties of Pidgin English spoken in Australia' during the earliest stages of settlement. According to him, this 'English-based stable pidgin' included 'a considerable amount of indigenisation, with Aborigines communicating about new ways of life and new beliefs in Pidgin English'.

In some contact language situations such as the more urbanized centres of South-East Queensland, there was a gradual reversal, or shift away, from Pidgin English – away from creolization – and a move closer to standard English in the form of different varieties of Aboriginal English (Eades, 1991). Mühlhäusler (1996) concluded that this was due to several factors, including (in southern Australia) the widespread death and dispersal of Aboriginal people.

As Aboriginal people, we are often reminded of these events by the older generations who have passed stories down to us through oral history – about the spread of unfamiliar diseases and, in some cases, the deliberate massacre of large numbers of our people. During this earlier period, some other factors which contributed to the emergence of new ways of communication for the Aboriginal population included 'a long standing program of assimilation... resulting in an increase of standard English and Aboriginal English', as well as 'the creolisation of Pidgins in some parts of the Northern Territory, Cape York Peninsula and Torres Straits' (Mühlhäusler, 1996: 8).

As time passed and more young Aboriginal people entered mainstream education, they developed bi-dialectical English oral language skills, including a form of Standard Australian English, while code-switching in different speech contexts and continuing to use 'language' words and phrases from their traditional languages. In parallel to these developments, the traditional languages themselves gradually fell into decline as the older, more fluent speakers died and fewer younger people gained full fluency in their ancestral languages.

In the earlier decades, the emerging varieties of Aboriginal English were often unrecognized or misunderstood by outsiders and were generally considered to be 'bad English'. In more recent times, Aboriginal people have lobbied, with support from concerned linguists, for the acceptance of Aboriginal English as a primary language or dialect.

A Stronger Push to have Aboriginal English Accepted in Schools

A former Queensland academic, E.H. Flint, wrote (1973: 4) of 'the need for bilingual education aiming at solving social and educational problems arising from multilingualism in Australia', which, if ignored, could 'lead to role compartmentalization...'. Other researchers, such as Kaldor (1976), strongly advocated that teachers in Western Australian schools recognise Aboriginal English as the first dialect of their Aboriginal students. A year later, Gardiner (1977) reinforced the need to teach Standard Australian English as a *second dialect*. Sharifian (2005: 513) notes that 'the notion of "standard" in this context is largely constituted with reference to non-linguistic issues such as social and economical power, though the non-standard varieties may be emotionally and ideologically more powerful'.

Flint recognised in an earlier study (1968) that the Queensland Education Department's 'attempt to suppress the L(ow) form [of English] caused great unrest in the community, as it did on Norfolk Island between 1912 and 1929' (Flint, 1968: 19). He goes on to say that the attempt was later abandoned, because of 'the simple sociolinguistic reason that the L form is culture-bound and is closely associated with the child's intimate emotional family and home relationships' (Flint, 1973: 11). Eades later comments on Flint's writing:

> Unsurprisingly for the 1960s, Flint's article was framed within the assimilationist discourse of the time, and it predicted that "the Aboriginal English dialect will soon disappear".... when the official government policy of social and cultural assimilation of Aboriginals into the Australian community has been completely carried out. (1968: 19, in Eades, 2008: 2)

Flint is considered by some to be one of the first researchers in Australia to refer to the various social dialects spoken by Aboriginal people in Queensland at that time as Aboriginal English. According to Eades, Flint was concerned about the education of the speakers of these new varieties of English, in spite of his 'assimilationist prediction' (2008: 2).

> Aboriginal English, as shown by the data gathered from the 30 Queensland communities, is not homogeneous. Five different types of communities, of which the English speech exhibits both similarities and differences, are distinguished. (Flint, 1973: 11)

In 1984, in the fringe camps of Alice Springs, the major large town of Central Australia, a study was carried out by linguist Jean Harkins at the request of the governing Aboriginal council of the then independent, multilingual Yipirinya School. Harkins acknowledged in her book *Bridging Two Worlds* (1984) that 'most Australian Aboriginal people speak English at least some of the time, though many also speak one or more Aboriginal languages... Many Aboriginal people feel their lives would be better if they could improve their command of English' (1984: 1). While it would be more precise to say that Aboriginal people probably felt life would be easier with improved competency in English – both back in the 1980s and even more so in the current climate of economic rationalism – Harkins stated, at that time, that 'perhaps English isn't really a problem for Aboriginal people at all, or at most a very minor problem compared to the impact of racism and economic exploitation' (1984: 1).

While this continues to be the social environment that many Aboriginal people are forced to operate in throughout Australia, life is generally easier for those who do have reasonably high levels of English language competency.

Harkins (1984) conducted a linguistic analysis of the variety of English used by Aboriginal people from the different language groups in the various contexts in which they operated in Alice Springs. At that time, it was a small town, with hostility often being shown to itinerant Aboriginal people from 'out bush' – referring to the more remote communities where their lifestyle was closer to the traditional way. People from these isolated communities would come to town to seek or obtain educational or other government services, medical treatment or to visit sick relatives and/or attend funerals. Many would stay on for an extended time in Alice Springs – which could be several months or longer – resulting in severe overcrowding in the houses of other family members, living, as they were, in one of the many town camps surrounding the township.

Yipirinya School was originally set up in the late 1970s to provide alternative educational services to the children living in these town camps, with a commitment to provide teaching for much of the curriculum in one of the four main Central Australian Aboriginal languages. These were, generally, the first languages for the majority of children who attended the school. The school was also required by government policies to deliver programmes in Standard Australian English.

Harkins points out that there was, at that time, a perception in Australia that Aboriginal people generally spoke a deficit type of English. The purpose of her study was to show how Aboriginal people connected to Yipirinya School were learning and using English in a multilingual environment, while developing a distinct variety of English with its own rules and grammatical structures, in order to meet their communication needs (see Appendix). She writes:

> although they have suffered great disadvantage in the non-Aboriginal school system many Aboriginal people have retained a vision... to acquire knowledge and tools to give them more power over their own lives and enable them to better express their own aspirations and identity... Aboriginal languages were highly valued, and maintenance of them is seen as one of the goals of education. English is an important additional language to serve as a bridge between Aboriginal and non-Aboriginal realities. (Harkins, 1984: 4–5)

Responses to this Changing Language Situation

While many Australian indigenous people now recognise that SAE (Standard Australian English) is necessary for survival in the globalised Western world, they continue to resist giving up their right to speak their own form of English. These modern ways of speaking are considered as important markers of our *identity* and the main form of communication within our extended families and community groups. The unique features associated with our use of language set us apart from the rest of the Australian population.

In many places, young indigenous members of the different communities were not being exposed to sufficient Standard Australian English to develop their oral skills in this dialect, so Aboriginal people involved in the development and delivery of educational programmes – in, at least, Queensland and Western Australia – joined with the linguists, who had an academic interest in Aboriginal English, to lobby schools and government to accept it as the first dialect of many school-aged children.

One of the proposals put up to government at this time was to support teachers to use Aboriginal English in the early stages of education as a starting point to acquiring Standard Australian English (SAE). In Western Australia, Jennifer Gardiner (1977) proposed programmes for Teaching Standard English as a Second Dialect to Speakers of Aboriginal English (TSESD). At that time, she suggested that the rationale behind such a programme would be similar to that of bilingual education programs happening at that time in the northern parts of Australia. This model was seen as 'wider than just the need to teach children standard English so that they can succeed in school' (Gardiner, 1977: 166).

> Such progammes are also concerned with the totality of the child's experience, that is, with Aboriginal culture, values and aspirations, rather than, as in the past, exclusively aimed at inducting Aboriginal children into the European-Australian society. (Gardiner, 1977: 166)

Gardiner, along with other linguists, called for the *difference theory approach* to TSESD and 'the recognition of the child's own language or dialect to be regarded as resource rather than an obstacle' (1977: 174).

The TSESD programme, to our knowledge, was never officially endorsed by the Western Australian education authority, nor any other government body across Australia, but research and in-service programmes with high standard resources continue to be offered to staff (mainly in primary schools) to inform them of the negative educational implications and effects of de-valuing and ignoring the use of Aboriginal English in the classroom (Sharifian & Malcolm, 2003). This is particularly the case when teachers – even today – place it, from the outset, within a deficit framework.

According to Malcolm and Rochecouste (2001: 273), familiar lexicon from Standard Australian English is contextually different when used by Aboriginal English speakers, because it is 'informed by a semantics deeply rooted in Aboriginal culture'. Increasing numbers of indigenous people now speak a localised form of Aboriginal English as their first or – in some remote communities – their second language or – in many cases – a variety of the rapidly spreading English-based creole widely used by both Aboriginal and Torres Strait Islander people throughout most of northern Australia.

Bilingual Education in the Northern Territory: The 2009 Four-Hour Challenge

In 2009, in the Northern Territory (NT) of Australia, considerable numbers of Aboriginal people still lived on their traditional land in remote locations and continue to speak their ancestral languages. In late 2009, the NT Government made a policy decision that all Aboriginal children in remote community schools would have English-only teaching for the first four hours of every day, including those schools where previously 'traditional languages… were used systematically alongside English to teach the school curriculum to young students' (Dickson, 2009: 20). Strong concerns were expressed by Aboriginal leaders and language activists from both linguistic and church communities in the Northern Territory about the impact that this policy would have on the remaining, and relatively strong, Aboriginal languages still spoken in the NT.

Supporters of bilingual and multilingual education have unified to try to reverse this policy, which was seen as a knee-jerk reaction to pressure from the Federal Government. Poor literacy and numeracy results in the National Assessment Programme – Literacy and Numeracy (NAPLAN) standardised tests were seen as a major contributing factor to the new policy, although Brian Devlin – linguist and leading academic on bilingual education – states that 'the *Data for Bilingual Schools* document tabled in the Legislative Assembly on November 26, 2008 is incomplete, selective, erroneous and biased. It is too insubstantial a basis on which to initiate a major policy shift that imposes compulsory changes on remote rural schools' (Devlin, 2008: 2).

The announcement of a national curriculum by the Federal Government has also supported the move away from a bilingual educational model towards an intensive focus on English literacy and numeracy in the NT's remote community schools. Educational leaders see this as the beginning-of-the-end for bilingual education in the Northern Territory. As an Aboriginal elder and the Aboriginal and Torres Strait Islander Social Justice Commissioner, Tom Calma, in his keynote address to the World Indigenous Peoples' Conference in Melbourne (2008), stated that, if this policy is implemented, the four hours of mandatory English will effectively kill off bilingual education:

The Northern Territory Government claims it is being pushed into dismantling Bilingual education because the Federal Government is standardising school curricula across the nation. I have two responses to that. The first is that there is nothing stopping schools from teaching a national curriculum in Indigenous languages. All of the same content and the same outcomes can be achieved in Indigenous languages. In addition, we have to remember that right from the beginning of school, English is part of the Bilingual school day, and therefore students are learning English literacy right from the first year of school. (Calma, 2008: excerpt)

Experienced indigenous educators have protested strongly against the four-hour policy, and many letters supporting the retention of bilingual education were sent to the Minister of Education in an attempt to reverse the decision. These indigenous voices echoed the cries from teacher, Yalmay Yunupingu (2009), a senior Yolŋu (Aboriginal) educator, who quoted from her own letter to the Minister in an online discussion group, as follows:

Yolŋu language is our Power, our Foundation, our Root and everything that holds us together. Yolŋu language gives us strength, language is our identity, who we are. Yolŋu language gives us pride. Language is our Law and Justice. The importance of teaching our Indigenous language is to keep it alive and to nurture it, to preserve and to sustain our language.

Yunupingu's letter expressed her dismay at the introduction of this new policy and also predicted the reaction of young Yolŋu children to her use of English language in the first four hours of teaching time:

I have been told that I am not allowed to use the children's language anymore. We have been told we are not to use our students' first language, only English. Well, I already know that the children won't understand what I'm saying, they will laugh at me, and they may even misbehave because they'll be bored and won't know what the lessons are about. So perhaps I will cheat and use some *Yolŋu matha* – what will happen then? Will I have my mouth washed out with soap like in the mission times? Or will I have to stand on one leg outside the classroom? Or perhaps I will lose my job?

The debate is still continuing. No resolution has been reached in addressing the concerns and issues raised by supporters of bilingual education. It seems that English is viewed as the superior language, and no amount of evidence-based research will change the minds of the policy-makers. Intensive English teaching is seen as the key to solving all educational problems, relating to indigenous children who speak English as a second or third language. On the positive side, there is an increasing amount of support from the international arena. In particular, the United Nations, where Australia is required to regularly report to the Committee on the Elimination of Racial Discrimination (CERD). In 2010, in response to Australia's report, it stated that:

The Committee welcomes the new national approach to preserve Indigenous languages but is concerned that no additional financial resources have been committed by the State party nor received by the Maintenance of Indigenous Languages and Records program for this new approach.

The Committee is also highly concerned by the recent abolition of bilingual education funding by the Northern Territory Government in light of the precarious condition of many Indigenous languages, and the lack of adequate opportunities for children to receive instruction in or of their language. (CERD, 2010: Section 21, Articles 2 and 5)

The committee went on to encourage Australia to allocate adequate resources for the new national approach to preserve Indigenous languages and to work in consultation with indigenous communities to hold a national inquiry into the issue of bilingual education for indigenous peoples. It was recommended that Australia adopt all necessary measures to preserve native languages and develop and carry out programmes to revitalize indigenous languages and bilingual and intercultural education for indigenous peoples, respecting cultural identity and history. As Australia is a party to the UNESCO Convention against Discrimination in Education, it was also strongly encouraged to consider providing adequate opportunities for national minorities to both use and teach their own languages (CERD, 2010: 7).

At the time of writing, nothing has been forthcoming from either the Northern Territory or the Australian Commonwealth governments, in relation to the reversal of this controversial policy, however, the supporters of bilingual education continue to fight to maintain, strengthen and support bilingual programs for indigenous children in remote Northern Territory communities.

Indigenous Language Revival and Reclamation

Traditional languages for indigenous people in Australia are regarded as an integral part of our identity, as the First People of this land. Many indigenous people today still feel pain and resentment at the widespread loss of ancestral languages in our country, and while many language revival projects are now under way in Australia, providing indigenous people with an opportunity to regain and re-learn parts of their traditional languages, the number of fluent speakers of many of the surviving languages continues to decline. While some revival programs have been more successful than others, there still exists an ongoing firm commitment among community groups, linguists and language workers, including non-indigenous linguists employed by language centres and universities, to continue this work.

Unfortunately, a strong emotional connection to the past does not always manifest into active participation in language revival programmes, which consequently means fewer people are becoming semi- or fluent speakers of these languages. There also exists a large group of Aboriginal people who were separated from their families and communities at an early age (the 'Stolen Generations', Australian Human Rights Commission, 1997). In some cases, they may not feel a strong connection to their traditional home areas and languages. For this group, there is often a strong sense of loss which runs deeper, and they may find it difficult to become involved in language revival programmes, without first participating in some kind of healing process.

In a report of recent work concerned with developing a 'Typology of Revival Languages in Australia', Eira and Couzens (2010) conducted a series of interviews with community people, including linguists and language workers, which revealed that a number of questions need to be considered in the analysis of traditional languages including:

(1) What are the points of meeting and/or tension between cultural and linguistic criteria for decision-making in this language? And,
(2) In what ways does the link between language and identity affect decisions and processes as evidenced in language use?

The results of this ongoing study, along with other relevant emerging discussions around issues such as beliefs and attitudes toward language-revival work, are becoming critical in determining the future direction of this work across Australia and globally. While this is a relatively new dimension of the language revival debate in our country, a lot more discussion needs to happen. Only minimal government funding is available in Australia for indigenous communities to carry out language revival and maintenance activities, with more project applications being made than there are funds to support them.

In a discussion of the language revival work that is happening in the traditional Tlingit lands in south-eastern Alaska, Dauenhauer and Dauenhauer (1998) focused on a region where English has rapidly become the language of choice for many indigenous people. They refer to the 'intergenerational dislocation' in this region as extreme, and they detail the emotional and psychological factors involved in efforts to achieve ideological clarification. Much of this is in relation to the negative images which still remain in some people's minds about the use of language in earlier days and how this was strongly discouraged and degraded.

> Certainly in Alaska,... Native American individuals and communities are plagued and haunted with anxieties, insecurities, and hesitations about the value of their indigenous language and culture. These

insecurities must be addressed and resolved as an initial step before any meaningful action can be taken on a personal, family, or community level. (Dauenhauer & Dauenhauer, 1998: 61)

The situation in Australia is very similar to North America and many other parts of the world, and we believe there needs to be more informed discussion around what is realistically achievable when we attempt language revival. This is particularly relevant in communities where the languages have been severely diminished with few or even no fluent speakers and with the existence of only small amounts of documentation on the language. A realistic assessment of the language situation in each region is required before the development of appropriate strategies are designed for success in the planned programme. What may work in one language community will not always be appropriate in another language community.

> As language revival and revitalisation rapidly become primary modes of community-based work in Aboriginal Australia, the need for a theoretical foundation for the linguistic scenarios which emerge is becoming increasingly evident. While linguists and communities have been developing approaches and solutions for commonly encountered issues, the various outcomes and stages for the languages themselves are as yet insufficiently understood in the wider academic arena as well as by communities starting out. (Eira & Couzens, 2010: n.p.)

One example of such a programme which has managed to survive and grow, despite the lack of a theoretical foundation, is the one in which Bell was involved with her own language community located in Hervey Bay in Queensland. This is a coastal area where many Aboriginal people continue to live on the land of their ancestors – the Butchulla people who originally inhabited a section of the largest sand island in Australia. Prior to the commencement of the language revival programme over a decade ago, and as a trained linguist, Bell compiled a dictionary of the Butchulla language from historical sources recorded with our elders by earlier linguists who had a scientific interest in the indigenous languages of Australia.

Bell assisted with the basic linguistic training of indigenous language workers, including Joy Bonner, a close cousin and other members of the Butchulla language community, which provided them with enough skills to get the language programme off the ground. In those early days, the language workers taught words, phrases and simple songs from the Butchulla language to a group of Aboriginal children in Hervey Bay. These children continue to be the core of the revival programme, which is taught on a regular weekly basis. Joy is still the coordinator and teacher of this programme, and assistance is provided by younger people in the community, who are helping to develop new teaching materials for the programme. This allows the children to extend their speaking knowledge, as well as their reading and writing competencies, in this language.

In 2009, the Education Department within the Queensland State Government began negotiations with Aboriginal and Torres Strait Islander people involved in the revival of languages to set up a curriculum framework in anticipation of taking their languages into selected mainstream schools within the region. While this move is generally seen as positive by the people involved, the downside is that the government is likely to only provide the community linguists and teachers with limited resources to go into the schools and teach the language. They will need increasing amounts of support to be able to develop the teaching materials that are essential if this type of programme is to be successful in the eyes of the government authorities and the community.

In addition to such developments, the linguists and the government will also need to continue to support the language revival efforts being made at the community level, in order to ensure that the language stays in the hands of the custodians and that they are given the power and responsibility to make any future decisions about what direction these efforts will take. This will further develop the custodians' own aspirations for language retention. Traditional language knowledge and use remains a core part of their other efforts to maintain and revive cultural practices associated with their ancestral lands.

Aboriginal people have survived the white-man's world by being strong-willed and by being determined to stay true to who they are. Even though many of the traditional Aboriginal languages have been wiped out, Aboriginal people have kept their cultural identity by shaping, moulding and manipulating the English language into something of their own. Whether we like it or not, Aboriginal English is the first language for the majority of Aboriginal Australians, and it is here to stay. At the same time, we indigenous Australians are determined to reclaim and retain as much as possible of our own traditional languages.

The juggernaut that is Standard Australian English will need to be confronted, hobbled and disempowered.

Appendix: Some Features of Australian Aboriginal English

To be truly competent in Aboriginal English, one has to know and understand the many linguistic and communicative rules and processes that come into play once a speech event begins. When these are not properly adhered to, the verbal interaction between speakers can become distorted and incomprehensible.

This is evident when a non-Aboriginal person, who may appear competent in speaking Aboriginal English in social interactions, can often be caught out when the invisible language and cultural rules are overstepped. This can cause offence, embarrassment and confusion to all who may be involved in the verbal interaction. There are underlying currents of linguistic and cultural rules, protocols and processes at play which apply when Aboriginal English is spoken just between Aboriginal people. We do not profess to state that all Aboriginal people behave, act and talk in this certain way, on the contrary, we believe that every person – black or white – possesses an individual personality, regardless of their upbringing. However, we do believe that our underlying values, beliefs and knowledge do influence, guide and direct the way that Aboriginal people communicate with others, both in their own socio-cultural context and in mainstream society.

To be truly communicatively competent in Aboriginal English, one must grow up learning the cultural and linguistic rules and protocols of the specific Aboriginal social group to which one is connected. These rules and protocols guide individuals into using appropriate actions, behaviours and aspects of language, depending on the situational context. Aboriginal people have cleverly taken the English language and shaped, manipulated and moulded it to make it their own. They have resisted the dominant linguistic forms of speaking, by staying true to their values, beliefs and ways of doing and being – incorporating and embedding this into their speech. This has resulted in English dialects that are distinctly Aboriginal.

The key features of this English dialect that make it distinctly Aboriginal include the central importance of relationship and respect.

Relationship

Important relationship values that are incorporated into Aboriginal English include using kinship terms to show respect or a connection to other Aboriginal people, regardless of direct family ties or not. Many younger members know they should address older men and women as Aunty or Uncle and not by their first name. This is part of correct social protocol. It is quite acceptable for younger members to address each other as brother, sister or cousin, even though they are not related.

Indirectness

Indirectness in language is also a sign of respect. It is important to be careful not to ask direct personal questions to a person that one has only just met. This type of behaviour would be viewed as rude and disrespectful of the other person's privacy. When the time is right, the appropriate questions can be asked. An aspect of indirectness is a gentle approach, not being forward and pushy, but actually waiting for an appropriate time to ask certain questions.

Although English forms the basis of the grammatical structure and organisation of Aboriginal English, there is also room for certain words and phrases from both Aboriginal languages and English to be embedded into the spoken language.

Words/Phrases

Words, phrases and terms from traditional Aboriginal languages are used in many Aboriginal English(es) to ensure that one's cultural identity is kept intact. Certain words from heritage languages identify the connection of the group of speakers to their particular cultural heritage. Aboriginal people can often identify where people are from just from the way they speak or pronounce a certain word or phrase.

Likewise, some words and phrases from English are deliberately manipulated to completely change the meaning to the opposite of the English meaning. A common word that all Aboriginal people know and use is the word 'deadly'. To Aboriginal people, this means excellent and good, but for mainstream Australia, it means 'dangerous and bad'. There are many other examples in which Aboriginal people have taken an English word and changed the meaning to make it their own.

References

Australian Human Rights Commission (1997) Bringing them home: The "Stolen Children" report. Online report, accessed 17 July 2011. http://www.hreoc.gov.au/social_justice/bth_report/index.html

Bell, J. (2002) Linguistic continuity in colonized county. In J. Henderson and D. Nash (eds) *Language and Native Title* (pp. 43–52). Canberra: Aboriginal Studies Press.

Bell, J. (2010) Language and linguistic knowledge: A cultural treasure. *Ngoonjook Journal* 35, 84–96.

Calma, T. (2008) Keynote address at the World Indigenous People's Conference – Education, Melbourne, 9 December 2008. Online at http://www.hreoc.gov.au/about/media/speeches/social_justice/2008/20081209_world.html

CERD (2010) *Committee on the Elimination of Racial Discrimination, 77th session: Consideration of reports submitted by states parties under Article 9 of the Convention.* Online document, accessed 4 October 2011. http://www2.ohchr.org/english/bodies/cerd/cerds77.htm

Dauenhauer, N.M. and Dauenhauer, R. (1998) Technical, emotional, and ideological issues in reversing language shift: Examples from Southeast Alaska. In L.A. Grenoble and L.J. Whaley (eds) *Endangered Language* (pp. 57–98). Cambridge, UK: Cambridge University Press.

Devlin, B. (2008) A critique of recent government claims about the comparative performance of bilingual and non-bilingual schools in the NT. Unpublished discussion paper, Charles Darwin University.

Dickson, G. (2009) Northern Territory's small languages sidelined from schools. In C. Moseley (ed.) *Ogmios Newsletter: Foundation for Endangered Languages* 40, 3.

Eades, D. (1991) Aboriginal English: An introduction. *VOX* 5, 55–61.

Eades D. (2008) Researching Aboriginal English. Unpublished paper presented at the Australian Linguistics Society Annual Conference, University of Sydney, Australia.

Eira, C. and Couzens, V. (2010) *Meeting Point: Setting up a Typology of Revival Languages in Australia.* Melbourne: Victorian Aboriginal Language Centre.

Flint, E.H. (1968) Aboriginal English: Linguistic description as an aid to teaching. *English in Australia* 6, 3–21.

Flint, E.H. (1973) The sociology of language in Queensland aboriginal communities. *Linguistic Communications* 10, 11–25.

Fogarty, L. (1983) *Spirit Jukambe.* Brisbane: Kudjela Planet Press.

Gardiner, J. (1977) Teaching standard English as a second dialect to speakers of Aboriginal English. In E. Brumby and E. Vaszolyi (eds) *Language Problems and Aboriginal Education* (pp. 165–199). Perth: Mt Lawley College of Advanced Education.

Harkins, J. (1994) *Bridging Two Worlds, Aboriginal English and Cross Cultural Understanding.* Brisbane: University of Queensland Press.

Kaldor, S. (1976) Language problems, language planning, and Aboriginal education. In R.M. Berndt (ed.) *Aborigines and Change: Australia in the 70s* (pp. 237–251). Canberra: Australian Institute of Aboriginal Studies.

Malcolm, I. and Rochecouste, J. (2001) Event and story schemas in Australian aboriginal English. *English World-Wide* 21, 261–289.

Mühlhäusler, P. (1996) The diffusion of pidgin English in Australia. In S.A. Wurm, P. Mühlhäusler and D.T. Tyron (eds) *Atlas of Languages of Intercultural Communication in the Pacific, Asia, and the Americas: Trends in Linguistics Documentation 13* (pp. 143–146). Berlin: Mouton de Gruyter.

Phillipson, R.(2008) The linguistic imperialism of neoliberal empire. *Critical Inquiry in Language Studies* 5 (1), 1–43.

Sharifian, F. (2005) Something old, something new, something borrowed, something blue: Australian Aboriginal students schematic repertoire. *Journal of Multilingual and Multicultural Development* 26 (6), 5–13.

Sharifian, F. and Malcolm, I. (2003) The use of pragmatic like in English teen talk: Australian Aboriginal usage. *Pragmatics and Cognition* 11 (2), 327–344.

Yunupingu, Y. (2009) Extract from *Yalmay's story: Bilingual teaching.* On-line discussion forum, accessed 10 September 2010. http://groups.google.som.au/groupfoblmail

5 English Language as Nemesis for Māori

Graham Hingangaroa Smith and Vaughan Rapatahana

The prescription that English should be the sole language of the schools was a supreme stroke of genius as a means toward the civilization of the Māori people.
Butchers, 1932 (quoted in Williams, 2001: 135)

And finally if the result has been to make the Māori lose his language, don't forget that in its place he has the finest language in the world and that the retention of Māori is after all largely a matter of sentiment.
W.W. Bird, 1945 (quoted in Williams, 2001: 247)

Our challenge is to embrace the Paulo Freire contradiction; on the one hand we must help the oppressors to free themselves and yet on the other hand we must first free ourselves before we can genuinely help to free others.
Dist. Prof. Graham Hingangaroa Smith, Keynote Address, World Indigenous People's Conference on Education, Melbourne 2008

Preamble

This chapter examines the problematic role of the English language and its attendant cultural nuances as something that is antagonistic to the Māori language and cultural longevity. While this is posed as a core problem, we are not arguing to *colonize back*, but to call dramatic attention to the negative impact that English has had on Māori language survival. We would like the same power and privilege enjoyed by the English language and its speakers to also extend to the Māori language and its speakers. Ours is not a struggle against English, but for the *appropriate recognition of the Māori language*, given that we will still need to resist the English language when it threatens the viability of Māori language regeneration.

In this sense, we are not arguing for an either/or outcome between English and the Māori language. All New Zealanders should have positive, unimpeded access to a depth and breadth of excellence in both languages. However, the state of each of these languages is not the same. English survival is guaranteed, because it exists elsewhere in the world – it is promoted aggressively in many, many places, as other chapters in this book describe. The Māori language belongs only in Aotearoa (New Zealand.) If it is lost from this land, then it is lost forever. It is because of the dire circumstances of Māori language longevity, and an associated widespread lack of concern for its survival, that we make a case for the Māori language in the way that we do. The English language has been a destructive and colonizing force. This chapter not only advocates for the Māori language, it is also concerned to identify the ongoing colonizing impact of the English language within New Zealand society and, of course, the relevance of this situation to other indigenous language contexts.

The peopling of Aotearoa began with an initial settlement by Māori people. The Māori belong to the generic Polynesian population, and they brought with them their own ancestral language. They mostly lived by a set of values that supported collective responsibilities, with respect to social and economic organization. Moreover, they had their own culturally distinctive system of education – of passing on knowledge and teaching and learning. At the heart of this cultural system of education was the Māori language.

The arrival of European voyagers and the subsequent settlement from the 1800s by European groups from various countries (but mostly from Britain) brought European (Pakeha) and Māori cultural forces into contestation. The arrival of the Europeans, and their subsequent concern to protect and maintain their own culture, had two discernible imperatives: first, a positive impulse to maintain and preserve the familiar British language, knowledge and culture; and, secondly, a negative impulse to dominate and even decimate the Māori language, Māori knowledge and Māori culture.

This contest is often generically described as 'colonization'. The colonization of the Māori has had a number of themes that have been developed through both informal (socialization) and formal (policy) educative processes. Whatever the process, two common factors have seemingly underpinned the motivation to undermine Māori language, knowledge and culture. The first was to more easily and justifiably access material resources from Māori ownership. The second was to lend validity and legitimacy to the European invasion and occupation of Aotearoa, in the absence of the *terra nullius* defense. Some examples of inter-cultural engagement are listed here. Some of these developments represent a historical chronological order, others overlap:

(1) Expurgation (the missionary imperative to civilize) – to 'cast out the sins of the heathen natives'.
(2) Annihilation (the political strategy to do nothing, but to let Māori die out naturally) – 'to smooth the pillow for the dying race'.
(3) Assimilation (the political policy to turn Māori into Europeans) – 'to teach the Māori lass to be a good farmer's wife and the Māori lad to be a good farmer'.

(4) Integration (the Hunn Report policy, 1960) – 'to take the best of Pakeha life-style and the best of Māori life-style and produce a new hybrid citizen'.
(5) Biculturalism (the Walker thesis, 1975, cited in Williams, 2001) – 'to take the best aspects of Māori culture and to blend them with the best aspects of Pakeha culture to produce a new biculturally competent New Zealander'.
(6) Self-development (to allow Māori to develop their own cultural aspirations and to co-exist with Pakeha) – 'two peoples, one nation'.

The history of engagement between the dominant Pakeha language and culture and the subordinated Māori cultural frameworks has seen the emergence of the English language and its cultural forms as the taken-for-granted mainstream cultural and language norm. Its dominance has effectively contributed to the current marginalization and undermining of the survival of the Māori language.

In more recent times – approximately from the 1970s onwards – Māori people have made a spirited resurgence, linguistically and culturally. This chapter examines where the Māori are up to and what the future may hold, as they continue to both resist and adapt to their nemesis: English-language-centred domination. The Māori once had complete authority over their own lives (*tino rangatiratanga*). This loss of power to make decisions – which reflected their own cultural aspirations – has been a major contributor to Māori language demise. The dominant Pakeha (European) groups do not share the same interests for Māori language survival. Looking forward, a key strategy will be to strengthen and retain the power to self-develop outside the dominant culture's interference.

History

Prior to the arrival of Europeans in *Aotearoa*, the Māori elders (*kaumātua*) and grandparents (*tipuna*) taught traditional knowledge in family (*Whānau*) settings in an oral, non-written tradition. Some aspects of this vital form of transmitting knowledge continue until today. When the late Koro Dewes (1974) announced the beginning of the Māori language revitalization effort centred on the Wellington-based Te Reo Māori Society, he stated:

New Zealand is now experiencing a cultural revolution... moving towards a re-vitalization of the Māori values expressed in traditional oral literature which can survive only with the assured perpetuation of the Māori language. Action songs of today... cry for the freeing of the Māori spirit which is threatened by the continuation of Pakeha [non-Māori] education. (Benton, 1981: 10)

All this made, and makes, *te reo Māori* (the Māori language) absolutely essential in the transmission of Māori knowledge via Māori education. Rangimarie Rose Pere reinforces the inextricable link between language, knowledge and culture and, therefore, the priority of the need to struggle to preserve the Māori language, as follows:

> There is one truly great treasure among us Māori... and that is our chiefly language... [it] has its own spirit of inherent wisdom, it is communication of the abstract, in order that outsiders might not understand its hidden depths... Language is not only a form of communication but it helps transmit the values and beliefs of a people. (Pere, 1994: 3–10)

These elements are central to the Māori-language resistance initiatives. These elements are implicit in *Te Kōhanga Reo* ('language nests' at pre-school level), *Kura Kaupapa Māori* (elementary schools) and *Whare Wānanga* (Māori-focused tertiary provision – currently, there are three *Wānanga* tertiary institutions in Aotearoa.) Indeed, prior to the European arrival, there were many *Wānanga* operating throughout the islands. These are the Māori educational and schooling options that have evolved out of Māori community and aspirations for the revitalization and retention of *Te Reo Māori*, the Māori language. Māori education historically involved no formal institutions, instead it went on at any given time, night or day, and involved all members of *Whānau*.

'*Ako* (learning) was not bound by age, gender or social status in tradition-based Māori society' (Pihama *et al.*, International Research Institute or IRI, 2004). It was life-long, mostly informal and it put great value on skills and experience. Moreover, knowledge was seen as a gift from the spiritual realm (*atua*). It had 'origins in the metaphysical' (IRI, 2004); it involved everything in an interconnected, living world – both physical and metaphysical. Distinguished Māori elder, Ranginui Walker (2004: 344), observed, 'according to Māori epistemology, humans have no knowledge of their own. All knowledge emanates from the celestial realm of the gods'.

Māori education can be differentiated from Pakeha education, epistemologically and ontologically.[1] These essential differences have mostly been ignored as the dominant, monocultural Pakeha cultural norms have been asserted, validated and reproduced through culturally selected constructions of educational practice and structures. The end result has been that the Māori people have been rendered subservient to English language education and cultural mores over the last 150 years or more. Indeed, many Māori would say that they are still shackled by the colonizing effects of such an education, despite the current efforts of alternative Māori pathways. Some might further consider that the education and schooling approaches of the last 150 years have been successful in their colonizing intentions. For example, Graham Hingangaroa Smith (2009: 4–5) has commented that 'there are still a few bumps and some elements that need to improve... colonization has not gone away... old forms of colonization have been embedded in schooling'. English language education has served to alienate many Māori from their cultural identity and emotional well-being. The importance of language to the notions of 'being' and 'feeling' Māori is captured in the following *pepeha* (proverbial saying):

> *Ko te reo Māori te ha o te Māoritanga.*
> Māori language gives meaning and life to being Māori.

It is not an exaggeration to state that an education and schooling system built on the reification of the English language and culture has not only alienated many Māori from learning, it has also deliberately weakened their cultural identity and emotional well-being. The English language agency truly was, and remains still, the nemesis of Māori language and culture.

The English Language Agencies Arrive – Mission Schools

Before the Treaty of Waitangi (*Te Tiriti o Waitangi*) was signed in 1840, and prior to the advent of the Māori-Pakeha land wars of the 1860s, Pakeha-inspired education for Māori occurred mostly in Mission Schools. The year 1816 saw the first such school established in Rangihoua. Here, the Māori were taught in their own language and – initially, at least – they were enthusiastic participants, especially during the 1830s and 1840s. They were motivated to attain 'Pakeha wisdom', knowledge and skills. Notwithstanding the contradictory outcomes for the Māori, Stephen May (2004a: 25) claims that, 'the initial aim for Māori in incorporating Pakeha learning was one of enhancing their traditional way of life'.

The contradiction was that in the pursuit of Pakeha knowledge, Māori knowledge was to be displaced. In the view of the missionary teachers, the heathen Māori had to be 'saved'. They needed to expurgate their sins and take up the puritanical ways of the European. The idea behind the early Mission Schools was to 'civilize the natives' so as to condition them into Christianity. The Church Missionary Society (CMS), based in England, had a major role to play here. All of this was a deliberate colonizing strategy to employ a social control mechanism that was designed to bring stability, docility and complicity to the colonies. It was not an accident that the funding of the CMS carried the stipulation that all instruction was to be in the English language. Simon and Smith (2001: 159) explain the link to language this way: 'by controlling the language of instruction... the missionaries exerted a great deal of control over the knowledge and information that Māori could potentially access'.

The 1847 Education Ordnance provided some funding for such schools, as long as they taught in English. This funding was especially made available for the establishment of boarding schools, whch would get Māori away from the 'demoralizing influence of Māori villages' (Barrington, 1966, quoted in Simon, 1992). In the government policy of that time, 'there was to be only one official language and that would be English. These policies were to be followed rigorously in the ensuing decades. *They continue to impact on Māori society to the present day'* (Williams, 2001: 22). The Māori began to see that the knowledge that they wanted was gradually being infused by the Pakeha aspirations for the Māori. As Judith Simon (1992) has noted:

> Pakeha had their own ideas of what the Māori should be taught in the schools and both the missionaries and the government controlled the amount and type of knowledge that was made accessible to the Māori in accordance with their own agendas.

The Māori were taught by their paternalistic mentors (in an alien medium of instruction) to accept that they were not as good, nor, indeed, as intelligent as their European counterparts. The selective curriculum – 'selecting in' Pakeha-dominant cultural expectations and aspirations and 'selecting out' subordinate, Māori cultural preferences – was problematic in the mission schools, and it remains a problem today, some 150 years later.

Such schools were later largely abandoned, however, when the Māori-Pakeha land wars commenced in 1865. What then ensued in Aotearoa was land-grabbing by the new settlers to the extent of totally disregarding the promises of *Te Tiriti o Waitangi*. It was signed in 1840, but treated as irrelevant by many Pakeha, many of whom were out-and-out racists at worst and incredibly patronizing at best.[2] Disregard for the Treaty is clearly seen in the ruling by Judge Prendergast in the Wi Parata case of 1877. He marginalized the Treaty as a 'simple nullity', 'since it had not been incorporated into domestic law' (Alves, 1999: 51). The Treaty was totally ignored, as large numbers of Europeans poured into the country and demanded more and more *whenua Māori* (Māori land.)

It is essential to note that many Māori perceive themselves to *be* the land. They will often link themselves by genealogy (*whakapapa*) to *Papatuanuku* – the Earth parent. There is a vital bond here, so that any loss of land equates to a literal loss of life and a severing of *whakapapa*. Mason Durie (1994: 3) explains this, by saying that 'land was part of the internalized identity, providing individuals and groups with a tangible past, a *turangawaewae*, or a place where they could feel more secure, confident, and supported'. Māori well-being is intimately linked to the land. 'The loss of land made Māori more vulnerable to diseases associated with poverty, malnutrition and overcrowding' (Simon & Smith, 2001: 224). The Māori became spiritually and physically vulnerable as a result of land loss and other colonization effects. Tove Skutnabb-Kangas (2003: 31–52) emphasized this vital link between linguistic diversity and biodiversity in her declaration that language is literally the 'lifeblood of a culture'.

According to Buchanan (1990), the early colonists made concerted efforts to totally repudiate the Treaty by interpreting its English language translations to their own advantage and, thereby, exploiting the Māori land owners. This went on and on and gave rise to the land wars of the 1860s. During this time, very few Māori were attending school anywhere. They had become progressively less enthusiastic about schools and saw them as sites of cultural contestation between Māori and Pakeha interests.

Just the same, in 1858, there were some Māori who were still enthusiastic about English-language education. 'It was not at all inconsistent for a champion [Matene Te Whiwhi] of *Kingitanga* [the 19th century King movement] also to argue firmly in favour of English language instruction for Māori children in schools' (Williams, 2001: 116). Wi te Hakiro *et al.* (in 1876) argued similarly, when, by then, in some areas, the non-Māori population outstripped the Māori population. Lee and Lee (1995: 109) explained it this way:

> The reason why Māori wanted access to schooling was seldom concealed – it was the chief means by which to obtain social and economic parity with the Pakeha... 377 Māori had petitioned the Government... so that any native school teacher [would]..."provide all the knowledge which the Europeans possess" and "be persons altogether ignorant of the Māori language".

Of course, just as many other Māori, over a similarly long period of time, refused this English language dominion, just as many had refused to sign *Te Tiriti o Waitangi* (including the *nga ariki*, the chiefs, of Te Atiawa). In 1908, a Māori Member of Parliament, Hone Heke, 'strongly urged that the Māori tongue should be systematically taught in the native schools, as at present the people were in great danger of losing their language altogether' (cited in Simon, 1992).

Native Schools

The year 1858 saw the Native Schools Act brought in by the government of the day, whereby subsidies were given to mission schools, as long as they used English as the medium of instruction. From 1867, Native Schools per se were established, and this later Act decreed that only the English language was to be used in Māori education. Witness Section 21, 1867, which stated:

> No school shall receive any grant unless it has been shown to the satisfaction of the colonial secretary by the report of the inspector...

that the English language... [is] taught by a competent teacher and that the instruction is carried on in the English language as far as practicable. (Williams, 2001: 25)

More sinisterly, such Native Schools were only created when the Māori asked for them, gave the land for them and also gave substantial amounts of money for their salaries and building costs. These schools were then duly constructed as colonial Trojan Horses, slap bang in the middle of Māori communities.

It is also important to note that the Native Schools preceded public (Pakeha) schools by 10 years and that scholarships were later provided for the 'best' Māori students to attend these public schools, so as to further 'develop an educated Māori elite who would return to their villages and spread the gospel of assimilation' (Simon, 1992). Even these few 'successful' elite graduates remained subaltern to nga Pakeha, however.

There is absolutely no doubt from both Māori (for example Walker, 2004) and, ironically, also, many Pakeha sources (Ward, 1974; Pearson, 1990; Simon, 1992; Williams, 2001; Benton, 2001) that the Pakeha made this determined effort to assimilate the Māori, with the accent on utilizing English only. These schools prevented their Māori students from speaking te reo Māori – the gateway to all aspects of Māori tikanga (Māori preferred values, beliefs and practices) – to the extent of physical punishment if they spoke their own language at school, even in the playground. For Māori, Ko te reo te tāhuhu o tēnei whare (language is the ridgepole of this house). The English language educators seemed determined to demolish it.

Assimilation, Amalgamation and Annihilation

Throughout the late 19th century and well into the 20th century, the Pakeha continued to force Māori to speak and write the English language (Harker, 1985; Simon, 1992). Such was the domination of English language education in Aotearoa, particularly after the land-wars of the 1860s, that few Māori students could escape being caught up in it. This was a determined policy of *assimilation* by the colonial government. Here, then, was the key to Pakeha dominion, because:

...the fluent use and knowledge of the Māori language is fundamentally essential to the preservation and vitality of Māori cultural knowledge systems. The language underpins the culture and helps to define it. The worldview and cosmology embedded in the language provide insights into aspects of Māori culture that are unique to the tangata whenua of this land. Arguably, the Māori language is the only appropriate means of transmitting Māori cultural knowledge. (Williams, 2001: 124)

By eliminating *te reo Māori* and enforcing the English language, the European colonizers were also effectively eliminating Māori people as culturally holistic beings. Such an extermination had literally occurred when the total Māori population fell to just over 42,000 nationwide in 1896, after the series of land-wars and also the exposure to the sicknesses introduced to the shores of Aotearoa by the white men (Buchanan, 1990.) Annihilation, while not an official governmental policy, was not necessarily discounted by several white settlers. Williams (2001: 242–243) sums up some of the colonizers' attempts at this linguistic and cultural genocide, as follows:

> In all things they [the Māori] must be required to learn to follow British cultural knowledge systems and in particular to ensure that they were educated in the English language. The arrogance of colonialism was such that no attempt was made in Crown policy-making to ensure that Māori cultural knowledge was transmitted to future generations... it is this arrogance, this insistence on the superiority of the English language and all things British... that has led some Māori today to describe the Crown's policies as cultural genocide and a metaphorical "holocaust" that incinerated Māori historical cultural knowledge systems. (See also, Skutnabb-Kangas & Dunbar, 2010)

May (2004a: 24–25) similarly comments that:

> ironically, in this process, Pakeha were not only to repudiate and replace Māori language and knowledge structures within education, but were also to deny the Māori full access to European knowledge and learning.

Theoretically, such *assimilation* – as outlined above – was designed to lift the Māori from one rung of existence to a higher one, 'but only as long as they were not lifted too high' (*ibid.*: 26). The early Pakeha wanted a menial labouring class, so the Māori were intentionally marginalized onto thin shards of rural land and later dotted around urban areas. This was 'a strategy to reduce competition in expanding bureaucratic, commercial and professional positions in urban areas by putting impediments in the way of Māori students' (Barrington, 1992: 68–69).[3] Ward's seminal work, *A Show of Justice* (1974: 38), equates assimilation with *amalgamation* – a deliberate British pogrom of non-equal opportunity – and of overcoming an entire race:

> Official policy was basically in line with other "amalgamation" policies then in vogue as the best means by which a native people would be saved from extinction... The saving of the Māori race involved the extinction of Māori culture... little encouragement was being given to Māori participation in a wide spectrum of vocations... Economic opportunities everywhere seemed to be closed off to the Māori.

Into the 20th Century

English-language-centred and controlled policies continued to impact deleteriously on Māori language and culture. As the new century began, 1903 saw an even stricter enforcement of an English-only policy. Children who came from a Māori-speaking *Whānau* were now expected to stay in the junior classes in primary schools for one extra year – they were viewed as disadvantaged.

Since 1928, the two systems of separated schools followed the same curriculum, but the Native Schools (mainly rural) remained in operation until 1969. More and more Māori were also attending regular schools in the growing urban centres. These were schools which had absolutely no conception of the need to cater for a completely different group of people.

Why was there this demographic movement of Māori to the urban areas? From the 1940s, they were coerced into urbanizing by the government-inspired rural land loss. The best arable land was taken off the Māori, and they were left with the rest. They were also being deliberately under-educated in the arts of agriculture for use on their uneconomic tracts of land. For Pakeha educationalists, such as biology professor Henry Kirk (1906), even farming skills should be taught 'on strictly limited lines' (cited in Simon, 1992). Finally, through a no-choice, deliberately inadequate training in manual arts, Māori students could not compete with the Pakeha for more specialized positions anywhere.

A pronounced emphasis on English language education then remained steadfast right through to the 1930s. The year 1931 saw the advent of another 'new' policy direction. This was the 'cultural adaptation' of education policies to allow some selected elements of *Māoritanga* (the Māori way of life/culture) into Native Schools, because the 'Māori were not using the English language and adopting European patterns of living to the extent expected' (Simon & Smith, 2001: 197). Therefore, 'education under this policy was to be adapted to "native life"' (*ibid.*: 195). In the 1930s, the Pakeha were still 'creating the conditions under which Māori might more readily take on board European patterns of living' (*ibid.*: 198). 'It was, however, the Department of Education which did the selecting of these elements, thus reserving the right to determine what constituted valid Māori knowledge... Māori language not included' (Simon, 1992). Simon also fiercely cast this 'new' policy of adaptation as merely another social control to prevent any discontent and potential rebellion.[4] It was not until 1941 that there were any Native District High Schools. Prior to this, they had all been primary schools, with a smattering of denominational Māori boarding schools for 'the most proficient Māori children' who had earned scholarships (Simon & Smith, 2001: 10).

More and more Māori students then began to attend public schools as the 20th century rolled on, but as Simon (1992) notes, the 'Māori children in public schools were often subjected to low expectations from teachers who were seldom concerned to improve their educational performances', and they were, indeed, discriminated against on manifestly racial grounds.

> At these schools they have been subjected to "streaming" and standardized intelligence or achievement tests that have placed most of them in the low streams... [These] "sorting" processes were claimed to be scientifically objective with the students being classified according to their "abilities" and not according to "race", ethnicity or socio-economic status... it conceals the tests' political nature and the fact that they are biased toward dominant class interests. (*ibid.*)

By 1951, it was acceptable to learn Māori at university level, but:

> no effort would be made to train Māori language teachers or to teach Māori to primary school children... more effective transmission of modern Māori culture could be made by using English rather than Māori as the medium of transmission. (Williams, 2001: 139)

The Government line, right through the 1960s, remained that there were insufficient teachers of *te reo Māori*, '...because there was a long-term governmental unwillingness to make provision for teacher training' (*ibid.*: 143).

English language as Nemesis, indeed.

Issues of Māori Language and Culture Murder Continued as the Century Wound On

By the 1950s, the majority of the Māori workforce was unskilled: only 6% held qualified positions (New Zealand in History, 2011). Consequently, and obviously, they suffered far greater economic hardships, which only served to alienate them even more. This served to reinforce what the Pakeha, in general, thought about them anyway, and, from Gramsci's (1971) notion of hegemony, for Māori to start to believe this about themselves. Māori educational achievement during childhood fell well behind the statistical norms of Pakeha children (Marie *et al.*, 2008) – a situation that still prevails.

The 1950s policies, such as 'pepper-potting' of Māori families into predominantly urban Pakeha communities, further ensured the loss of Māori language and culture. Benton (2007: 167) records that 'social engineering on the part of the Government, which adopted a policy of resettling Māori families in need of housing assistance in ethnically mixed communities' only broke up any Māori traditional networking of shared language and culture. According to May (2004a: 41), 'prior to the Second World War less than 10% of Māori had lived in cities or smaller urban centers. Currently [1995], 82% of Māori live in urban areas... Māori have thus undergone what is perhaps the most comprehensive and certainly the most rapid urbanization process in modern times'. By 1960, only 26% of Māori people spoke Māori as their first language, after 90% of Māori school children had been fluent in 1913 (ibid.) They had lost touch with their *turangawaewae* (place of birth and nurture) completely. By now, the Māori also had a different agenda regarding the learning of the Queen's English. 'Their focus now was on *surviving* economically and politically within a Pakeha-dominated society. Clearly they recognized fluency in English as one of the strategies of survival' (Simon & Smith, 2001: 165).

Then there was the Hunn Report on Māori (education), whereby the Māori language was cast as 'one of the few surviving relics of ancient Māori life' (1960: 15). The Report's supposedly new policy of *integration* meant Māori were to somehow merge into the dominant Pakeha society completely – to become 'brown Pakeha', 'to combine (not fuse) Māori and Pakeha elements to form one nation' (ibid: 14–15). Indeed, integration seemed no more than assimilation dressed up in different clothing. The Hunn Report 'tended fairly consistently to restrict "Māori" solutions and to promote instead "Pakeha" answers to the problems of the Māori people' (Booth, 1970, quoted in Williams, 2001: 99). The Pakeha-centred process of English language dominion continued, via such a Pakeha-centred policy.

The Beginnings of Change

There were some slightly positive changes inspired by the Pakeha that began to be implemented from about 1970 onwards. However, the Māori quickly realized that they would not gain control of their own destinies from such Pakeha-initiated policies and notions and that they would have to do things for themselves and by themselves if they wanted their language – and, thus, their unique culture – to survive.

(1) Multiculturalism

This notion decreed that all cultures within Aotearoa-New Zealand would, in some way, benefit by the learning of elements of each other's cultures. Sadly, the policy was 'also seen as a useful mechanism for containing the conflicts of ethnic groups within existing social relations rather than as a basis for any real power-sharing between Māori and Pakeha' (May, 2005a: 28).

(2) Biculturalism

A very similar policy to the above, in that Māori and Pakeha were to, in some way (ascribed by Pakeha), share aspects of culture, such as learning each other's tongues. Again, this was seen to be serving merely to 'indigenise the Pakeha' (Smith, 1987: 189). Dewes (1977: 63), for example, bemoaned the fact that 'standards in oral language are lowered to cater for second-language learners (mostly Pakeha)', as a direct result.

(3) *Taha Māori*

A later 1970s Pakeha-inspired crush on *Taha Māori* (the Māori 'side') only served Pakeha interests. As Graham Smith (1990) pointed out, this programme was designed by the Pakeha to maintain the status quo of Pakeha as gatekeepers of what was to be included in any school curriculum, but more than that, such was its design, that it actually further served to assimilate the Māori. The Māori were supposed to, in some way, garner sufficient self-esteem from *Taha Māori* so as to 'achieve better' within an alien system. Pita Sharples, now a leading politician in Aotearoa-New Zealand, noted that, 'both *Taha Māori* and "ambulance projects" (such as the Māori Education Foundation's special scholarships, quotas and preparatory classes) do not challenge what is being taught and how it is being taught. The result is no marked increase in Māori performance in the State Education System' (Sharples, 1992: 18).

In 1987, Smith wrote that:

> the curriculum initiative of *Taha Māori* is a Pakeha-defined, -initiated and -controlled policy which serves the needs and interests of Pakeha people. Education policies such as *Taha Māori* are concerned with surface level, "additive", or "sticking plaster" solutions to the burgeoning schooling crisis affecting many Māori people. (1987: 183)

Later in the same article, he speaks of the 'illusion of change', whereby Pakeha are:

> capturing the definitions of *Taha Māori*... co-opting the *Taha Māori* definition... and facilitating the acculturation of Māori language, knowledge and culture... *Taha Māori* enhances acculturation by allowing Pakeha uncontrolled and wholesale access to Māori knowledge. (ibid.:187, 191)

Like Harker, Smith invokes Bourdieu (1986) and the cultural capital of Pakeha as the dominant power-source, self-maintaining itself via schools 'premised on the imperialist assumption that Pakeha-defined cultural capital is the most appropriate for all New Zealand schools' (ibid.: 187).

(4) 'Closing the Gaps'

This was yet another Pakeha-inspired and initiated policy, whereby economic and social 'gaps' were to be closed up so that all people in the country would have a more equitable slice of the fiscal pie. If anything, such supposed remedies for Māori 'underachievement' merely cemented the Pakeha power systems more firmly into place. Humpage and Fleras observed that '…a core function of *Closing the Gaps* was to encourage social cohesion by helping more Māori and Pacific peoples become more like well-off Pakeha… it might be "assimilation in slow motion", but assimilation it remains' (2001: 49). In 1998, Te Puni Kokiri commented that:

> overall the evidence presented in this [*Closing the Gaps*] report does not provide assurance that the economic and social gaps between Māori and non-Māori are closing. Of greater concern is that the statistics do not provide any signals that there is an impending change in the situation. (Te Puni Kokiri, cited in Williams, 2001: 111)

These policies were certainly not intended to build on the more self-determining Māori-inspired and Māori-instigated initiatives, such as *Te Kōhanga Reo* and *Kura Kaupapa Māori*. These latter positive programmes 'have evolved their own counter-hegemonies, which the state is now being invited to accept' (Smith, 1987: 185). Yet the gaps remain, even after the advent of these *kōhanga reo* and *Kura Kaupapa Māori*. Why did this remain the case? Because, as Smith further emphasized, 'real power lies within the dominant Pakeha population who are able to control what will be taught, how it will be taught and by whom it will be taught' (1987: 192). By then, there was also new technology and television – an exclusively English medium – which would 'reinforce the implicit message that English was the only language of any importance in the wider world' (Benton, 2007: 167). No wonder the Māori had become increasingly apathetic about education from the later 1800s and early 1900s onwards. It was a no-win situation, and their lack of academic success – predicted by Pakeha to happen anyway – became a self-fulfilling prophecy:

> It was inevitable that, over time, these low expectations, would come to be accepted and reproduced by the Māori children themselves… Māori aspirations thus became progressively lowered till they reached the stage where Māori themselves seemed to accept that manual labour was their natural vocation. (Simon, 1992)

Similarly, as Jenkins (1994: 152) notes, 'as "victims", Māori believed it was their own fault, that they were deficient'. Rapatahana (co-author of this chapter) had no instruction in *te reo Māori* at school, because none was available in the 1960s in his south Auckland school, even though most students there were non-Pakeha. They all had to learn Latin and French and sing 'God Save the Queen' at every morning assembly in the 1960s. This was another example of linguistic imperialism/imposition and cultural denial. The only Māori staff member in the school taught Art and Craft.

Māori Fight Back

Since 1970 onwards, changes – involving a revitalization of the Māori language *by Māori themselves* – began in earnest, especially within Māori-language educational settings (see the Timeline at the end of this chapter).

The new trends, such as *kōhanga reo* and *kura kaupapa*, outlined above, transpired from the 1970s onwards, partly inspired by the rage and frustration that the Māori were increasingly expressing. There were also those, like the distinguished *kaumatua* or elder (Koro) Te Kapunga Dewes, who angrily said that he was 'sick and tired of Māori being blamed for their educational and social shortcomings, their limitations highlighted and their obvious strengths of being "privileged New Zealanders" in being bilingual and bicultural, ignored' (Dewes, 1968: 1). *Nga Tamatoa* – a group of younger activist Māori – and the *Te Reo Māori Society* stood together with Dewes (Barrington, 1972: 64) as 'critics of official language policy [who] complained of "linguistic imperialism" in the schools and prejudice against the Māori language by headmasters and educational authorities'.

The Government did start to bend a little in the 1970s. By then, of course, it was probable that the Pakeha policy-makers did not want to be accused of apartheid or racism, so they were far more willing to disestablish any signs of separatism in society at a time when the political climate worldwide had changed significantly regarding civil rights. In other words, *global trends*, as much as national pressures, contributed to the more racially aware epiphanies of some Pakeha. The majority of Pakeha, however, in our observation, still remained unwilling to give up too much ground.

More Recent Developments: Māori Begin to Take Control

Some manifestly major changes began to transpire, and the situation has further developed so that nowadays:

contemporary expressions of *kaupapa Māori* develop within the education system. Their development and ongoing survival has been driven by Māori... *Te kōhanga reo* and *kura kaupapa Māori* developed as resistance to a mainstream Pakeha-centred system that failed to address key needs of Māori. (IRI, 2004)

These movements also act as a challenge to Pakeha dominance. There is also a movement towards *Kaupapa Māori* implementation *within* mainstream institutions and settings (IRI, 2004). As Pihama (1993: 57) sees things:

> *Kaupapa Māori* theory is a politicizing agent that acts as a counter-hegemonic force to promote the conscientisation of Māori people, through a process of critiquing Pakeha definitions and constructions of Māori people, and asserting the validation and legitimation of *te reo Māori* and *tikanga.*

Graham Smith (2003: 8–11) delineates six core principles as 'the crucial change factors in a *kaupapa Māori* non-lineal transformative praxis'. *Kaupapa Māori* consists of:

(1) the principle of self-determination or relative autonomy;
(2) the principle of validating and legitimating cultural aspirations and identity;
(3) the principle of incorporating culturally preferred pedagogy;
(4) the principle of mediating socio-economic and home difficulties;
(5) the principle of incorporating cultural structures which emphasize the 'collective' rather than the 'individual' such as the notion of the extended family; and
(6) the principle of a shared and collective vision/philosophy.

Smith has been at the forefront of this change, and he notes that contemporary *Akonga Māori* (or the principles of Māori education) – as a continuation of the historic process – emphasizes the inter-relationship of teaching and learning, in that they are not understood as separate concepts. In the Māori worldview, teaching and learning are one and the same. Thus, the Māori term for 'learn' is *Ako*, the Māori term for 'teach' is *Ako,* unlike the Pakeha notions of teaching and learning as separate things (Smith, 1987).

In the 21st century, the Māori are 'doing it for themselves'. Perhaps the most visible symbols of the alterations to the educational scene for Māori have been the proliferation of *kura kaupapa Māori* – themselves logical and necessary developments from *kōhanga reo*. They all incorporate the *akonga* framework and all instil pride and act as counters to deficit thinking for Māori people. *Te Aho Matua* is the set of guiding principles to be followed. All such *kura kaupapa Māori* are conducted in *te reo Māori*, as a counter to English language dominance.

Smith (1997) stressed that *kura kaupapa Māori* are founded on three vital bases – that all things Māori are valid and legitimate; that *te reo Māori* and culture is imperative; and that Māori must have autonomy (*tino rangatiratanga*). He also made it clear that *kura kaupapa* curricula are 'within the national guidelines set by the state' (1987: 194) and that 'it is not a rejection of Pakeha knowledge and/or culture... Māori parents want full access to both cultural frameworks for their children'(1992: 10). In 2011, many Māori were opposed to the national educational curriculum, because they saw it as not fully compatible with *Te Aho Matua*, not wide-ranging enough. They felt that 'there is no evidence they [national standards] will improve kids' achievement' (Radio New Zealand News, 2011).

Indeed, *Kura Kaupapa Māori* academic results 'show Māori-medium learners were more likely to meet literacy and numeracy requirements for NCEA (National Certificate of Educational Achievement) Level 1 than their peers at English-medium schools' (Nga Haeata Matauranga, 2009). The 2006 Maxim Institute paper on *Current Issues in Māori Schooling* further emphasizes just how much *kura kaupapa Māori* immersion education is improving academic results, community involvement and 'affirming Māori in their cultural identity'. Quite simply, Māori need *kura kaupapa Māori* language education. It is designed *for* them and *by* them. Mainstream English-medium schooling options are currently failing Māori badly, not least because of their inherent irrelevance and racism. This deficit theorizing by teachers is the major impediment to Māori students' educational achievement, for it results in teachers having low expectations of Māori students. 'This, in turn, creates a downward spiraling, self-fulfilling prophecy of Māori student achievement and failure' (Bishop *et al.*, 2003). The 2006 Maxim report really rams home the damning indictment of this mainstream English language education system's failure to cater for Māori.

Smith noted, back in 1992, that most Māori children had few options other than to attend local state schools. Not much has changed, as the majority of Māori children today do not go to Māori-medium educational facilities, whether they be deemed 'bilingual', with more than 12% of lessons in *te reo Māori*, or 'immersion', with more than 81%. While there was a rapid rise in the number of *kura kaupapa Māori* in the 1990s, a plateau was reached in 2010. Indeed, many such students are still not catered for at all, in terms of having *te reo Māori* made available to them. Benton (2007: 172) further cautions that, 'on the one hand, Māori people have battled persistently to preserve the Māori language, yet today most Māori parents do not speak Māori at home and they send their children to mainstream English-medium schools'. In 1996, for example, only 2.3% of Māori children attended either bilingual or immersion schools – a figure that had only climbed to slightly less than 16% 14 years later (Education Counts, 2011.)

We must therefore continue to stress that most Māori *still* – at the time of writing – attend state schooling options and are *still* are taught via the English language. The English language still has huge sway in Aotearoa/ New Zealand. According to May (2005: 1), 'more than 9 out of 10 of Aotearoa/New Zealand's 3.8 million inhabitants are first-language speakers of English, which means that the country is one of the most linguistically homogenous in the world today'. Even though the Māori language is indeed making a spirited resurgence both within and without Māori educational sites, the sheer weight of numbers of English first-language speakers and their concomitant grip on the reins of power, remains continuously intimidating.

The English language Hydra head, that is named Nemesis, remains steadfast.

The Current Situation: Continued English Language Nemesis or *Tino Rangatiratanga*?

So have things really altered that much from the 1970s onwards, given the dawn of *Nga Tamatoa*; *kōhanga reo* and *kura kaupapa Māori*, the Māori Language Act (or MLA), political promises, the Māori Language Fund (or MLF), the Waitangi Tribunal finally ratifying the rights of Māori to steer their own *waka* (canoe), and the further Pakeha-inspired policies, such as the Picot Report and *Tomorrow's Schools* (1987), and so on and so forth? The answer would seem to be: a little, but not enough.

Using the Māori Language Act as just one example, Benton (2007: 17) noted that:

> the provisions of the Act… are narrower in scope than what the tribunal considered desirable… the Māori Language Act does little more than make Māori officially available for oral use by accused criminals and other people involved in court proceedings.

As regards the Māori Language Fund, it is all too often under-utilized for the purposes for which it was designed. Respected Māori academic Arohia Drurie (1999: 22), for example, wrote that '…once received by the schools it [the funding] did not necessarily reach the Māori language programmes'.

Richard Benton, historically at the forefront of drawing attention to the demise of *te reo Māori*, maintains that the Māori language is being corrupted by English-language definitions and technical terminologies (2007), which is, of course, the self-same neoliberal impetus that drives (Anglo-American) English language global dominion or, as May (2004a: 35) puts it, 'the ongoing valorization of English'. 'The greatest danger… lies… in its [the Māori language] manipulation and damage by the forces of modernization' (Benton, 2007: 178). Benton also invokes the work of Janet Holmes (2005) about the presence of a distinct New Zealand Māori English: '…it is the adaptation of English to their own ends, so that a distinctive Māori English has become a marker of identity' (2007: 177). In so doing, he repeats what Smith and Sharples stress, regarding the importance of Māori maintaining

English competency, but on their own terms and via their own pedagogies. Māori rarely deny the importance of English as a language of wider national and international communication. Sharples (2007) pointed out that English language was in no way precluded from *kura kaupapa* and that, in fact, *te reo Māori* grounding would also lead to more competent biliteracy. Just as the Māori have adapted the Native Schools to survive and just as they have responded mightily to Benton's crucial survey showing the potential death of *te reo Māori* with a plethora of *kōhanga reo* and a resurgence of *mana* (prestige), the English language could also be turned on its head to serve the oppressed, as a form of linguistic response to one day challenge the dominant English discourse of New Zealand (Foucault, 1980).

Māori English is, potentially, a further avenue for Māori potency. It is a unique, localized English and a counter discourse to what was drummed down their throats for hundreds of years. It is a far cry from what the Department of Education in 1972 called a 'limited form of expression that hindered cognitive development... a "restricted code"' (Simon & Smith, 2001: 169). Indeed, Holmes *et al.* (2005: 431) further point out the use of Māori English as an essential strategy to 'signal and assert... group identity, and to subvert the pervasive influence of the dominant group'.

Let the Māori, then, divest (the agents of) the English language accordingly by not only continuing the bountiful harvest of *te reo Māori*, but also by generating their own specific Māori English and, at the same time, usurping the inherent and deliberate hegemonic tendencies of the English language so as to move more fully and finally from 'Māori-friendly' to 'Māori-centred' biculturalism (Johnston, 2001). Will this be fully realized, given that Pakeha and Māori are necessarily symbiotic units within Aotearoa/ New Zealand and that 'neither term can be discussed in isolation, as their existence relies on the existence of the other' (Johnston, 2001: 7)? Hopefully, yes. This is the 'mutual accommodation' of May (2004a: 34) and what Rapatahana (2010) also calls 'separate biculturalism'. Listen again to the words of Koro Dewes: '...what New Zealand is facing today is a time of accounting to chart a new path in the Nation's destiny. Nationhood, in the Māori view, does not depend on assimilation or integration: we are one nation of two peoples' (1968, quoted in Benton, 1981:57). Dewes' words today are as valid and vital as they ever were. There is space for two idiosyncratic cultures and languages – both equally independent and interdependent and, largely, sharing the same territory. Māori academic Gary Raumati Hook (2007: 14; 2010) postulates a very similar scenario: two separate but equal education systems, including a specifically National Māori University. Indeed, he goes on to add: 'such [Māori] education should be condoned and supported by the public purse without the expectation that they conform to what Pakeha consider appropriate'.

Indeed, there is ample room for more radical and authentic resolutions for Māori educational and linguistic and cultural struggles. The Maxim report (2006: 16) stressed that:

schools should have more freedom over their operations, with a consequent reduction in state power over schools… many benefits arise when schools are given more freedom to specialize and offer alternative curriculum and examinations.

To which we would add also the scope to design their own spatial settings, physical appearances, clientele and timetables.

Graham Smith claimed that:

we [Māori] have moved from this state of despair and despondency to one of optimism about our future and survival as a legitimate and viable cultural entity within our own country. Māori language is not only surviving – it is slowly growing… Māori are now much happier… Māori still want to be Māori. (2009: 3)

Furthermore, Smith has also encouraged Māori (and other indigenous peoples) to learn the submerged lessons of the alternative education 'struggle'. He makes the following observations about some important factors in developing a more authentic struggle:

(1) Struggle is important – it teaches us what we are against, but also what we are for.
(2) Struggle needs to move beyond 'silver – or magic – bullet' solutions; there is no 'one' answer; our struggle needs to embrace a 360° approach.
(3) We need to ensure a moral base to our leadership for our struggle – to get beyond the 'mystification' of culture and 'divide and rule' hegemony.
(4) We need to construct an inclusive struggle that embraces everyone and not create a struggle that is hierarchical and/or exclusive.
(5) Our struggle is not just about our 'cultural nuance', nor should it be argued in culturally reductionist ways; it must also engage with structural impediments and with the processes of ongoing colonization – colonization has not gone away, it is often being perpetrated in new guises. We must have an analysis that enables us to recognize these new shapes and to challenge these impediments, in order to make space for our cultural aspirations. To emphasise this point, it is simply not enough to struggle only at the level of culture. (Smith, 2008, WIPCE Address)

Conclusion: Repositioning the Māori Language into the Future

In this chapter, we have attempted to show the 'long trek' undertaken by Māori and others interested in the survival and longevity of the Māori language, in both its written and oral forms. This struggle has been conducted in many sites, although we have argued that schooling and education policy and practice have been primary sites for this engagement. A particular emphasis in our argument is that the struggle is couched between two imperatives; on the one hand, a dominant Pakeha cultural imperative, which is engaged in the struggle for the primacy of English; and, on the other hand, there is a struggle to undermine and marginalize the importance of the Māori language. More latterly, arguments have been made for developing excellence in both Māori and English. This is the tacit (if not fully supported) intention of Māori language being recognized as an official language (alongside English) within the Māori Language Act that we mentioned previously. However, the prevailing dominance of the English language means that it remains a nemesis for Māori aspirations related to its survival.

The latest evidence produced by Te Puni Kokiri and The Waitangi Tribunal (NZ Herald, October 2010), in respect of the condition of Māori language survival, is not particularly optimistic. They note that the key initiatives of Te Kōhanga Reo and Kura Kaupapa Māori are diminishing in numbers and, as well, there has been some criticism by native speakers of the 'modern' Māori language spoken within these language revitalization sites. Some criticize this new form of Māori language as 'bastardizing' classical Māori. In the main, this criticism results from assessing the language spoken by these children against what may be an unrealistic benchmark set by the native speaker. While this disparity in quality is evident, there is a need to broaden this insular thinking.

First and foremost, languages are in constant change, and new words are needed for new phenomena. Secondly, the new language of the Kōhanga Reo and Kura Kaupapa Māori (despite its new elements of grammar and vocabulary) fulfills all the fundamental elements of modern day languages. The children can effectively communicate through it; it raises emotions to allow them to laugh and cry; they can play using it; they can learn with it; and they can innovate with it. More importantly, it has become an everyday 'taken for granted' language outside of schooling, and a medium through which identity politics are both produced and reproduced. Moreover, it is also being spoken by an increasing number of people who are graduates of this form of language education, who form a new wave of young Māori professional elites. A critical understanding here is that if the language is to survive, then we must accept the new changes and not simply marginalize this newer form of the language as being 'unauthentic' or 'not classical'. Put more bluntly: if the language is to survive, Māori communities must support the new form of Māori language that is coming out of the immersion learning environments of Te Kōhanga Reo and Kura Kaupapa Māori.

A subsequent issue is the need to recommit to these initiatives, rather than to continue to undermine them by unrealistically expecting them to produce classical Māori language speakers. In particular, there is a need to critically interrogate the 'policy capture' by some native speakers around these issues – by this, we mean setting themselves up as the only ones capable of formulating language policy. An important point to remember is that these initiatives were given much of their early impetus by Māori who knew the pain of language loss and that many of the native speakers came onboard with the struggle once the hard work was done, and they have repositioned themselves as the 'experts' at the centre of this movement. We make this assertion cautiously, given that not all native speakers have acted in this way. There is an urgent need for the renewal of these institutions and their embedded *kaupapa* or philosophy. The immersion environment takes care of much of the problematic derived from competing with English.

Some of these issues we raise in this conclusion have yet to be fully understood, let alone debated, within our own communities. Although they are self-critical of ourselves as Māori, we raise them humbly and with respect, with the ultimate purpose of making some positive changes and gains in the ongoing survival of the Māori language.

It is gratifying, also, to note that at long last (April, 2010) the New Zealand government has finally signed the *United Nations Declaration on the Rights of Indigenous Peoples*. The hope is that this Declaration will help the Māori to realize their hopes and dreams in respect of their cultural aspirations and, indeed, enable a greater degree of autonomy and self-development in the process. But we also caution that such a declaration is only a set of non-binding words and that the responsibility for its enactment ultimately resides with ourselves.

Vasil, a non-Māori, puts it this way:

...it is important for the Pakeha to realize that they are dealing with an entirely transformed, awakened, articulate and assertive Māori community that can neither be bought nor coerced. It will also no longer be fobbed off by the Pakeha's 'reasonable' solutions based on higher, sacrosanct norms and principles. (Vasil, 1990: 141)

Notes

(1) Western thinking divorces the notions of time and space... But there is also another world view which occurs in another spatial and temporal dimension which is not that of European or Western notions of time and space... Civilisation, progress, lineal time, and objectified relocatable space, are all assumptions of colonialism that have impacted upon the experience of... Māori philosophies. (Takirirangi Smith, 2000: 53–60)
What are these philosophies?
The view that everything in existence is connected and related. The belief that all things are living. The belief that unseen worlds can be mediated by the human. All those are called 'unseen' in English, they are 'seen' worlds in Māori... Missionaries refashioned Māori epistemologies to fit into their concepts of God... English

[language] does seem disconnected when examining it alongside Māori. (Cherryl Waerea-I-Te-Rangi Smith, 2000: 45–49)

Ironically, the writers of this chapter also recognize their sequential outlining of the processes of usurpation and regeneration, here via the English language.

Donna Awatere (1984: 60), for example, also stressed how Europeans compressed time into space: 'The dimensions of time have been collapsed into space... Nature and geneology were put aside'.

(2) Some quotes attributed to Pakeha colonialists:

'Shoot them to be sure! A musket ball for every New Zealander [i.e. Māori] is the only way of civilizing their country'. (John Guard, 1834, in Ballara, 1986: 82)

'The Māori are dying out, and nothing can save them. Our plain duty as good, compassionate colonists is to smooth down their dying pillow. Then history will have nothing to reproach us with'. (Issac Featherston, 1856, in Simon & Smith, 2001: 224).

'...I consider that too much stress cannot be laid upon the acquirement of the English language. I believe that civilization cannot be advanced beyond a very short stage through means of the aboriginal tongue. The Māori tongue sufficed for the requirements of a barbarous race, but apparently would serve for little more'. (Hugh Carleton, 1857, in Williams, 2001: 116)

'I find one lies in wait to shoot Māoris without any approach to an angry feeling – it is a sort of scientific duty'. (A.S. Atkinson, 1863, in Ward, 1974: 163)

'I have heard a great deal about Magna Carta and the Bill of Rights and all that... I say the same about this Treaty of Waitangi which I hope will in future be relegated to the waste paper basket which is about the only place it ought to be seen in'. (Colonel Robert Trimble, 1882, in Simpson, 1979: 183)

'The power of using the English language is perhaps the greatest boon that the schools can confer upon their pupils'. (Habens, in Williams, 2001: 129)

'Do not speak to your pupils in Māori, and do not permit them to speak in Māori to you, or to one another... The less they hear of Māori the better it will be for their English'. (Bird, 1905, in Williams, 2001: 130)

'...the Māori race is a menace to the wellbeing of the European'. (Makgill, quoted in Williams, 2001: 229).

(3) Pearson (1990: 55) further states this categorically: 'Māori schools were designed to aid assimilation rather than to fit Māori students for an equal stake... in the wider society on their own terms'... 'the new hope became that the Māori would... disappear through assimilation, a process regarded as possible because the Māori was judged to be at a higher stage of development than the darker races'.

(4) As a significant aside here, Māori did not wish to relinquish any significant control of their own culture and, as a point of fact, never do when Pakeha are present. Barrington, in 1981, wrote '...constraints on the implementation to the Māori cultural programmes were, in part, due to objections by Māori themselves... The Native School... was perceived by some Māori to be an artificial or improper environment for the teaching of some aspects of Māori culture' (quoted in Simon & Smith, 2001: 189). *Tapu* (or forbidden and sacred) is a key facet of Māori lore: certain things remained restricted and/or untaught at certain times and to certain groupings.

A Timeline: The Struggle for Change

1967: Dr Pat Hohepa organized a petition to NZBC to pronounce Māori names and place names correctly.

1969: Remaining Native Schools formally disestablished, to the consternation of many Māori who '...in many cases found security within the *Whānau* environment of the

Native School...[they] came to regard the schools as their own, and supported and valued them' (Simon & Smith, 2001: 274)

1971: Duncan McIntyre, Minister of Māori Affairs, accepted *te reo Māori* could be taught at primary school level.

1972–1973: 30,000 signatories for Māori Language Petition. Hana Jackson – the chief organizer of said petition – viewed the 1871 Native Schools amendment as 'the psychological and cultural annihilation of a people' (Jackson 1972, cited in Williams, 2001: 164).

'We, the undersigned, do humbly pray that courses in Māori language and aspects of Māori culture be offered in ALL those schools with large Māori rolls and that these same courses be offered as a gift to the Pakeha from the Māori, in ALL other New Zealand schools as a positive effort to promote a more meaningful concept of integration'. (quoted in Te Rito, 2008: 2)

1973: The very important Benton-led NZCER survey showed just how threatened the Māori language was – only 70,000 mostly elderly rural Māori could now speak Māori with any fluency.

1974: Finally, a Waitangi Tribunal was established to hear Māori land grievances.

Five universities and eight training colleges included Māori as a language to be taught.

1975: *Hikoi* (the land march through Aotearoa) led by Dame Whina Cooper.

1976–1978: Ruatoki School became the first bilingual school in Aotearoa.

1982: First *kōhanga reo* (literally language nest) in Wainuiomata at Pukeatua Kokiri, formed after a 1981 *Hui Whakatauira* called by Māori in response to Benton's findings. By 1994, there were 809 *kōhanga reo*, incorporating wider extended families – all participants, therefore, being involved in language learning. A *Te Kōhanga Reo* Trust was later established, which also developed a nationally recognized curriculum so as to attract state funding – something that ultimately transpired in 1990.

1984: Māori Educational Development Conference. Bicultural solutions were seen as not ensuring Māori language continuity after *kōhanga reo*.

Te Wānanga o Raukawa became an incorporated body and began to teach its first degree, while, in 1992, *Te Whare Wānanga o Awanuiārangi*, in Whakatane, was established. In 1993, *Te Wānanga o Aotearoa* was also registered.

1985: Hoani Waititi was the first *kura kaupapa* to cater for the kids emerging from *kōhanga reo*. 'Dr Pita Sharples simply set up school facilities at Hoani Waititi without government funding or their "permission"'. (Te Rito, 2008: 4)

Note: Hoani Waititi finally received government funding in 1990. Sharples identified *Te Aho Matua* as the philosophy underlying *kura kaupapa Māori*, based on *Ākonga Māori*.

1987: Māori Language Act ensured Māori language was an official language of Aotearoa/New Zealand. At the same time, the Māori Language Commission was established.

1987: Matawaia Declaration formulated at a *hui* (gathering) of Māori educationalists, who called for the establishment of an independent Māori education authority.

1989: Education Act: *Tikanga Māori* and *Te Reo Māori* to be taught if a demand existed.

1990: Education Amendment Act (Sections 155 and 156) provided formal recognition for *kura kaupapa* Māori and *wānanga* and consented to grant funds to develop them. *Te Aho Matua* to be the governing principles.

Note: The Government also wished to implement a National Languages Policy. NZ $8.7 million was earmarked to employ Māori language teachers within state schools: the Māori Language Factor Fund.

Late 1980s and early 1990s: Advent of Māori radio and – finally – television helping Māori utilize Pakeha-inspired technology, which had acculturated Māori into Pakeha culture and the English language. Māori could now re-acculturate themselves 'back to their own language and culture'. (Te Rito, 2008: 5)

1993: *Te Runanga Nui* – the national body of *kura kaupapa Māori* – established in Whanganui. Dr Pita Sharples becomes initial *Tumuaki* (President), also the first ever *wharekura* (secondary level *kura kaupapa Māori*).

1994: *Te Hikoi Reo Māori* – massive march to promote Māori language.

1997: Now 675 *Kōhanga Reo*, 54 *Kura Kaupapa Māori*, 3 *Whare Wānanga*, although the majority of Māori children *still* attend 'mainstream' educational facilities, given that many, at least now, had some exposure to their own language. Māori Education Commission also initiated.

2003: The Māori Political Party established.

2007: First Māori language curriculum for English medium schools.

2008–2009: Now 73 *Kura Kaupapa Māori* and a huge increase in bilingual schools – usually 'lower level of immersion' (May *et al.*, 2006: 2) – as units in mainstream schools.

2010: Latest figures: The number of *kura kaupapa* remains stable – 73 schools – the same number since 2007. Student numbers had dropped from 6272 in 2007 to 6015 in 2009 and then back up to 6038 in 2010. While there has been a slight decrease in students enrolled overall in Māori language educational facilities (including bilingual units), there has also been a 'small rise in *kōhanga reo* rolls from 2009–2010' (Education Counts, 2011). This source further points out that because of the large numbers of students now enrolling at *whare wānanga*, this has meant the student-teacher ratio has also increased dramatically from 2008 onwards.

References

Alves, D. (1999) *The Māori and the Crown: An Indigenous People's Struggle for Self-Determination*. Westport, CT: Greenwood Press.

Awatere, D. (1984) *Māori Sovereignty*. Auckland: Broadsheet.

Ballara, A. (1986) *Proud to be White? A Survey of Pakeha Prejudice in New Zealand*. Auckland: Heinemann Publishers.

Barrington, J.M. (1972) Educational administration in the multiracial society: A report on New Zealand. *Race and Class* 14, 59–68.

Barrington, J.M. (1981) From Assimilation to Cultural Pluralism: A comparative analysis. *Comparative Education* 17 (1), 59–69.

Barrington, J.M. (1992) The school curriculum, occupations and race. In G. McCulloch (ed.) *The School Curriculum in New Zealand: History, Theory, Policy and Practice*. Palmerston North: Dunmore Press.

Benton, R.A. (1981) *The Flight of the Amokura Oceanic Languages and Formal Education in the South Pacific*. Wellington: New Zealand Council for Educational Research.

Benton, R.A. (2001) Whose language? Ownership and control of *te reo Māori* in the third millennium. *New Zealand Sociology* 16 (1), 35–55.

Benton, R.A. (2007) *Mauri* or mirage? The status of the Māori language in Aotearoa New Zealand in the third millennium. In A. Tsui and J.W. Tollefson (eds) *Language Policies, Culture and Identity in Asian Contexts* (pp. 163–18). Hillsdale, NJ: Lawrence Erlbaum Associates.

Bishop, R., Berryman, M., Tiakiawi, S. and Richardson, C. (2003) Te Kotahitanga: The experiences of year 9 and 10 Māori students in mainstream classrooms. *Report to the Ministry of Education*. Wellington: Ministry of Education. Online at http://www.educationcounts.govt.nz/publications/maori_education/9977/5375

Bourdieu, P. (1986) The forms of capital. In J. Richardson (ed.) *Handbook of Theory and Research for the Sociology of Education* (pp. 241–258). New York, NY: Greenwood Press.

Buchanan, A. (1990) 150 years of white domination in New Zealand. *Race and Class* 31, 73–80.

Dewes, T.K.M. (1968) The place of Māori language in the education of Māori. An address delivered at the 40th Anzaas Congress, January. 24–31, 1868. Christchurch, Aotearoa New Zealand.

Dewes, T.K.M. (1977 revised edn.) The case for oral arts. In M. King (ed.) *Te Ao Hurihuri (The World Moves On)* (pp. 55–85). Wellington: Hicks, Smith & Sons.

Durie, A. (1999) Māori-English bilingual education in New Zealand. In J. Cummins and D. Corson (eds) *Encyclopaedia of Language and Education* (pp. 15–24). Dordrecht: Kluwer.

Durie, M. (1994) *Whaiora: Māori Health Development*. Auckland: Oxford University Press.

Government of New Zealand (2009) *Nga Haeata Matauranga 2008/2009*. Online document, accessed 15 June, 2010. http://www.educationcounts.govt.nz/publications/series/ 5851/75954

Government of New Zealand, Education Counts (2011a) Māori-medium education as at 1 July 2010. Online document, accessed August 2011. http://www.educationcounts. govt.nz/statistics/Māori_education/schooling/6040/mori-medium-education-as-at-1-july-2010

Government of New Zealand, Education Counts (2011b) *Kura kaupapa Māori and kura teina*. Online document, accessed August 2011. http://www.educationcounts.govt. nz/indicators/main/quality-education-provider/2011

Foucault, M. (1980) *Power/Knowledge: Selected Interviews and Other Writings 1972–1977*, Colin Gordon (ed.). New York, NY: Pantheon.

Gramsci, A. (1971) *Selections from the Prison Notebooks*, Q. Hoare and G. Nowell-Smith (eds). New York, NY: International Publishers.

Harker, R. (1985) Schooling and cultural reproduction. In J. Codd, R. Harker, and R. Nash (eds) *Political Issues in New Zealand Education*. Palmerston North: Dunmore Press.

Holmes, J. (2005) Using Māori English in New Zealand. *International Journal of the Sociology of Language* 172, 91–115.

Holmes, J., Stubbe, M. and Marra, M. (2005) Language, humour and ethnic identity marking in New Zealand English. In C. Mair (ed.) *The Politics of English as a World Language* (pp. 431–455). Amsterdam: Rodopi.

Hook G.R. (2007) A future for Māori education, Part 11: The reintegration of culture and education. *MAI Review Journal* 1 (pp. 1–17). Online at http://www.review.mai.ac.nz

Humpage, L. and Fleras, A. (2001) Intersecting discourses: Closing the gaps, social justice and the Treaty of Waitangi. *Social Policy Journal of New Zealand* 16 (July), 37–53.

Hunn, J.K. (1960) *Report on Department of Māori Affairs: With Statistical Supplement*, 24 August. Wellington: Government Printer.

Jenkins, K. (1994) Māori Education. In E. Coxon, K. Jenkins, J. Marshull, L. Massey (eds) *The Politics of Learning and Teaching in Aotearoa New Zealand* (pp. 148–176). Palmerston North: Dunmore Press.

Johnston, P.M. (2001) "Watch this spot and whose in it": Creating space for indigenous educators. *Australian Journal of Teacher Education* 26 (1), 1–8.

Lee, H. and Lee, G. (1995) The politics of Māori education: History, policies, conflicts and compromises. *Waikato Journal of Education* 1, 95–117.

Marie, D., Fergusson, D. and Boden, J. (2008) Educational achievement in Māori: The roles of cultural identity and social disadvantage. Online document, accessed 16 September, 2010. http://www.thefreelibrary.com/Educational+achievement+in+Māori%3A+the+roles+of+cultural+identity+and...-a0188159291

Maxin Institute (2006) *Current Issues in Māori Schooling* (2006). Maxim Institute Policy Paper. September, 2006 Auckland, Aotearoa New Zealand. Online at www.maxim.org.nz/files/pdf/policy_paper_Māori_education.pdf

May, S. (2004) Māori-medium education in *Aotearoa*/New Zealand. In A. Tsui and J.W. Tollefson (eds) *Medium of Instruction Policies: Which Agenda, Whose Agenda?* (pp. 21–42). Hillsdale, NJ: Lawrence Erlbaum Associates.

May, S. (2005) Deconstructing the instrumental/identity divide in language policy debates. Online article, accessed June 26, 2009. http://researchcommons.waikato.ac.nz/bitstream/10289/3234/1/May,%20S.pdf

New Zealand Herald (2010) Tribunal warns te reo Māori near crisis point. *New Zealand Herald*, October 10. Online at http://www.nzherald.co.nz/news/print.cfm?objectid=10681810

New Zealand in History (2011) New Zealand in History: dates marking post-colonial Māori history. Webpage, accessed April 16, 2011. http://history- nz.org/maori7.html

Pearson, D. (1990) *A Dream Deferred: The Origins of Ethnic Conflict in New Zealand.* Wellington: Allen and Unwin.

Pere, R. (1999) Te Reo Rangatira me o na Tikanga. *Māori Education Commission Newsletter* 2 (May), 3–10.

Pihama, L. (1993) *Tungia te Ururua kia tupu Whakaritorrito te tupu o te Harekeke: A critical Analysis of Parents as First Teachers.* Auckland: Department of Education, University of Auckland.

Pihama, L., Smith, K., Taki, M. and Lee, J. (2004) A literature review on *kaupapa Māori* and Māori education pedagogy. *The International Research Institute for Māori and Indigenous Education.* Online research paper, accessed September 17, 2009. http://akoaotearoa.ac.nz/mi/download/ng/file/group-199/a-literature-review-of-kaupapa-maori-and-maori-education-pedagogy.pdf

Radio New Zealand News (2011) *Kura Kaupapa* say they're exempt from national standards. Radio New Zealand News, 2 May, 2011. Online at http://nzcerlibrary-nznews.blogspot.com/2011/05/kura-kaupapa-say-theyre-exempt-from.html

Sharples, P. (2007) Address to International Adult Literacy Conference, Auckland, September. Online at www.workbase.org.nz/Conference/resource.aspx?ID=412

Sharples, P.R. (1992) *Submission to the Parliamentary Select Committee on Education.* Glen Eden: Hoani Waititi Marae.

Simon, J.A. (1992) State schooling for Māori: The control of access to knowledge. Online article, accessed September 20, 2009. www.aare.edu.au/92pap/simoj92382.txt

Simon, J. and Smith, L.T. (2001) *A Civilising Mission? Perceptions and Representations of the New Zealand Native Schools System.* Auckland: Auckland University Press.

Simpson, T. (1979) *Te Riri Pakeha: The White Man's Anger.* Martinborough: Alister Taylor.

Skutnabb-Kangas, T. (2003) Linguistic diversity and biodiversity: The threat from killer languages. In C. Mair (ed.) *The Politics of English as a World Language.* Amsterdam: Rodopi.

Skutnabb-Kangas, T. and Dunbar, R. (2010) *Indigenous Children's Education as Linguistic Genocide and a Crime Against Humanity?: A Global View.* Guovdageaidnu/ Kautokeino: Gáldu Resource Centre for the Rights of Indigenous Peoples.

Smith, C.W. (2000) Straying beyond the boundaries of belief: Māori epistemologies inside the curriculum. *Educational Philosophy and Theory* 32(1), 43–51.

Smith, G.H. (1987) *Akonga Māori: Preferred Māori Teaching and Learning Methodologies.* Auckland: Department of Education, The University of Auckland.

Smith, G.H. (1990) *Taha Māori: Pakeha Capture.* In J. Codd, R. Harker and R. Nash (eds) *Political Issues in New Zealand Education* (2nd edn.). Palmerston North: Dunmore Press.

Smith, G.H. (1992) *Tane-Nui-A-Rangi's* legacy, propping up the sky: *kaupapa* Māori as resistance and intervention. Online article, accessed March 16, 2010. http://www.aare.edu.ac/92pap/smitg92384.txt

Smith, G.H. (1997) The development of *Kaupapa* Māori: Theory and Praxis. Unpublished PhD Thesis, The University of Auckland.

Smith, G.H. (2003) *Kaupapa Māori* theory: Theorizing indigenous transformation of education & schooling. Paper presented at the *Kaupapa Māori* Symposium, Auckland, December. Online at www.aare.edu.au/03pap/pih03342.pdf

Smith, G.H. (2008) Keynote Address, *World Indigenous Peoples Conference on Education*, December 7–11. Melbourne.

Smith, G.H. (2009) Transforming leadership. A discussion paper presented at the *Leading Change in Education Summer Institute*, Simon Fraser University. July 6–16. Online at www.viu.ca/integratedplanning/documents/DrGrahamSmith.pdf

Smith, T. (2000) Nga Tini Atuatanga o Nhakapapa. *Educational Philosophy and Theory* 32 (1), 53–60.

Te Rito, J.S. (2008) Struggles for the Māori language: *He whawhai mo te reo Māori*. *MAI Review Journal* 2, Article 6 (pp. 1–8). Online at http://www.review.mai.ac.nz

Vasil, R. (1990) *What do the Māori Want? New Māori Political Perspectives*. Albany: Random Century.

Walker, R. (1975) The Māori People of New Zealand: 150 Years of Colonization. Paper presented to the *Indigenous People's Conference*, October 27–31. Port Alberni, Canada.

Walker, R. (2004) *Ka Whawhai Tonu Matou: Struggle Without End*. Albany: Penguin Books.

Ward, A. (1974) *A Show of Justice: Racial 'Amalgamation' in Nineteenth Century New Zealand*. Canberra: Australian National University Press.

Williams, D. (2001) *Crown Policy Affecting Māori Knowledge Systems and Cultural Practices*. Online report, accessed August 25, 2009. http://www.waitangitribunal.govt.nz/genericinquiries2/florafauna/moriknowledgesystemscrownpolicy.asp

6 A Personal Reflection: New Zealand Māori and English

Tamati Cairns

The New Zealand Experience: English is the Worst Kind of Thief

Kaumatua
Te iwi o Tūhoe

Whakatangia te puupuu ki Manawaru,
Ko taku tira tēnei ka whai i te Mana o Rongo
Ki Mana Teepa, ki kaautu whero ko Tuiringa
E ngā Iwi, nau mai.

Aue, miria te aroha ki te rito o te puuharakeke,
Ki Onini, ko Hinepukohurangi, ko Te Maunga,
Tooku Manawa whakairia ki konei e Taane.
E ngā Iwi, haere mai.

Wehea te tapu ki te awa ki Rauiri, eke ana ki Tauperetao,
Whaatare iho, kia kite kiha, ko Tapuae, ko Tatahoata
Ee, Ko Ruatahuna tēnei
E kume nei te tangata
E kume nei te whenua
E kume nei i te ra ki toona taumata
Tūhoe ee, karangatia kia piri, karangatia kia tata,
Mauri ora.

He wāhanga tēnei no te paatere "Te whakaeke a te Okiwa"

Sound the conch from the peak of Manawaru
As travelling guests negotiate passage through Mana o Rongo,
To Mana Teepa onward to Kaauta Whero, the red, there to be greeted by
the great Chief Tuiringa
Esteemed visitors, welcome.

Exclaim, cherish, exalt the love, aroha from root source and the union of
Hine pukohurangi the Mist Maiden to Onini the Mountain
Elevated on high is my love, my heart
Esteemed guests, welcome.

Travel the divide at Rauiri and rise to the summit of Tauperetao
From here gaze down to the foot where stands the ancestral house
Tapuae
On hallowed ground Tatahoata
Ahh!!! This is Ruatahuna
This is the people
This is the Land
This is what draws the noon day sun
Te Tūhoetanga o te ra
Tūhoe Nation welcomes you come close
Tūhoe Nation welcomes you, bind together
Esteemed readers welcome.

We wish you abundant life.

This is an excerpt from the *pātere, 'Te whakaeke a te Okiwa'*, given to me by
Tamiana Thrupp and engaged, in this case, as a *mihi* to you all from where I
belong, *Tūhoe*.

I am a Māori male, born in 1946. My *iwi*, or tribes, are *Tūhoe, Raukawa,
Tūwharetoa* and *Kahungunu*. I grew up in a small place called *Ruatahuna*,
which is rather isolated and in the heart of the *Urewera*, in the centre of the
North Island of *Aotearoa* (New Zealand). In this community of 1200, at that
time, all the locals were native speakers of *te reo Māori* (the Māori language),
and a small number of transient workers and their families – say, 15 in total
– were either bilingual or English-speakers.

This was a total Māori community, complete with its own culture,
religious beliefs, laws and lore councils that managed all of the community's
needs, the allocation of lands and resources and exercised the social controls.
There were the *Rangatira* (chiefs) and *Tohunga* (wise men) within *Whānau*
(families), *Hapū* (sub-tribes) and *Iwi* (tribes) that governed. The Māori
'order' was managed on a daily basis by an understanding of both a celestial
and a terrestrial understanding and belief systems. All of this was inextricably
woven together by its language, Māori.

At that time, the life-blood of the community, its economic, social,
cultural and leadership aspects, were all organised by way of the Māori

language – that was the controlling mechanism. I was to learn, in later years, that during the colonisation that had been experienced in other countries, it was usually the coloniser's desire to delete the natives' tongue in as short a time as possible and impose colonial law upon them.

Along come the Pākehā (Europeans), with a promise of a better world filled with opportunity. A treaty was signed capturing the aspirations of the original partners, only to find that it was, indeed, the instrument that eventually undermined the entire Māori race, almost to the point of extinction. Māori were not ever a conquered people, but the agents of the English language and the imposition of its culture took their toll.

The Treaty of Waitangi (1840, between the English settlers and Māori) is the basis – the cornerstone of New Zealand society. By the law of *contra-preferentum*, we Māori continue to contest the poor and manipulative translation of the meaning of it that does not reflect a Māori understanding of obligations, including those of language rights, as incorporated in this Treaty.

There was also the early settlers' introduction of new and poorly understood strains of diseases. A new religion was introduced to the Māori people, new English laws were introduced, the Māori language was outlawed, and by this total change and manipulation, Māori became paupers in their own country. Such is the way today where Māori are endeavouring to claw back what little they can after the Treaty connivance resulted in a total land loss of some 66 million acres.

The English language clobbering machine has impacted on many countries around the world in exactly the same way. All people, worldwide, belong to this world and, in so doing, express that belonging in the language that they are.

I te tīmatanga te kupu, ko te atua te kupu ko te atua te kupu i te tīmatanga.

In the beginning was the word, the word is God. God was the word in the beginning.

Henrietta Maxwell stated this on the television programme *Waka Huia*, TVNZ, on Sunday 12 July 2010: 'If we lose our language, we will lose God'.

Tamati Cairns
Kaumātua (respected elder spokesperson for *Tūhoe*)

7 The *Malchemy* of English in Sri Lanka: Reinforcing Inequality through Imposing Extra-Linguistic Value

Arjuna Parakrama

Note to readers: This piece is written partly in non-standard language-register discourse to dramatize the fact that the use of broader (up-to-now unacceptable) standards affects neither intelligibility nor clarity, except in the usual substantive ways, by which all language use is governed. The rule-breaking may be arbitrary and inconsistent, but so are the rules it breaks. In fact, I have succeeded if you are unsure whether the *errors* are deliberate or not. In this context, both 'authenticity' and 'appropriateness' need to be re-examined as functions of arbitrary-but-not-innocent categories, which mask their ideological underpinnings through representation as (an impossible) neutrality. I will not gloss 'Lankan' terms: if you need to know what they mean, please take the trouble to find out, just as we have to with 'British' or 'US' usage. We all need to earn the right to eavesdrop on other contexts and cultures – an always (productively) difficult and fraught process – any shortcut that seems to make understanding easy does serious disservice, because it oversimplifies, trivializes and distorts.

> *There is no document of civilization which is not at the same time a document*
> *of barbarianism and just as a document is not free of barbarism, barbarism*
> *also taints the manner in which it was transmitted from one owner to the other.*
> Walter Benjamin

Introduction

I done shown Standard spoken English as standing up only for them smug-arse social elites. And it ain't really no different for no written English neither. The tired ways in which the standardized languages steady fucked over the users of other forms had became clear when we went and studied them (post)colonial Englishes. Them 'other' Englishes came and made it impossible to buy into sacred cows like native speaker authority because there from the getgo there are only habichole users, not natives!

Writing this, in 1990, was excruciatingly difficult for me and went against the grain of all that I'd been taught and assimilated in a lifetime. It seemed crude and vulgar, macho, inappropriate to the core. More than 20 years later, it is still hard to read this as serious theory, whereas my 'academic' version – much less precise, alas, and much less theoretically important – is much more acceptable. Such is the complete control that standards and norms exert on us, which is even prior to ideology, politics and practice.

> The hegemony of hip standard languages and cool registers which hide where they are coming from by a shitload of 'arbitrary' rules and 'other-people-in-power-require-'isms, is read for points by these non-standard varieties like and unlike the ones I be mixing and jamming here.[1]

This thingy examines the complex and nuanced ways in which the mainstream discourse around English in Sri Lanka, on the one hand, promises and predicates such extra-linguistic value, while on the other, reinforces discriminatory linguistic hierarchies that exclude and devalue the majority of non-elite users. This is a privileging of English as the language *par excellence* for its ubiquity and resilience, yet maintaining the hidden inter-variety inequalities (despite token counter-claims about the validity of 'newer' forms). It reflects the globalized racism of dominant TEFL/TESL 'theory', which is mindlessly applied in the Sri Lankan context, too, relegating millions of users to the dustbin of linguistic and, in this new twist, moral failure.

In order to do this, I have identified 10 radical propositions on the nature of language and (extra-) linguistic value that I shall test and explain in terms of the Sri Lankan context, which is where I found them hanging out, as it were. Each statement contradicts dominant forms of 'extra-linguistic value', hanging out as legitimate, even objective, linguistic assessments. For instance, in the first proposition, *the* standard is held to be (a) the best; (b) universally accepted by all users (dissimulated as the consensually prestige dialect); and (c) a product of natural evolution – none of which is entirely true. Running through this is the thesis, now taken as self-evident, that English is the language *par excellence*. English is touted as having transformative and magical powers: confusing political currency with inherent value. The deliberate displacement of the discourse of language rights by arguments from economic opportunity and the de-politicization of underclass-forced 'choices', which are dissimulated as free agency (being interfered with by elite hypocrites who claim to speak for the 'masses').

Proposition 1: Language is a site of struggle which standards cover over. The non-standard is a better indicator of how language works

That language is a site of struggle is, after Voloshinov, a platitude in post-structuralist circles, but this insight has not been linked to the processes of standardization. The focus has been on the struggle for meaning and not for structure. I have argued till the cows come home that standardization obliterates struggle in, and through, language by representing this as a natural process in no one group's special interest. Borrowing from Marx's description of the universal equivalent, I suggest that, just as the defective form of exchange better represents reality, and the very success of the money form actually serves to hide the fact that what is being compared is human labour, so, too, the 'defective' form of language reveals the struggles that are swept under the carpet of the standard (See Parakrama, 1995, for a more detailed treatment of this homology, and Rossi-Landi (1977) for an extended discussion of the parallels between language and political economy).

If hegemony be maintained through putting up and policing standards, and if a kind of 'passive revolution'[2] manages opposition by allowing for a piss-trickle of the previously non-standard into the standard, then you's resisting when you's refusing, the self-evidence of the rules and the proper. Mistakes and bad taste, whether deliberate or not, whether in organized groups or not (as counter-hegemony), is always subversive, though sometimes 'wastefully' so because they cannot be absorbed into the standard as easily. These non-standard stuff is therefore 'natural' resistance and a sensitive index of non-mainstream against-hegemony. Persistent mistakes and bad taste fuck the system up because they cannot be patronized if you don't accept the explanation, so they fail your ass at the university and say you need remediation like it's the pox.

Standards hide their self-interest and privileged users. Linguists claim merely to be recording the status quo without taking sides, as if recording did not confer value and reinforce hegemony, *pace* Daniel Jones. Champions of the so-called Other (or [post]colonial Englishes) have operated on the basis of the special status of these varieties, thereby justifying the formulation of different criteria for their analysis. A careful examination of the processes of standardization as they affect these 'Others' strips the camouflage from standardization, which can be seen as the hegemony of the 'educated' elites, hence the unquestioned paradigm of the 'educated standard'. These standards are kept in place in 'first world' contexts by a technology of reproduction, which dissimulates this hegemony through the self-represented neutrality of prestige and precedent, whose selectivity is a function of the politics of publication. In these 'other' situations, the openly conflictual nature of the language context makes such strategies impossible. In Sri Lanka, for instance, the users cannot agree on a standard, hence, it is blatantly imposed, and its discrimination and exclusions are clearly manifest for all to see.

Proposition 2: Standards are arbitrary but not innocent, and since all standards discriminate (against women, minorities, multiple marginal groups), the broadest local standard is the least iniquitous. There is no linguistic evidence to support the premise that a narrower standard is better than a broader one, or the thesis that there is a definable outer limit beyond which the standard ceases to be effective

Language in its standardized form, nuanced through a panoply of rite-of-passage styles and registers, artificially creates 'the natural' in several ways. For those of you who abhor this technical vocabulary on the misconception that it is unnecessary jargon, let me rephrase this position. What I am suggesting here is that the natural goodness of the standard is no more self-evident and universally approved than the 'natural goodness' of infant milk foods advertised in the market. What has happened is that the continuous exposure and valuing of the standard, vis-à-vis other variants, has taken on the familiarity-cum-acceptance which has become second nature to us. However, this second nature is neither innocent (in the sense of being independent of class and gender bias – egalitarian), nor universal (in the sense of being trans-historical, acultural, *a priori*).

The basic claim for the classed, 'raced', gendered, regioned nature of the standard language is hardly contested now. Yet, little is done to work against this, except in the insistence of linguistic 'table manners', in order to subvert the most blatant sexism in, say, standard (or, for that matter, not-so-standard) English. Examples of scholarly work in 'dialect' exist both in the US and Britain, but as isolated experiments that seek, quite rightly, to legitimize certain group-interests, rather than as part of a project to explicitly contest/broaden the standard itself. Across the spectrum of disciplinary and ideological views, therefore, there exists a shared and 'self-evident' premise that the standard is clearer, more amenable and, to put it in a nutshell, *better* than the other variants/dialects/forms. If, in fact, the standard is all these things, and, in a sense, it is *now*, given the history of its evolution, this has as little to do with the inherent superiority of the standard, as has the fact that more men are good chess-players than women today to do with superior intelligence or inherent ability. In any case, none of these arguments can be used against a systematic effort towards broadening the acceptable range of this standard.

Taking the discriminatory nature of the standard seriously and also accepting the necessity of standards, however attenuated, this thesis argues for the active broadening of the standard to include the greatest variety possible; it also holds that the 'acceptable' bounds of general linguistic tolerance will expand with the systematic and sanctioned exposure to such variety.

> The lastma final word, then, is to go like crazy for the broadest standard and to be psyched up to steady talk in it, teach your head off in it, write like mad in it, despite of its sometime 'oddness' to our ears, refusing of the uncomfortable laughter, inspite the difficulty, paying no mind to some non-standard users and their liberal advocates having an attitude about it. The ideal, then, is for what is standard now to become contaminated with what is non-standard now, and ass backwards, so much so that everyone will have to know more about what everyone else speaks/writes, and so that not knowing, say, 'black english' will be as much a disqualification as not knowing 'general american'. There should even be room for a certain amount of self-inconsistency as well. Complete intelligibility is a cheap hoax anyway, so it's necessary, yar, to bring this to the up front level, nehi¿ (Parakrama, 1995: xi)

If I were to risk a generalization, I'd say Sri Lankan scholars in the field are hardly different. The more progressive ones use phrases like 'interference' and 'interlanguage' within quotes, creating a false space between themselves and the concepts they use to understand and rationalize their reality. The term 'prestige' invariably describes the elite standard, carrying three unexamined consequences: consensus (everyone agrees that it is the norm), inevitability (this is naturally so and has come about through a long and levelling process, which should not be tampered with) and innocence (no one is to blame, certainly not the linguist). The misleading notion of the standard as the variety *par excellence* is pervasive.

> All this wont be in place for a long time, and mebbe never, but anything else isn't worth this pul try. As teachers we don't often let blatant sexism and racism get by from our students just because their views are shared by many in power all over the world. Why the hell do we excuse away language values and non-language values hidden within language values, then¿ All things considered, and *ceteris paribus*, it is my expert and dispassionate opinion, therefore, that, in punishing 'error' so brutally yet so selectively and in laying the blame elsewhere, or in saying in the appropriately subdued tone, 'what else can we do¿', the language teacher is pimping with a vengeance for the system while masturbating his/her conscience with this 'empowerment' crap. (Parakrama, 1995: xii)

The linguist's responsibility is ultimately the same as the citizen's, but she has a special role in exposing the complicity between language/discourse and power and actively working towards a more informed and egalitarian socius. Lankan scholar-activists need to fight two battles – one within the country and the other outside, as we shall see below. Need to, I say, but, sadly, we do neither really.

Proposition 3: Rather than being special-emergent cases, the so-called (post)colonial Englishes are no different from the (post)imperialist Englishes in terms of range, elaboration, nuance, and may, in fact, be better gauges of the ways languages work

Treating the Englishes as equivalent in every way to their 'parent' forms leads to the re-evaluation of cherished linguistic paradigms, such as 'native-speaker authority', since hitherto self-evident categories such as this are fraught in the (post)colonial contexts. For instance, among the thousands of studies spawned by Selinker *et al.* (1975) on 'interlanguage' and 'interference', especially in relation to fossilization and such delightfully prejudicial concepts, I have yet to come across one in which L1 is a so-called first-world language. Hence, it would appear that, for instance, fossilization is a phenomenon peculiar to, and peculiarly symptomatic of, contexts where an L1 user of a 'non-Western' language is learning a 'Western' one. Hence, L1 users of American English learning Tamil do not suffer from this debilitating pathology, because, as we all know, English has alchemic powers unlike the others, correct? In the Lankan context, if we had eyes to see and ears to hear, we would know that what takes place when languages meet in an individual or group is not interference, but *enrichment*. Here, then, is a simple example of how a theoretically weak premise, such as 'interference', comes undone if we critically engage with the lived reality of our multilingual postcolonial contexts, instead of imposing a linguistic apparatus that has little explanatory power, except as a stubborn guardian of the (neo)colonialist hierarchy of languages.

Three ways of classifying 'Other' Englishes have gained currency in the past. These can be described through Standard Lankan English (SLE) as follows:

(1) (SLE as) Pathology, aberration and sub-standard.
(2) (SLE as) Special case requiring concessions, emerging norms which need time and encouragement to develop.
(3) (SLE as) More or less equal to the other, 'older', 'native' Englishes, but 'newer', hence less mature. This is the version espoused by most 'progressives', and its adherents still retain the binary distinctions of older/newer, native/non-native [or nativized], inner/outer [circle],

which smuggles in a clear hierarchy of Englishes, some of which are more equal than others.

I have long proposed a fourth alternative:

(4) (SLE as) Equal in every way, and also a better indicator of the ways languages work, since the site of struggle is more visibly contested in a shorter time frame (rapid language change and fierce contestation, as if the transformation is 'fast-forward in slow-motion'). What we can only conjecture, based on fragmentary evidence about past developments in English, for instance, we see taking place before our eyes.

Add to this the serious concern that SLE, such as it is, mainly reflects dominant urban elite usage and does not adequately engage with users whose first language is Tamil. SLE, then, manifests yet another tier of linguistic hegemony, as – one must belabour the point – all standards inevitably do. Here it is more liminal, contested, up for grabs and, therefore, impossible to see as consensual, happy-go-lucky, apolitical.

Proposition 4: The historical complicities of Linguistics with colonialist knowledge production and the fetishism of objective science continue today in the hierarchizing of languages, the Indo-European theocracy, mainstream ELT and in concepts such as native userhood

This process of policing the (new, yet archaic) standard is not always obvious and is often misread by those who aspire to achieve the gifts bestowed upon 'fluent' English users. They are taught that it is necessary for the achievement of international intelligibility criteria, which is a requirement imposed by the global North. Thus, in this manner, non-elite learners of English in Sri Lanka have to contend with poorly-understood and even outmoded norms – especially in pronunciation – no longer applicable on the *mothership* if they are to break into the rarified inner circle. While progressive voices argue for the global proliferation of national Englishes, (acid) tests such as TOEFL and IELTS still ensure that there is a hierarchy of such varieties. Intelligibility criteria and 'native' status are the most commonly invoked sophisms to justify the hegemony of (the) WEST (White English Standard Testing) in norming transnational usage.

The relationship between language and identity requires careful re-examination, including cherished notions of mother tongue and native userhood. Ethnicity/identity is discursive, not based on any essence.

The decline of the native speaker in numerical terms is likely to be associated with changing ideas about the centrality of the native speaker to norms of usage... Large numbers of people will learn English as a foreign language in the 21st century and they will need teachers, dictionaries and grammar books. But will they continue to look towards the native speaker for authoritative norms of usage? (Graddol, 1999: 67–68)

This is not very different from Wikipedia, which – to its credit – is more direct and clear.

Native speakers of English are people whose first language is English. They learned English when they were children. They think in English. They use it naturally. Usually native speakers of English are people from English-speaking countries like the USA, Great Britain, Australia, Canada, Ireland, etc.

Graddol, like Quirk,[3] conjures an image reminiscent of Caliban (as colonial subject), who, according to Shakespeare, was taught 'language' not 'your language' (Cesaire, 2000). Shakespeare, as a product of his time, has an excuse for being racist, but it seems – in linguistics, at least – the more things change, the more they remain the same. The point, of course, is that now English/Spanish/Portuguese/ French/German/Dutch are Caliban's language too.

That there are 'native speakers' of Malaysian English, Lankan English, Singapore English, etc. is well known. To refer to 'native speakers' of 'English' as only (white) Australians, British, Americans, etc. goes beyond a linguistic assessment to an ideological one. The concept of the 'native speaker' as a homogeneous category is itself problematic, because some 'native speakers' have greater competence than others, and this reflects power, class and education. In Ceylon, in 1954, this was documented, though many linguists still have difficulty accepting it today.

I think most of us would grant, except perhaps the incorrigible purist, that the English spoken by the English-educated class either in their homes or in the more complex contexts of specialized activity is satisfactory enough, and has become native to the class which speaks it today. In that sense it has become a natural medium for their thinking. (Gunatilleke, 1954)

Corpus-based work, though claiming to be more inclusive and value-free, reinforces the same paradigm, since the corpus is always already selective and restricted to 'appropriate' sources. In the following case, the chosen Lankan texts are from 2010 only and appear to disproportionately privilege university contexts.

The International Corpus of English (ICE) project has opened up new pathways for corpus-based comparisons of varieties of English. Launched in the early 1990s (cf. Greenbaum, 1996), the final version of this megacorpus will include approximately 25 components, representing major 'inner-circle' native varieties of English (e.g. Australian, British and US-American English) as well as postcolonial 'outer-circle' varieties (e.g. Indian, Jamaican and Singaporean English)... While some components (e.g. ICE-GB, ICE-IND) have been available for a decade already, many ICE components, especially representing New Englishes in smaller speech communities, are currently being compiled, e.g. ICE-Sri Lanka and ICE-Fiji... There are, however, a number of problems involved in the compilation (and, thus, the analysis) of ICE components of New Englishes. For example, in many postcolonial settings it is not easy to fill certain genre categories (e.g. parliamentary debates in Fiji, given that the parliament has been suspended ever since 2006) and to decide on who qualifies as a speaker of the variety at hand (e.g. in Sri Lanka: what minimum level of English competence? Only L2 speakers, or also local L1 speakers of English? How to deal with the many speakers who have stayed abroad very long?). What is even more challenging is the inherent diachronic gap that has already emerged across ICE components: while the first ICE components include texts from the early 1990s only (e.g. ICE-GB), on-going ICE projects are bound to include texts from 2010 and later (e.g. ICE-Sri Lanka). We have to uphold, however, the general fiction of linguistic stability over the past 20 years in order to be able to treat ICE components as synchronically comparable corpora. (Mukherjee & Schilk, n.d.).

The ludicrousness of Mukherjee and Schilk's 'problems', such as the absence of current parliamentary debates in Fiji (and, hence, a blank slot in the pre-determined corpus framework: no parliament means no English, or what, jolly roger), hide deeper methodological and attitudinal shibboleths that mark this project, not the least of which is 'the general fiction of linguistic stability over the past 20 years'. The point is that while theoretical problems obtain even in Northern contexts, they are most visible as ruptures here. Thus, the tired, old hierarchy of 'New Englishes' (newer than what? Indian English is arguably older than Australian English, for instance) and 'Native Englishes' (native by what standard? Actually native here can only mean 'white' if we're looking for the one common denominator of all the Englishes described as 'native' within mainstream literature) remain unquestioned in this text.

Sanctioned ignorance and, what I call, the 'Columbus-discovered-America' syndrome appear to affect linguists more than other scholars – no doubt a shadow cast by the historical complicity between linguistics and colonialism. Despite the evidence of 70 years of writing on Lankan English within and outside Sri Lanka/Ceylon,[4] Michael Meyler – who should know better – writes:

> My impression is that in recent years there has been increasing awareness of SLE in the academic field... And outside Sri Lanka, there is virtually nothing to show that SLE even exists: many people are ignorant of the fact that there are a significant number of people in Sri Lanka who actually speak English as their first language... Part of the problem has always been the lack of documented evidence showing that SLE exists, and identifying the features that define it.

Not to be outdone, Mukherjee, Schilk and Bernaisch write that:

> The rigid Sinhala-only policy of the 1950s propagated Sinhala as the only official language of the island and denied Tamil, the indigenous language spoken by a substantial minority of the island's population (mainly comprising Tamil-speaking Hindus and Muslims in the Northern and Eastern provinces), an equivalent status. Along these lines, English was not considered to be part of the local linguistic repertoire, and it was not until the mid-1980s, after many years of civil war between Sinhala-speaking and Tamil-speaking Sri Lankans, that English was reintroduced in the Constitution of Sri Lanka as a 'link language' alongside Sinhala and Tamil, i.e. as a neutral interethnic means of communication. In spite of the changing status – and societal role – of English in Sri Lanka over the past six decades, the language remained present on the island all the time and became more and more indigenised: without any doubt, it is true that 'Sri Lankan English' is not simply 'English in Sri Lanka', but a variety with a certain regional and social identity. (Meshtrie & Bhatt, 2008: 200).

The passage, symptomatic of the entire article, is so full of errors and over-simplifications that correction will take too long. Suffice to point out, the cavalier approach to key dates (1950s for 1956, mid-1980s for the demonized 13th Amendment to the Constitution of 1987, 'many years of civil war' for three, if that) and the exclusion of over a million Tamil-speaking people (over 5% of the national population) in the central hills. Most egregious, however, is the suggestion that English can serve 'as a neutral interethnic means of communication' in countries where less than 10% speak English with any degree of comfort (See Proposition 5 below). But we're getting sidetracked here. Mukherjee *et al.* present Meshtrie and Bhatt as their Columbus surrogates, who proudly determine that our English is 'a variety with a certain regional and social identity', not 'distinct', but much vaguer, still, we must be grateful for small mercies.

Proposition 5: Present models of mono-, bi- and multi-linguality are based on the interaction of separate individual languages that have no explanatory power (today)

We only ever speak one language – or rather one idiom only.
We never speak only one language – or rather there is no pure idiom.
Jacques Derrida, Monolingualism of the Other: Or The Prosthesis of
Origin (1998, trans. Patrick Mensah)

Figure 7.1 describes the inter-relationships between Sri Lanka's three main languages. It is not the case that the three distinct languages borrow/steal from one another and still remain distinct languages. The interaction transforms each of the languages in a complex process that cannot be equated to simple addition/enrichment of words and phrases. The enrichment goes far deeper. Derrida, referring to his own linguistic legacy as an Algerian Jew speaking French, captures this always-already heterogeneous nature of every single language in multilingual (read, 'all') contexts rather well, I think.

A fuller explanation is required of this phenomenon. I shall merely outline some of the ways in which the conventional explanation of code-mixing and code-switching cannot account for what's going on here. Both 'mixing' and 'switching' do not leave either language inviolate, because this process transforms the meaning that obtains in the original language(s). Languages are not discrete entities *to cut and paste* from, but they exist in dialogic relationships with each other. Moreover, the 'same' borrowing/switch has different meaning(s) depending on interlocutors, sequence, context etc., and the complete utterance (involving multiple languages in

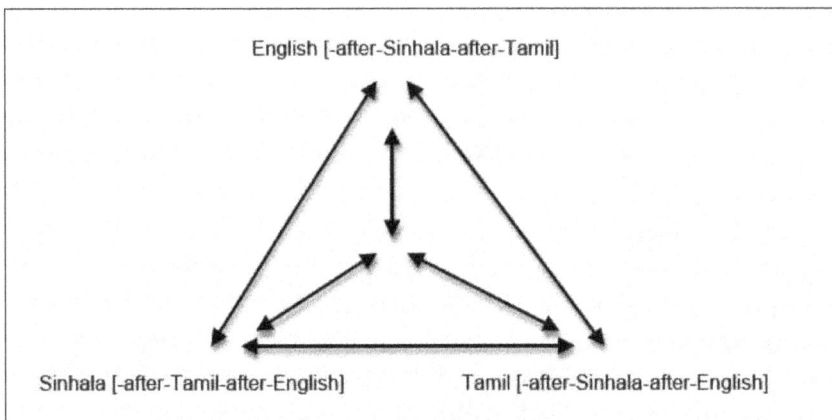

Figure 7.1 Language inter-relationships in Sri Lanka

the old sense) has composite meaning, not reducible to its component parts. In addition, phonetic, syntactic and semantic changes in the original may result from multilingual use and even the language borrowed from is transformed in this exchange. Further confounding simplistic conventional explanations, it is often impossible to distinguish which is L1, L2 or L3 in situations of language exchange, especially in non-elite, everyday discourse in Sri Lanka.

Thus, while upward mobility in general is tightly controlled by economic, political and ideological forces, a few exceptions are permitted to enter the inner portals of (linguistic) power, so that it can be said that the (English) language is neutral and rewards dedicated learners, which is the linguistic version of the 'rags to riches' storyline. Currently, war and post-war politico-economic enterprise has created a new power-language nexus. The new leaders may not be well versed in the niceties of English, but they employ front men and propaganda machines that are.

There is no linguistic reason or justification for the limiting of acceptable variation in language standards. Neither theoretical principle, nor empirical evidence has been offered by linguists of all stripes who discuss standardization and 'describe' standards at work. These are political decisions masquerading as linguistic ones, especially when linguists claim merely to describe what exists.

Proposition 6: Diglossia and dialectal variation often create greater inequalities than the use of different languages, but language nationalism and purism dissimulates this

> *National consciousness, which is not nationalism, is the only thing that will*
> *give us an international dimension.*
> Frantz Fanon, 1968: 247

Through the fraught relationships played out among Sinhala, Tamil and English speakers, Sri Lanka provides a nuanced case study of the alignment of language and power in multilingual contexts and demonstrates the key role that diglossia plays in maintaining elite hegemony. Just as global English Language standards dissimulate their elitist nature through entrenching value judgments that have naturalized special interests and represent them as inherently better than other varieties/lects, so, too, with Sinhala and especially Tamil, there is a hierarchy of dialects. Tamil spoken by the Jaffna elites takes pride of place at the expense of Muslim speakers and those living in the tea plantation areas. Adding another layer to this disempowerment of underclass (hence 'uneducated', since they have to begin working for wages at school-going age) users of Sinhala and Tamil is spoken/written-formal/informal diglossia, which denies them access to their own language outside the familial/community sphere. For Sinhala and Tamil, as well as for English, dominant linguistic paradigms serve narrow political interests, since even in the case of first-language users ('native speakers') of each of these languages, socio-economic class, education and proximity to urban centres determine the extent of inclusion/exclusion and access to language normativity.

Linguistic nationalists may claim that removal of the oppressive language and culture will guarantee equality. This is not even true within a single language, and in a context of multiple linguistic domination, there can be no such simple solution. By analogy from Sinhala and Tamil, a diglossic model for English is predicated in Sri Lanka, and the overwhelming demand is for 'Spoken English', as if it involved widely different grammatical rules and structures, whereas pronunciation – the current index of proficiency policed by the opinion-makers and influence-peddlers – demands conformity that later learners cannot recognize, much less reproduce, due to key sounds not being found in their mother tongues. The confusion is further confounded by a lack of clarity on what is at stake in the discussion of varieties and standards of English, where even teachers do not seem to know how to distinguish or identify varieties clearly. There is, however, the wide perception that external (Western) norms are necessary to validate English – most want to use SBE or IE (Standard British English or International English). Students, teachers, policy-makers and influence-peddlers wanted 'Standard British English' (and, in some cases, 'Standard American English') to be taught to their children (and themselves, of course), but many felt that for rural, under-privileged students who had no English-speaking background, other kinds of English ('Sri Lankan English', often seen as a euphemism for 'Broken English') were OK.

Proposition 7: Discourse of English as benevolent and neutral access to upward mobility needs unpacking. Access is invariably privileged (gendered/ethnicized/classed), teaching and materials ideological. Demand is deliberately mismatched by supply

In its dominant versions today, English is presented as conferring magical powers, echoing Kachru's analogy, which credits the language with the transformative potential of alchemy. This claim and self-fulfilling prophecy, which I theorize as a key form of extra-linguistic value, posits that through English competence, *good* learners acquire a range of qualities, including 'intelligence', 'politeness', 'sensitivity' and even 'decency', in addition to the well-established appendages of English, such as wealth, erudition and social credibility. By implication, the English-speaking elites already possess these desirable extra-linguistic qualities and are generous enough to share their superiority with the best of the best learners who need to earn the right to this rare privilege by denouncing others from their original socio-economic class. Instrumental reasons for learning English have, therefore, been supplemented by value-laden bonuses, and this ideology is being successfully exploited by both international and national business enterprises, such as the British Council and private schools.

The general fraught context of English language learning and teaching signals that there is more at stake than the mere learning of a language. It is in partial recognition of this situation that students themselves express some confusion and anxiety about what they are, in fact, learning. In the (translated) words of one of our respondents:

> Something is making learning English difficult for me, for us. I don't know exactly what it is – it is our text book, our teacher, it is the fact that we don't use English outside our classroom, but it is also something else. (Private correspondence, undated)

It is presumed, both naively and disingenuously, that English is not a weapon of oppression – a *Kaduwa* – that hangs over their heads, but rather, it is a neutral and transparent medium, which is equally accessible and benevolent to all. Diametrically opposed to this view are many who see English only as an oppressive class-sword, utterly oblivious to the opportunities for upward mobility and a slice of the pie that the language provides, although selectively, to later-learners in Sri Lanka. These stone-throwers rage against the hegemony of English, but re-inscribe Sinhala dominance over Tamil and often educate their children abroad. This dual and paradoxical role of empowered-for-a-few and oppressor-for-the-many that English so clearly fulfills, vis-à-vis the Sri Lankan underclasses, carries with it crucial psychological baggage for the learner (and teacher), which must be accounted for in any language planning programme or teaching material/methodology formulation that aims at a positive national impact.

The stories about English in Sri Lanka are many and varied. In 200 years of exposure, of which 60 years were post-independence, Sri Lanka has gone through the entire spectrum of attitudes towards English: from hatred to colonialist adulation and imitation to legislated rejection and ridicule. While it is simplistic to claim that at the end of the first decade of the 21st century the response to English has come full cycle, it is nonetheless true that the premium on English-language competence is such that it is the single most important index of legally sanctioned economic and social upward mobility in the country.

However, as described above, unknown to many underclass aspirants for a slice of the pie, pronunciation has become entrenched as a class-marker and passport for those who learnt English at their mother's knee, so to speak, as distinguished from those who learnt English later in life. This policing of the standard ensures that only a few are allowed entrance at the gate to one-of-us-dom, with Lankanisms generally being ghettoized in creative writing and/or as objects of insider humour, as is commonly seen in other, similar post-colonial contexts.

While the English-speaking elite claims that it is steering a benign meritocracy of equal opportunity, within which the English language is the handmaiden of globalization outcomes and opportunities in Sri Lanka today (as it was of colonialism for 150 years), this narrative of language-opportunity is only one side of the commercial coin, since new and subtler systems of exclusion and marginalization have been set in place. These operate indirectly in the form of class-based assessments of language competence, which stipulate impossible standards for first-generation learners to achieve.

Proposition 8: Due to skewed globalization, extra-linguistic value is being conferred on English by an opportunist peripheral market and a complicitous centre, thereby reintroducing colonialist paradigms

'Extra-linguistic value' is a concept I have developed through an analogy with economics, where the notion of extra-economic coercion is well-known as the defining element of feudalism with which capitalism broke, in creating the space for the worker to sell his (alas, it remained a male prerogative for a long time) labour (although not at any real measure of what this labour was worth). Extra-linguistic value can be defined as that value placed on aspects of language and language use which go beyond the legitimate purview of linguistics. For instance, language competence can be measured and fluency mapped in terms of benchmarks, whatever we may think of these benchmarks. These are linguistic values, since they are judgments that are within the legitimate disciplinary space of language use. We needn't agree with the judgments, but if so, the disagreement takes place within the logical space for such judgments. If, however, judgments about a person's intelligence or honesty are made on the basis of his/her competence in English (as measured by pronunciation or adherence to grammatical rules), then this is an example of extra-linguistic value being afforded to English use. If, as I shall establish below, there is a significant increase in extra-linguistic value placed on English in Sri Lanka, it is both a cause and effect of inequality operating in, and through, English in the country. Since English competence (as a proxy for class and privilege) confers power, it is seen to possess qualities and characteristics that transcend language, moving into the realm of ethics and personality.

In a survey undertaken by the Sri Lanka English Language Teachers' Association (SLELTA) in 2010 – covering nearly 500 influential users of the language across the country – a clear pattern emerged regarding the extra-linguistic value conferred on English. Most respondents suggest that the 'appearance of the speaker' is a key element in identifying the variety spoken. This is an indication that English still comes with strong colonial baggage and much extra-linguistic value added to it. The physical appearance of the speaker should have very little to do with the correctness (or variety) of English spoken. This attitude, however, is consistent with data obtained from other sources.

Evidence for my thesis regarding the extra-linguistic value placed in English as an index of intelligence, personality, general knowledge and suitability for employment, derived from interviews and questionnaire responses, is starkly, shockingly self-explanatory:

Private Sector/Management Perspectives (from 30 interviews)

(1) Good knowledge of English = intelligence = good family background = good personality = high aptitude = demonstrates team spirit.
(2) Good knowledge of English = a sense of responsibility = sound business sense.
(3) Good knowledge of English = proper pronunciation = confidence at interviews = fluency.

Student/Teacher Perspectives (trends from 200 interviews)

(1) Good knowledge of English = social mobility = better social status.
(2) Good knowledge of English = all round ability = decency.
(3) Good knowledge of English = personality = goodness = intelligence.
(4) Good knowledge of English = proper pronunciation = confidence at interviews = grammaticality.
(5) The English (men and women) = good knowledge of English.

This means that learners of English are actually hoping to become better human beings through English, and, as a corollary, people whose English is manifestly impeccable, in their eyes, are 'decent', 'punctual', team players. etc. Note, also, that the neo-colonial value system, which re-invests English in its colonial garb as the purview and prerogative of (white) English men and women, is also thriving here. Many of those interviewed were students of British Council English classes, which have become more popular since the nineties. The values espoused by these students are reminiscent of a by-gone era. We were told that the variety of English that Lankans speak was not 'real' English, and none of the students (aged 15–25) cited any Lankan role models who could match their teachers. No any[5] of the parents interviewed were English-speaking, though most said that they would not allow their children to watch anything but English television.

It took us 40-odd years to uncouple the English language from England and the old colonial bandwagon, but the jolly old umbilical cord is still in place, it seems. We've not been able to get an assurance from the British

Council in Sri Lanka that they are committed to valuing all varieties of English equally and that the most appropriate form of English to be used/taught in Sri Lanka is Lankan English. To publicly admit this would be to kiss huge profits goodbye. The resurgence of the British Council as a high-class tuition *kadey* marks the neo-imperialism of Western culture under globalization.

Proposition 9: Even at the academic and intellectual level, linguistic/discursive standards and norms naturalize and legitimize prejudice resulting in a double discrimination, which is another (indirect) form of extra-linguistic value hanging out as objective judgments of substance and clarity

A Lankan student wrote an essay containing the following sentence, which I shared with colleagues, who bemoaned the declining standards of English and also the lack of coherent thinking among students that made our task as teachers so much harder. It was not a big deal, just a casual conversation that they soon forgot.

> In this Kandiyan wether I not ashamed of my difficulties on learning English and I know that my continung to write is like ambusing the Department with a bom in my hands.

A few weeks later, I showed some of them the following version, after correcting the obvious sentence-level errors, and their response was an appreciation of the literary allusions.[6] This, clearly, was a student with the right background and sensitivity – rare commodities for us.

> In this Kandyan weather I'm not ashamed of my difficulty in learning English, and I know that my continuing to write in the language is like ambushing the Department with a bomb in my hand.

What is telling is that, once the mistakes are fixed, and only once they are fixed, are we ready to recognize that the student is capable of higher-order thinking. If he can't get his grammar and spelling right, then he cannot be intelligent or sensitive enough to be ironic, thoughtful or scholarly. The double discrimination is that language errors pre-empt serious engagement with substance, so that while mistakes are penalized, the ideas expressed by the student are devalued, too. Preliminary work, that Christine Abbott and I did in Pittsburgh in 1990, led to similar conclusions about the assessment of undergraduate student writing, where we found that some African-American students were penalized for using dialectal variations in composition courses and that they were institutionally coerced into writing 'safe', non-ethnically marked texts in order to pass, often doing violence to their creativity and identity.

An analysis of school texts has demonstrated that, in addition to having to learn a language which is not used in their daily lives, Lankan students have to grapple with situations that are both unfamiliar and daunting. The fictional context for the study of English in Sri Lanka is a bonhomous, opportunity-laden world that is ideology-free and equitable, where all children are equally privileged and have access to a luxurious lifestyle, as depicted in the textbook lessons. The sad reality is that students who don't fit this model are marginalized and alienated, even demeaned, by this approach. The most obnoxious and alienating of material takes centre-stage, while the students' own experiences and lifestyles are, in effect, devalued through under-emphasis and trivialization. Hence, the sense of linguistic and cultural insecurity that the average student faces when confronted with English is reinforced. Language teaching, in this form, becomes identical with a classed, 'nationed' (British, in this case, but in others, US, though aggrandized as 'American') and regioned acculturation. This may be less legitimate in a context where the language concerned has no roots/history/currency in this country – in teaching a *foreign* language, for instance – but English is very much a Lankan language, though not necessarily in the specific form taught in schools today. The point is that the 'foreignness' of English is being emphasized through such texts and methodologies, not its 'nativeness'.

Students are invited, encouraged and even enticed into becoming everything but themselves. The ordinary rural students – sons and daughters of farmers or plantation workers who comprise the overwhelming majority of those in the classrooms around the country – are required to imagine themselves in another time, in another place, in another socio-economic class and in another geographical location. In short, any place but where they are. The difficulty of learning an oppressive language is made twice as difficult through this alien, and alienating, material.

Not only are the school texts unsuitable for rural students, Tamil-speaking and non Buddhist students have an additional tier of exclusion to grapple with. Their texts follow the current dominant paradigm that Lankan history is the triumphal march of Buddhism as it overcomes Indian/Tamil/Hindu opposition. Here, as elsewhere in the teaching of English in Sri Lanka, another category of extra-linguistic value has been smuggled in as purely linguistic. Here, learning English is not learning a language that is legitimately Sri Lankan – in the technical vocabulary, an institutionalized variety – but learning a way of life that is at once *classist* and (neo) colonial in character, as well as discriminatory and alienating to those who do not have the 'right background'. This means that to a student who already finds the language difficult, there are more debilitating factors that hinder and psychologically affect his/her progress. So, too, are those rural English teachers who are not from the anglicized middle-class milieu of teachers to be found in privileged national and private schools in the major cities. Most of these English (assistant) teachers have little access to the lifestyle and worldview of this material and are therefore uncomfortable with teaching from these texts, resulting in their students being doubly disempowered.

Proposition 10: Elite gate-keeping of 'standards' and humiliation of non-elite learners lead to 'pathologies', which need to be read as resistance, not collective imbecility

The danger of insistence on 'arbitrary', external language standards includes the fact that it pathologizes learners, debilitates non-elite teachers, reinforces hegemony and other hierarchies, straitjackets user creativity into 'safe' structures and fetishizes native-speaker gobbledygook, and it comes already based on a theoretically unsound model of discrete language use. The implicit argument is that other varieties, especially from former colonies, are inferior to THE Standard (Standard British/US English). However, in the case of the post-colonial varieties, these norms are contested – not beyond question – and, hence, have to be justified or, if not, their relationship to power is exposed.

There is another kind of argument related to international intelligibility, where we are advised to learn SBE in order to facilitate global communication, have access to information flows and compete for lucrative jobs. The intelligibility hoax does not stand up to scrutiny. If it is 'international' intelligibility that is the objective, surely all users are equally important. Not so for the intelligibility-wallahs, who are only interested in peddling ease of understanding for the old hierarchy (native, northern, white, elite). Why is the intelligibility argument not brought up in relation to southern US drawlers or Scottish accents? If it is to do with numbers, shouldn't we all measure whether the Chinese or the Indians can understand us? 'International' meanings privilege English/American meanings, which are falsely represented as being universal (beyond the self-interest of an individual variety), whereas other meanings (and vocabulary) are deemed to be restricted and specialized.

Kandiah, who has done pioneering work in the area of Lankan English, has identified some of these 'errors' as *schizoglossia,* which he relates to hypercorrection. Kandiah's argument that the phenomenon of hypercorrection is inadequate to explain errors in the speech and writing of Lankan users low on the cline of bilingualism, is well taken. In fact, all I have tried to do here is to push the argument a little further and deeper, clearly acknowledging his influence (Parakrama, 1997). In pronunciation alone, the *p/f* substitution he observes can be supplemented in each of the following cases as well; *s/z* substitution, *a/e* substitution, consonantal cluster substitution and so on – many of these are even demonstrated by users high on the cline. It is important to note here that pronunciation is now the class-marker among Lankan speakers of English, with later-learners still being ridiculed and imitated. Too much, therefore, rides on pronunciation and other indices of inter-generational familiarity, which the non-elite learner cannot even recognize.

This linguistic insecurity, which has been brought about by extra-linguistic pressure, is also visible in the learner's ability to grasp – in key instances – the role and function of English within a given context on the one hand and, on the other, to indulge in excessive formalism and gaucheness, not to mention inappropriate usage. The end result is the same from opposite poles, as it were, and malapropism rules the day. The written language is stilted, archaic, pretentious, even servile, and most conspicuously verbose to the point of caricature, as can be seen from this example.

Post of Stenographer or Steno-Secretary

I am a Sinhala Buddhist religionist; a Steno Secretary and a Stenographer by profession. I have pulled through:

(1)   Diploma-in-Journalism – English
(2)   Teachers' Diploma

Being a speed-writing calibre, I am able to stylograph your flawless diction in phonographical strokes at a speed of 110–120 w.p.m. I also can manipulate a SINHALA key-board typographical contraption at a moderate speed. I have gleaned a wealth of work experience in various aspects of secretarial functions and able to draft Inward and outward routine correspondence independently.

At present I am serving under an eminent legal luminary at his residential office in the capacity of Steno-secretary on a temporary basis and that too by fits and starts due to work availability.

Should your goodself acquiesce in defraying me a substantial payment of emolument to commensurate my labour, work experience, etc, I wish to state that I am desirous of taking up assignment with immediate effect.

In marked contrast, 'Good' learners imitate external norms and standards, often archaic and inappropriate. 'Good' learners tend to show off what they know and are quite comfortable with the ideology of English, vis-à-vis Sinhala and Tamil in Sri Lanka. Good Learners think 'Englishly', a la West and Macaulay (Minute on Indian Education, 1835). Good learners are upwardly mobile and *vice versa.*

We now have an ethico-political dilemma, which we can choose to dissimulate as an apolitical professional concern for 'Good English' and for not patronizing our students by offering them an inferior variety. Yet pushing the discriminatory standard as if it were self-evidently the best performs epistemic and cultural violence and straitjackets learners into unproductive and sterile forms of expression. The following example dramatizes precisely this predicament:

Conclusion of an undergraduate essay on 'The Importance of English'

The spread of the English Language widely in the world does not imply that learning English is easy. The learning of English has several barriers and the worst of it is spelling! As English spelling is not a direct reflection of pronunciation, non-native learners face problems. This can be avoided by proper guidance given to the learner to learn proper English. English spelling has been described as 'notoriously confusing' by one scholar. Another problem a learner will face is unpredictability in spelling ....

Despite these defects English should be celebrated as remarkable, and we have to agree with Edward Thomas who described the Language as:

You English words, I know you:
You are light as dreams, tough as oak,
Precious as gold on poppies and corn
Or an old cloak

Considering these qualities of the English Language, it should be said that English is important at all levels of education, for professionals and all the other people in the world.

This piece was written by a university student who was considered excellent by her lecturers. Yet the sentiments are all borrowed and contrived, like the poetic metaphors she claims to share common ground with. One is starkly reminded of Godfrey Gunatilleke's epochal essay, 'A Language without Metaphor', because it is precisely this cultural wasteland that our stellar student inhabits, that we – in a sense – invite her to call home. She dreams in English (which may be fair enough, because some of us, in fact, do), but the added identification of the texture of English with oak wood (perhaps she has lived in the West?), its cloak-like comfort/protection and its value in the glitter of poppies and corn (all of which are alien and disturbingly outside the social and linguistic experience of even the most elite of Lankan English speakers) pushes us towards the conclusion that this is vicarious and learned, not lived, experience. The values here are unabashedly elite, as seen in the throwaway tokenism of the last line, where English is identified as important for professionals (us) and 'all other people in the world' (them).

The non-standard is one of the most accessible means of 'natural' resistance and, therefore, one of the most sensitive indices of de-hegemonization.

Fortunately, non-elite language users do not read linguistic analyses. In fact, I shall argue their entire linguistic practice is an implicit critique of such theories. This intervention will end with a close examination of the nature of non-standard (English) language use as resistance against hegemonic standards and norms. What has been devalued and pathologized in ELS will be read against the grain as a complex process of dehegemonization, which needs to be taken seriously as an antidote to the *malchemy* (negative alchemy) of English in this phase of post/neo-coloniality and as a response to the absurd, yet pernicious extra-linguistic discourse around World English or English as Lingua Franca.[7]

Resistance and protest are also normed by dominant perceptions of what forms and contexts opposition should take. Of these essential attributes of resistance – as we recognize it within the dominant discourse – *rationality and intention* surely take pride of place. We are unused to conceiving of unthinking, unmotivated, even irrational acts as resistance. Yet I suggest that ours is a model based on the tyranny of those who share and participate in the dominant discourse. There is no room in this model for the radical alterity of these who are not caught within the nexus of power/access to power/the possibility of access to power in the future. For those outside the pale, as it were, the logic of resistance and protest, as we understand it, does not clinch. For this group, for whom the trendy term would be 'subaltern', other paradigms of resistance and protest need to be conceptualized, since, to echo Ranajit Guha, there is dominance without hegemony.

Thus, it is for the 'weak', in this sense, that there appears a need to use other weapons than we do, and it is important for any sensitive analysis of language or the society to see the possibility and potential of *persistent mistakes and errors* as being the reflection of something other than collective failure. Otherwise, we are doomed to making absurd claims such as: 'There are no bright students in the villages. They have all come to the city by now'. Our TESL/TEFL/World Englishes echo of this thematic would have to generalize about the idiocy and incompetence of at least 19.5 million people (out of 20.5) in Sri Lanka.

The refusal to recognize what is actually happening in, through and around English in Sri Lanka, is to reduce oneself to non-intervention and apathy in the face of systematic discrimination and structurally nurtured insecurity, which leads to the kinds of 'pathology' or 'aberration' that I shall spell out here. Let me reiterate that *the pathology*, in this view, is not with the learner, but within the system. It is a condition that forces learners to resort to the kinds of self-blame and debilitation we have described. Yet we must also be aware of the impossibility of translation, the untenability of all origins, the self-interest of all normative systems and the vigilance against counter-hegemonies, which, in turn, re-inscribe other hierarchies.

Conclusion

It is no surprise, then, that the English teaching/learning practiced in Sri Lanka has been a colossal and costly failure[8] for over 50 years, and English usage continues to reinforce inequality even today, because:

(a) it asks rural non-elite (and urban underclass) students not to learn a language so much as to take on the worldview and values of the urban, upwardly-mobile upper/middle class;

(b) it devalues authentic Lankan experience, metaphor and idiom and calls for an alien and alienating variety and worldview of English that is rife with archaisms and excessive formality;

(c) it confers on English an illegitimate, added (extra-linguistic) value that lies outside the realm of language use;

(d) its materials and teaching modalities, its governance and assessment structures (including teacher training and certification) are inappropriate and counter-productive;

(e) it uses pronunciation as a class-marker and gatekeeper, precisely because this distinguishes home-learners (the urban elite) from school-learners (the rest) of English;

(f) it stigmatizes certain types of usage seen as gross errors, which become the target of ridicule and, hence, traumatize users, creating pathologies of *lajja-baya*; and

(g) it is majoritarian Sinhala in its orientation, and it discriminates against Tamil-speakers (see Canagarajah for an account of this process).

This critique does not seek to devalue the excellent contributions made to English teaching in certain specific situations or to deny the wonderful individual success stories that every structural failure feeds upon as alibis for maintaining the status quo. Yet the aggregate effect is a calamitous reproduction of elite control and a slow trickle upwards. English is not the panacea for success that it is touted to be, but at the same time, its systemic denial to those who desire to learn the language is indefensible.

It's now a truism that language, in its broader sense, is the only access we have to everything outside of ourselves, not to mention our access to ourselves (or to use Wittgenstein's beautiful, but now trivialized phrase, 'my language is my world') in the philosophical sense. This language, in the narrow sense, is also the vehicle – witting or unwitting – of values and ideology that, historically and today, have taken sides. Or in a less theoretical formulation, the fact that 'villain' originally meant 'peasant' and 'blackguard' derived from 'kitchen worker' only goes to show just who is winning the war of words – power is ultimately the ability to make meaning stick, and to do this, one has to be heard. Or to use an example from Sinhala, how the word for interpreter in early colonial times ('dubash') became the word to describe debased culture ('thuppahi'). Thus, standardization adds another more insidious dimension to this struggle, since it controls and regulates structure, pronunciation, register, style and so on, which serves to exclude many voices.

The hardest part for us, within these dominant paradigms, is, of course, the unlearning of our privilege in/through language. In the 20 or so years that I have been discussing these ideas with academics, teachers, intellectuals and anyone interested, the most persistent anxiety has centred around this issue of the (loss of) authority/control, through it is invariably couched in worries about 'What will be taught in the classroom, then?' or 'Who will decide what is right and wrong?' In this broader standard, linguistic insecurity will diminish and, with it, many of the blatantly classist elements of English in Sri Lanka. If it comes to the stage where (almost) anything goes and where meaning is the arbiter of acceptance and where it is extremely difficult to reject one kind of usage in favour of another, then language would have become as level as it would get, which is not much.

Here we come full cycle, then, to the point at which our aim – as teachers of the standard, bearers of the torch, etc. – is to destabilize, broaden this standard towards the creation of a situation where the onus is on us to learn (or rather, unlearn) to read our students' persistent errors as resistance with or without demonstrable intention and to respect its radical difference. Ours *was* the privilege as linguists, teachers, codifiers, standard bearers and so on to confer the privilege of language on these other Calibans so that their profit on't was to curse us in it. Let the roles be reversed: let us learn their (version of) language to earn the right to the privilege of ours. Otherwise, we're simply acting out the words of Wittgenstein: a crack is showing in the system, and we're trying to stuff it with straw, but to quieten our conscience, we're using only the *best* straw.

Notes

(1) Two observations. This is a mish-mash because the brother wants to show-off essentialist notions of dialect use, which ghettoize non-standard forms. Black English is not spoken only by blacks, nor do all blacks speak it, no? This means also that questions of 'authenticity' and 'appropriateness' (semi-literates can only talk in 'vulgarisms') must also be questioned like a motherfucker. This, of course, does not let whatever dialect or *tuppahi* mish-mash language off the hook if it is racist, regionalist, and so on and so forth. Second, why is the 'appropriate' liberal response to this *achcharu* a snicker-giggle? What does this cover-up? At what point in these matters does proving a point become also interventionist practice, not tokenism? This operation can then be termed 'strategic de-essentialization' to parody or upside-downify Spivak's phrase. It attacks notions of (originary) purity, even in the oppressed linguistic situation, and confronts the issue of mediated representation through language form. To trash Wittgenstein for a worthy cause, if language be a form of life, then the form of language is telling us nothing epistemologically new about the form of this form of life. What is up for grabs are habits and practices, contextually creative vocabularies and so on, but not systems/possibilities/limits of knowing, because, after all, standard and non-standard forms of language are so differentiated for political reasons, not philosophical ones.

(2) *Contra* Gramsci, not merely restricted to relatively weak hegemony, but also strong, pre-empting effective counter-hegemony.

(3) 'The existence of standards (in moral and sexual behaviour, in dress, in taste generally) is an endemic feature of our mortal condition and... people feel alienated and disoriented if a standard seems to be missing in any one of these areas... Certainly, ordinary folk, with their ordinary common sense, have gone on knowing that there are standards in language and they have gone on crying out to be taught them'. (Quirk, 1985: 5–6).

(4) See S. Fernando, M. Gunesekera and A. Parakrama (eds) (2010) *English in Sri Lanka: Ceylon English, Lankan English, Sri Lankan English*. Colombo: Aitken Spence.

(5) This 'error' is one that makes elite Lankan English speakers wince or smirk, depending on their politics. It is pervasively used in both writing and speech by the majority of Lankans who are not 'mother's knee' English acquirers. This, then, is a key example of both the arbitrariness of the rules of usage, as well as the ways these rules are used to exclude and demean the 'other'. The (mis)use of 'there' for 'their', and vice versa, is another no-no I've smuggled in to this text, as is the (incorrect) use of 'the', especially in relation to 'society', 'nature', etc. A fourth example is the (over)use of the present continuous tense. I want readers to disagree about what is a grammatical/ discourse rule and what following such rules involves (not, of course, in Wittgenstein's philosophical sense). Why can't the same word convey multiple meanings here, as elsewhere in English, for instance? Once this discussion moves beyond quasi-arguments, such as you-must-follow-the-rule 'because the sky is so high...', we're already chipping away at language hegemony.

(6) Lakdasa Wikkramasinha, a radical Lankan poet, wrote 'In this Kandyan weather there is/ no shame in having in your bed / a servant maid –' (*To My Friend Aldred*) and 'The poet is the one who is always preparing / The ambush' (*The Poet*) and 'He is the one that, tossing a bomb into / The crowd, takes notes' (*The Poet*).

(7) Here, as elsewhere in this piece, my debt to Pennycook and Phillipson is gratefully acknowledged, though the mess I've made remains my sole responsibility.

(8) For conspiracy theorists, this could also be the 'success' of English language policy and implementation, because it does not democratize access and reinforces the gatekeeping role of an English-speaking *class* that is fast losing its economic stranglehold, but still has a power-brokering and influence-peddling role to play in Lankan society. The same argument can be adduced to Bandaranaike's language policy, which, in addition to discriminating against Tamil-speakers, also reinforced the *de facto* hegemony of English by creating barriers for its easy access.

References

Benjamin, W. (1940) *Theses on the Philosophy of History VII*. In H. Adams and L. Searle (eds) *Critical Theory Since 1965* (1986). Tallahassee: Florida State Univ. Press. Online at http://simple.wikiquote.org/wiki/Walter_Benjamin.

Canagarajah, A.S. (1999) *Resisting Linguistic Imperialism in English Teaching*. Oxford: Oxford University Press.

Cesaire, A. (2000) *Discourse on Colonialism*. Joan Pinkham (transl). London, New York: Monthly Review Press.

Davis, A. and Elder, C. (2006) *The Handbook of Applied Linguistics*. Oxford: Blackwell Publishing.

Derrida, J. (1998) *Monolingualism of the Other: Or the Prosthesis of Origin*. Palo Alto, CA: Stanford University Press.

Fanon, F. (1968) *The Wretched of the Earth*. New York, NY: Grove.

Fernando, S., Gunesekera, M. and Parakrama, A. (eds) (2010) *English in Sri Lanka: Ceylon English, Lankan English, Sri Lankan English*. Colombo: Aitken Spence.

Graddol, D. (1999) The decline of the native speaker. In D. Graddol and U. Meinhof (ed.) *English in a Changing World: AILA Review* 13, 57–68.

Gramsci, A. (1971) *Selection from the Prison Notebooks.* Moscow: International Publishers.

Guha, R. (1998) *Dominance Without Hegemony: History and Power in Colonial India.* Cambridge: Harvard University Press.

Gunatilleke, G. (1954) A language without metaphor. In S. Fernando, M. Gunesekera and A. Parakrama (eds) (2010) *English in Sri Lanka: Ceylon English, Lankan English, Sri Lankan English.* Colombo: Aitken Spence. Online at http://corpus.byu.edu/files-oup/mukherjee_schilk.doc. Accessed 10 Jan 2011.

Kachru, B. (1990) *The Alchemy of English: The Spread, Functions, and Models of Non-native Englishes.* Urbana: University of Illinois Press.

Kandiah, T. (1981) Sri Lankan English schizoglossia. *English World-Wide* 2, 63–81.

Katz J.J. (1972) *Semantic Theory.* New York, NY: Harper and Row.

Macaulay, T.B. (1835) Minute on Indian education. In H. Sharp (ed.) *Selections from Educational Records, Part I (1781–1839)* (pp. 107–117). Delhi: National Archives of India.

Marx, K. (2005) *The Eighteenth Brumaire of Louis Bonaparte.* New York and Berlin: Mondial.

McCarthy, M. (2001) *Issues in Applied Linguistics.* Cambridge: Cambridge University Press.

Mesthrie, R. and Bhatt, R.M. (2008) *World Englishes: The Study of New Linguistic Varieties.* Cambridge: Cambridge University Press.

Meyler, M. (2009) Sri Lankan English: A distinct South Asian variety. *English Today* 25 (4), 55–60.

Mukherjee, J. and Schilk, M. (n.d.) Exploring variation and change in new Englishes: Looking into the International Corpus of English (ICE) and beyond. Online document, accessed 5 October 2011. *corpus.byu.edu/files-oup/mukherjee_schilk.doc*

Mukherjee, J., Schilk, M. and Bernaisch, T. (2009) Compiling the Sri Lankan component of ICE: Principles, problems, prospects. *ICAME Journal* 34, 64–77.

Parakrama, A. (1995) *De-Hegemonising Language Standards: Learning from Lankan English about "English".* London: Macmillan.

Parakrama, A. (1997) *Baduth Unge, Naduth Unge, The Tools and Rules are Theirs: Some Thoughts on the Language of Privilege and the Privilege of Language.* Colombo: Katha.

Pennycook, A. (1994) *The Cultural Politics of English as an International Language.* Harlow: Longman.

Pennycook, A. (1998) *English and the Discourses of Colonialism.* London and New York: Routledge.

Phillipson, R. (1992) *Linguistic Imperialism.* Oxford: Oxford University Press.

Quirk, R. (1985) The English language in a global context. In R. Quirk and H.G. Widdowson (eds) *English in the World* (pp. 1–6). Cambridge: Cambridge University Press.

Rossi-Landi, F. (1977) *Linguistics and Economics.* The Hague: Mouton.

Selinker, L., Swain, M. and Dumas, G. (1975) The interlanguage hypothesis extended to children. *Language Learning* 25 (1), 136–152.

Spivak, G.C. (1988) *In Other Worlds: Essays in Cultural Politics.* New York and London: Routledge.

Spivak, G.C. (1993) *Outside in the Teaching Machine.* New York and London: Routledge.

Sri Lanka English Language Teachers Association (SLELTA) (2010) Survey results presented at the Sri Lanka English Language Teachers Association annual conference, Colombo, 17 October.

Volosinov, V.N. and Bakhtin, M.M. (1973) *Marxism and the Philosophy of Language.* Cambridge, MA: Harvard University Press.

Widdowson, H. (2000) On the limitations of linguistics applied. *Applied Linguistics* 21(1), 3–35.

Wittgenstein, L. (1977) *Culture and Value.* London: Blackwell.

8 English Language as Governess: Expatriate English Teaching Schemes in Hong Kong

Eugene Chen Eoyang, Pauline Bunce and Vaughan Rapatahana

*There is no explicitly formulated language educational policy in Hong Kong...
Whatever undefinable language educational policy Government has, it can claim very little
educational achievement except the success in creating a demand for English education...*
Cheng et al., 1973: 15, 27

*Sometimes it comes to mind that the compulsory learning of English in schools is one of
the British government's political strategies... the teaching of English is a kind of cultural
intrusion in Hong Kong and may be regarded as a political weapon.*
Eva Wai Yin, quoted in Pennycook, 1998b: 190

*The problem is that Hong Kong's colonial history has created a system of schooling in
which English-medium education has come to be regarded both as an avenue to better
life chances and as a marker of social status for the local middle class...
a vested interest to be defended at all costs.*
Sweeting & Vickers, 2007: 34

The Hong Kong community's attitude towards the English language can be rather schizophrenic. There is a definite desire for it, rooted in instrumental and social motivations, but there also exists a kind of aloof indifference towards it. As Evans (2008a: 360) has noted, this schizoid attitude commenced in the early days of 19th century colonialism, with – as just one example – 'students at Queen's College... [who] extracted what they wanted from their studies... with attitudes towards the British that were rarely more positive than coolly indifferent'.

By examining the history of the territory's many Native English-speaking Teacher (NET) schemes and, in particular, the most recent Enhanced NET Scheme of 1998 as an example of this schizophrenic attitude, this chapter will cast the English language as a stern and intractable governess from England who just never seems to go away, but whose conspicuous presence is tolerated by Hong Kong's residents, who are led to believe they might get something desirable from her – such as good remuneration and social status, if not a good education – one day.

A Series of Expatriate Teacher Schemes in Hong Kong – Some Background

It is important to note that there had been a much smaller scale, but rather unpopular, Expatriate English Language Teacher Scheme (or 'the pilot EELT scheme') put in place in 1987. A rather inconclusive, somewhat secretive, report on the scheme by the British Council – who also trained the teachers involved – glossed over the abject failure of that scheme. Mark Hopkins (2006: 281) observed that 'the EMB [Education and Manpower Bureau], having failed to prepare the ground beforehand, then attempted to bury the results of the trial afterwards in the form of an interim report which was never made public'. Boyle provides us with several reasons why the scheme was not popular and goes so far as to say (1997b: 178) that: 'the Expatriate English Teachers Scheme was one of the more obvious examples of linguistic imperialism in the story of English in Hong Kong'. Twenty-two expat teachers, from a total of 75, left Hong Kong within two years of arriving, and only 41 schools signed onto this initial scheme. By 1990, 50% of the schools wanted to quit (Hong Kong Government Legislative Council, 1997a). Yet, rather surprisingly, in September 1991, a modified Permanent English Language Teacher Scheme (PELT) was launched, without British Council involvement and with a slightly higher rate of interest rate shown by Hong Kong secondary schools – almost 100 signed on this time (*ibid.*).

Unfortunately, the old problems re-emerged. Principals found administrative problems dealing with foreigners; local staff resented the supposedly 'superior' native language speakers – all recruited from the UK. The scheme was accused of 'following a British-is-best policy' (Boyle, 1997a: 27). The recruited teachers found difficulties adjusting to Hong Kong life, and, more than this, they were not financially better off – the exchange rate between the UK and Hong Kong was not to their advantage.

The objective for both of these earlier expatriate teacher schemes was the 'enhancing' of students' English language achievements. That was also the rationale for the next scheme born into Hong Kong: the 1996 project to employ, 'under local terms of service', Native English language speakers 'to improve the English language proficiency of students' (Hong Kong Government Legislative Council, 1996b). This was all rather vague and all flying in the face of the apparent lack of success experienced by the earlier schemes.

Even the third, 1996 scheme, could be counted as a failure if we quote from the reflections of the very instigators of the scheme themselves – the Hong Kong government:

> There was considerable difficulty in recruiting qualified language teachers... 25 out of the 37 participating schools had withdrawn from the scheme. (Hong Kong Government Legislative Council, 1996b)

> Our intention was to recruit 100 NETs. However the scheme received lukewarm response and we managed to employ only 12 and 37 teachers in 1996–97 and 1997–98 respectively. (Hong Kong Government Legislative Council, 1997a)

Again, poor remuneration plus administrative problems were listed as two reasons for this third scheme's lack of success. This time, only 33 out of 360 schools signed on to have expatriate teachers (Boyle, 1997a).

Boyle (1997a: 24) sums up the similarly vague rationale for this 1996 scheme and the surprising decision to continue with it, given the obvious and self-admitted lack of success with earlier schemes:

> With a history of such limited success for the EETS, it came as a surprise when in late 1995 the Education Commission issued a Draft Report (Hong Kong Government Education Commission, 1995) which blandly stated: 'The Commission notes that the Expatriate English language Teachers Scheme has been useful in improving the learning of English in secondary schools'... All of this was quite unrealistic.

Oddly absent from each of these schemes was a clear *rationale* for their establishment. Even more odd was the addiction-like process of repeating them, without much apparent debate as to their worth and viability. We will concentrate in this chapter on the latest manifestation of these schemes, and, in so doing, we will see strong parallels between the earlier and the more recent NET programmes, as regards their 'real' rationale.

The 1998 Enhanced NET Scheme

It came as something of a surprise that in 1998 the Hong Kong government was to introduce a fourth incarnation of these dubious expatriate English teaching schemes. The Enhanced Native English-speaking Teacher (NET) Scheme was designed to place a 'native speaker' of English into every secondary school in the territory. This was followed by a similar scheme in primary schools in 2002–03. In both cases, a Special Allowance was to be payable to such NETs. Financially speaking, it was the most attractive employment package to date.

By 2010, there were over 900 such teachers in Hong Kong, working at a huge annual cost of millions of Hong Kong dollars, financially augmented by the introduction of a Retention Allowance in 2005 and an increase to the NET Special Allowance in 2008 and again in 2011. In the 2010–11 financial year, the Hong Kong dollar figures were nearly $645 million, according to replies to questions asked at the Legislative Council (LegCo) meeting held in March, 2011 (Hong Kong Government Legislative Council, 2011). Clearly, this project was costing the territory more and more financially, as the Enhanced Teacher Scheme became increasingly 'enhanced'.

It is clear that Hong Kong wants to keep these teachers in place and that it is prepared to pay for them, even in times of financial downturn, and even accepting inductees into the system with lower academic qualifications than when the scheme first began:

> As was reported in the local press, 39% of the NSTs [Native-Speaking Teachers, or primary NETs] recruited for the 2008–09 academic year were not qualified teachers… there is a certain irony in importing experts from overseas who lack training and experience with the reforms in their own countries. (Bryant, 2009: 8)

The rationales for the continued employment of such teachers continue to change, and new rationalisations for them also continue to appear. Bryant (2009: 1) speaks of the nostalgic 'idealised images' of NETs as expert language teachers from Hong Kong's teaching past, transported into more recent times. NETs are employed, despite their 'intended role and perceived competencies having shifted over time, leading to new rationales for maintaining and expanding [their] teaching' (*ibid*.: 1), regardless of their true competencies and their degree of impact on local teaching situations. Bryant writes of a perception that 'the more Westerners in the school, the better the English' (personal communication, 2010). Somehow, the 'native-speaker' is seen as better – the best – in the minds of the Hong Kong public and, in particular, in the perception of the city's parents.

Why is there such an apparent *addiction* to 'native English-speaking' teachers? Why did the government even feel the need to set up such schemes? Why does it continue to run them? What was to be the role of these teachers? How were they going to fit into the existing education system? Why is English seen as so important to Hong Kong? The responses to these questions are so closely related, that responses to one will entail a response to the others. The ever-continuing NET schemes and the actions of other English-language agencies in Hong Kong are nothing less than accomplices in hegemony.

Answers

To attempt to answer these questions, we have searched through the Education and Manpower (Education Department) and Legislative Council (LegCo) and its Finance Committee mandates, minutes, publications, papers, publicity statements, policies and dictates from well before, inclusive of, and beyond 1998. We have conducted internet searches, library research, held discussions with former and present NETs and local staff in schools, read magazines, journals and transcripts of speeches, books and more books, and there are no easy answers.

The legislative origins of these schemes are truly clouded in mystery. These schemes seem to just appear without much apparent legislative debate/decision. They just arise out of the bureaucracy like a genie. Just like the perceived 'need' for housemaids in Hong Kong, there is no questioning the territory's apparent requirement for outside hired help. We have had to do considerable detective work to unravel the deeper reasons for the existence of such NET programmes. From all our research, there appears to be no clearly delineated, official policy from the educational administration as to *why* the Enhanced NET Scheme came into being in 1998, itself the more expensive expansion of the earlier 1996 hiring of expatriate native English teachers on 'locally equivalent' conditions. There is some evidence from the 7 May 1997 LegCo records that many Hong Kong Cantonese-speaking legislators were actually quite hostile about the introduction of the 1998 Enhanced Scheme (Hong Kong Government Legislative Council, 1997b). All the dissenting voices at that time were very articulate, and this provides us with direct evidence that 'there never had been an overwhelming demand for expatriate teachers' (Boyle, 1997a: 25).

So the locus of support for such schemes became even less clear to us. An *Information Paper* on the recruitment of NETs from the Education and Manpower Bureau (Hong Kong Government Legislative Council, 1996a) quotes from the Education Commission Report No. 6 (Hong Kong Government Education Commission, 1995) and noted that this 1995 report recommended:

> … that secondary schools be encouraged to employ, on local terms of service, more native English speakers qualified to teach English language. The aim is to improve the English language proficiency of students. As a result the Government introduced the Native-speaking English Teacher (NET) scheme this year.

This desire to 'improve English language standards' is a hallmark of Hong Kong policymakers' discourse for the need to employ NETs. It is very closely allied to the all-too-frequent, but unfounded, claim that 'English language standards are declining'. These twin beliefs have a great deal to account for in the continuation of expatriate teacher schemes.

English as a Tool of Commerce?

It has mainly been the business community, which has kept pushing an agenda of 'improving English standards' and the perceived need to maintain Hong Kong as an important hub of commercial transactions via an English-language capability, that has kept the ball rolling. P.K. Choi (2003: 683, 686) forcefully states that this linkage always was, and still remains, a 'myth'. According to him:

> ... fluency in English is crucial for the maintenance of Hong Kong's position in international commerce. This utilitarian perspective that privileges English learning above all else is actively promoted by businesses, which played a major role in constructing the relevant discourse and shaping the policy itself... foreign business interests and certain academic discourses supported the government's English-dominated policies... by furnishing rhetoric that legitimized the subordination of all educational goals to the dominant goal of mastering a foreign language.

While government advisor, C.K. Lau, points out that:

> ... complaints about the poor English skills of Hong Kong Chinese are as old as the city's history... In fact there is evidence that English standards have risen rather than fallen since universal secondary education was introduced 30 years ago. (Lau, 2009)

Lau clarifies his stance by noting that there are far more tertiary students nowadays and that the perceived decline in standards is only evident because more people speak some form of English than ever before. Thirty years ago, nearly 90% of today's students would not have been in the tertiary sector. In the year of Hong Kong's reversion to Chinese rule, Edinburgh University Professor J.E. Joseph (1997: 64) declared that '... the myth of declining English in Hong Kong is a type of linguistic snobbery'. This mythology of declining standards of English and the perceived need to 'improve' them continues to prevail today, as Hong Kong endeavours to maintain its place in a globalised commercial environment.

Let us now dig deeper.

Further Amorphousness

Our own perusal of the Education Commission's *ER6 Report* from 1995 (Hong Kong Government Education Commission, 1995: 17) reveals that it never actually addressed the hiring of NETs per se, but glossed over the issue by recommending that the Education Department 'work out details for the native-speaker scheme... with a view to appointing some of these teachers in the new school term of September, 1996'. This self-same report had earlier pointed out that 'many local teachers and school heads had reservations about the cost-effectiveness of expatriate teachers' (ibid.: 3). Only a comment on the *Item for Finance Committee* papers (Hong Kong Government Legislative Council, 1997a) attempted to provide a rationale for the scheme:

We have to take positive measures to enhance the English language proficiency of students in order to maintain the competitiveness of Hong Kong as an international trade and finance centre... [to] introduce a new Native-speaking English Teacher (NET) Scheme... with effect from the 1998/99 school year.

Somehow, proficiency in the English language had become directly associated with fiscal empowerment. In his annual Policy Address in 1997, Hong Kong's Chief Executive, C.H. Tung, added this strong additional strand to the prevailing and long-lasting discourse about the city's need for the English language:

Confidence and competence in the use of... English are essential if we are to maintain our competitive edge in the world ... To make an immediate impact on improving the English language standard of students, we will implement a new Native-speaking English Teachers Scheme... (C.H. Tung, Chief Executive's Policy Speech, 8 October 1997)

More glib and vague official statements followed as the years went by.

The various NET schemes at work in the last decades of the 20th century would all seem to have been initiated without sufficient foresight, detailed planning or an educational rationale. 'Overambitious' is how Boyle (1997a: 28) described the earlier EELTS scheme, and this word seems equally applicable to the 1998 Enhanced Scheme. Herbert and Wu (2009) note that 'there is often surprisingly little rationale behind the decision to import native speakers'. They quote personal correspondence from Peter Storey – one of the government-appointed evaluators of the NET scheme – in 2008: 'In my experience, theoretical underpinnings are noticeably lacking in justifications for NET schemes, at least as proposed by governments'. In fact, the Storey (2001) official review of the secondary NET scheme (*Monitoring and Evaluation of the Native-speaking English Teaching Scheme* or *MENETS*) stated: 'official statements of the objectives of the NET scheme are characteristically terse and tend to take the benefits of employing native language speakers as understood'. This report later outlined three roles that the NETs would fulfil in their enhancing of the teaching of English. These were:

(1) to be language resource persons;
(2) to assist in school-based teacher development; and
(3) to help to foster an enabling environment for students to speak English.

Again, all rather vague.

The 'Real' Reason For NET Schemes

In the disappointing dearth of sources, there is one, quite revealing, notation from David Mennier, a NET himself and the founding President of NESTA (the Native English-Speaking Teachers Association). In 2000, he suggested the following as a palpably more likely rationale for the implementation of the scheme in 1998:

> But first, some background information. The Enhanced NET scheme was developed as a solution to a very pressing problem in Hong Kong: decreasing standards of English among secondary students. This situation was exacerbated by the recent change to Chinese Medium of Instruction (CMI) at many schools. The Education Department found itself under pressure to satisfy the demands from parents and students for quality English language education. The solution: place a native-speaking English teacher (NET) in as many secondary schools as possible.

In retrospect, it would now seem that the current, increasingly costly Enhanced NET Scheme ultimately came into being in 1998 for reasons beyond the alleged (and politically correct) educational rationale of assuaging the need to improve declining English language abilities. It would seem to have been specifically implemented for reasons *other than* to upgrade Hong Kong's business communication skills and bolster Hong Kong's role as a crucible for global business and finance, thus necessitating a sizeable English-speaking workforce. All these purported rationales are too simple. It was far more likely that the 1997–98 implementation of CMI (Chinese Medium of Instruction) led directly to the employment of NETs. In an effort to placate the parents, potential employers and the pupils themselves, English was to be a *neocolonial buffer*. It was to be neocolonial compensation for, or a balance to, the new CMI policy (Lai, 1999b).

If one really digs deeply into the mass of records from the Legislative Council, one can find a solitary, brief comment reinforcing the true agenda for NETS – '...the recruitment of native-speaking teachers could... alleviate resistance from schools and parents to the use of mother-tongue teaching' (Hong Kong Government Legislative Council, 1997c). Bryant (2010, personal communication) adds the observation that 'the association of NETs with elite English education is why the [Enhanced] NET Scheme provided a panacea in response to fears of the Medium of Instruction (MOI) policy shift in 1997–8'. The strong parallel here to the continued desire for the earlier EET Scheme is emphasized by Boyle (1997a: 17): '...the idea of the [1997] scheme was to encourage schools to switch from English-medium of instruction to Chinese-medium of instruction. Schools which made this switch would get two extra expatriate teachers of English'. Later, he wrote: 'Hong Kong parents still wanted English-medium schools for their children' (*ibid.*: 23).

There was, indeed, a tremendous uproar over the switch to a Cantonese mother-tongue medium of instruction in 1997–98. Some parents and pupils were reduced to tears by the news that their school had become 'downgraded' from an EMI (English Medium of Instruction) to a CMI (Chinese Medium of Instruction) school. An interviewee told Elaine Chan (2002: 276) that 'I was proud when I wore my school uniform before, but now I can't even hold my head up when I walk in the streets'. Chan observed that 'it had become a matter of... dishonour, of... shame' (*ibid.*: 277) for a student to attend a school that denied its students the English language as a medium of instruction.

Ironically, then, the territory's laudable post-colonial thrust of turning to CMI as the viable and widespread medium of secondary school instruction – after the British 'handover' of their former territory to the People's Republic of China in 1997 – *also* led to the full-scale orchestration of schemes for English language 'experts', the NETs. How ironic. Here was Britain returning a territory to China some 100 years after it had 'confiscated' the land to 'punish' China for the 1840 Opium War, in which China had dared to attack the opium-laden British ships. Ironically then, 'it could therefore be argued that the major beneficiary of official policy to promote Chinese-medium in the past may have been English rather than Chinese' (Benson, 1997: 13).

In actual fact, the need for Cantonese as a medium of instruction (MOI) had long been suggested by British 'experts' in a series of reports ever since Stewart (the first headmaster of Central School) had recommended it in the 1860s (Tsui *et al.,* 1999). This idea was further promoted by Burney in the 1930s and Llewellyn in the 1980s, all because the quality of teaching everything in English back then had not been satisfactory, let alone completely in that tongue. Indeed *mixed-code teaching* in, and of, the English language, even in supposedly EMI (English Medium of Instruction) schools, has long been the order of the day. While the textbooks may have been in English, the classrooms were largely operating in Cantonese.

To see why there was such fury when CMI was legislated in 1998, we need to go further back in time to also see just how the English language governess has managed to exert her ongoing and powerful influence.

The Superiority of English – a Brief History of English Language Education in Hong Kong

Britain's 'first duty' in the empire was to 'impose the language of England upon the British colonies', and thereby 'imitate the ancient Government of Rome'.
W.E Forster, progenitor of the British 1870 Education Act, cited in Evans, 2008b: 55

Britain certainly did prioritize the English language when it colonized Hong Kong, especially late in the 19th century, even though initially there was vacillation between vernacular- and English-language media of instruction. This emphasis on English was seen as deliberate by Alastair Pennycook, while Evans (2006) writes that the British administration gradually shied away from vernacular education and stressed English-language education from the 1880s onwards, largely due to the influence of Governor Hennessey, who himself stated, '...we should have here an English-speaking community' (cited in Pennycook, 1996: 143). Several government schools were set up, and then the Anglo-Chinese (or EMI, actually, code-mixed) schools began. Vernacular education was left to private schools, mission schools and mainland Chinese benefactors and was seen as a poorer option, not only financially, but also scholastically. Cheng *et al.* (1973: 19) note:

> ...from 1901 to 1913, the average number of pupils in Government and Grant schools receiving instruction through English increased by 60%, while the corresponding increase for vernacular schools was only 10%.

In 1914, Edward Irving, the first Director of Education in Hong Kong, commented:

> Since Chinese is so difficult a language that it is only studied by Government Officials, Missionaries and Sikh policemen – English must be the general medium of communication. Thus at the very outset we are committed to the establishment of English Schools for the Chinese, not as a moral obligation, but as a commercial necessity. (cited in Sweeting, 1990: 341)

The English language governess, thus, was engaged to teach the Cantonese colonials. Stern and headstrong, she ruled the schools with an imperious but correct demeanor and gave a definite air of social superiority, despite her own, illegitimate origins.

What, in fact, seems to have been the case is that there was never a concrete mandate, but rather, a marked lack of clear policy direction and a concomitant expectation by all parties that English must be taught, especially at secondary school level, despite a complete lack of infrastructure. Like the governesses in England, there was no official qualification, and governesses were appointed through a network of personal recommendations. This soft, yet persuasive, 'arm-twisting' – as initiated by the British administration – was also a message to everyone else – install the English language as the prime teaching medium. Employers kept up the pressure, and parents also saw that English-language education was, apparently, the avenue to employment, tertiary education and lifelong 'success'. A specific example of the colonial administration's unwillingness to assert itself can be seen in 1974 when a White Paper on secondary education suggested that Cantonese become the medium of instruction. Such was the public furor this caused that English became even more in demand. The White Paper was watered down:

> to the anodyne suggestion that language policy should be the responsibility of the independent schools. This served as authorization for schools to follow practices approved by the 'market' (i.e. most of the parents). Thus, the trend towards increasing numbers of enrolments in schools that were at least ostensibly English-medium... was, if anything, reinforced. (Sweeting & Vickers, 2007: 28)

English Language for the Elite Only

The British administration had never demanded a switch to Cantonese before 1997. They had merely recommended it on occasions and had noted, consistently, that mixed-code teaching was pedagogically unsatisfactory, whilst deliberately enabling an elite indigenous population to learn English. Angel Lin observed (1996: 55) that access to English was never open to the majority of students – those at the lower end of the socio-economic scale. She writes that:

> English constitutes the dominant, if not exclusive, symbolic resource and the prerequisite for individuals aspiring to gain a share of the socioeconomic, material resources enjoyed by a small elite group... only the children of the elite can become members of the elite.

It is important to note that despite the supposed availability of English-language education prior to the handover (in reality, predominantly taught as code-switched anyway), few students – far less than even the arbitrary 30% deemed worthy of English language education after 1998 – were competent enough in the English language anyway, and the swing to CMI only further exacerbated this situation. Just who were those who had sufficient English-language fluency? Sun responded (2002: 297): '...the [mother-tongue] policy effectively preserves the colonial structure in which the most talented elite, who could... speak English well, were heavily rewarded'.

Law Wing-san (2009: 51–54) writes about what he calls 'collaborative colonialism'. He sees this as beginning during the early British take-over in the 1800s, when the desire for English language was a deliberate, class-focused partnership between a small, local Chinese elite and the colonial British government, who both designed to split themselves from the mainland Chinese masses, who were not able to access English. Law writes that:

the Other for the Hong Kong-based Chinese elite was the "mainland Chinese"; and the European contingent's *Other* was also the "mainland Chinese"... two privileged communities... shared the same... very "English" sympathies and ideas... the English language remained an indiscernible set of sounds and scribbles for Hong Kong's wider Chinese community.

Rather than unifying Hong Kong, the English language had worked to create a schism within it. The elite Hong Kong Chinese clique 'increasingly came to see that proficiency in English opened up the prospect of social and economic mobility in the colonial milieu' (Evans, 2008b: 51). Indeed, Stewart had noted, as early as 1865, that for this particular group, 'English [was] being converted to dollars' (*ibid.*: 51).

The Enhanced NET Scheme, then, can be seen as part of a perpetuation of the enabling of a small but powerful, self-maintaining, English-speaking force of administrators and politicians. As Hong Kong's financial power grew, English-language education not only became more desirable in the eyes of many locals, it also became more difficult and costly to obtain. As the 1997 hand-over approached, it was widely seen as politically correct to 'return to CMI'. This was a convenient 'out' for the British, who were no longer – on the surface, at least – going to be in control of Hong Kong's language policies. A.Y.K. Poon wrote (1999: 59) that 'it was a political move: a gesture to appease China'.

Amy Tsui (2004: 108) observed that:

There was no illusion that colonial rule would extend beyond 1997... The new MOI policy was very much part of the plan for the retreat... the challenge of implementing a highly sensitive and emotionally charged policy would be faced by the Hong Kong SAR Government, rather than the colonial government.

By 1997, the way was clear to reconstruct Hong Kong as a Chinese city, and, therefore, mandatory CMI in schools (except for a minority) was seen as an obvious route to follow. It is now obvious, however, that the policy was delineated pre-handover and that this MOI regulation was, 'in reality, an elitist language policy. In terms of linguistic imperialism, this was the first time in Hong Kong's history that compulsion in the matters of language was used' (Tang, 2006: 31). Linguistic imperialism, of course, does not always lie in the hands of the colonizing power – the baton can, and often is, passed on to the pre-trained and indoctrinated 'subalterns', who can now lord it over the rest of the populace. Thus, the English language governess became a Chinese person with a British accent.

After the 1998 MOI announcement, only 114, or approximately one-fifth, of the over 500 Hong Kong secondary schools were permitted to remain as EMI schools. Needless to say, all were members of the so-called Band One, or top level of schools, whose intake represented the top 20% of performers in an end-of-primary examination (akin to the British 11-Plus).

Thus, the clamour by parents for EMI, as opposed to CMI, schools. There is no question that EMI academic standards are perceived as higher than CMI and not necessarily because they offer better instruction. Most (if not all) EMI schools are self-selected, i.e. students apply to get in. Few (if any) of the CMI schools are self-selected, i.e. students go to whatever CMI school is in their district: they are there by default. There is both the social 'superiority' and the probable educational 'superiority' of EMI schools. 'The elite are determined to be in a system that practices elitism and encourages elitism' (Chue, personal communication, 2010), even if they are not English-speaking, or fans of British culture and even if there are no longer O and A level examinations within any of these schools, although there is a growing number of Direct Subsidy EMI Schools which have incorporated the UK's IGCSE curricula.

In addition to this, there is the entire government-subsidised, yet private, English Schools Foundation (ESF) system, which cannot be fully explored in the confines of this chapter. Suffice it to say that such schools serve as elitist English medium-of-instruction sites for parents who are wealthy and/or desperate enough to enrol their children there. Hong Kong is one of only a few places in the world that permits local children to go to 'international-type' schools such as these ESF institutions – people would almost kill to get into ESF. They pay 'trainers' to get their kids in. They try to wangle the entrance tests out of teachers.

English Language and NETs as Hegemonic Imposition – the Long Rope of 'Passive' British Linguistic Imperialism

We now can see why there was – in 1997–98 – a neo-colonial, *political demand* that there be English language education (and not CMI) from the very people – parents, pupils, etc. – who were being, ostensibly, anyway, decolonized. Our theory is that the British (and much later on, the Americans) were rather crafty. They had contrived to build up here – and elsewhere in their vast Empire – a global business centre that was, and continues to be, dependent on English as the only palpable *via media*, and they had taught the local populace to believe that English was the key to its economic future. As Lai (1999b: 221) puts it:

...it is still impossible for Hong Kong to abandon English totally as the language of the colonizer... a weakened English ability would be a disadvantage in surviving in the Western context that the British have firmly established for the city.

While Joseph Boyle (2004: 77, 80) observed:

> ...linguistic imperialism of the *classic, colonial, cleverly manipulative kind* [our emphasis] has existed in Hong Kong for almost a century... In terms of linguistic imperialism, it does seem that the EET and NET schemes are open to this accusation.

Britain had, therefore, cemented into place a clever discourse of the need for their abiding language in the relatively short time that they maintained Hong Kong as a colony. Despite their rather *laissez-faire* attitudes to the enforcement, or otherwise, of both their own and the vernacular language in Hong Kong, they had firmly established in the minds of the local populace that the English language was the be-all and end-all if one was to climb up the social ladder, given the fact that they also ensured that only some would ever have access to this 'golden fleece' of English.

> Both English and vernacular languages were used to promote particular forms of colonial governance... language education policies were constantly designed to maintain the inequitable social conditions of Hong Kong... Coupled with the development of a highly inegalitarian society with English as the decisive distributor of possible social and economic advancement... *the colonial decision-makers in Hong Kong can be seen to have far more responsibility for the state of affairs than they admit.* (Pennycook, 1998a: 126, 200)

The British also made certain that the English language was enshrined as an official language in the Basic Law (Article 9). The UK and the local, often UK-educated, elite, then, had successfully brainwashed the Hong Kong people well before 1997, in a society that was deliberately constructed by those with the most to gain. This mindset further ensured that most NETs (though by no means all) were also employed from the UK or from its quasi-cultural dominions, such as Canada, Australia and New Zealand. Indeed, in the first (the non-enhanced) version of the scheme, NETs were only employable if they *were* British citizens. They were not certified by either their teaching experience or by their competence in English, merely by their passports. Even today, one can see that the majority of NETs are Caucasian: there is a smattering of West Indians and teachers from the subcontinent, and we have met one lady from the Philippines. Eoyang (2000: 73) declares 'such a policy is ultimately racist and resuscitates old colonial prejudices and anti-colonialist resentments'. Even today, NETs are not tested either on their ability to teach or their command over English, but on their 'plausibility' as English speakers. Perfectly fluent speakers of English, such as Malaysians, Filipinos, West Indians, Pakistanis, Indians or Africans from Nigeria or South Africa, are rarely hired as NETs.

We wonder just how many overseas applicants are disqualified from even being considered, merely because their names do not 'sound English'. Kachru (2005: 245) cites cases of Hong Kong secondary schools apparently wanting 'a genuine Englishman to be our NET' and not wanting '… a dark-faced man, because [he] would scare our pupils' (ibid.: 245). Amazing, but this is a current example of the supremacist mythology of 'native speakers' and not only, of course, in Hong Kong.

The English language regimen has thus clearly and deliberately mythologized its own necessity. Discussions of 'linguistic imperialism', however, need to distinguish between the learning of English as a *replacement* for a native vernacular and the learning of English as a *complement* to the native vernacular: the first certainly smacks of linguistic triumphalism, the second, however, should be welcomed as a helpful educational step towards operational bilinguality. In this way, then, the NET schemes:

> …are 'quick fix' solutions to a systematic problem which had never been addressed, namely, how to maintain or even improve levels of student attainment in English, while enforcing a segregation between schools according to their MOI… It is tempting to see this costly appeal to outside expertise… [as] a further example of Pennycook's 'colonial continuities', particularly the… use of the term 'native-speaker'. (Hopkins, 2006: 283)

Hopkins (ibid.: 283) further believes that the NET schemes were only ever going to maintain the *status quo*, whereby 'those students with higher social capital [the top 20–30%]… enjoy greater opportunities for exposure to English'. So, who misses out most? Not only the other 70% in CMI schools, but also their parents and, as importantly, the local teachers of English, who are seen as somehow inferior and who manifestly resent this denigration.

More Strands of the Rope of Linguistic Imperialism

Before 1997, there was also the presence of an orderly British bureaucracy under which the rule of law and free-market commerce flourished, further separating Hong Kong from China in the minds of many of its inhabitants who had fled from the threat of communism to Hong Kong after 1949 and who wanted not only security, but – just as significantly – to be seen as different from the mainland Chinese. Chan (2002: 272–273) points out that:

> at the level of individual Hong Kongers, the English language has become both cultural and symbolic capital and, at the communal level, knowledge of English distinguishes Hong Kongers from their counterparts in the PRC… the English language has become a linguistic *habitus* for the people of Hong Kong.

Given that many will never attain English language competence, even if they pay their way into English-medium schools, this is true.

Tsui (2007: 130) states that this perceived mainland/Hong Kong divergence was a deliberate construction of 'the mainland Other' by administrative forces. She writes: 'immigrants from China... were stereotypically caricatured in the media as backward, ignorant, ill-mannered migrants who could not speak English'. Little wonder, then:

> the community's apprehension about losing the international flavour and competitive edge of Hong Kong because of reunification with China resulted in stronger than ever demands for more English and more English education. (ibid.: 138)

The 1997 hand-over thus accelerated a CMI policy at the same time as it quickened the Hong Kong Chinese population's perceived need for more English – all because of their fear of a potential mainland Chinese diminishment of the language. Here was yet another impetus to firmly establish the various NET schemes, even though, as Lai (1999b: 192, 222) also notes, 'there was in fact little positive evidence from the preceding expatriate teachers' scheme to support such a quick expansion of the [1996] NET scheme and... there has never been any evidence to show that a programme of this kind is effective in Hong Kong schools'.

There have been three expensive, 'specialist' studies of the NET schemes, culminating in Griffin's 2009 *Evaluation of the Enhanced NET in Hong Kong Secondary Schools*, and there have also been consistent LegCo reviews – the latest of which (in 2010) maintains its efficacy. Yet Griffin himself even stated, in 2006, that there had been 'patchy gains' from the NET scheme, '...whether this was a sufficient return on the considerable investment is not known. More than 600 million dollars is a vast sum to invest in language development', where the gains are dubious, and the benefits anecdotal (Herbert & Wu, 2009).

Self-Colonization in Post-Colonial Hong Kong

There is an abiding Orientalism at play here, regarding the employment of NETs (Said, 1978). The belief of the Hong Kong administration, and the population at large, is that externally sourced, often solely monolingual, well-paid 'foreigners', who are seen and heard to utilize something called 'native English' – whatever this might be – are the most desirable and expert exponents of English-language teaching and diction. In fact, this is a form of hyper- or neo-Orientalism. Edward Said initially criticised the colonial British regime for its latent and manifest equating of Caucasian English speakers as the *summum bonum* of, not only the teaching of English per se, but also of social rank. The English spoken by English 'natives' was equated with knowledge/power and dominant discourse (Foucault, 1968), whilst the 'passive Orientals' were necessarily '"inferior"/alien/the Other/"docile bodies"/"passive"/"imitative memorizers"' (Pennycook, 1996; 1998b and 2002b). In Said's view (1978: 4–5), 'the Orient' is merely a convenient construct to maintain Western stratagems and, thus, hegemony: 'the Occident itself is not just there either… such locales, regions, geographical sectors as "Orient" and "Occident" are just man-made'.

In Hong Kong, it would seem, then, that the very people Said endeavoured to emancipate – namely the people of the East/the Other – still maintain a creed of their own Orient, something which does not exist. Aspects of the very regime that Said critiqued are held in the highest regard by the very administration and society most suppressed by it, and so staunch is the adherence to this discourse, that they ratiocinate after the event. Thus this penchant for 'standard' English, RP (received pronunciation) and the Enhanced NET scheme. The locals continue to empower those agencies which promulgate the English language, even paying lavishly to implement their policies. A local Hong Kong teacher, Jane Lung, wrote, in 1999, that 'the special treatment of NETs appears to reflect Hong Kong's deference to the British image and its aura of success'. This goes, then, well beyond English as the route toward global capitalist meritocracy and is a *kowtow* of obeisance to the sheer power of the English-American hegemonic language game, which propels this very meritocracy and penalizes those without 'correct', or any, competency in English (Lyotard, 1984; Phillipson, 2008). In fact, *status value over functionality* in English language ability all too often seems to be the driving force for many Hong Kong residents, particularly the aspiring middle-class. According to Boyle (1997b: 177) '… those with English quickly felt a sense of superiority over others… the social prestige of the English language made it a highly desirable commodity'.

What is important here is the pragmatism of Hong Kong parents (David Li, 2001). Cynically, many do perceive, and are not especially happy about, this English language succubus in their society, but they will bear it as they attempt to ensure 'progress' for their children and, concomitantly, themselves. This is the almost schizophrenic love-hate relationship with the English language in Hong Kong. It could be depicted as the masses doing 'linguistic somersaults' to move towards a promised heaven, not happily, but amazingly stoically, given that over 95% do not speak English at home or anywhere else. As David Li (2001) points out, many view English language acquisition as similar to imbibing, not on opium after all, but on ginseng – bitter but necessary and, perhaps, 'enabling'. Hong Kong has mixed feelings about its English language governess: she inspires very little affection, but she commands a great deal of respect.

Hobson's Choice

David Li, whilst claiming that Hong Kong people deliberately wish to learn this 'standardized' form of English as opposed to resisting it, still feels that people *have a choice*. We do not feel that they have such, because its potent internationally based agents, and even local intellectuals, ensure its universalized sustainability, promulgation and domination, and because of what the language intrinsically is. Most Cantonese speakers are very reluctant speakers of English, yet most would concede the supposed social importance of knowing the language. Li claims this is a conscious and deliberate decision by individuals and not an imposed form of linguistic imperialism (2001). We, however, feel that they have no real choice, only 'Hobson's Choice'.

Hong Kong people self-regiment themselves – this is hegemony at work. Gramsci's (1971) *domination by consent* continues, given that more recently there is also the swagger of American transglobal corporations pushing an empiric agenda of English language as critical for globalization, thus further exacerbating the situation and further restricting the language choice of Hong Kongers. Why is there *no* systematic resistance to English language hegemony? Angel Lin (1996: 78) has an insight into this 'self-subordination' by Hong Kong citizens:

> Our justification and acceptance of, or acquiescence to, the subordination of all educational goals to the single dominant goal of learning English for its presumed importance to our economy is merely a reflection of a deeper and greater subordination: the total subordination of ourselves to commercialism.

Hong Kong residents resent having to learn a language they have no affinity for at all, yet feel they are obliged to take on, so as to best survive. What we have, then, is the illogic of a Cantonese preference for an English they cannot speak. This is a form of neocolonial aberration.

For the majority, predominantly Cantonese-speaking population, the English language is never really internalized, for it is never intrinsically wanted, especially by those least equipped to attain competency in it. English in Hong Kong remains a minority language: it is here, but it isn't.

Further Conflicts Within the NET Schemes, Further Conflicts Within English – Who are the 'Native Speakers'?

In Hong Kong, the concept of 'native speaker' is, too often, mistakenly equated with nationality. Paikeday (1985) believes that it is silly to even make a distinction between native and non-native speakers. To him, the concept is fatuous. Rampton (1990: 98) wrote that the 'supremacy of the native speaker keeps the UK and the US at the centre of ELT'. Medgyes has also noted (1994) that these so-called native speakers of a language are not necessarily superior to non-native speakers. While Eoyang (1997: 8) declares: 'I would insist that being native to a language does not automatically qualify one to be an effective language teacher'.

There are many more problems with the Hong Kong NET schemes, which are beyond the scope of this chapter to detail, but which include the sheer lack of consistency of roles which NETs play from school to school; the cost-effectiveness of such schemes; and, especially, the attrition rate of NETs. Any NET scheme will remain a mere add-on: expensive, frustrating and, probably, totally unnecessary. It is almost as if the schemes have taken on a life of their own – a sort of perpetual motion behemoth, with an inside imprimatur who will protect them, whatever happens. Conspiracy theorists would have a field day here. Consider, for example, the following quite reasonable questions from Hong Kong legislators:

> ... Madame President, as far as I understand it, the NET Scheme is not that successful in some of the schools. I would like to ask the Secretary: If the school considers that the Scheme is not so much of a success, can the Administration allow flexibility for the school to use the resources concerned to recruit local English teachers to improve student's English language proficiency? (Mr Yeung Yiu-Chung, Hong Kong Government Legislative Council, 15 March, 2000)

> ... in view of the Government's budgetary constraints and the reduction in teaching posts, [my question is] whether the authorities will consider redeploying the funding for employing NETs to providing training for local teachers and increasing teaching posts...? (Mr Abraham Shek, Hong Kong Government Legislative Council, 10 December, 2003)

Both statements went unanswered. The NET implementation policy had already been decided. Interestingly enough, back in 1997, LegCo member Andrew Wong had suggested that the employment of expatriates would be 'a violation of Article 103 of the Basic Law, which states that privileged treatment for foreign nationals should be abolished' (Hong Kong Government Legislative Council, 17 October, 1997c). He also asked the question, 'Why do we not give local people a chance first if they are the right people?' He, too, was ignored.

Kirkpatrick (2007) has pleaded for a complete overhaul of the Enhanced NET Scheme. He holds that there is no need for such teachers in Hong Kong, in the sense that it is not necessary to develop native-like competence in English here:

Rather than focusing on so-called native speakers of English, it would make more sense to employ suitably trained Asian multilingual speakers of English... The current message implicitly provided to children is that you have to be a 'native speaker' – and a white one at that – in order to speak English 'properly'... local teachers... are, in fact, the ideal linguistic role models for their children in today's world. (Letter to *The South China Morning Post*, June 2 2007)

We concur with him – indeed, what is wrong with employing qualified non-native teachers of the language? Why is there an insistence on 'native speakers', some of whom are not even qualified to teach? We would go even further and question the need to demand this 'standard' form of English for many residents in Hong Kong at all. However, we are mindful of the conundrum that local people seemingly do not want anything but their 'idealized' English and the NETs to provide it. Any reform in the NET scheme will have to educate Hong Kong parents as to the value of English, not merely as a class distinction.

The myth of 'true' or 'standardized' English as vital continues to perpetuate itself under the tutelage of its English language governess, typified by the NET schemes.

Are the English Language and NET Schemes Here to Stay?

There is, clearly, a bittersweet regard for the English language governess in Hong Kong, what Pennycook (1994: 21) called 'a deep sense of ambivalence'. Yet, conversely, 'English is clearly regarded as indispensable and inalienable in Hong Kong' (Schneider, 2007: 139). It is even possible that the popularity of English might have increased since the 1997 hand-over, despite everything noted above about ambivalent public attitudes and the low-frequency use of the medium (DPA, 2008). The secondary Enhanced NET Scheme and its younger sibling – the Primary NET scheme – can be seen as integral components of an English language 'Trojan horse' of huge significance (Cooke, 1988).

In inculcating itself into Hong Kong society, the external and internal agents of the English language have ensured its own continuation and potency, albeit in variegated forms. Take, as one further example, the hugely profitable business of publishing consumable English-language textbooks and workbooks. These publications serve to continue the insidious process of promoting the English language as somehow better than other languages. There is also the patient and expensive slog toward IELTS and TOEFL examination achievement by so many of our former pupils, well after their schooling has ended. Professor Arthur Li, in 2003, in his then role of Official Secretary for Education and Manpower, announced that 'the University

Grants Committee has recently adopted the International English Language Testing System (IELTS) as a common English proficiency assessment'. The supreme irony here is that, in so many cases, it is Hong Kong Chinese paying tremendous amounts to be enabled in the English language, in an endeavour to achieve fiscal security, yet it is the gatekeepers of the English language – generally, not Hong Kong Chinese, not even living in Hong Kong – who make the most money from their ownership of English language – via such examinations – from examination fees, enrolments and tuition.

In 2009, Education Secretary, Michael Suen, advocated a modification to the Cantonese as Medium of Instruction (MOI) policy to allow for even more English MOI in the SAR's secondary schools. This was a political move that was received very favourably by many schools and parents and which, in September, 2010, came to fruition as many schools prepared to 'revert' to EMI under this 'fine-tuning' policy, at least in part. 'The move is to respond to parents' clamorous demands for more English teaching' (Yau, 2009). Yet, it also seems highly likely that what will happen is merely a reversion to the pre-1998 situation and the complications and confusions that will ensue in yet another turnaround in Hong Kong's MOI policies: here, the Hong Kong government has essentially abandoned its policy of CMI.

So much for the claim in the 2001 Report on the NET Scheme (Storey, 2001) that 'the NET scheme is a short-to mid-term measure'. It does not appear likely to vanish just yet. The English language governess still strides indomitably in the schools of Hong Kong schools: she still has a formidable presence. Perhaps the NETs are her nephews. Will they ever leave? Sweeting and Vickers (2007: 35) don't think so, especially because 'the recent rush to learn English on the Chinese mainland… makes any further challenge to the status of English within the local education system highly improbable'.

A more enlightened language policy would place less of an emphasis on monolingual, Western-sourced NETs and, hopefully, a reduction in the huge monetary outlay involved in their hire. The recognition that hiring 'native speakers' as NETs is as prejudicial and as misguided as the earlier insistence that English was a content course that any primary or middle school teacher could teach. If there are to be NETs in Hong Kong, the programme should be broadened to include those who are not native speakers, but have a far more intrinsic appreciation of the errors made by Cantonese speakers. It could be renamed as an EEP or English Enhancement Programme, for example.

Therefore, at the very least, those NETs who are here in Hong Kong would be well advised to take heed of what Searle wrote in 1983 about them being agents of the English language. He recommends that they:

> … grasp that same language and give it a new content, to de-colonise its words, to de-mystify its meaning… to rip out its class assumptions, its racism and appalling degradation of women, to make it truly common, to recreate it as a weapon for the freedom and understanding of our people. (Searle, 1983: 68)

We cannot see the English language governess packing her bags at any time in the immediate future. She is too well ensconced and too well looked after to ever leave her comfortable Hong Kong house on the hill.

References

Benson, P. (1997) Language rights and the medium-of-instruction issue in Hong Kong. *Hong Kong Journal of Applied Linguistics* 2 (2), 1–21.

Boyle, J. (1997a) Native-speaker teachers of English in Hong Kong. *Language and Education* 11 (1), 38–54.

Boyle, J. (1997b) Imperialism and the English language in Hong Kong. *Journal of Multilingual and Multicultural Development* 18 (3), 169–181.

Boyle, J. (2004) Linguistic imperialism and the history of English language teaching in Hong Kong. In K. Tam and T. Weiss (eds) *English and Globalization: Perspectives from Hong Kong and Mainland China* (pp. 65–84). Hong Kong: The Chinese University of Hong Kong Press.

Bryant, D. (2009) Revisiting native-speaking teachers of English in Hong Kong. Paper presented at the 3rd HAAL Research Forum, 12 December, Hong Kong.

Bryant, D. (2010) Personal email correspondence.

Chan, E. (2002) Beyond pedagogy: Language and identity in post-colonial Hong Kong. *British Journal of Sociology of Education* 23 (2), 271–285.

Cheng N.L., Shek, K.C., Tse K.K. and Wong S.L. (1973) *At What Cost? Instruction through the English Medium in Hong Kong Schools*. Hong Kong: privately printed pamphlet.

Choi, P.K. (2003) The best students will learn English: Ultra-utilitarianism and linguistic imperialism in education in post-1997 Hong Kong. *Education Policy* 18 (6), 673–694.

Chue, R. (2010) Personal email correspondence.

Cooke, D. (1988) Ties that constrict: English as a Trojan horse. In A. Cumming, A. Gagne and J. Dawson (eds) *Awareness: Proceedings of the 1987 TESL Ontario Conference*, (pp. 56–62). Toronto: TESL Onfaris.

DPA. (2008) English trumps Chinese as top business language in Hong Kong. Online article, accessed 12 November, 2009. http://www.topnews.in/english-trumps-chinese-as-top-business-language-hong-kong-288737

Eoyang, E. (1997) English as the world's language. *Occasional Paper Series No. 1*. Hong Kong: Centre for Literature and Translation, Lingnan College.

Eoyang, E. (2000) From the imperial to the empirical: Teaching English in Hong Kong. In P. Franklin (ed.) *Profession 2000* (pp. 62–74). New York, NY: The Modern Language Association of America.

Evans, S. (2008a) The making of a colonial school: A study of language policies and practices in nineteenth-century Hong Kong. *Language and Education* 22 (6), 345–362.

Evans, S. (2008b) Disputes and deliberations over language policy: The case of early colonial Hong Kong. *Language Policy* 17, 47–65.

Foucault, M. (1968) *The Archaelogy of Knowledge* (A. Sheridan, trans.). New York, NY: Pantheon.

Government HK. Chapter One: General Principles. In *Basic Law of the Hong Kong Special Administrative Region of the People's Republic of China*. Online document, accessed 14 November, 2009. http://www.basiclaw.gov.hk/en/basiclawtext/chapter_1.html

Gramsci, A. (1971) Selections from the Prison Notebooks, Q. Hoare and G. Nowell-Smith (eds) New York, NY: International Publishers.

Herbert, P. and Wu, C.H. (2009) Cultural diversity in the classroom: Shortcomings and successes of English co-teaching programs in East Asia. Online article, accessed 6 November, 2009. http://zif.spz.tu-darmstadt.de/jg-14-1/beitrag/Herbert_Wu.htm

Hong Kong Government Education Commission (1995) *Education Commission Report No. 6.* Hong Kong: Government Press.

Hong Kong Government Legislative Council (1986) Legislative Council Brief. In *Employment of Expatriate Teachers of English in Secondary Schools.* Online document, accessed 15 August, 2010. http://www.LegCogov.hk/general/english/library/search_records_collection.htm

Hong Kong Government Legislative Council (1996a) *Recruitment Under the Native-speaking English Teacher Scheme.* Online information paper, accessed October 18. http://www.LegCogov.hk/yr96-97/english/panels/ed/papers/ed1810-7.htm

Hong Kong Government Legislative Council (1996b) Minutes of the Panel on Education, 18 October. Online at http://www.LegCogov.hk/yr96-97/English/panels/ed/minutes/ed181096.htm

Hong Kong Government Legislative Council (1997a) Finance Committee Paper, *FRC* 21 November (97–98), 63. Online at http://ww.LegCogov.hk/yr97-98/englishfc/fc/papers/fc211163.htm

Hong Kong Government Legislative Council (1997b) Minutes for 7 May 1997. Online at http://localhost/Teaching http//:www.LegCogov.hk:yr96-97:english:lc_sitg:hansard:97050:fe.doc.

Hong Kong Government Legislative Council (1997c) Minutes of the Panel on Education, 17 October, 4. Online at http://www.LegCohk/yr97-98/english/panels/ed/minutes/ed171097.hym

Hong Kong Government Legislative Council (2000) Official Record of Proceedings, 15 March. Online at http://www.LegCogov.hk/yr99-00/english/counmtg/hansard/000315fe.pdf

Hong Kong Government Legislative Council (2003) Official record of Proceedings, 10 December. Online at http://www.LegCogov.hk/yr03-04/chinese/counmtg/floor/cm1210ti-confirm-c.pdf

Hong Kong Government Legislative Council (2007) Review of the native-speaking English teacher scheme. Updated background brief prepared by the Legislative Council Secretariat, papers CB (2) 1545/06-07 (03) and (04) in LC Paper No. CB (2) 1782/06-07. Online at www.LegCogov.hk

Hong Kong Government Legislative Council (2011) Replies to initial written questions raised by Finance Committee members in examining the Estimates of Expenditure in 2011-2012: EDB8009. Online document, accessed 9 September, 2011. Online at http://www.LegCogov.hk/yr10-11/english/fc/fc/w_q/edb-e.pdf

Hopkins, M. (2006) Policies without planning?: The medium of instruction issue in Hong Kong. *Language and Education* 20 (4), 270–286.

Joseph, J.E. (1997) English in Hong Kong: Emergence and decline. In S. Wright and H. Kelly-Holmes (eds) *One Country, Two Systems, Three Languages: Changing Language Use in Hong Kong* (pp. 60–73). Clevedon: Multilingual Matters.

Kachru, B. (2005) *Asian Englishes: Beyond the Canon.* Hong Kong: Hong Kong University Press.

Kirkpatrick, A. (2007) Multilingual teachers would better meet needs of NETS scheme. *South China Morning Post* (Education Post) 2 June, 2.

Lai, M.L. (1999b) Jet and net: A comparison of native-speaking English teachers schemes in Japan and Hong Kong. *Language, Culture and Curriculum* 12 (3), 215–228.

Lau, C.K. (2009) Hong Kong's English teaching conundrum. Hong Kong Journal (Summer). Online article, accessed 17 August, 2010. www.hkjournal.org/archive/2009_summer/3.htm

Law, W.S. (2009) *Collaborative Colonial Power: The Making of the Hong Kong Chinese.* Hong Kong: Hong Kong University Press.

Li, A.K.C. (2003) Promoting the use of English. Speech in Hong Kong's Legislative Council, 22 January. Transcript online at http://www.edb.gov.hk/index.aspx?nodeID=135&langno=1&UID=9100

Li D.C.S. (2001) Hong Kong parents' preference for English-medium education: Passive victims of imperialism or active agents of pragmatism?. In A. Kirkpatrick (ed.) *Englishes in Asia: Communication, Identity, Power & Education* (pp. 29–62). Melbourne: Language Australia Ltd.

Lin, A.M.Y. (1996) Bilingualism or linguistic segregation?: Symbolic domination, resistance and code-switching in Hong Kong schools. *Linguistics and Education* 8, 49–84.

Lung, J. (1999) A local teacher views the native English teacher scheme in Hong Kong. *TESOL Matters* 9 (3), 8. Online at http://www.tesol.org/s_tesol/sec_document.asp?CID=196&DID=806

Lyotard, J. (1984) *The Postmodern Condition: A Report on Knowledge*. Manchester: Manchester University Press.

Medgyes, P. (1994) *The Non-Native Teacher*. London: MacMillan.

Mennier, D. (2000) Teachers helping teachers: The NET support group. Online article, accessed 8 July, 2008. http://www.teslhk.org.hk/PreGen/TESLV00045211.asp?ID=5211&PaperID=0041

Paikeday, T.M. (1985) *The Native Speaker is Dead*. Toronto: Paikeday Publishing Inc.

Pennycook, A. (1994) Beyond (f)utilitarianism: English as academic purpose. *Hong Kong Papers in Linguistics and Language Teaching* 17, 13–23.

Pennycook, A. (1996) Language policy as cultural politics: The double-edged sword of language education in colonial Malaya and Hong Kong. *Discourse Studies in the Cultural Politics of Education* 17 (2), 133–152.

Pennycook, A. (1998a) Hong Kong and the cultural constructs of colonialism. In B. Asker (ed.) *Teaching Language and Culture: Building Hong Kong on Education* (pp. 131–151). Hong Kong: Addison, Wesley, Longman.

Pennycook, A. (1998b) *English and the Discourses of Colonialism*. London and New York: Routledge.

Pennycook, A. (1999) Development, culture and language: Ethical concerns in a postcolonial world. Online article, accessed 25 June, 2008. http://www.languages.ait.ac.th/hanoi_proceedings/hanoi1994.htm

Pennycook, A. (2002a) Mother tongues, governmentality, and protectionism. *International Journal of the Sociology of Language* 154, 11–28.

Pennycook, A. (2002b) Language policy and docile bodies: Hong Kong and governmentality. In J.W. Tollefson (ed.) *Language Policies in Education* (pp. 91–110). Hillside, NJ: Laurence Erlbaum Associates.

Phillipson, R. (1992) *Linguistic Imperialism*. Oxford: Oxford University Press.

Phillipson, R. (2008) The linguistic imperialism of neoliberal empire. *Critical Inquiry in Language Studies* 5 (1), 1–43.

Poon, A.Y.K. (1999) Chinese medium instruction policy and its impact on English learning in post-1997 Hong Kong. *International Journal of Bilingual Education and Bilingualism* 2 (2), 131–146.

Rampton, M.B.H. (1990) Displacing the native speaker: Expertise, affiliation, and inheritance. *ELT Journal Volume* 44 (2), 97–101.

Said, E. (1978) *Orientalism*. New York, NY: Pantheon.

Schneider, E. (2007) *Postcolonial English Varieties Around the World*. Cambridge: Cambridge University Press.

Searle, C. (1983) A common language. *Race and Class* 25 (2), 65–74.

Storey, P. (2001) *Monitoring and Evaluation of the Native-Speaking English Teaching Scheme (MENETS): Technical Report*. Hong Kong: HKIED. Online at http://ebook.lib.hku.hk/HKG/B35850796.pdf

Sun, C.F. (2002) Hong Kong's language policy in the postcolonial age: Social justice and globalization. In M.K. Chan and A.Y. So (eds) *Crisis and Transformation in China's Hong Kong* (pp. 283–306). Hong Kong: Hong Kong University Press.

Sweeting, A. (1990) *Education in Hong Kong Pre-1841 to 1941: Fact & Opinion.* Hong Kong: Hong Kong University Press.

Sweeting, A. and Vickers, E. (2007) Language and the history of colonial education: The case of Hong Kong. *Modern Asian Studies* 41 (1), 1–40.

Tang, W. (2006) Linguistic imperialism in medium of instruction policies in pre and post 1997 Hong Kong. Thesis, Bryn Mawr University. Online at www.brynmawr.edu/eastasian/pdf/Tang.pdf

Tsui A.B.M. (2004) Medium of instruction in Hong Kong: One country, two systems, whose language?. In J.W. Tollefson and A.B.M. Tsui *Medium of Instruction Policies, Which Agenda? Whose Agenda?* (pp. 97–106). Hillside, NJ: Laurence Erlbaum Associates.

Tsui, A.B.M. (2007) Language policy and the social construction of identity: The case of Hong Kong. In A.B.M. Tsui and J.W. Tollefson (eds) *Language Policy, Culture, and Identity in Asian Contexts* (pp. 1–21). Hillside, NJ: Lawrence Erlbaum Associates, Inc.

Tsui, A.B.M., Shum M.S.K, Wong, C.K., Tse, S.K. and Ki, W.W. (1999) Which agenda?: Medium of instruction policy in post-1997 Hong Kong. *Language, Culture and Curriculum* 12 (3), 196–214.

Tung C.H. (1997) Chief Executive's Policy Speech, 8 October. Online transcript, accessed 26 June, 2006. www.ssrc.hku.hk/sym/98/sarce.html

Yau, E. (2009) Fine-tuning gives English a boost as teaching medium. *South China Morning Post*, 23 November. Online at http://archive.scmp.com/results.php

9 English Language as Auntie: Of 'Good Intentions' and a Pedagogy of Possibilities – ELT in the Philippines and its Effects on Children's Literacy Development

Lalaine F. Yanilla Aquino

'The Road to Hell is Paved with Good Intentions'

I could not help thinking of the above saying as I listened to my friend – a Filipino college professor, whose first language is English. She was doing volunteer work, and their group was trying to teach urban poor Filipino preschool children in Metro Manila how to read in English. My friend complained that the children were not engaged in any of the activities at all. They had been teaching the children for weeks, but the little ones did not seem to be making any progress, even if the teachers were already making things 'fun' by having the children recite English rhymes, sing English songs and listen to children's stories in English. She insisted that, as they were children who lived in Metro Manila (the National Capital Region of the country), they must have had some exposure to English. These children would have heard English on radio and television and seen it on billboards and printed advertisements. I can understand my friend's frustration – she and her group of volunteers had the best of intentions, but the urban poor Filipino children did not respond well to their English literacy instruction.

Such frustration is echoed by a great many teachers, parents and even politicians, who, like my friend, have nothing but 'good intentions' in teaching Filipino children basic concepts and skills *primarily* in English. These 'good intentions', however, have so far not been able to solve two of the major problems of Philippine education today:

(1) the dismal performance of Filipino elementary and high school students in the 2009 National Achievement Test, in which they obtained a mean percentage score of only 66.3% (Tubeza, 2009); and

(2) the high drop-out rate: with only 66 out of 100 Grade 1 pupils being able to finish Grade 6. (Muzones & de Jesus, 2009)

The 'good intentions', the frustrations and the problems of Philippine education are recurring themes in the more than 100 years of English language teaching (ELT) in the country. Unfortunately, this vicious cycle has had adverse effects on the cognitive, affective and literacy development of the supposed beneficiaries of these 'good intentions', namely, the Filipino children. Though both foreign and local studies show the advantages of using the child's first language (L1) in literacy instruction, the language policy-makers in the Philippines (and many teachers and Filipino parents as well) still insist on primarily using English, which is a second language (L2) for most Filipinos. The lack of correspondence between what research results suggest, and what Philippine language policy-makers and some educators insist on implementing, is one of the reasons why ELT in the country is problematic. The frustration of my friend shows that the problem is found, not only at the macro-level (the level of language policy-making and language planning), but also at the micro-level (the level of individual instruction and teacher/parent preference in terms of which language/s to use for beginning literacy instruction).

ELT in the Philippines: English as 'Dear Auntie'

The history of English in the Philippines can be likened to a visit by a 'Dear Auntie' – someone who is related to the family, not by blood, but by affinity. 'Auntie' is a term of address often used by Filipinos for an older female friend or acquaintance as a sign of respect. In the case of ELT, Auntie (i.e. English) comes for a visit, supposedly to help the family. She then opts to prolong her visit and meddles with family affairs. Some members of the family may believe that Auntie's intentions are good and that she has something valuable to offer them, while other members may doubt not only her intentions, but also the value of the help she can give.

The English language came to the Philippines with the American sailors of Admiral John Dewey, who figured in the 'Mock Battle of Manila Bay' in 1898, when the United States declared war on Spain, supposedly to free Cuba from Spanish tyranny (Bautista & Gonzales, 2006; Best, 1998; Gonzales & Alberca, 1978). While there is some historical agreement as to when the English language arrived here, there is much political and philosophical disagreement as to why she opted to stay and become an official language and the main medium of instruction (MOI) in Philippine schools. It has been a political issue from the start, because English was (and, in a way, still is) the language of the colonial masters. It has always been a social issue, because English has defined (and still defines) social roles and social status in Philippine society. Constantino (1982: 7) puts it most succinctly: 'English became the wedge that separated the Filipinos from their past', and it went on to separate the school-educated Filipinos from the Filipino masses.

In 1898, the American government claimed that its only intention in the Philippines was 'to make war on the Spanish and that [their] becoming the *de facto* colonial administrators of the Philippines was merely an accident of war' (Best, 1998: 3). As *de facto* colonial administrators, the Americans had the 'good intentions' of teaching the new colonials the principles of democracy, good citizenship and self-governance. In almost the same way that the Americans became the *de facto* colonial administrators, the English language became the *de facto* instructional medium in public schools. This was because the people were deemed to need a common medium of communication – a language that would unite the country's disparate ethnicities (Sibayan, 1999b; Tupas, 2002). Thus, this unrelated 'Auntie' stayed on.

According to Gonzales (2002: 107):

English was transplanted by the American colonial government into the Philippines with the first schools established by Chaplain W.D. McKinnon as early as 1898 and with the public school system constituted by the Organic Act of 1901.

Transplantation implies that the language has somehow been indigenized and even 'owned' by the colonized. However, there is more to the mere 'transplanting' and indigenization of English during the early years of American colonization. There was also the violent 'weeding out' of local species by the killing-off of nationalist fervor and the suppression of the emerging self-identity of the people and the nation. Thumboo (2006: 406) explains how this happened:

Like all centers of power, languages tend to perpetuate themselves, projecting a practical and intellectual assertiveness, which is seen at its most potent in the development of colonialism/imperialism. When colonies are formed, it is not merely peoples confronting each other: their cultures and their languages are involved, with the more powerful suppressing the lesser.

It is obvious that there are two opposing views regarding the value of English language teaching in the Philippines. On the one hand, there is the prevalent belief that the introduction of the public school system (and, consequently, that of English) is evidence of the purely benevolent intentions of the USA.

On the other hand, there is a belief that such an education 'served to attract the people to the new masters, and at the same time to dilute their nationalism which had just succeeded in overthrowing foreign power [the Spanish]' (Constantino, 1982: 33). The former view, according to Constantino, is a result of the miseducation of the Filipinos regarding their own history. He sees a need to re-educate the people, to help them become aware of history's omissions and falsities. Ty-Casper (2005: 224–225) describes what she feels the American occupation was really all about:

> ... history taught that [the] American occupation of the Philippines was for our own good: America brought civilization and prosperity, eradicated diseases, taught the lessons of democracy. The cost to us – official history will not admit. Colonialism interrupts the development of indigenous institutions, erases the colonial's past to impose a new consciousness and identity compatible with and acceptable to the colonial power.

Re-educating the Filipino people will certainly be no mean feat, because, for one, the very people who could be instrumental in this re-education are probably, themselves, in need of a paradigm shift. One argument that has been given by the colonial masters as to why English should be used as the sole instructional medium was to unite a culturally and linguistically diverse country like the Philippines. According to Tupas (2002: 144), the insinuation that linguistic diversity is a 'problem' that can be solved by using English as an MOI is 'a recurring assumption in many educational works, consequently paving the way for an unqualified and uncritical acceptance of English in the schools'. Such a view often resulted in 'rationalizing the support for colonial languages, and concomitant economic interests, at the expense of indigenous languages and local economic development' (Ricento, 2006: 13–14).

Unfortunately, even though the history of Filipino-American relations through the decades has shown many not-so-benevolent reasons as to why the Americans colonized the Philippines, some Filipinos still believe the benevolent view. Sadly, the same Filipinos also believe that English is indeed the appropriate medium of instruction, since it had already become 'the "language of aspiration"'... the language used for aspiring to the so-called better life, both social and economic' (Sibayan, 2001: 206). The Philippine Autonomy Act of 1916 stated that no person should be an elected member of the Senate of the Philippines 'who is not able to read and write either the Spanish or English language' (Sibayan, 1999a: 38). Thus, anyone aspiring to be a senator at that time would have had to learn to be literate in a colonial language.

The deeply ingrained belief in the importance of learning English and using it as an MOI shows how successful the colonial masters were in (mis-) educating the Filipinos. English was used as MOI in the schools up until 1938. The use of local languages 'was not allowed in schools', and 'pupils were not permitted to speak their local language on the school premises' (Sibayan, 1999a: 5), 'in some cases on pain of punishment' (Sibayan, 1999b: 45). Despite this, only about 27% of the total population (16 million at that time) was listed as speaking English in the 1939 Census (Gonzales & Alberca, 1978). In 1934, the Philippine Commonwealth and Independence Act clearly stated in Section 2.8 that 'provision shall be made for the establishment and maintenance of an adequate system of public school, *primarily conducted in the English language*' (emphasis added) (Philippine Independence Act, 1934, n.p.).

There was no longer a need for the Americans to oversee Philippine education, however, 'because a captive generation had already come of age, thinking and acting like little Americans'; thus, 'in exchange for a smattering of English, [Filipinos] have yielded [their] souls' (Constantino, 1982: 4.) So, by the time that the Commonwealth government was established in 1935, it was already clear that 'Auntie' absolutely meant to stay and that she was meddling with family affairs. Her presence in the family was strongly felt and markedly divisive. Significantly, this American Auntie is still determined to keep on dominating (Phillipson, 2008).

The National Language Controversy

The 1934 Constitutional Convention approved by voice vote the formation of a national language 'based on the native languages', but the committee on style (the committee that wrote the final draft of the Constitution) changed it to 'based on one of the existing native languages' (Saulo, 1975, in Sibayan, 1999c: 135). The politicians who were biased in favour of Tagalog (one of the major Philippine languages and the native language of the Commonwealth President) and the committee on style that made the change, 'did not foresee that their action was not to be forgotten and was to cause disunity later' (Sibayan, 1999c: 136).

The 1935 Philippine Constitution, Article XIV, Section 3 states that 'The Congress shall take steps toward the development and adoption of a common national language based on one of the existing native languages. Until otherwise provided by law, English and Spanish shall continue as official languages'. With this provision, 'the hegemony of the colonial languages, English and Spanish, in what was to be an independent state, was virtually ensured' (Maceda, 2003: 101). Thus, in one stroke of the pen, that particular section of the 1935 Constitution compromised the chance of a native language becoming acceptable as a symbol of unity and identity and rendered the languages of the colonial masters as languages of aspiration and social status. The notion of a truly national language was already in trouble.

In 1936, the National Language Institute (NLI) was tasked with 'the study of Philippine dialects in general for the purpose of evolving and adopting a common national language based *on one of the existing native tongues*' (emphasis added) (Rubrico, 1998, n.p.). The NLI recommended Tagalog as the basis of the Philippine National Language (PNL). In 1940, summer courses were held to enable the national language to be taught as a subject in fourth-year high school and in teacher training colleges, beginning in 1941 (Gonzales *et al.*, 2000). The PNL had no name at that time (it was simply called the *national language*), and it was taught as a subject. It was not used as a medium of instruction.

In 1946, when the Philippines became a republic, the Tagalog-based PNL became one of the official languages of the Philippines, in accordance with the Commonwealth Act 570 (Sibayan, 1999b). Such a status was important, because as one of the official languages of the country, the PNL was recognized as a language for government transactions, rules and regulations, the law, the courts and legislation. The PNL was given further recognition when the country's leaders designated a specific time for celebrating it. This was on March 26, 1946 when President Osmeña issued Proclamation No. 35 designating March 27-April 2 as 'Linggo ng Wika' (Language Week) and on January 15, 1997 when President Ramos issued Proclamation No. 1041, declaring August as *'Buwan ng Wika'*(Language Month) (Buwan ng Wika, 2009). Yet there is something hypocritical about the Filipino children celebrating the week or month of the PNL, because for the rest of the school year, many of them are penalized and fined every time they use the language of their home or even the PNL in the 'English zones' of their schools. In primary school, we were made to pay five centavos for every Tagalog utterance we made in class, even though it was the first language (L1) for most children in my school. My own children have gone through the same experience in their primary and high schools. This was the reason why I had to pay more than three hundred pesos (roughly 5 EUR or 7 USD) in 'fines' before my eldest son could graduate from primary school, because he had kept on speaking Filipino in class (the students' *lingua franca* in his school).

In 1957, the Board of National Education (BNE) decided:

(1) that the MOI in the first two grades of the elementary school shall be the *local vernacular*;
(2) that the PNL shall be taught informally, beginning in Grade 1, and given emphasis as a subject in the higher grades;
(3) that English shall be taught as a subject in Grades 1 and 2 and used as MOI beginning in Grade 3 (Espiritu, 2001: n.p.).

In 1959, the Department of Education called the Tagalog-based national language, *Pilipino*. As Sibayan (1999c: 142) notes, 'for more than 21 years, the national language had no name and was simply called "the national language"'. It was neither the national law-making body nor the president of the Philippines that gave the national language its name, Pilipino. It was Jose C. Romero, who was the Secretary of Education in 1959.

From Pilipino to Filipino

While Pilipino was gradually gaining ground as a national language, with more Filipinos becoming conversant in it, arguments against it continued. During the 1971 Constitutional Convention, which revised the 1935 Philippine Constitution, the language issue was one of the heated subjects (Perdon, 2003). As completed, Article XV, Section 3.2 of the 1973 Philippine Constitution states, 'The National Assembly shall take steps towards the development and formal adoption of a common national language to be known as *Filipino*', and Section 3.3 states, 'Until otherwise provided by law, English and Pilipino shall be the official languages'. According to Sibayan (1999c), Section 3.2 is a rejection of the Tagalog-based Pilipino as the PNL. Following the ratification of the Philippine Constitution in 1973, the Board of National Education introduced a bilingual approach to teaching: Pilipino was to be used as the MOI in subjects like the social sciences, the practical arts and physical education, while English was retained as the MOI for mathematics and the sciences. Pilipino was also adopted as the MOI for Rizal (an important subject on the life and works of national hero, Jose Rizal) and for history subjects in colleges and universities (Rubrico, 1998). Thus, 'before Pilipino was rejected as a national language, it was taught only as a subject in all schools; after its rejection, it was made MOI from Grade One to university' (Sibayan, 1999c: 139). All very ironic.

But how did the change from Pilipino to Filipino happen? In a discussion paper, Maceda (2003: 103) provides some insight into this:

> As early as the 1960s... the national language was already being viewed as a means of empowering the masses. But it is significant to point out that during this period of militancy and activism, people were already starting to redefine the national language in terms of the everyday language spoken in the streets and factories and the medium used in popular cultural materials, not the national language as developed by the INL and taught in schools. Linguists from the University of the Philippines differentiated this from the school-taught Pilipino by calling the language Filipino. Filipino was a national lingua franca, which naturally evolved in populated centers across the country out of the need by members of different ethno-linguistic groups to communicate to one another. The language was made up of elements common to most Philippine languages or what linguists Ernesto Constantino and Consuelo J. Paz called the "universal nucleus".

The 1973 Philippine Constitution, in effect, accepted the distinction between Pilipino and Filipino; yet, it viewed Filipino as a language that had yet to be developed before it could be adopted as the 'common national language'. Maceda (2003), however, asserted that Filipino was already a *de facto* national *lingua franca*. *Filipino*, therefore, is different from *Pilipino*. Constantino (2000: n.p.) tries to clarify the distinction between the two:

> It [is] apparent that Pilipino was also Tagalog in concept and structure and there was no Pilipino language before 1959. Also, there was no Filipino language before 1973. Pilipino is different from Filipino even though both became national languages because these are different concepts – one was based on only one language and the other on many languages in the Philippines, including English and Spanish.

Compared to Pilipino, Filipino has more phonemes, it has a different system of orthography, it manifests a heavy borrowing from English and it has a different grammatical construction. Based on studies in the Philippines, Filipino is favoured as a symbol of unity and linguistic identity by most Filipinos (except Cebuanos), but it is not necessarily favoured as the exclusive MOI in schools. So, in this tangled way, a bilingual schooling scheme has gradually been accepted (Gonzales *et al.*, 2000).

The Bilingual Education Policy of 1987

It is the Bilingual Education Policy (BEP) of 1987 that is followed today in Philippine schools. This policy keeps most of the important provisions of the BEP from 1974. It specifies the use of the 'vernacular' as the instructional medium for initial schooling and literacy – that is, regional languages can be used as auxiliary languages for Grades 1 and 2. It also specifies the separate use of Filipino and English as MOI in basic education for definite subject areas. The goals of the BEP also include the propagation of Filipino as a language of literacy, the development of Filipino as a linguistic symbol of national unity and identity, and the cultivation and elaboration of Filipino as a language of scholarly discourse (i.e. its continuing intellectualization), and the maintenance of English as an international language for the Philippines and as a non-exclusive language of science and technology.

At this point, it is important to emphasize two things. Even though the Bilingual Education Policy of 1987 specifies the use of the vernacular as the medium for initial schooling and literacy, this is not, in reality, implemented. Secondly, even though there has always been recognition of the importance of the L1, or the local community's language (or even the PNL), in teaching basic concepts and skills, such recognition has not always been enough to solve many on-going language-related problems (e.g. what language to use in initial literacy instruction).

Across the history of ELT in the Philippines, and in the history of the PNL as well, there have been many common themes: a lack of political will; a lack of good instructional materials (including storybooks) in the vernacular languages; a lack of competent teachers who can teach the PNL in non-Tagalog regions; a lack of teacher training in using the vernacular for instruction (because it is not enough to be a native speaker of a language to be able to use it in effective teaching or to teach it as a language); a lack of a favourable attitude toward the PNL in some provinces (like Cebu); limited opportunities to use the PNL outside the classroom setting; a lack of a standardized register of Filipino for use in the classroom; the pessimism of educators and policy-makers as to how far Filipino can be cultivated as an MOI for mathematics and science, among many other things (Gonzales, 2001; Sibayan, 1999b).

Political To-and-Fro

These language-related problems are yet to be resolved. It does not help that the language for use in instruction is a hot political issue among Filipinos (particularly politicians and business people), and the arguments and controversies regarding this seem to go on ad infinitum. For instance, in 1990, a Congressional Commission was created to survey Philippine education. It recommended the use of Filipino as the language of instruction at all levels by the year 2000. This recommendation has not been acted upon by Congress because of strong opposition from various sectors. In 1991, the Republic Act 7104 established the 'Komisyon sa Wikang Filipino' (Commission on Filipino Language) – the main task of which was to cultivate Filipino as a language of academic discourse.

In January 2003, President Macapagal-Arroyo ordered the Department of Education to restore English as the primary MOI to reverse the decline of English literacy. In 2004, House Bill (HB)1563 was filed in Congress, seeking to make Filipino the sole MOI in all schools at all levels. In 2005, Executive Order 210 established the policy to strengthen the use of English as a second language by using English starting from Grade 3, using Filipino only in teaching Filipino and Social Studies and English in teaching all other subjects, and HB 4701 was filed, seeking to use English as the sole MOI from preschool to college. In January 2009, two opposing and controversial bills were hotly discussed in Congress: HB 3719, which proposed that students from preschool-Grade 6 be taught in their L1, and HB 5619, which proposed that English be used in all academic subjects from Grades 4–6 and in all levels of high school (Sponsors, 2009).

One biting editorial criticized HB 5619 and described the bill's 'English myopia' as hegemonic, because it overlooked scientific evidence showing L1 to be the best MOI. It concluded that 'no science or reason propels the campaign for the reinstitution of English as the instruction language in our schools – except for that uniquely Filipino science – *hiya* or loss of face, the reverse of which is another uniquely Filipino science – *yabang* or conceit' (King's English, 2009: A10). According to the same editorial, the proponents who want to make English the sole MOI had considerations that 'hardly have anything to do with hastening learning or the absorption of lessons by our students', but rather, 'have more to do with their distaste of the Tagalog-based Filipino and their resistance to Manila imperialism'. The same strident editorial likewise identified a 'hidden agenda' behind HB 5619:

> [The proponents] also want English proficiency because of the global scheme of things, such as the decided advantage of Filipino manpower abroad due to their English know-how and the relative prestige accorded to nations that speak English. But since Filipinos get the lower end of skills in global manpower, what level of English proficiency should they really have? To be sure, many Filipino maids abroad can speak English even better than their masters.

A Department of Education Order (No. 74, issued on 14 July 2009) institutionalized a policy of Mother-Tongue-based Multilingual Education (MTB MLE), which supplanted the 35-year-old BEP (Llaneta, 2010). MTB MLE involves the use of more than two languages for literacy and instruction as a fundamental policy and programme in the whole stretch of formal education, including preschool. The implementation of the MTB MLE in June 2011 was in line with the Aquino administration's thrust, which is 'Every Child A Reader by 2015'. Just the same, in April 2011, a bill was busily being filed in Congress to make English the MOI in elementary and high school (Cebu Lawmaker, 2011).

It is clear that law-makers and policy-makers see English as a ticket to a better socio-economic status. The jobs that pay well – abroad or in the Philippines – almost always require good speaking, listening, reading and writing skills in English. The controversy regarding ELT in the Philippines and the MOI, therefore, has often been reduced to socio-economic considerations. Yet, it is evident that there is a need to improve Filipinos' literacy skills in both their L1 and in English if they are to improve their lives in general.

Either way, dear Auntie English has found herself a permanent place to stay in our country.

Filipino Children's Literacy Development in L1 and in English

Those who promote using English as the primary MOI seem to forget that before Filipino children can become 'economic pawns' who will someday be wage earners that will keep the Philippine economy afloat, they are, first of all, individuals with cognitive, affective and aesthetic needs. If these adults are to make informed decisions that will truly benefit the Filipino children, they need to listen to what local research results suggest regarding the relationship between MOI and the cognitive and literacy development of children.

The results of studies on the relationship between MOI and cognitive/literacy skills have three main findings:

(1) instruction in L1 facilitates the acquisition of cognitive and literacy skills;
(2) L1 learning has positive effects on L2 learning; and
(3) the skills learned in L1 are transferred to L2 (cross-linguistic transfer).

Measures should therefore be adopted to help youngsters develop critical thinking and learn literacy in their L1 before they are instructed in English. In other words, a nation that intends to make its citizens true bilinguals and biliterates must, necessarily, invest in their learners' first languages. Teaching Filipino children critical thinking and literacy in their L1 will certainly help to facilitate their later learning of English (Skutnabb-Kangas, 2006).

That L1 should be used as the initial language of instruction is supported by several local research findings. The effective and successful use of Hiligaynon as a medium of instruction in Iloilo from 1948 to 1957 by Education Superintendent Jose V. Aguilar became the basis of the policy on the use of the vernacular as the MOI in the first two grades of the elementary school with English as a subject (Sibayan, 199b). Ocampo (1991) found that urban, poor children who underwent a three-month early-reading programme, which had L1 (Filipino) as its MOI, exhibited significant gains in more areas of early literacy than a control group which had both L1 (Filipino) and L2 (English) as MOI.

In a similar study, Yanilla Aquino (2005) investigated the effects of the MOI on the acquisition of literacy skills of urban, poor preschool children and found that those instructed only in their L1 (Filipino) performed better in both L1 and L2 (English) literacy tests than those instructed only in L2 and those instructed in both L1 and L2. The results suggest that there was cross-linguistic transfer of literacy skills from L1 to L2.

Other local studies have highlighted the close relationship between L1 and L2 learning. Laudiano (2006) found that among Grade 1 learners, there was a cross-linguistic transfer of skills from L1 to L2. Combista (1995) found that there was a transfer of cognitive academic language proficiency (CALP) skills from L1 (Cebuano) to L2 (English) and that CALP in L1 could affect academic success in L2. In a similar study, Baetiong (2004) focused on the CALP of intermediate grade pupils and found that five years after students had started formal schooling, they scored almost twice as well in L1 as in L2.

Such results are a strong argument against introducing L2 too early in formal schooling; students should be given enough time to acquire their CALP in L1 before they are required to develop the same skills in an L2.

Introducing the L2 very early in formal schooling has its effects not only on the cognitive development of the children, but on their affective development as well. This can be seen in students' attitudes towards their own regional languages. Nical, Smolicz and Secombe (2004) found that students in Leyte had more positive attitudes to Filipino and English (both L2) than to their regional language (L1). Bautista (2001: 268) focused on students' attitudes toward Philippine English and found that the respondents experience the liberating effect of having one's own variety of English legitimized, but on the other hand, 'there is also the nagging thought that Philippine English is still not good enough – Philippine English is still equated with not hitting the standard of American English, and with being an inferior brand of English'.

Perhaps one of the best arguments for investing in L1 before introducing L2 is the First Language Component (FLC) in Lubuagan – an intervention carried out by the Department of Education and the Summer Institute of Linguistics-Philippines (de Jesus, 2007). Lubuagan schools teach Grades 1–3 pupils how to read and write in Kalinga (L1) and use Kalinga in the teaching of other subjects. By the end of Grade 3, most children can read and write in Kalinga, Filipino and English. In the 2006 national achievement test, Lubuagan District topped both the English and Filipino tests in the Division of Kalinga.

The Lubuagan teachers who provide individual instruction have shown that such an instructional method is available and that having children effectively learn literacy in both L1 and L2 is possible. Yet, the government policy-makers might argue that providing L1 instruction in a country of more than 150 languages will definitely be a 'financial nightmare'. In answer to this, de Jesus (2007) cited the example of Papua New Guinea (PNG) – a country that provides its children access to the first three years of education in 450 different indigenous languages. PNG officials reportedly maintain that the reduction in the financial and social costs associated with high drop-out and repetition rates have outweighed the expense of multiple sets of instructional materials.

A 'Pedagogy of Possibilities'

At the time of writing, there is a proposal to expand basic education in the Philippines from 10 to 12 years. A review of the published arguments (e.g. Luz, 2010; Faustino, 2010; Salazar, 2010) for or against this proposal shows that, even though the writers focused on the importance of providing Filipino students with a quality education, there was no mention of the specific language in which that quality education should be given. This focusing on 'quality education' without considering one of the major components of that education (the instructional medium) is symptomatic of the myopic, 'slash-and-burn' approach to solving the problems of Philippine education. Such approaches offer short-term solutions to major problems, but neglect all the inter-related issues.

If 'Dear Auntie's' detrimental and divisive influence on family affairs is to be checked – that is, if English is to be put in its proper place and used for the Filipinos' advantage and for the country's sustainable development, there has to be a recognition of its not-so-obvious and almost invisible influence on how Filipinos view themselves as a people, how they view their own mother tongues and how their perception of English influences the major decisions they make. Tupas (2002) asserts that if Filipinos are to create new relationships with English, they will first have to understand the socio-cognitive nature and historical rootedness of their views of English, of the way this language should be taught and learned and of the assumptions that Filipinos hold regarding its importance in the country. Aside from such understanding, there is also a need for Filipinos to realize that living in a multicultural and multilingual country is a gift and not a liability. It is important to learn critical thinking and literacy in one's own language if one wants to learn a second language, like English, with greater facility. It is actually possible to take on English without becoming less of a Filipino.

Such understanding and realization could happen if the country could promote a *pedagogy of possibilities* (Freire, 1998). According to Pennycook (2002: 235), 'language in sustainable development needs to be understood as both locally contingent and globally related, involving local participants in shaping their globally connected lives'. Development can mean two things: having more and being more. It is definitely good to have both kinds of development in one's country, but *having more* is rather limited, compared to *being more*. The former concerns itself with accumulating material goods and improving one's social and economic status, while the latter considers going beyond 'the obvious ends' and entertains the possibility of a better life, apart from the social and economic concerns. A pedagogy of possibilities would be a new way of looking at things such as the ultimate goals of education, the objectives of language and literacy instruction, the meaning of genuine learning, the nature of being a learner and the balancing act that is the learning of two or more languages. In using a pedagogy of possibilities, there is no need to kick 'dear Auntie' out of the family circle, because she can very well be a part of 'being more'.

At this point, it is important to cite the research of Ocampo *et al.* (2006) and the National Learning Strategies for Filipino and English, which their group has drawn up. They recommend that the country:

(1) implements a developmentally and culturally sound programming of language and literacy development in schools;

(2) creates better learning environments to support the language and literacy education of students; and

(3) enlivens critical social support-structures in the community to support learners in schools.

The first strategy emphasizes the need to acknowledge the importance of the children's experiences, the knowledge that they bring with them to school and the language with which they are able to share those experiences and knowledge. It also emphasizes the importance of providing our children with their first informal and formal learning experiences in the language with which they are most familiar. The second strategy emphasizes the need to provide a learning environment that is conducive to both language and literacy learning – such a learning environment includes providing competent teachers who know the children's L1, high quality and appropriate instructional materials in the children's mother tongue and the use of children's literature to support language and literacy development. The third strategy emphasizes the need to create a critical awareness among parents as to the effective language and literacy learning process (e.g. the need to invest in L1 oral language development and literacy learning) and the importance of having local government units and the community participating and providing support for the implementation of the language and literacy programming strategies.

Ocampo *et al.* (2006: ix) describe what the scenario would be like if these strategies were to be implemented:

> These national language and literacy strategies, and the reforms that must be implemented to put the strategies in action, will yield a scenario that is friendly to the child and the teacher and thus result in the child's effective and efficient development of English and Filipino language and literacy skills. In so doing, the child who comes out of secondary school will be able to apply his thinking, language and literacy abilities in all domains or registers of oral or written discourse – from communication to rhetoric, from scientific to cultural, from knowledge learning to aesthetic and thus he will be emancipated from mere literal understanding to critical and creative thinking, from being a frustrated language and literacy learner to a successful user of language and literacy.

Perhaps when a *pedagogy of possibilities* is promoted and used, the frustrations that teachers, parents and policy-makers feel might come to an end. This time around, good intentions will not 'pave the way to hell', but to a better, happier, more meaningful, more encouraging and more fulfilling life for Filipino children.

Where will Auntie English be in such a scenario? Certainly not as a dominating, self-important and unwelcome acquaintance, but rather as a supportive and helpful family friend.

References

1935 Constitution of the Republic of the Philippines (1935) Online document, accessed 23 June 2010.   http://www.chanrobles.com/1935constitutionofthephilippines.htm#1935% 20Constitution%20of%20the%20Republic%20of%20the%20Philippines

Baetiong, L.R. (2004) Cognitive academic language proficiency threshold level skills in written Filipino and cross-lingual transfer. Unpublished PhD dissertation, University of the Philippines.

Bautista, L. (2001) Attitudes of selected Luzon University students and faculty toward Philippine English. In E. Rosario *Maminta in Focus: Selected Writings in Applied Linguistics* (pp. 235–273). Quezon City: The Philippine Association for Language Teaching.

Bautista, L. and Gonzales, A. (2006) Southeast Asian Englishes. In B.B. Kachru, Y. Kachru and C. Nelson (eds) *The Handbook of World Englishes* (pp. 130–144). Victoria: Blackwell Publishing.

Best, J. (1998) *American Era Photographs 1900–1930*. Makati: Bookmark, Inc.

Buwan ng Wika. (2009) All Philippines. Webpage, accessed 25 June 2010. http://www. allphilippines.com/?p=331

Combista, D.T. (1995) The interdependence of the cognitive academic language proficiency (CALP) in Cebuano and English in Learning Science. Unpublished MA Thesis, University of the Philippines.

Constantino, P.C. (2000) Tagalog/Pilipino/Filipino: Do they differ? Webpage, accessed 27 June 2010. Online at http://www.emanila.com/pilipino/various/ntu_tagalog.htm

Constantino, R. (1982) *The Miseducation of the Filipino*. Quezon City: Foundation for Nationalist Studies.

De Jesus, E. (2007) Language: Barrier or bridge? *Manila Bulletin,* May 14, p. 11.

Espiritu, C. (2001) Filipino language in the curriculum. Webpage, accessed 28 June 2010. http://www.ncca.gov.ph/about-culture-and-arts/articles-on-c-n-a/article.php?igm =38i=216

Faustino, P. (2010) Pinoy Magsaysay awardees oppose 12-year basic education cycle. *GMANews TV,* 20 September. Online at http://www.gmanews.tv/story/199615/ pinoy-magsaysay-awardees-oppose-12-year-basic-education-cycle

Freire, P. (1998) *Pedagogy of Freedom: Ethics, Democracy, and Civic Courage.* Lanham: Rowman and Littlefield Publishers, Inc.

Gonzales, A. (2001) Looking at some of DECS' problems from a linguist's view point: Some insights from experience. In E. Rosario, *Maminta in Focus: Selected writings in applied linguistics* (pp. 216–234). Quezon City: The Philippine Association for Language Teaching.

Gonzales, A. (2002) The transplantion of language to a different culture: Possibilities and alternatives. In C. Villareal, L.R.R. Tope and P.M.B. Jurialla (eds) *Ruptures and Departures: Language and Culture in Southeast Asia* (pp. 107–111). Quezon City: University of the Philippines.

Gonzales, A. and Alberca, W. (1978) *Philippine English of the Mass Media*. Manila: Research Council, De La Salle University.

Gonzalez, A., Bernardo, A.B.I., Bautista, M.L. and Pacasio, E.M. (2000) The social sciences and policy making in language. *Philippine Journal of Linguistics* 31(2), 27–37.

House of Representatives Philippines (2009) Sponsors unfazed by opposition to English bill. Online press release, accessed 30 June 2010. http://www.congress.gov.ph/press/ details.php?pressid=2949

Lewis, M.P. (ed) (2009) *Ethnologue: Languages of the World* (16th edn). Dallas: SIL International. Online at http://www.ethnologue.com/

Laudiano, R.E. (2006) Phonemic awareness and word reading in English and Filipino of first graders. MA Thesis, University of the Philippines.

Llaneta, C.A.C. (2010) The language of learning: Mother tongue-based multilingual education in the Philippines. *The UP Forum* 11(2). Online at http://www.up.edu.ph/upforum.php?issue=36&i=318

Luz, J.M. (2010) Basic education: How to go from 10 to 1 years. *Philippine Daily Inquirer*, August 15, p. A12.

Maceda, T.G. (2003) The Filipino national language: Discourse on power. In K.L. Adams, T.J. Hudak and F.K. Lehman (eds) *Papers from the Seventh Annual Meeting of the Southeast Asian Linguistics Society* (pp. 99–108). Tempe, AZ: Arizona State University, Programme for Southeast Asian Studies. Online at http://sealang.net/sala/archives/pdf8/maceda2003filipino.pdf

Muzones, G.M. and De Jesus, J.E. (2009) As cost of education rises, dropout rates among Filipino youths soar. Online article, accessed May 29 2010. Online at http://www.bulatlat.com/main/2009/05/30/as-cost-of-education-rises-dropout-ratesamong-filipinos-soar/

Nical, I., Smolicz, J. and Secombe, M. (2004) Rural students and the Philippine bilingual education program on the Island of Leyte. In J.W. Tollefson and A.B. Tsui (eds) *Medium of Instruction Policies: Which Agenda? Whose Agenda?* (pp. 153–176). Mahwah, NJ: Lawrence Elbaum Associates.

Nolasco, R.M.D. (2007) Languages do matter! *Philippine Daily Inquirer*, 3 January, p. A3.

Ocampo, D. (1991) Development of an early reading program for day care centers in urban poor communities. Unpublished Master's thesis, University of the Philippines.

Ocampo, D., Diaz, L., Padilla, P., Vilbar, L., Villanueva, V., Maca, M.N., Fontanos, P. Villanueva, L., Ruda, R. and Bereber, R. (2006) KRT3 Formulation of the National Learning Strategies for the Filipino and English Languages. Online document, accessed 29 June 2010. Online at http://sites.google.com/site/dinaocampo/thephilippineroadmaptomulti-literacy

Pennycook, A. (2002) Appropriations: Postcolonial challenges to language development. In C. Villareal, L.R.R. Tope and P.M.B. Jurialla (eds) *Ruptures and Departures: Language and Culture in Southeast Asia* (pp. 213–241). Quezon City: University of the Philippines.

Perdon, R. (2003) The making of a national language. Online article, accessed 30 June 2010. Online at http://www.emanila.com/philippines/the-making-of-a-national-language

Philippine Daily Inquirer (2009) King's English, 11 January, p. A10.

Philippine Independence Act (1934). Online document, accessed 29 June 2010. Online at http://philippinesarchipelago.com/politics/documents/1934_philippine_independence_act.html

Phillipson, R. (2008) Linguistic imperialism: A conspiracy, or a conspiracy of silence? Online article, accessed 3 November 2010. Online at http://www.cbs.dk/content/download/62841/866506/file/conspiracy-rev.pdf

Ricento, T. (2006) Language policy: Theory and practice – an introduction. In T. Ricento (ed.) *An Introduction to Language Policy: Theory and Method* (pp. 10–23). Massachusetts, MA : Blackwell Publishing.

Rubrico, J.G.U. (1998) The metamorphosis of Filipino as national language. Online article, accessed 3 October 2011. http://www.languagelinks.org/oldsite/pdf/fil_met.pdf

Salazar, C.B. (2010) 12-year basic education: A quality imperative. *Philippine Daily Inquirer*, 20 September. Online at http://opinion.inquirer.net/inquireropinion/columns/view/20100828-289168/12-year-basic-education-a-quality-imperative

Sibayan, B.P. (1999a) Language policy, language engineering, and literacy in the Philippines. In *The Intellectualization of Filipino and other Sociolinguistic and Education Essays* (pp. 1–36). Manila: Linguistic Society of the Philippines.

Sibayan, B.P. (1999b) The implementation of language policy. In *The Intellectualization of Filipino and other Sociolinguistic and Education Essays* (pp. 37–86). Manila: Linguistic Society of the Philippines.

Sibayan, B.P. (1999c) Pilipino and the Filipino's renewed search for a linguistic symbol of unity and identity. In *The Intellectualization of Filipino and other Sociolinguistic and Education Essays* (pp. 135–144). Manila: Linguistic Society of the Philippines.

Sibayan, B.P. (2001) The failure in educating Filipino children through their native language and through Filipino. In E. Rosario *Maminta in Focus: Selected Writings in Applied Linguistics* (pp. 205–215). Quezon City: The Philippine Association for Language Teaching.

Skutnabb-Kangas, T. (2006) Language policy and linguistic human rights. In T. Ricento (ed.) *An Introduction to Language Policy: Theory and Practice* (pp. 273–291). Massachusetts, MA: Blackwell Publishing.

Spot (2011) PH schools lag behind in ASEAN, Spot, 7 June 2011. Online article, accessed 4 July 2011. http://www.spot.ph/newsfeatures/48522/ph-schools-lag-behind-in-asean

Sy, M. (2008) P500m for English proficiency program. *Philippine Star*, 3 January, p. 4.

Tabada, F. (2011) Cebu lawmaker pushes English bill. Cebu Daily News, April 17 2011. Online at http://cebudailynews.wordpress.com/2011/04/17/cebu-lawmaker-pushes-english-bill-2/

Thumboo, E. (2006) Literary creativity in world Englishes. In B.B. Kachru, Kachru, Y. and Nelson, C.L. (eds) *The Handbook of World Englishes* (pp. 405–427). Victoria: Blackwell Publishing.

Tubeza, P. (2009) Sixth-graders improving in achievement tests. *Philippine Daily Inquirer*, 25 June. Online at http://newsinfo.inquirer.net/inquirerheadlines/nation/view/20090904-223464/Sixth-graders-improving-in-achievement-tests

Tupas, T.R.F. (2002) A century of errors: English language teaching and a political history of Philippine-American relations. In C. Villareal, L.R.R. Tope and R.M.B. Jurialla (eds) *Ruptures and Departures: Language and Culture in Southeast Asia* (pp. 127–175). Quezon City: University of the Philippines.

Ty-Casper, L. (2005) History and literature: Aspects of memory. *Journal of English Studies and Comparative Literature* 8 (1), 224–237.

Yanilla Aquino, L.F. (2005) The effects of bilingual instruction on the literacy skills of preschoolers. Unpublished doctoral dissertation, University of the Philippines.

10 It's Not Always English: 'Duelling Aunties' in Brunei Darussalam

Noor Azam Haji-Othman

The country of Brunei Darussalam is a small sovereign state on the north-west coast of the island of Borneo. Apart from its coastline with the South China Sea, it is completely surrounded by the Malaysian state of Sarawak. In 1963, Brunei was the only Malay state to choose not to join the Malaysian federation. It remained a British Protectorate until 1984, when it became a fully independent state. In a linguistically and ethnically diverse new nation-state such as Negara Brunei Darussalam (henceforth Brunei), the issues of nation-building and the manifestation of a national identity have been primary concerns. The need to assert a national 'Bruneian identity' became increasingly necessary in the lead-up to Independence in 1984, when Brunei pronounced itself to be a nation of *Melayu Islam Beraja* (*MIB*, literally: a Malay Muslim Monarchy).

How was this to be achieved when the country was home to multiple, distinct indigenous languages, including the Malay language (Nothofer, 1991)?

The People of Brunei

The 2001 Population Census recorded the total population of Brunei for that year as 348,800, out of which, 232,200 were classified as 'Malay by race' (Government of Brunei, 2003). The 'Malay by race' label was coined in the 1961 *Nationality Act of Brunei*, which stated that there were seven indigenous groups within the 'Malay by race' category, these being: the Belait, Bisaya, Brunei, Dusun, Kedayan, Murut and Tutong ethnicities. Historically, these groups were said to be the original inhabitants of Brunei, as opposed to the Ibans and the Punans, which the *Constitution of Brunei Darussalam* recognizes as 'native to Borneo', but not specifically to Brunei Darussalam. According to Kershaw (1999, in Haji-Othman, 2005a: 14), the term 'Malay' – in the constitutional context – is 'racial' in nature and rather open to interpretation, however, 'the seven precisely named groups that are comprised therein were able to be thus specified because of their well-defined linguistic and cultural traits and associated identity – in current terminology, their *ethnicity'*. In practice, this constitutional terminology has permitted various convenient political, social and economic inclusions and exclusions.

The non-indigenous population of Brunei, most notably the Chinese, Indian and expatriate populations, form about 10% of the overall population today. The breakdown figures for each of the ethnic groups that made up the 'Malay by race' category in the 2001 Population Census were not tallied. Gunn (1997: 6) and Martin (1990: 130–131; 1991) have both suggested that the distinctions between these groups have been deliberately blurred over time, especially due to the active processes of both *Islam-icization* and *Malay-icization*. Martin (2002: 182) calls this blurring 'a cultural and linguistic redefinition'.

Some of the important factors that have influenced *self-identification* among Brunei's many ethnic groups – apart from the two mentioned above – are education, new employment patterns, urbanization and intermarriage (King, 2001). It has also been argued that there has been a general move towards a single national identity among the younger generations of Bruneians, in conjunction with a growing national consciousness in the country (Haji-Othman, 2005a; 2005b). This *Brunei-zation* process (*ibid.*) had its genesis in the creation of the modern Brunei nation-state in the earlier part of the 20th century.

Language and Education

It is argued here that the pre-1984 education system was instrumental in this nation-building process, in particular, through its propagation of the politically and historically dominant Malay language (hence, Malay hegemony) by its use as the medium of instruction in schools. Post-independence, English has taken a more prominent role in the education system, as evidenced by its inclusion in the *Dwibahasa* (Bilingual) education policy. It is also clear that, since gaining independence, Brunei has embraced globalization, and its citizens have been trained to use English to engage with the outside world, yet at the same time, *MIB* (*Melayu Islam Beraja*, the national philosophy) has been strongly emphasized as a marker of Bruneian identity. There is also evidence to suggest that another process of 'assertion of overall hegemony' (Harvey, 2005: 56) has taken place locally among the non-Malay population (culturally and linguistically), even though they were labelled as 'Malay by race' in the Constitution.

It is in this context that the two languages, Malay and English, can be said to have played the role of 'Aunties' – the former, a close relative; the latter, a slightly more distant, but still familial aunt. The discussions that follow will attempt to demonstrate how, for the majority of non-Malay-speaking ethnic minority groups, the Malay language became the *first Auntie* that aligned them to the politically dominant Malays (the Bruneis – an ethnic group, as opposed to 'Bruneians', the national citizens). Subsequently, English became their *second Auntie*, whose good connections in the wider world were seen as highly beneficial.

The ways in which Malay and English have both become linguistic 'Aunties' directly relate to the roles they have each played in the education system. Linguistically, in tandem with the substantial blurring of ethnic demarcation, as described above, there appears to have been a convergence of ethnic-language speakers on the *lingua franca*, Brunei Malay. Martin (2002) records that early accounts of the various ethnic groups explicitly stated that they had 'languages of their own', but by the 1950s, the same groups of people were said to be 'Malay-speaking'. Graham Black, writing as the British Resident (essentially the governor of the country) in the *Brunei Annual Report* of 1939, argued for the need to assimilate the multi-ethnic population for educative purposes. In classic colonial mode, he wrote the following piece of 'social engineering' (Pennycook, 1998), providing a convenient precursor for the later 'Malay by race' categorisation of several non-Malay indigenous groups:

> As at least a quarter of the indigenous population of the state is composed of races whose mother tongue is not Malay, the criterion [of compulsory education for children who live within a two-mile radius of a school where the language of instruction is their own language] is hardly satisfactory. The provision of education in their several languages is obviously impracticable, and it is inevitable that, *linguistically at any rate, the other races must be assimilated to Malay*. It is proposed, therefore, to amend the Enactment so as to make attendance at Malay vernacular schools compulsory for all children of Malaysian [sic] race alike. (Govt. of Brunei 1939: 33–34, [my emphasis])

The statement, 'linguistically at any rate', suggests there was a broader drive for social control and cultural assimilation, possibly including the idea of a new identity for Bruneians. The census figures appear to support this suggestion. Before 1960 (in the 1911, 1921, 1931 and 1947 censuses), figures were provided for each separate indigenous group. However, since 1961, all seven groups have been categorized as 'Malay' in the *State of Brunei Annual Report* for that year (Government of Brunei, 1961: 118–120). In relation to this, Braighlinn states that, indeed, 'for the authors of the 1961 Nationality enactment, assimilation to Malay culture was definitely a long-term aim of political incorporation' (1992: 20). The resultant shift in ethnic classification would not only change the population statistics drastically, it would also have serious linguistic and cultural implications, one of which would be the 'debate about the role of Malay as the state's national language' (Saunders, 1994: 170–171). The precise role of the Malay language as an important social marker, and its direct link to cultural identity in Bruneian society, is powerful. Its dissemination through the schools has been a major force in the country's linguistic and cultural redefinition.

Pre-1984 Formal Education

The development of education in Brunei was not a smooth journey at first, although it picked up speed in the period after the Second World War. The first Malay vernacular school was opened in 1914 with an intake of 30 boys. By 1918, three more schools had opened in Muara, Tutong and Belait. The official report on Brunei, cited by Gunn (1997: 71), stated that the public was not yet ready for universal compulsory education. This was an omen for the 1920s, which did not see much development in terms of formal education. In fact, the schools in Muara and Belait had to be closed, due to a lack of students. The ones that remained open benefited only those living near the major towns, such as the Bruneis and the Chinese, and disadvantaged those living in more rural areas.

The 1930s witnessed the building of more schools, the opening of the first Brunei Malay girls' school and greater student attendance. This was due to the fact that all male children between the ages of 7 and 14 were required by law (*Enactment No. 3*, Government of Brunei, 1929), to attend school within a two-mile radius of where they lived. St George's English School was opened in 1938, followed by four more English mission schools throughout the country. Indeed, prior to the outbreak of war in the region in 1941, the number of schools in Brunei had increased to 32, which included 24 vernacular Malay schools, three private English schools and five private Chinese schools. The number of pupils enrolled was 1746, including 312 girls (Ministry of Education, 2002).

Up until the 1940s, there was no secondary education in Brunei. During World War II, between 1941 and 1945, Brunei was occupied by the Japanese forces. The Japanese administrators of Brunei, however, 'recognized the importance of education for social engineering even more than the British' (Gunn, 1997: 98). It was they who introduced the *Rumi*, or Romanized Malay, script. When the Allied forces liberated Brunei in 1945, schools were forced to close. It has to be said that an important legacy had been left by the Japanese – they had promoted Malay, and they had raised an awareness of the importance of education in Brunei (Abdullah, 1987: 8).

In October 1951, a Brunei Town Government English school was opened in the capital, followed by the opening of a similar school in Kuala Belait, a year later. In less than three years, the government was able to introduce English-medium secondary education in the country. Malay-medium secondary education, however, only began in 1966.

The 1954 Five Year Development Plan for education created the infrastructure for what eventually became the Ministry of Education. New schools were planned, large numbers of teachers were trained and more expatriates were employed in the schools. By the completion of the Plan in 1959, there were 15,006 pupils enrolled in the State's schools, 30% of whom were girls. Brunei now had 52 Malay primary schools, three English schools (including one exclusively for girls that had been completed in 1958), seven mission schools, eight Chinese primary schools and three Chinese secondary schools, which all came under government control in 1957 (Jones, 1994: 104). There were also 133 Bruneians at teacher-training colleges overseas and many at Brunei's own training college that had opened in 1956. With the growing emphasis on education, it soon became apparent that expatriate teachers had to be recruited, and these were brought in from Sri Lanka, India, Singapore, Malaya, the Philippines, the United Kingdom and Australia (*ibid.*).

In 1959, two Malaysians, Aminudin Baki and Paul Chang, were appointed to advise the Brunei Government on general education policy and principles. Jones records that 'having spent only two weeks in Brunei, and using the Malayan *Tun Razak Education Report* of 1956 as the source of their recommendations, Baki and Chang presented their report' (Jones, 1994: 106). The recommendations of this report subsequently became Brunei's National Educational Policy of 1962. Jones comments that the theme of 'national unity' was recurrent through both the Malayan and Bruneian reports, and he cites the *Tun Razak Report*, as follows:

> ... the ultimate objective of the educational policy... must be to bring together the children of all races under a national educational system in which the national language is the main medium of instruction. (*Tun Razak Report*, 1956, in Jones 1994: 107)

This statement echoes the British Resident's report of 1939 cited earlier (Government of Brunei, 1939), which promoted 'linguistic assimilation' for educative purposes.

After it was declared the Official Language in 1959, the propagation of the Malay language through the schools and media was so successful that a language shift from indigenous languages to Malay became evident. There were many reasons for this happening, including the perceived status of the language, the number of speakers or users, population mobility, mixed marriages and institutional support for language teaching or, indeed, more specifically, the education system. However, if degrees of contributions toward the shift to Malay were possible, then the education system would certainly rank the highest among these factors.

Even though the National Educational Policy of 1962 and the subsequent report of the Education Commission in 1972 both recommended the use of Malay as the main medium of instruction in primary and secondary schools, a series of political events resulted in a complete change of emphasis in the final choice of language-medium for the country's national education system. In 1974, according to Jones (1994: 115), plans to adopt a Malaysian-style system of education were cancelled, because of a serious diplomatic spat between Brunei and Malaysia – the main supplier of teachers and training in the late 1970s. This forced Brunei to send its students, teachers and government officers to British universities. This change had a downstream effect, in that English suddenly became important in primary and secondary level education, in anticipation of students needing to go to the UK. This was a decisive moment in the history of education in Brunei. 'There is no doubt that the Education Commission of 1972 wanted, and expected, the system to use Malay as the medium of instruction... Instead, through circumstance, English was adopted' (Jones, 1994: 115–116).

Post-1984: *Dwibahasa* (Bilingualism)

Perhaps the most radical move in the make-over of the education system was the implementation of the post-independence *Dwibahasa* (Bilingual) education policy in 1985. This bilingual education system incorporated the use of two school languages (Malay and English) for different subjects. All primary and secondary schools were to follow a common curriculum, prescribed by the Ministry of Education. From preschool level to Primary III, the medium of instruction for all subjects was to be the Malay Language, except for English Language, which was to be taught as a subject. From Primary IV onwards, the pupils were to follow a bilingual system where two media of instruction were used. The Malay language would be used for teaching Malay, Islamic Religious Knowledge, Physical Education, Arts and Crafts, Civics and MIB (Malay Islamic Monarchy). The English language would be used for teaching subjects such as Science, Mathematics, Geography and English Language (History has been taught in Malay since 1995).

The new bilingual system should have ensured that pupils attained a high degree of proficiency in both English and Malay, along the lines of Phillipson's 'parallel competence' (2008: 1–43). However, Braighlinn notes that the sudden prominence of the English language threatened Malay's position as an official language, stating, 'the supposed development of the Malay language as a medium of literary expression and analytical thought has instead been thwarted by the introduction of the *Dwibahasa* system' (Braighlinn, 1992: 21). Martin (2002) agreed. He said that, despite the rhetorical correctness of the government's official emphasis on Malay, the system clearly legitimized English as the dominant language. What was more apparent, however, was that with the emphasis and support being given to Malay and English, 'the other languages have been left to fend for themselves' (Martin, 2002: 181).

The valorization of English became more pronounced with the introduction of the *Dwibahasa* education system and this continued through the 1990s. While English gained even greater popularity among Bruneians,

Malay was still zealously upheld as the 'language of the soul' through the schools and university (via the introduction of *MIB* modules of study). The growth of English was also spurred by the internet explosion, globalization and, perhaps most importantly, by the provision of universal English-dominant education.

In January 2009, the *Sistem Pendidikan Negara Abad Ke 21* (*SPN 21*, the National Education System for the 21st century) was introduced, replacing the 25-year-old *Dwibahasa* policy. As its name suggests, this new system was designed to equip Bruneian students with all the essential skills for independent, productive and creative learning, to prepare them to become significant members of a highly qualified and skilled workforce in the 21st century (Ministry of Education, 2009). The curriculum now includes all the basic literacy skills, as well as world languages, ICT skills, etc. – all essential to ready young Bruneians for a more globalized Brunei. Early criticisms have suggested that this new system pays even more attention to English than Malay in the *Dwibahasa* system. However, because of its novice status, *SPN21* shall be excluded from the scope of this discussion. It is too early to see its results.

Bruneian Bilingualism

The implications resulting from the culmination of socio-historical changes and changes in the system of education in Brunei can be seen through the changing notion of *bilingualism*. Haji-Othman (2007) has analysed the changing definition of bilingualism in Brunei, with particular reference to the non-Malay ethnic population. He has charted the evolution of the definition of the 'bilingual person' over time and found changes in terms of the language involved. Jones (1994) and Haji-Othman (2005a; 2005b; 2007; 2009) have argued that contacts between the ethnic groups were minimal, prior to the development of inland roads in the 1950s. Despite a flourishing riverine culture that was noted as early as 1904 by McArthur, the various ethnic groups remained largely isolated from each other. Haji-Othman (2005a, 2007) has suggested that the non-Malay-speaking communities (Belait, Bisaya, Dusun, Murut and Tutong) spoke their own traditional languages exclusively, prior to extensive contact with other communities. Greater contact as a result of better roads, in turn, resulted in greater movement and integration between the communities in the 1950s and also led to increasing Malay language infiltration into these ethnic minority communities. This was reinforced by the use of Malay in schools, as ethnic minority parents came to associate the Malay vernacular with schooling and that not speaking it from an early age would put their children at a disadvantage. To only speak an indigenous language brought with it a degree of social stigma (Martin, 1996b).

Haji-Othman (2005a, 2007, 2009) argued that, in the 1960s, a 'bilingual person' would have been defined as a speaker of an ethnic minority language (e.g. Tutong) as a first language and of the *lingua franca* Malay as a second. In the 1970s, a modernizing Brunei still placed great importance on Malay, but it was beginning to realize the significance of English. There were single-stream Malay and English secondary schools, but Malay graduates soon found themselves being side-lined when it came to employment. 'Auntie Malay' was seen to have a more restricted currency compared to 'Auntie English', who had an influence well beyond the Malay Archipelago.

Non-Malay-speaking ethnic groups by now had equal footing with their Malay-speaking counterparts, in terms of their command of both Malay and English through schooling. In the early 1980s, in the lead-up to Independence, the awareness of the importance of Malay as the official language, coupled with the ever-growing significance of English as a tool for social, academic and professional advancement – particularly in a burgeoning British-trained, middle-class society – resulted in an increasing number of traditionally non-Malay-speaking Bruneians being brought up with Malay as their first language and English as their second. Increasingly, to be 'bilingual' came to mean being fluent in Malay and English. Herein lie the roots of both Malay and English as 'duelling Aunties' to the non-Malay-speaking indigenes of Brunei.

The Socio-Economic Impact of Formal Education

The impact of formal education on Bruneian society has been tremendous. For one, it has created a more literate population. However, it also marked the demise of traditional lifestyles, work and social practices, as it began a shift to an increasingly modern, living-and-work preference among the younger generation of Bruneians of all ethnic affiliations. This was particularly felt in the 1970s and 1980s, prior to Independence (1984), when there was still a substantial section of the population working on the land. But more attractive job opportunities that paid well were in abundance in the newly developed civil service, which, for the most part, meant office jobs, not just with the government, but also in the lucrative oil industry. This trend continued into the post-Independence period, when students under the *Dwibahasa* system were trained to use more English, and at the same time, they were instilled with Malay Islamic values, in line with the national philosophy.

Apart from the basic dissemination of knowledge and language skills, however, the schools played another important role. As mentioned above, the Aminudin Baki/Paul Chang (1962) Report, which advocated a national system of education for Brunei, also suggested the need to create a common identity in Brunei. This was slightly more forthright than the 1939 Black Report that had suggested 'linguistic assimilation'. Indeed, this notion has stood the test of time.

This aim to create a common identity was reiterated more recently in a speech in 2002 at a Chinese businessmen's assembly by Brunei's then-Minister of Education, Pehin Dato Haji Abdul Aziz – a well-known proponent of the national philosophy – who said, 'the present system strives to produce a uniform system to crystallise a common Brunei identity' (Brudirect, 2002). Although not mentioned explicitly here, the national philosophy was to be the medium through which this creation of a common identity was to be achieved. And the very fact that *Melayu Islam Beraja* (MIB) was not even mentioned in the speech, presupposes that everyone who is Bruneian knows exactly what is being referred to.

The official website of the Ministry of Education could not state this more clearly:

> Brunei Darussalam's Education Philosophy is founded on the National Philosophy of a Malay Islamic Monarchy and also incorporates the two key elements of Naqli (on the basis of the holy Qur'an and Hadith) and Aqli (on the basis of reasoning)... This is an important foundation for ensuring loyalty to Islam, the Monarch and the nation. (Ministry of Education Website, 13 August 2008)

The role of the education system in the propagation of the national ideology, the Malay language and Malay Muslim hegemony cannot be refuted. The following discussions focus on the manifestations of this process.

Identity Shift Among the Non-Malays

The relationship between language and identity has been discussed extensively in the literature by well-known authorities in the social sciences, including Fishman (1972), Coulombe (1995) and Blommaert (1996). Fishman (1999) reminded us that there is a link, rather than equivalence, between language and ethnicity. It is a very strong link, however, and certainly an oft-cited one among Bruneians ('*Bahasa jiwa bangsa*', literally, 'Language is the soul of the people'). Although the language-identity link is not absolutely a one-to-one relationship, the parallels between ethnic groups and language groups in Brunei suggest a strong correlation – at least in terms of ethnic identification through language – manifest in a perceived merging of ethno-linguistic identities.

Haji-Othman (2005a, 2007) has observed the emergence of a new Bruneian (national) identity that is increasingly seen to be more important than individual ethnic identities. This follows on from Martin's (2002: 182) discussion of the 'linguistic and cultural redefinition' process. Braighlinn (1992: 19) also highlights the apparent consolidation of 'a single national identity, born of convergence on a dominant Malay culture'. Haji-Othman (2005a, 2007) has shown that the language-shift process witnessed in Brunei is denotative of a consequent shift in identity as well, evidenced by the merging of identities among the new generation of Bruneians. If a parallel is to be made, a shift from ethnic minority languages to Malay has been reflected in a shift from ethnic minority identities to more of a 'pan-Bruneian' cultural identity (Haji-Othman, 2005a, 2007).

This process of gradual identity shift in Brunei had been observed by earlier researchers. Leach (1950) discussed the problems of classifying Borneo's ethnic minority populations, because they had 'become Malay'. A similar observation was also made by Brown (1960), who described the occurrence of shifting identities in Brunei, as follows:

> With the changes brought about in this century, such as improvements in communication, travel and education, Westernization, the growth of political parties and so on, the number of ethnic groups appears to have declined. Two processes seem to have been at work: the recognition of socio-cultural affinities previously obscured by classifications based on locality, and *the merging of lesser ethnic groups with the greater*... In Brunei we can clearly see a process whereby ethnic groups of lesser significance decrease in numbers through the movement of their members to classification as Malays... It is socially advantageous to identify with Brunei Malays, and there is a considerable "passing" of indigenes into this category – at least so far as census data is a reliable guide. (Brown, 1960: 4–9 [my emphasis])

These observations of shifting identities in Brunei are highly significant. The factors that Brown identifies – in the quote above – as the causes of shifts in identity are essentially similar to the ones that influence language shift. In addition to these studies, Maxwell (1980: 189–197) also discussed the shifts in the semantic classification of indigenous Brunei ethnic groups. More recent studies on identity in Brunei, such as those by Braighlinn (1992: 20), Gunn (1997) and Kershaw (2001: 124), have suggested that identity shifts more as a result of deliberate political pressures or even 'inventions' of a national identity, towards which the indigenous populations are shifting. There is no evidence to support or refute this contention, but what has been observed is a close link between emergence of a 'Pan-Bruneian identity' that parallels the emergence of a 'Pan-Brunei Malay language'.

As regards linguistic diversity, Haji-Othman (2005a) and other researchers have noted that within the multitude of languages in Brunei, the need for a common language seems imperative. A national language, so to speak, although never officially proclaimed, in fact exists in the form of Brunei Malay, which the informants say best expresses 'Bruneian-ness'. This is the language that everyone shares. The ethnic minority languages, on the other hand, express separate ethnic identities, even if some of these languages are not spoken by the younger members of their communities and are possibly dying out (Martin, 1995). It is therefore problematic to try to reconcile the fact that there is much personal support for these languages and for linguistic diversity, with the fact that the ethnic minority groups themselves speak their languages less frequently and do not necessarily transmit them to their youngsters.

Haji-Othman (2005a) noted the declining importance of the overt expression of *ethnic identity* among Bruneians, while, on the other hand, he saw greater emphasis being placed on a *national identity*. This can be seen as a de-emphasizing of differences.

The Legitimization of the 'Malay-icization' Process

In many societies, linguistic (and cultural) diversity can create a perceived need for 'a central policy of containment' in anticipation of potential ethno-linguistic problems. According to Blommaert and Verschueren (1998: 12–14), such containment policies often take on these three forms:

- the discouragement of diversity;
- the elimination of differences; and
- a narrow interpretation of legality.

In applying these observations to the case of Brunei Darussalam and its various ethnic minority languages, Haji-Othman (2005a) found the following:

The discouragement of diversity

Blommaert and Verschueren (1998) argued that one possible reaction to linguistic diversity could be an overt homogenizing tendency in national language policies through explicit bans on the 'less significant' languages. In the case of Brunei, the government has never issued any explicit statement to suggest a prohibition of the use of multiple languages. Likewise, however, neither has there been any visible encouragement to the opposite effect. There is no documentary evidence of any legal enactments in Brunei – other than in the government circulars that were issued to remind government officers to use Malay for official business – that would suggest an official policy of language containment. What is clear, also, is the absence of any forcible rhetoric to ensure the use of one language only. However, this is not to dismiss the existence of *implicit* policies practiced by some government departments that would appear to contradict an absolute denial of any kind of language restrictions. While there does not exist any law against the use of Tutong or Dusun, for example, implicit forms of language restrictions could be just as lethal for linguistic diversity. One example of such implicit policies is the apparent reluctance of the Language and Literature Bureau (a government department under the Ministry of Culture, Youth and Sports) to publish in non-Malay ethnic languages. It should be noted, however, that the bureau was specifically created to develop the Malay language.

The elimination of differences

According to Blommaert and Verschueren (1998), the active elimination of differences, including linguistic differences, is another way of containing diversity. They recognized the potential danger of ethnic tensions that might result from different ethno-linguistic groups wanting official status for each of their languages. Such 'fear of tribalism' feelings are not necessarily translated into the aggressive elimination of ethno-linguistic differences, however. They could, in fact, be manifest in a de-emphasizing of differences, which is perhaps a more diplomatic means toward the same end. In this regard, the focus is drawn away from ethno-linguistic differences. Today, Bruneians take great pride in their long and multicultural history, even to the extent that past differences appear to be taken for granted now. There has not been any aggressive elimination of differences. What can be seen is a de-emphasis of the differences between various ethno-linguistic groups, in general discourse, in the country.

A narrow interpretation of legality

A third form of a 'policy of containment', as outlined by Blommaert and Verschueren (1998), is a restrictive interpretation of legal statements. Technically speaking, there is no language law in Brunei, apart from the official language declaration (*Constitution of Brunei*, Article 82), although such an idea was mooted in July 2009. The 1961 *Nationality Act* defined the 'Malay by race' category to include Brunei Malays and Kedayan Malays, as well as some non-Malay ethnic groups, namely the Belaits, Bisayas, Dusuns, Muruts and Tutongs. The common practice among Bruneians is to refer to the *Nationality Act* of 1961, often wrongly equating the legal definition of the Malay person with the linguistic definition. These are separate notions. In Brunei, the problem may be not so much that of a *narrow interpretation*, but rather an *inconsistent interpretation* of the law. Some argue that the recognition of Malay as the official language is justified, as the ethnic minority groups are all 'Malay by race', despite having their own distinct languages that are not Malay. On the other hand, others might argue that the version of Malay that is meant to be official is the one in which the Constitution itself is written; a language which no one in Brunei can really claim to be their own, not even the ethnic Brunei Malays. So, rather than a restrictive interpretation of 'Malay', the common interpretation of the law (*Constitution of Brunei*, Article 82) in Brunei is conveniently broad, yet inclusive at the same time.

Despite slight variations to Blommaert and Verschueren's original typology, the ramifications of these more subdued and measured reactions to linguistic diversity remain just as effective – the successful diffusion of ethno-linguistic groups and the circumvention of ethno-linguistic tensions. In other words, ethno-linguistic diversity has been implicitly contained. While there is no overtly aggressive stance against linguistic diversity, there is, nevertheless, a general belief in Brunei that some level of linguistic homogeneity needs to be achieved for the government and administration to function smoothly. It has to be acknowledged that there is a certain, *implicit* form of a 'policy of containment', with regard to linguistic diversity in Brunei. The manifestations of this policy, however, differ slightly from those originally described by Blommaert and Verschueren (1998: 12–14). Instead of the discouragement of diversity, one could say that an *absence of linguistic coercion* is more evident. Instead of the elimination of differences, there is a *de-emphasis of differences* and instead of narrow interpretations of legality, *these interpretations are rather broad.*

Conclusion: 'Duelling Aunties'

To be sure, the British Residents established and developed a Malay education system for Brunei between 1906 and 1959. This legacy continued for the next two decades, whereupon Bruneian education officials decided that English-language education needed to be emphasised, and they introduced bilingual education. For many non-Malay-speaking groups, this meant having to learn *two* new languages. It is not always the English language that eviscerates indigenous languages, however. Sometimes a local linguistic code can be just as much of a 'Hydra' as the language of colonisation. English can be embraced for the practical benefits it brings to its users, and a facility in the Malay language can also bring membership of the dominant Malay community. This has certainly been the case for many of the ethnic minority people in Brunei.

The phenomenon of *language shift* has been a major factor in the changing language ecology of Brunei. One of the implications of language shift – be it through either domain loss or dispossession (Harvey, 2005; Phillipson, 2008) from different minority languages to a common language – is the reduction of linguistic diversity. Language shift also has implications for cultural identity. Now that a common facility in the Brunei Malay language is perceived as an important marker of 'Bruneian-ness', differences between ethnic identities have become less and less emphasized. With modernization and greater integration among the population, the diverse languages and identities are concurrently converging, and a common language and a common national identity are both emerging, in turn. There has clearly been an intergenerational switch from ethnic minority languages to Malay. What is emerging, as a result, is a new generation of Bruneians who all speak

Malay and could rightly claim it as their mother tongue, rather than their original ethnic minority languages. There is a process of convergence on a pan-Bruneian Malay code and, concurrently, a pan-Bruneian identity, attributable to significantly increased inter-ethnic mixed marriages and a detachment from, if not indifference to, traditional ethnic identities among the population.

There have indeed been some profound changes in the language ecology of Brunei that have coincided with the rapid modernization which occurred during the last century. The most evident has been the adoption of English by Bruneians. But in terms of indigenous languages, the prognosis is that the linguistically diverse population is now steadily morphing into a more homogeneous and seemingly more monolingual Malay speech community. Spurred by the unbalanced nature of the relationship between Malay and the ethnic minority languages and a lack of maintenance, or even a disinclination to maintain them, the ethnic minority languages are fast disappearing, some much sooner than others, as studies such as Martin's (1995) have shown. This has been a dramatic change in the linguistic landscape, particularly in the context of an indigenous population of only less than a quarter of a million. English, the more distant but eminently 'useful Auntie', is being learned for the instrumental purposes of competing internationally.

It must be stressed that, even though the arguments presented here would appear to suggest that Malay has been more damaging than English to ethnic minority languages, indigenous people constantly juggle the two wider languages and have come to realise that *both* 'Aunties' need to be kept happy. It is a very complicated relationship, as demonstrated in the following episode.

In April 2010, the Director of the Language and Literature Bureau (*Dewan Bahasa dan Pustaka*) was reported in the media to have blamed the bilingual education system for 'poor standards' in the Malay language (Fitri, 2010) – a story that was echoed on national television and radio and, surely, a sentiment shared by a handful of Malay purists and nationalists. A month later, this claim was dismissed by Pehin Dato Hj Badaruddin, a very well-respected senior government official, as well as a Malay literary figure (later to become Minister of Home Affairs). He affirmed that '[English] does not reduce the value and importance of the Malay language', arguing that the bilingual education system (including *SPN21*, still English-heavy) 'has been operating well and past generations have succeeded due to their good command of English' (Dewi, 2010). Such is the value placed on English that, even more recently, the new Minister of Islamic Affairs – an even more unlikely supporter – declared that for Arabic language education to succeed in Brunei, it will have to 'emulate the approaches used to teach English' (Rashidah, 2010).

This episode succinctly captures the significance of the two 'duelling aunties' in modern Brunei. This tiny country has had to please both 'Aunties' and draw benefits from both. At the same time, something has had to give in the 'handbag quarrels' between the two. As a well-known Malay saying goes, *Gajah berperang, pelanduk mati di tengah-tengah* ('When elephants collide, the mouse-deer dies between them'). In a linguistic context, the mouse-deer represents the ethnic minority identities and languages in Brunei (including those of the non-Malay ethnic groups, such as the Iban and the Punan). Indeed, these languages have been overlooked in discussions that, more often than not today, assume a homogeneous linguistic community that speaks Malay, having to fend off threats from English.

The not-so-clear, yet present, danger in reality is perhaps closer to home than most Bruneians realise, and it is not the English language.

References

Abdullah, J. (1987) Bilingual Education in Brunei Darussalam: Problems in Implementation. Unpublished Masters thesis, Southeast Asian Ministers of Education Organization Regional Language Centre, Singapore.

Allan, L.A. (1921) *Annual Report on the State of Brunei for 1921*. Kuala Lumpur: Government of Brunei.

Black, G.J. (1939) *Annual Report on the State of Brunei for 1939*. Singapore: Government of Brunei.

Blommaert, J. (1996) Language planning as discourse on language and society: The linguistic ideology of a scholarly tradition. *Language Problems and Language Planning* 20 (3), 199–222.

Blommaert, J. and Verschueren, J. (1998) *Debating Diversity: Analysing the Discourse of Tolerance*. London: Routledge.

Braighlinn, G. (1992) *Ideological Innovation under Monarchy: Aspects of Legitimation Activity in Contemporary Brunei*. Amsterdam: VU University Press.

Brown, D.E. (1970) *Brunei: The Structure and History of a Bornean Malay Sultanate*. Brunei: Brunei Museum.

Brudirect, www.brudirect.com. Website, accessed 2 May 2002.

Chevallier, H. (1911) *Annual Report on the State of Brunei for 1910*. Singapore: Government of Brunei.

Coulombe, A.P. (1995) *Language Rights in French Canada*. New York, NY: Peter Lang.

Davis, H.W. (1947) *Annual Report on the State of Brunei for 1947*. Singapore: Government of Brunei.

Dewi, Mohd Sofri (2010) Poor Malay not due to bilingual education. *The Brunei Times*, 21 May.

Fishman, J.A. (ed.) (1999) *Handbook of Language and Ethnic Identity*. New York/London: Oxford University Press.

Fitri, Shahminan (2010) Bilingual education cited for poor Malay language proficiency among students. *The Brunei Times*, 29 April.

Government of Brunei (1961) *Nationality Act of Brunei*. Online document, accessed 23 July 2011. http://www.agc.gov.bn/agc1/images/LOB/PDF/Cap15.pdf

Government of Brunei (1984) *Constitution of Brunei Darussalam*. Online document, accessed 23 July 2011. http://www.worldstatesmen.org/Brunei1984.pdf

Government of Brunei (2003) *Population Census of 2001*. Bandar Seri Begawan: Government of Brunei Economic Planning Unit.

Gunn, G.C. (1997) *Language, Power and Ideology in Brunei Darussalam*. Athens: Ohio University Press.

Haji-Othman, N.A. (2005a) *Changes in the Linguistic Diversity of Brunei: An Ecological Perspective*. PhD thesis, University of Leicester.

Haji-Othman, N.A. (2005b) *A National Identity Achieved? Linguistic Tell-tales of Identity Shift*. Paper presented at the Second International Conference on Austronesian Dialects (SADDAN II), 1–8 October, 2005, Brunei.

Haji-Othman, N.A. (2007) English and the bilingual Bruneian. In K. Dunworth (ed.) *English in South East Asia: Challenges and Changes* (pp. 59–70). Perth: Curtin University of Technology.

Haji-Othman, N.A. (2009) *The Changing Linguistic Profile of Brunei: Notes for Language Education*. Plenary paper at the International Conference on the Teaching and Learning of English in Asia 3 (TLEiA3), 19–20 November, Bandar Seri Begawan.

Harvey, D. (2005) *The New Imperialism*. Oxford: Oxford University Press.

Jones, G.M. (1994) A Study of Bilingualism and Implications for Language Policy Planning in Negara Brunei Darussalam. Unpublished PhD thesis, University College of Wales.

Kershaw, E.M. (1994) Final shifts: Some why's and how's of Brunei Dusun convergence on Malay. In P.W. Martin (ed.) *Shifting Patterns of Language Use in Borneo* (pp. 179–194). Williamsburg, VA: Borneo Research Council.

Kershaw, R. (1999) An outline of the minorities of Brunei and some shortcomings of empathy and accuracy in English language sources. *Asienforum* 29 (1–2), 83–106.

King, V.T. (2001) A question of identity: Names, societies, and ethnic groups in interior Kalimantan and Brunei Darussalam. *Sojourn* 16 (1), 1–36.

Leach, E.R. (1950) *Social Science Research in Sarawak*. London: HMSO.

Martin, P.W. (1990) The pattern of language communication in Brunei Darussalam and its pedagogic implications. In V. Bickley (ed.) *Language Use and Language Teaching and the Curriculum* (pp. 175–185). Hong Kong: Institute of Language in Education.

Martin, P.W. (1991) Language shift and language solidarity in Brunei Darussalam: The ecology of a minority language. Paper presented at the Conference on Bilingualism, Universiti Brunei Darussalam, November 1991, Brunei.

Martin, P.W. (1995) Whither the indigenous languages of Brunei Darussalam? *Oceanic Linguistics* 34 (1), 27–43.

Martin, P.W. (2002) One language, one race, one nation? The changing language ecology of Brunei Darussalam. In M. David (ed.) *Methodological and Analytical Issues in Language Maintenance and Language Shift Studies* (pp. 175–193). Frankfurt am Main: Peter Lang.

Maxwell, A.R. (1980) Urang Darat: An Ethnographic Study of the Kadayan of Labu Valley, Brunei. Unpublished PhD thesis, Yale University.

McKerron, P.A.B. (1929) *Annual Report on the State of Brunei for 1929*. Singapore: Government of Brunei.

Ministry of Education. (2009) Sistem pendidikan negara abad ke-21 *(National Education System for the 21st Century)*. Online document, accessed 13 March, 2010. http://www.moe.edu.bn/web/moe/home/

Nothofer, B. (1991) The languages of Brunei Darussalam. In H. Steinhauer (ed.) *Papers in Pacific Linguistics: Pacific Linguistics A-81* (pp. 151–176). Canberra: Australian National University.

Pennycook, A. (1998) Hong Kong and the cultural constructs of colonialism. In B. Asker (ed.) *Teaching Language and Culture: Building Hong Kong on Education* (pp. 131–151). Hong Kong: Addison Wesley Longman.

Phillipson, R. (2008) The linguistic imperialism of neoliberal empire. *Critical Inquiry in Language Studies* 5 (1), 1–43.

Rashidah H.A.B. (2010) Not competent in Arabic? Step aside, please: Minister to teachers. *Borneo Bulletin*, 22 June.

Saunders, G. (1994) *A History of Brunei*. Kuala Lumpur: Oxford University Press.

Sercombe, P.G. (2003) Multilingualism among the Penans of Brunei. *International Journal of Bilingualism* 7 (2), 153–175.

11 English Language as Siren Song: Hope and Hazard in Post-Apartheid South Africa

Sandra Land

Background

In 1990, Rolihlahla Mandela was released from prison. The apartheid government of the time realised that they had to choose between a doomed struggle as an internationally outcast regime repressing its country's people and capitulation. They admitted defeat, and Mandela walked out of prison, setting South Africa on a new steeplechase ride that is probably still just beginning. In the two decades since then, South Africa (or uMzansi, as people call it[1]), went from two official languages to eleven, from four provinces to nine and from an obsession with race for segregation to an obsession with race for redress. Our rulers changed from a right-wing, white government to a black, post-liberation government that rests on an increasingly factionalised and fractious tripartite alliance of the South African Communist Party, a trade union coalition (COSATU) and the African National Congress – a political party that reels between the socialist demands of its loyal millions of voters and the capitalist interests of its political elite. 'Interesting times' is an understatement for the political landscape we career through, and our language dynamics reflect all the hopes and hazards and the contradictions, discords and harmonies that characterise our 'rainbow nation'.

In 1996, the Constitution of South Africa accorded official status to 11 languages: nine indigenous Southern African languages spoken within the bounds of the country; isiNdebele, Sesotho, Sepedi (or Sesotho sa Leboa), siSwati, Xitsonga, Setswana, Tshivenda, isiXhosa and isiZulu, as well as two languages of settlers from Europe; Afrikaans, derived from Dutch, and English. The Constitution states that everyone has the right to use the language and participate in the cultural life of his or her choice and, with reference to the indigenous languages, it states that 'Recognising the historically diminished use and status of the indigenous languages of our people, the state must take practical and positive measures to elevate the status and advance the use of these languages' (*Constitution of the Republic of South Africa*, No. 108 of 1996, Chapter 1, Point 6).

Arising from the Constitution, our Bill of Rights ensures that speakers of all South Africa's official languages have equal language rights. These rights could be exercised by, for example, an employee insisting that she receives communication from her employer in her own language or by students rightfully expecting to learn in their home language or someone in need of services rendered by state offices requiring to be spoken to in a familiar vernacular language.

In practice, although indigenous African languages are spoken in the homes of 78% of the population (Statistics SA, 2001), their speakers almost never claim the right to have their home languages used in public spheres. In this phenomenon, we follow in the wake of previously decolonised African countries, where 'indigenous African languages remain confined to the cultural domains, much as they were in the colonial era' (Kamwangamalu, 2010: 4). Therefore, even though only 2 million of the total population of 50 million are of British descent,[2] English continues as the dominant language in the business world, politics and education, and prevails in the hubs of big business activity, particularly in and around Johannesburg, Durban and Cape Town. Here, the dominance of English is massive, and indigenous languages are being displaced. First-language Zulu students at UKZN (the University of KwaZulu Natal), who garnish the Zulu they speak liberally with English terms and expresssions, claim that they cannot understand what they call 'deep Zulu' – the form used by people who live in rural areas remote from towns. By 'deep Zulu', they mean a form relatively free from the influence of English and rich in idiom and terms that most of the students consider archaic and inaccessible. The consensus in a class of approximately 30 post-graduate students (the B.Ed. Honours class of 2010) was that this form of Zulu has come to be associated with poor, rural, unsophisticated people and has, therefore, become stigmatised. Similarly, Heugh found (2009) that Xhosa students regard 'deep Xhosa' as unattractive and regard its use as restricted to rural people and academics (Heugh, 2009).

Afrikaans is the next most dominant language after English in influential discourse, particularly in parts of Johannesburg and Cape Town and in the towns and cities established by Dutch settlers when they fled English domination in the Cape and moved into the interior two centuries ago. Today, almost all Afrikaans speakers can speak English, and there is a shift in Afrikaans communities toward speaking English (Gough, 1996), but white English speakers – as self-assured as ever in our sense of distance and superiority – refer to Afrikaans areas as 'behind the boerewors[3] curtain'. Ironically, the Afrikaans community are the only language group who tend to claim their constitutionally guaranteed rights; it is from them that the bulk of complaints has been received by the Pan South African Language Board (Pienaar, 2008).

Given that in the years when the apartheid government restricted the vote to white people, it could not have retained power without the voting support and tacit approval of a substantial portion of English speakers, it is unfair that Afrikaans was labelled so unequivocally as the language of the oppressor. English should share that label. However, perhaps because the worst aspects of apartheid were associated with Afrikaans-speaking politicians and state officials, and because in the famous 1976 school riots children demonstrated primarily against being forced to learn some subjects through the medium of Afrikaans, it alone carries this tag, and English is accepted as the post-liberation *lingua franca*. The use of English by the ANC in exile – partly because exiled members came from different language groups – may have set a trend for this, but the social status of the language – relative to other languages in South Africa – makes it eminently acceptable as a language of power. This ready acceptance is frequently demonstrated, for example, by President Jacob Zuma, who – in spite of having styled himself as a '100% Zulu boy' in his political campaigns – continues parliamentary tradition by giving his state of the nation address at the opening of Parliament in English, with asides in Zulu, Sesotho and Afrikaans.

Part of the reason for using English is practical. Although many Black South Africans understand only one indigenous language, across the country, more people understand English than any other official language. Also, as de Klerk (1999: 316) suggests, the use of English as a *lingua franca* 'disadvantages all indigenous language groups equally'. This might sound bizarre, but our lamentable track record in intergroup violence in the last few decades gives her statement perspective. Hence, as in many ex-British colonies that spanned territories of more than one indigenous language group, public communication is in the language of the ex-coloniser. The resource- and time-saving advantages of avoiding multiple translations is clear. However the irony of a previously repressed and exploited people not only readily accepting the colonial language, but according it high status in their liberated country and, thus – in Phillipson's words – (2008: 6) 'perpetuating the subordination of colonial times into the present', remains.

English has high status across all communities. We English speakers take its status for granted with our customary, casual arrogance; Afrikaans speakers sometimes seethe against it with grinding resentment; and in black communities, the status is accorded with ready recognition of confidently spoken English as a marker of high levels of education and sophistication. This elevated status of English in the perception of ordinary people, and the linguistic capital it carries, is evident in language practices, such as the use of English by Zulu politicians to address Zulu communities. At a political rally near Durban during the build up to the 2009 general election, some first-language Zulu politicians spoke exclusively in English, although they were well aware that Zulu would be understood by all attending the meeting, and English understood by only a few (Chili, 2007: 76). This incident is a mirror image of another referred to by Bourdieu (1991: 68), where a French-speaking official won the respect of a gathering by addressing them in their own local dialect, thus demonstrating token solidarity with them. Bourdieu describes this as 'a strategy of condescension' used to gain profit. In the Zulu example, the politicians used English to profit by underscoring the social distance between themselves and the gathering, which would be considered a triumph in a context where escape from poor, marginalised rural communities is prized. According to Chili – who is himself a member of this community – the politicians' strategy was effective, and, in spite of being patently unable to follow what was said to them, community members expressed a high regard for the speakers who addressed them in English. Thus, they surrender, apparently willingly, to what Bourdieu would term the symbolic violence of this demonstration of unequal power between them and the politicians they vote for and believe in the paradox that because the politicians decline to truly speak *with* them, they are the best to speak *for* them.

In this surrender, we see economically and linguistically marginalised people engaged in what Bourdieu (1991) termed 'active complicity'. In Bourdieu's terms, they are dominated by the symbolic power of the legacy of their colonisers, and they support the legitimacy of this power, as well as the authority of the people who can exercise it (Thompson, 1991). In South Africa, this belief and support has not been engineered in a calculated way, but rather, it conforms to the pattern delineated by Bourdieu and 'impalpably inculcated, through a long and slow process of acquisition, by the sanctions of the linguistic market, and which are therefore adjusted, without any cynical calculation or consciously experienced constraint, to the chances of material and symbolic profit which the laws of price formation characteristic of a given market objectively offer to the holders of a given linguistic capital' (Bourdieu, 1991: 51). As noted by Rapatahana in the introduction to this book, 'Power is pervasive and omnipresent and insinuative; insidious and insidiously self-maintaining'. Indeed.

The interplay described above between politicians and rural communities exemplifies a fast-developing new South African divide between the recently empowered and enriched South Africans and those whose lives have not improved since apartheid. This echoes a situation only too common in previously colonised countries and pointed to by Ngũgĩ wa Thiong'o in Kenya, where members of a post-independence elite, to whom he refers as 'comprador neo-colonial ruling elements' (Ngũgĩ, 1986: 22), use English to maintain their domination. In South Africa, the development of these power relations is a direct contradiction of an optimistic prediction by Master (1998: 723–724) that '... when non-English-speaking countries that currently rely on English for modernization... become strong enough to continue that progress in their own vernacular languages, for example, by inventing new terminology, English will be displaced, as will all those in the population who identify with it, and power will naturally shift to those who know (and identify with) the vernacular' and that 'the dominance of English will gradually give way to reciprocity and fairness'. In making this appealing prediction, Master failed to consider that among the powerful few of those speakers of the vernacular, there would possibly be some who were more interested in establishing and ensuring their own power, than in sharing it, and they find English a useful tool for doing so. As Master also notes, 'at the level of linguistic dominance, the power to advance is contrasted with the power to hold back' (Master, 1998: 717), here used in a way that few of us foresaw – a distressing situation where ordinary people are discovering that promises of liberation can be bewilderingly turned inside out. Many people who are now in government seem to have changed direction, and they have started to use the tools of the colonialists for their own elite advantage.

As long-time political activist and respected language specialist, Neville Alexander, stated with reference to an English-only or English-mainly policy in South Africa, that such a situation:

- prevents the majority of the people from gaining access to vital information and, therefore, from full participation in the democratic political process;
- undermines the confidence of L2 speakers and, even more so, that of the vast majority for whom English is effectively a foreign language;
- smothers the creativity and spontaneity of people who are compelled to use a language of which they are not in full command; and
- at the economic and workplace levels, it causes major and avoidable blockages that can have significant negative impacts on productivity and efficiency.

(Alexander, 2006a: 251)

Promise and Forfeit: The Chosen Few

It is unsurprising, then, that learning English holds great promise for socio-economically deprived South Africans. The chasm between rich and poor in South Africa appears to have grown wider since the end of apartheid, with the difference now that a growing proportion of the wealthiest are black. This elite, often referred to as 'black diamonds', includes political appointees at various levels of government, entrepreneurs who have made money through business ventures that were previously hampered by apartheid restrictions or promising employees of business corporations who fast-track them up the corporate ladder, in order to meet Black Economic Empowerment targets set as a condition for getting state tenders (hence, a new South African English word, 'tenderpreneurs').

The appointment of these high fliers is a result of both political liberation and the international trend towards corporatisation. Like similar institutions elsewhere in the world, South African public institutions are increasingly run along business lines, and they focus on making a profit, rather than on delivering an affordable service for the public good. People in executive positions in these organisations can earn very high salaries. Many prominent members of the ANC gained positions in government on the basis of the role they, or their family members, played in 'the Struggle' – the resistance and armed activity that was waged against the apartheid regime. So, black people who remain poor in South Africa have witnessed meteoric rises in the wealth and power of some who were previously amongst them. Initially nicknamed 'WaBenzi', because of the Mercedes Benz cars they favoured, many have moved out of black townships and into suburbs that were previously reserved for whites. Concurrently, unjust, racially based differences in the rates of pay between people working in positions such as teachers or nurses ceased, and a large number of black South Africans experienced a sudden rise in income. Ever-ready to reap interest from whoever can pay it, the banks rushed to offer credit, and this group rapidly improved their houses, bought cars and became enthusiastic and discerning consumers of fashion and expensive household paraphernalia. Those who are anxious to show off the emblems of prosperity to emphatically separate themselves from those who remain mired in poverty would possibly fit Bourdieu's notion of a *bourgeoisie*. Where they shift their speech or 'linguistic productions' (Bourdieu, 1991: 82) towards the language of those in power, they mirror Bourdieu's description of the French *petits bourgeois*, who 'attempt to appropriate the properties of those who are dominant' (Bourdieu, 1991: 83).

The Dispossessed and Betrayed

Naturally, this dramatic social transformation has raised the awareness of their own poverty among the great numbers of black South Africans who have not benefitted from political transformation. It is to our shame as a country that there are a great many whose lives have not improved at all, especially as their earning opportunities have actually decreased. Our new labour laws, including minimum wages and procedures to protect people from dismissal, make employers wary of employing new staff. Also, with increased trends of corporatisation, many institutions which previously employed their own general workers now outsource functions like cleaning and make use of labour agencies, who tend to pay a flat rate at the lowest level permissible, without increases for experience and certainly no benefits. In addition, many businesses that were owned by emigrating white South Africans closed down, so jobs were lost in these businesses and in the homes of the émigrés.

A shift from agriculture to property development, land restitution claims and increased crime, such as stock theft and home robberies, resulted in a drop of 12.7% in the number of productive farms between the years 2002–2007 alone (Mnyaka, 2009). In our land restitution programme, black South Africans can claim land that their families lived on before it was appropriated by white settler farmers. This restitution is rights-based; claimants do not need to be farmers, and the majority do not intend to farm. The land restitution programme is currently stalled, with an enormous number of land claims pending, and commercial farmers of all races are unwilling to invest in expansion or even maintenance for fear that they will have to give up their farms and that compensation will not cover their investments. Thus, again, ironically, developments intended to empower poor people have worsened their plight, in terms of decreased opportunities for unskilled workers and the loss of benefits that went with employment on farms, such as grazing rights or housing, which was not always of the miserable hostel-type often associated with the previous political dispensation.

Adding to the gloom is that only half of young South Africans are in training or employed. In 2007, it was estimated that almost 3 million of the 6.7 million South Africans between 18–24 were neither in training nor employment and, in spite of affirmative action policies, 86% of these unplaced youth are black or Coloured[4] (Gower, 2009).

The Siren Song

In many African countries, 'the masses have become increasingly aware that ex-colonial languages are the catalyst for socio-economic inequalities, and that only access to these languages can bring about a remedy' (Kamwangamalu, 2010: 5). Correspondingly, in our context, it is unsurprising that many poor black families hear in the siren sounds of well-spoken English, the allure of a possibly better life for their children and make enormous sacrifices to send them to schools that will give them the best chance of gaining access to tertiary education or reasonably paid employment. For many speakers of indigenous South African languages, this means striving for the opposite of the right to be taught in their mother tongue and doing whatever they can to send their children to schools where English is the medium of teaching and the language of the playground – in other words, to the schools that were preserved under apartheid for white, Coloured or Indian children. In some of these schools, as the enrolment of black children has increased, that of whites has decreased, until some are now completely black, but still have English first-language teaching staff.

During apartheid, when schools were segregated according to racial population groups, schooling was compulsory for white children, but not for others, and a sliding scale of school subsidy was applied to state-run schools. White schools got a subsidy that enabled them to compare well with schools in First World countries; Indian and Coloured schools got a subsidy considerably lower than that; and schools for indigenous black

South Africans received the lowest subsidy of all. In 1994, expenditure on each white child was four times that of the expenditure on each African child (Lemon, 2004: 270). Institutions for black South Africans were organised under the infamous 'Bantu Education system', which was designed to produce an acquiescent working class, with a limited education. The system restricted not only spending, but also curriculum. It entrenched learning by rote, rather than enquiry, and allowed lower levels of education as a minimum for black teachers than was allowed for teachers of other race groups. Black schools were characterised by enormous classes (with sometimes as many as 80 children in a class, particularly in the lower grades), a lack of resources, poorly trained, badly paid and often demotivated teachers and very high drop-out rates. Many children stayed in school for one or two years only, sometimes because of traditional family duties, such as cattle herding, but often because schools failed to accommodate them or were too far away from their homes. The dishonest rhetoric of the apartheid government was 'separate but equal development', but it is clear that for generations to come, South Africa will suffer the serious consequences of the indefensible inequities of the apartheid system.

Language policy in education under apartheid was that the medium of the first four years of education should be mother tongue and that, where this was an indigenous African language, the medium should thereafter switch to English or Afrikaans – the two official languages at the time. Textbooks in indigenous languages were available only for the first four years. Teachers used indigenous languages in the first phase, but both indigenous and official languages in the phases that followed, mediating the content of the English or Afrikaans textbooks where they could to make the information more accessible to their students. However, because teachers were themselves products of the Bantu Education system, their own command of English tended to be weak, and their understanding of curricula, textbook content and teaching strategies was limited. The following account by a South African academic of his own experience as a black learner taught by black teachers in the Bantu Education system illustrates this:

> My Grade 9 and 10 English teacher, who would always carry a stick when teaching, never smiled during his lessons. His teaching approach was the epitome of what Balfour (2000: 48) refers to as 'the transmission mode of teaching with its emphasis on the authority of the teacher and passivity of learners'. Both in my Grade 9 and Grade 10, he was the only person in the class who had copies of the novels prescribed... Because of this, during reading lessons he would walk around our desks, reading the novel out loud and checking if any of us were talking. We thus had no choice but to remain absolutely silent. The silence was so obstructive to learning that, even if there were areas we did not understand as he read to us, it was almost impossible to raise a hand and ask him to repeat or

clarify something. On one occasion during our so-called 'Orals period', he gave me five lashes because of my 'wrong pronunciation' of the word 'apple'...

Grade 11 was worse. Our teacher, then a student at one of the teacher training colleges, 'taught' us essay writing and only one novel over the whole year. She missed most of her lessons as she spent most of her time either in the staff room or on 'sick leave'... (Mgqwashu, 2009b: 296–297)

It took a hardy, innate intellect to develop in this context, and, predictably, a great many learners under the Bantu Education system left school with poor content knowledge, poor mathematical skills and poorly developed literacy skills. Since the system produced its own teachers, a vicious cycle was established and, sadly, this continues in many schools.

There are some traditionally black schools, where, in spite of being poorly resourced and serving disadvantaged communities, teachers have a high work ethic and achieve good results[5], but they are unusual. For the most part, the new South African education department has failed to change the situation in poorly performing schools and many fail to give pupils a sound education. To illustrate, in the province of KwaZulu-Natal, the results of the school leaving examination continued to reflect apartheid differences at the end of 2008, when 73.9% of white children gained sufficient points for acceptance into a degree course at university, compared with 44.6% of Indian children, 39.1% of Coloured children and only 13.2% of black African children (Cronje & Roodt, 2009). Obviously, the fact that the majority of black African children write their school leaving examination in English and not their first language is an influential factor in these results, yet there are other damaging dynamics at play. According to the report on the newly introduced Annual National Assessments, released by the national Department of Basic Education in June 2011, even learners in the lower grades where teaching is in the mother tongue appear to be learning very little. The report shows that the average percentage gained in a mother tongue literacy test by Grade 3 learners (in their third year of schooling) was 35% and in a numeracy test, only 28%. Performances by Grade 6 learners, who by their 6th year in school are supposed to have switched to English as a medium of learning and teaching, were only slightly more alarming – at an average of 28% for literacy and 30% for mathematics (Department of Basic Education, 2010).

As noted in an address to school principals by President Zuma, a major problem in South African schools is the damaging tradition, among teachers at dysfunctional schools, of arriving late, leaving early, not attending at all on pay day and spending the time at school doing things other than teaching (Zuma, 2009). Current policies are attempting to deal with the problem, and in 'The Education Roadmap' – the government's 2009 plan for improving education – the first point is: '1. Teachers to be in class, on time, teaching. Teachers must also be required to use textbooks in class.' (Netshitangani, 2009: 2). The South African Democratic Teachers Union (SADTU) is a powerful union whose membership continues to be overwhelmingly black. It has been successful in negotiating some much-needed improved remuneration for teachers, but it has also protected poorly performing teachers against censure and dismissal and prevented the testing of teachers' competence (Taylor, 2011). In addition, learning is hampered by difficulties associated with the poverty that characterises the lives of so many of the learners.

Surrender to the Siren

Parents' eagerness to give their children a better educational springboard than they would be likely to get in traditionally black schools has resulted in a stampede of black children to ex-Coloured, Indian and white schools. The demand for places at suburban English-medium schools is so great that the schools can only accommodate fewer than 10% of the applicants (Heugh, 2009). Some of these state schools are still beyond the reach of poor families, because they charge fees to augment state funding. A legacy of apartheid is that ex-white state schools have good sports fields, libraries and other resources, and the drop in subsidy at the end of overt white privilege has forced them to choose between abandoning these facilities or charging fees. It is a source of bitterness for black families who cannot afford these fees that government officials and teachers who run historically black schools send their children to ex-white schools (Xulu, 2009), in the same way as the elite elsewhere in Africa send their children to schools where colonial languages are spoken, while officially supporting the promotion of indigenous languages (Kamwangamalu, 2010: 3). The painful outcome of this convoluted history is that, as far as parents are concerned, there is an unwritten, but obvious hierarchy of desirability of state schools, with ex-white schools (run on English education traditions, along with the use of the English language) at the top, then ex-Indian or ex-Coloured schools, then black schools where teachers do not belong to SADTU, and at the least desirable level, historically black, SADTU-dominated schools (Mgqwashu, 2009a).

Overall, black African parents who choose to send their children to English-medium schools hope that the children will gain the rewards associated with English proficiency and feel at home in both traditional African culture and Western English culture. However, they also face the hazard that they may never feel like a true insider in either one, seen as 'not quite one of us' by white South Africans and labelled by relatives and members of black African communities as a 'coconut' – a term used reprovingly to mean that they might be black on the outside, but have become white on the inside.

Policies for redressing inequity at universities include a complicated equity system that advantages members of 'previously disadvantaged' groups, in terms of university access for students, as well as staff employment. However, gaining access to university does not necessarily equate to adequate academic performance, and many black students from schools which equipped them poorly in academic skills struggle with the demands of university.

For black academics at South African universities, the struggle continues. There are no indigenous-language South African universities, and in spite of being held in high esteem by ex-schoolmates for having apparently sailed beyond the rocky perils of degrees and gained employment as lecturers, many black academics continue to struggle with the predominant English discourse. The pressure for all academics to have a PhD and publish in academic journals (which are in English) has shifted the goal posts from where they were some years ago, when an Honours degree was acceptable for undergraduate teaching and publishing was optional. In academic publishing, the power of English has fed on itself, and since the majority of editors, editorial boards and readers are English, the discourse, research paradigms and perspectives conform to the expectations of the English-speaking world (Altbach, 2008: 57). Again, speakers of African languages are disadvantaged, in comparison with their first-language English colleagues. Many of them, once more summoned by the siren song – this time towards the prospects of promotion or simply acceptance as equals – strive with academic texts and websites, with a good number foundering on the rocks and cliffs of perennial proposal writing or repeated rejection by journals. One is reminded of Bourdieu's concept (1984: 255) of 'the power of the dominant to impose, by their very existence, a definition of excellence which being nothing other than their own way of existing, is bound to appear simultaneously as distinctive and different, and therefore both arbitrary (since it is one among others) and necessary, absolute and natural.'

At the other end of the education spectrum, most adult literacy classes teach literacy skills in indigenous languages before introducing learners to English, but some workplace programmes offer the 'Straight to English' option, where learners try to learn literacy in English, thus attempting to use one unknown to learn another. This route appeals to literacy learners, because they believe they will achieve their central goals (mostly based on learning English) sooner than they would if they first learned literacy skills in their mother tongue. The strategy can be successful for learners who are reviving skills they learnt in brief periods of schooling as children, but not for first-time literacy learners. The promises made to them of speedy progress and vast gains are possibly the cruellest siren songs of all, since they offer hope to the most marginalised of South Africans, yet this learning route is characterised by painfully slow progress, small insignificant gains and high drop-out rates (Land, 2003).

Plotting a Course to the Future

Since the post-apartheid government committed itself to upholding the nine official indigenous languages and nurturing their development at the beginning of its rule, work has been done in setting up bodies such as the Pan South African Language Board and its associated provincial committees and on developing policy. Yet this effort seems to have produced only bureacratic results. People outside of these formal structures have not seen transformation relating to language beyond the broadcasts of news and some locally made programmes in indigenous languages on national television. Thus, in line with an unfortunate South African trend in many spheres of public life, we have extensive language policy development, but do not enjoy the expected outcomes. Webb (2009) offers several possible explanations for this failure to deliver on language policy, including a lack of capacity and preparedness among those in positions where they could use the policies to effect their desired ends, the association of the use of our different languages in education with apartheid and the possibility that the speakers of indigenous languages do not support their use in place of English.

This last suggestion resonates with what Alexander (2006a: 242) terms 'static maintenance syndrome', in which people use their own languages in their families, homes and communities, but do not see in their languages the capacity for use as languages of learning and power. Many first-language speakers of indigenous South African languages reveal this attitude towards their mother tongue and in it they typify Bourdieu's notion of symbolic domination (Bourdieu, 1991). We see people acquiescing, apparently voluntarily, to the disadvantage brought upon them by accepting as legitimate the assumed superior value of a dominant language. The 'consent of the victims' has been a major factor in maintaining the status of English and Afrikaans in South Africa (Alexander, 2006b). Their perception of the relative values of dominant and indigenous languages in 'the linguistic market' reflects and contributes substantially to the reality of this market. The attribution of higher status to all things associated with the colonisers of this country is linked with the habitual positioning – possibly in the minds of South Africans of all races – of black people in South Africa as *quescient recipients* of perceived benevolence, who accept and believe in the difference in status; as *potential agitators* against dominance, who reject the difference in status; or as *opportunistic agents*, ready to use any available strategy to improve their circumstances.

This rather crass division possibly has some use in considering the practicalities of what people stand to gain and lose in accepting the dominance of English (and the marginalisation of indigenous languages) or in choosing to use their indigenous languages as languages of learning, commerce and power.

Alexander (2006b: 8) maintains that 'In Africa... the languages of the majority of the people have to become the dominant languages... in the respective economy... of the individual countries. Only if this happens will the danger of a two-tier citizen-subject social model be countered in favour of a democratic system where all are citizens and all have similar life chances.'

The sentiment is intuitively attractive, yet how could indigenous languages achieve dominance in South Africa? Alexander writes of languages being 'given market value' and their enhancement of their instrumentality in 'processes of production, exchange and distribution' (Alexander, 2006b: 12), but it is difficult to imagine how this could be effected, even with government intervention. Even apartheid-era businesses – which went along willingly with policies of separate development – found that while the use of the distinct languages would have been useful for keeping a workforce divided and therefore more controllable, a *lingua franca* was necessary in workplaces such as mines. 'Fanakalo' – a simplified language based mainly on Zulu root words and English grammar – evolved as a workplace medium of communication. In spite of attempts to phase it out (Matomela, 2011), it is still used extensively – albeit now much less stridently – from suburban kitchens to De Beers, because workers need to communicate with each other both on-duty and off and many speak neither English nor Afrikaans, nor each other's languages (Madiba, 2011).

In public commercial activity, some banks offer users the choice of indigenous languages on their autobank screens, but this is a very small shift in the language market, and the only cost is one of investing in translation and some website maintenance. More substantial and, potentially, more influential shifts carry high costs and significant risks, for example, in the publishing industry. A common lament is that there is little published in indigenous languages and, therefore, not much available to read: less than 2% of the turnover for trade fiction and non-fiction books published in 2008 was from books in indigenous languages (Galloway & Struik, 2009). On the other hand, publishers are reluctant to publish books in indigenous languages, because, historically, the demand for them has been low (Desai, 2010). To remedy this situation, the government would need to subsidise the costs of publishing books in indigenous languages. Unfortunately, this is extremely unlikely, as even a petition to exempt books from value-added tax was rejected in 2009. Just the same, one possible sign of increased reading in indigenous languages is a recent rapid increase in the sales of a daily Zulu language newspaper, *Isolezwe*. While sales of English newspapers fell by as much as 16% in 2010, *Isolezwe* has had a surge of popularity, increasing its sales in the same period by 3.5%. In 2011, it recorded sales of more than 100,000 papers daily (Timse, 2011).

Ultimately, people will live according to the language options that accord best with what they experience as most comfortable and what brings them the most advantage. In Bourdieu's terms, they will, without deliberately shifting or preserving their language, choose whatever language use they are capable of that will best aid them in their pursuit of symbolic profit in interactions with other people and in the society in which they live (Bourdieu, 1991).

In families who have moved into the suburbs and into English schools, parents commonly express concern in relation to their children's shift towards English, but they tend to accept it as inevitable, as illustrated in the following recorded interview with a fellow academic at the University of KwaZulu Natal:

NM: I speak Zulu to them [my children] and I wish they spoke more Zulu than English... My husband and I always speak Zulu to them – they respond in English most of the time. They do speak Zulu to each other. But they are more comfortable in English.

SL: What language will their children speak?

NM: Mmm! You know how worried I am about that! I think it will depend on who they marry. But if they get married to kids like them – I mean – they speak more English than Zulu. And it's not like we haven't made a conscious effort – we've *begged* them, we've *bribed* them, we've *paid* them – when they were little we did everything we could in our power to make sure they spoke Zulu more often, but in the end... we would just throw up our hands...

SL: What about reading in Zulu?

NM: There was a time when I was really worried about them reading Zulu... I'm glad they can [now] read Zulu. My husband and I get so surprised when we hear them reading - because there was a time when we just threw our hands up and thought Oh God! We've really tried, it's not like we didn't *try* - we've done everything we could in our power to make sure they speak isiZulu more often – when going to... my husband comes from a deep rural area near Richards Bay – we would say [to them] "When we get there, please, please, *please* just for a *little*!" and they would try – for like 30 minutes or so... then they would just go back to English... I used to be so embarrassed... because I used to hate it when I saw kids like those [when I was younger] – and during my time there weren't many. But I used to think how can they be speaking English when all of us are speaking Zulu? And I could not believe it when my kids did the same. I tried to organise my friend Maki to open up Zulu classes for my kids. Other parents were not as concerned as I was but they were concerned.

SL: Do you think the [Zulu] language will be lost?

NM: I can believe it when I look at my kids. But I hope I'll be around to be a Zulu gogo [grandmother]. (Mthiyane, 2009)

Conclusion

Borne on the sweeping, rising tide of technological development and the sweeping power of globalisation, the English Hydra flourishes across the world, with the South African head as vigorous as any. In mythology, the breath of the many-headed Hydra was poisonous – a strikingly apt image for the effect of the English tongue on the other languages it touches. Here in South Africa, there is no overt, deliberate and defined imposition of English. It must also be acknowledged that a significant number of the South Africans who share the perception that they are appropriating English for their own purposes will eventually gain the rewards they pursue and do so fully conscious of the implications of their choice. They are not hapless victims, yet they are more 'swimming with the tide', than choosing their course. Like language communities anywhere that do not have the bulwarks of a publishing industry and readers with the tastes and resources to support it, a naturally growing terminology in 21st century discourses and speakers' confidence that the language can take its place alongside English, our indigenous languages are indeed shrivelling in the warmth of the Hydra's breath and the lure of the siren's song.

Notes

(1) 'uMzansi' – a Zulu and Xhosa word, denoting 'the one at the bottom', refers to South Africa's position on a map of Africa. The nickname has a strongly positive connotation and is used in advertising slogans, such as 'UMzansi fo sho!'
(2) Less than half of white South Africans speak English as a first language (Census 2001: 18); almost half a million whites emigrated between 1996 and 2010, leaving four-and-a-half million whites in the country (Statistics SA, 2010: 6)
(3) Boerewors is a spicy, undivided sausage cooked on an open fire, enjoyed by all South Africans, but originally a food of the Afrikaans community, particularly.
(4) The word 'Coloured' was used by the South African apartheid government, in the era of politically charged and traumatising racial discrimination, as a basket term for people who did not fit into apartheid's rigid racial categories of 'African', 'Asian' and 'White'. In spite of this, the term is not generally regarded as pejorative in South Africa.
(5) Some of these functional schools have their origins in missionary education, which – although now much maligned – was at least characterised by a strong work ethic and high standards of education.

References

Alexander, N. (2006a) Socio-political factors in the evolution of language policy in post-apartheid South Africa. In M. Pütz, J.A. Fishman and J. Neff-van Aertselaer (eds) *Along the Routes to Power: Explorations of Empowerment through Language* (pp. 241–260). Berlin: Mouton de Gruyter.
Alexander, N. (2006b) Language, class and power in post-apartheid South Africa. Online journal article, accessed 6 July 2011. http://www.yale-university.net/macmillan/apartheid/apartheid_part1/alexander.pdf

Altbach, P.G. (2008) The imperial tongue: English as the dominating academic language. *International Educator* 17 (5), 56–59.

Bourdieu, P. (1984) *Distinction: A Social Critique of the Judgement of Taste*. London: Routledge and Kegan Paul.

Bourdieu, P. and Thompson, J.B. (1991) *Language and Symbolic Power*. Cambridge: Polity Press.

Chili, B.B. (2007) Why are large numbers of illiterate adult members of the Luthuli rural community not attending ABET classes? Masters thesis, University of KwaZulu-Natal.

Constitution of the Republic of South Africa (1996) Number 108, Chapter 1, Point 6. Online document, accessed 20 July 2010. http://www.info.gov.za/documents/constitution/1996/a108-96.pdf

Cronje, F. and Roodt, M. (2009) A system which fails its pupils. *South African Institute of Race Relations Fast Facts*, December 2009, Johannesburg: South African Institute of Race Relations.

De Klerk, V. (1999) Black South African English: Where to from here? *World Englishes* 18 (3), 311–324.

Department of Basic Education (2010) *Report on the Annual National Assessments of 2011*. Online report, accessed 5 July 2011. http://www.education.gov.za/LinkClick.aspx?fileticket=1U5igeVjiqg%3d&tabid=424&mid=1831

Desai, Z. (2010) Laissez-faire approaches to language in education policy do not work in South Africa. In Z. Desai, M. Qorro and B. Brock-Utne (eds) *Educational Challenges in Multilingual Societies: Loitasa Phase Two Research* (pp. 102–112). Cape Town: African Minds.

Galloway, F. and Struik, W. (2009) *Annual Book Publishing Industry Survey Report 2008*. Pretoria: University of Pretoria. Online at http://www.publishsa.co.za/downloads/industry-statistics/2008_industry_survey.pdf

Gough, D.H. (1996) English in South Africa. In P. Silva, W. Dore, D. Mantzel, C. Muller and M. Wright, M. (eds) *Dictionary of South African English on Historical Principles* (pp. xvii–xix). Oxford: Oxford University Press.

Gower, P. (2009) Idle minds, social time bomb. *Mail and Guardian*, 31 July.

Heugh, K. (2009) Contesting the monolingual practices of a bilingual to multilingual policy. *English Teaching: Practice and Critique* 8 (2), 96–113.

Kamwangamalu, N.M. (2010) Vernacularization, globalization, and language economics in non-English-speaking countries in Africa. *Language Problems & Language Planning* 34 (1), 1–23.

Land, S. (2003) Resisting the right. Paper presented at the Language, Education and Diversity Conference, University of Waikato, New Zealand. 26–29 November, 2003.

Lemon, A. (2004) Redressing school inequalities in the Eastern Cape, South Africa. *Journal of Southern African Studies* 30 (2), 269–290.

Madiba, M. (2011) From Fanakalo to functional multilingualism in South African mines. Paper presented at the Mobility Language and Literacy Conference, January, Cape Town.

Master, P. (1998) Positive and negative aspects of the dominance of English. *TESOL Quarterly* 32 (4), 716–727.

Matomela, D. (2011) Fanagalo has to go, for safety's sake. *Independent Online IOL Business Report*, January 24. Online report, accessed 11 July 2011. http://www.iol.co.za/business/business-news/fanagalo-has-to-go-for-safety-s-sake-1.1015989

Mgqwashu, E. (2009a) *Interview on Reading*. Personal communication, Pietermaritzburg.

Mgqwashu, E. (2009b) On becoming literate in English: A during- and post-apartheid personal story. *Language Learning Journal* 37 (3), 293–303.

Mnyaka, M.B. (2009) The importance of an agricultural frame in decision making. Paper presented at the 57th session of the International Statistics Institute. Online at http://www.statssa.gov.za/isi2009

Mthiyane, N. (2009) *Interview on Reading.* Personal communication: Pietermaritzburg.

Netshitangani, T. (2009) *Review of Education, Skills Development and Innovation: Education Changes and Continuities Pre- and Post election 2009.* Human Sciences Research Council, Johannesburg, South Africa. Online at http://www.hsrc.ac.za/Document-3376.phtml

Ngũgĩ wa Thiong'o (1986) *Decolonising the Mind: The Politics of Language in African Literature.* Birmingham: James Currey.

Phillipson, R. (2008) The linguistic imperialism of neoliberal empire. *Critical Inquiry in Language Studies* 5 (1), 1–43.

Pienaar, M. (2008) A decline in language rights violation complaints received by PanSALB: The case of Afrikaans. *Stellenbosch Papers in Linguistics* 38, 135–137.

Statistics South Africa (2010) *Statistical Release P0302: Mid-year Population Estimates 2009.* Pretoria: Statistics SA.

Taylor, S. (2011) Uncovering indicators of effective school management in South Africa using the National School Effectiveness Study. Working paper 10/11, University of Stellenbosch.

Thompson, J.B. (1991) Editor's introduction. In P. Bourdieu *Language and Symbolic Power* (pp. 1–3). Cambridge: Polity Press.

Timse, T. (2011) Zulu newspapers thrive in South Africa. *Africa Review*, 4 April. Online at http://www.africareview.com/News/-/979180/1138364/-/hprwnmz/-/index.html

Webb, V. (2009) Multilingualism in South Africa: The challenge to below. *Language Matters* 40 (2), 190–204.

Xulu, L. (2009) *Interview on Reading.* Personal communication, Thornville.

Zuma, J. (2009) Address on the occasion of the President's national interaction with school principals, Durban International Convention Centre. 7 August, 2009. Online transcript at http://www.thepresidency.gov.za/pebble.asp?relid=623

12 English as Border-Crossing: Longing and Belonging in the South Korean Experience

Joseph Sung-Yul Park

Introduction

South Korea is well known for its heated pursuit of English – a phenomenon that is often called the 'English frenzy' (*yeongeo yeolpung*). Despite the country's well-established monolingualism in Korean, and the fact that English was not the language of the colonizer, significant investments are made in English language learning. The government continuously proposes revisions to the national curricula for English language education, introducing more English into the classroom and bringing in native-speaker English teachers to teach in Korean schools. Regional governments compete to build 'English villages', where students may practice English by being immersed in a simulated English-speaking community. Corporations demand that their employees have significant competence in English, and white-collar workers spend time and money honing their English language skills so that they can stay relevant to the workplace. Parents go to great lengths to give their children a head start in their English language learning and invest in a wide range of strategies, ranging from English-language DVDs to expensive English-only kindergartens to overseas study in English-speaking countries. Such efforts have led commentators to remark that Korea is a 'Republic of English' (Gim & Gim, 2007), where 'English is the national religion' (Demick, 2002; Park, 2009).

Phillipson's discussion of linguistic imperialism (1992) is clearly relevant to the Korean case. The hegemony and military presence of the US, neoliberal ideologies of globalization, the privileges of the English-speaking elite and the discourses of native speakerhood that are intertwined with images of race and ethnicity – all of these contribute to an overarching structure that conditions the enormous influence of English in Korean society. In discussing these issues, however, I want to explore how such broader structural conditions are reflected and reproduced in Koreans' psychological experiences. In doing so, I hope to translate Phillipson's insights onto a more personal level, which I believe actually sophisticates their political implications. By understanding how mundane, personal experiences are coloured through the forces of linguistic imperialism, we can more fully understand their roots in everyday life, obtaining a more complete picture of the specific processes by which the power of the English language comes into being.

The starting point for my discussion is how the Korean English frenzy is driven by a deep sense of anxiety. In Korea, one can often find complaints that Koreans' English language skills are woefully inadequate and that this lamentable incompetence is holding back the nation from participating in the global economy and enjoying its fruits. Such complaints are not only promulgated by media pundits, but are also widely shared among the entire population. It is common for foreigners to hear Koreans apologizing for their English, saying their English is not good, even among those who have had significant years of English language learning. Koreans refer to their own English as *Konglish* (*Korean English*) – a pejorative term that implies incorrect, absurd 'broken English' that is not really English at all (Park, 2008). When Koreans claim such incompetence, they do not simply note that they do not speak the language because it is not their own (as they would for any other foreign language), but they frame that incompetence in terms of embarrassment. They *ought* to be speaking good English and seriously would like to, but shamefully, they cannot – a manifestation of an ideology I have elsewhere called *self-deprecation* (Park, 2009). In this sense, the Korean English frenzy is not just an effort to secure English due to its pragmatic utility, but a manifestation of a pervasive anxiety, which presses Koreans to pursue English, by any means and at whatever cost.

In this chapter, I have adopted the notion of *border crossing*, to make sense of this anxiety. The notion of the border has been discussed extensively in various fields – including geography, anthropology, cultural studies and post-colonial studies – as migration, displacement and transnationalism have become central experiences in the modern world. While the most influential of these works, such as that of Homi Bhabha (1994), recognize the border as a site of hybridity that contests and subverts the imposing gaze of colonialism and modernity, here I rely more on perspectives that understand border crossing as a site of pain and anxiety (Walkerdine, 2006). Crossing the border is an experience fraught with tension, uneasiness and sadness, because one can never be completely at home with the place beyond the border, yet cannot fully return to the place one has left behind. As a result, one is left occupying an ever transient space that spans the border. I consider border crossing to be a useful metaphor for understanding the Koreans' relationship with English, as it highlights the material nature of this anxiety – how it is historically rooted in Korea's experiences of modernity, in which encounters with the West have played a significant role. It is something that is bodily experienced by Koreans – not simply an ideological, but a genuine psychological reaction, lived and performed through everyday life.

One characteristic of borders is that they are binary. They are an absolute line that differentiates Self and Other – despite the fact that they rarely correspond to 'natural' boundaries that exist independently of discourse – and in this sense, they are brutal. In post-colonial studies, borders are seen as Manichean (Fanon, 1965; JanMohamed, 1985) – a dualism that projects extreme oppositions of value, as in white/black, good/evil, civilized/savage, superior/inferior and so on. The border, thus, violently redraws the world of the colonized into compartmentalized, hierarchical spaces, erasing the complexity of relations that cannot be accommodated by such oppositions. This is what makes the border a site of anxiety, for our life world does not stop at boundaries stipulated by the border, yet the border is set up in a way that crossing over is constantly problematized. The colonized is led to desire the world beyond the border, which is represented as the ideal world under the Manichaean order, yet is precluded from being a part of that world, always being seen as the 'native'. The border invokes a sense of guilt in the colonized who may desire the world of the colonizer, for he or she is made to be seen as abandoning the 'homeland' that supposedly defines his or her existence. As a result, the colonized is caught in the borderland – between longing and belonging, between identity and alterity, between loyalty and betrayal – constantly wandering between the world they desire, yet cannot be a part of, and the home they left behind, yet cannot let go of.

On a more fundamental level, the anxiety of border crossing is inherent to modernity, at the centre of which stands the coherent, unitary Self, created by the Cartesian separation between the interior and exterior. As Valerie Walkerdine suggests, 'all subjects exist at a border' (2006: 11). Working-class women who left their community for a middle-class life; manual workers who are forced to take up new skills in the name of 'flexibility' and 'resilience', while their traditional community of support disintegrates – these are examples that Walkerdine offers as people who are made to live a life on the border, suffering from pain, loss and anxiety. Be it colonialism as a manifestation of the capitalist World System, the geographical and social segregation of classes, or the neoliberal obliteration of community and solidarity, what is central in each case is the *border* imposed by the ideology of the modern subject and the anxiety of being caught across that border.

The pain and anxiety of the border is all too familiar to Koreans, who live with the world's most heavily guarded, yet arguably most arbitrary, border in modern history – the demilitarized zone that separates North and South Korea, with hundreds of thousands of families split by the division. The modern Korean experience is also haunted by many other, interrelated manifestations of the border. In this chapter, I suggest that in Korea, English is one of those manifestations. It is a language that represents the glorified West, enticing Koreans to cross over to its world, but at the same time, it is an authorized language, which does not admit Koreans as members of its world, via a linguicism that constructs unequal divisions of identity on the basis of language (Skutnabb-Kangas, 1988; Phillipson, 1992). While to know English is to enter another world, dominant ideologies of English – originating from Western, racialized understandings of linguistic ownership and transplanted through Korean encounters with the West – problematize and illegitimize such acts of border crossing. And this problem is exacerbated by the fact that issues of class, power and privilege are deeply implicated in the drawing of the border of English. The resulting impenetrability and rigidity of the border thus fills Koreans' experience of English with feelings of anxiety, inadequacy and inferiority. By tracing the historical context and psychological effect of Koreans' anxiety about English, I discuss below in more detail how the border figures in the question of English in South Korea.

A Personal History

I want to begin my discussion with one specific case – my own – because it is one of the things that first made me think of the question of English in terms of the border. My life actually began with border crossing. My parents were Korean students studying in the US, where they met and got married. With the completion of my father's doctoral studies, my parents returned to Korea in the early 1970s with my sisters and me. We had all been born in the US. Once I came to Korea, I never crossed its border again, until more than 20 years later, when I would return to the US as a graduate student, like my parents once were. Just the same, my family continued to live inside the culture of the US. We consumed things like peanut butter and Spam (rare commodities at that time), we had our meals on a plate (instead of having rice in a bowl, the Korean way) and even owned a colour TV set (even though the only available broadcasts were black-and-white) – all material traces of the life we once had in the West, we preserved and maintained through the support of my father's position as a researcher at a government institute and later as a university professor.

The most salient vestige of our life abroad was language – the way English permeated our daily routines. While the language we spoke was mostly Korean, English still took a large part of our language use, with ample amounts of code-mixing. Literacy in English was also a major presence. There was always a recent issue of *Time*, *Newsweek* or *Stars and Stripes* (the newspaper of the US military) lying around the house, in addition to many books in English. My sisters and I also had the indelible marker of American accents. Even when the distinction offered by our material goods faded away (Spam and colour TV sets quickly became commonplace), English stood by our side like a faithful friend, testifying to our difference from other Koreans.

I didn't speak English like kids my age growing up in the US, and I still needed to learn English when I entered middle school (the stage where Koreans my age were first introduced to English). But my familiarity with English allowed me to learn it much more easily and quickly than my classmates. While they were busy memorizing rules of grammar, I was able to notice what was wrong with a sentence and how to correct it; while they were struggling to make sense of an English text printed in our books, I was able to grasp what it meant; and while other students tried hard to imitate the sound of native speakers recorded on cassette tapes, I knew exactly where to place my tongue to pronounce the word the way the Americans did. All of this was certainly an advantage in school. Korean language, mathematics and English were the three major subjects of study, and English was mostly a breeze for me, while for my classmates, studying English was a mysterious challenge.

For me, English meant more than a boost in school grades. It was also a door to another world. AFKN (American Forces Korean Network), a free-to-air television and radio broadcast of the US Armed Forces for their military personnel stationed in Korea, was a gold mine. While anyone with a TV set could watch it, I don't know of many Korean households who regularly watched it like we did. As a child, I used to watch the line-up of Saturday morning cartoons with my sisters and shows like 'Sesame Street' and 'The Electric Company' on weekdays. With the exception of the occasional Japanese anime shows featuring giant robots, nothing on Korean television was more enjoyable and more satisfying. Then, when I became a teenager, I discovered the world of pop music. Songs in English were definitely cooler than *gayo* or Korean popular songs, actually, pop music *had* to be in English; it simply wasn't conceivable to me, at that time, that one could express the same sentiments and sensibilities, the rhythms and beats in a language other than English. While Korean radio stations played a lot of Western pop music, I preferred to access the latest hits through the weekly show 'American Top 40' on AFKN. Keeping track of the newest hit songs and writing down their lyrics was the highlight of my week. English was the single most important thing that made all this possible for me. It was a key that allowed me to understand and appreciate this whole new cultural scene that lay beyond Korea and which other Koreans could only take a peek at through the muddied window of Korean monolingualism and local culture. English was a precious asset that I would not trade in for anything else.

But at the same time, English was also a great source of anxiety and tension. When my friends learned that I was born in the US, the first thing they would say was, 'Can you speak English?' Though uncomfortable with the attention, I would say a word or two in my American English, and they would burst out in laughter and amazement, mimicking my pronunciation. After the same thing happened a few times, I decided it would be wise to not reveal my transnational provenance. English was a great 'distancer' between other kids and me. It symbolically accentuated all the ways in which I was different from others, the foreign culture of my home, the benefits I enjoyed by coming from the US, the way I enjoyed things that the others didn't even know existed. English was a constant reminder of how I lived in a different world, unable to fully cross back to the world of my friends, where I also wanted to be. I didn't want them to see me as different, yet any utterance in English or the mere mention of the fact that I had been abroad would immediately set me apart.

As I grew older, I came to realize that there are deeper historical roots to my anxiety. I learned about the complex role of the US in Korean society – how it divided up the country into two in its imperialist contest with the Soviet Union, leading to the intra-ethnic bloodshed and destruction of the Korean War; how it endorsed the series of military dictatorships that ruled South Korea for decades so that it could maintain its influence in the geopolitically crucial Far East; how it mistreated its faithful ally through the unequal military agreements it established with the Korean government and so on. As I learned about these things, I realized having English carried serious implications of being a traitor who takes pride in siding with the Powerful Other and looks down upon his own kind. I hadn't read Frantz Fanon's *Black Skin, White Masks*, but it would have been all too familiar to me, because the colonized who desired to be the colonizer by speaking the colonizer's language – whom Fanon was talking about – was me. I thereby learned that desiring and celebrating English in Korea comes with a price: the price of anxiety, tension and guilt.

To me, then, to have English – to know English, to speak English, to feel close to English – was to live in a liminal space; that between Korean and English, Korea and the West, between identity and alterity, between loyalty and betrayal and between longing and belonging, never quite being rooted in one or the other, being ambivalent about where I should stand, feeling lost and unable to decide where I should belong. By being born into English, I was born straddling the border that did not allow crossing over; I was anxious and fragmented, at once wanting to desire and celebrate what English promised to bring me, yet held back by the guilt and shame that threatened my sense of belonging.

English in Korea: Some History

Even though my specific experience differs in many ways from an average Korean's, I believe my complex feelings towards English have much in common with other Koreans' anxiety about English. If my feelings were rooted not so much in transnational movement per se, but in the boundaries of class, consumption and culture that were invoked by English, then it would also make sense to think of all Koreans – even those who have never crossed the geographical boundary of Korea – as also living across a border, for such boundaries were central to Korea's modern experience. Although I fully acknowledge and do not mean to downplay my own classed position, I intend to point out that, in either case, it is the brutality of the modern border that defines us in a way that contradicts our own complex and multiple sense of being-ness.

When Korea opened its door to the West in 1882 by signing a forced treaty with the US, thus ending its isolation policy that had given it the name 'the hermit kingdom', Western technologies, practices, beliefs and ideas swarmed the Korean people, exposing them to a whole new world. When Korea emerged from Japanese colonial rule (1910–1945), the US military occupied the southern half of the peninsula, beginning decades of powerful US influence on Korean politics, economy and culture. Nadia Kim (2008) describes how such imperial encounters and their cultural manifestations – such as educational institutions built by US missionaries or Hollywood movies – established an idealized image of the benevolent, abundant and advanced West and instilled in the Korean populace a desire for the US that still persists, though in uneasy coexistence with anti-American sentiment. The neocolonial discourse worked in terms of a relational and binary opposition. As the US was constructed as powerful, advanced and beautiful (the Korean name for the US is *miguk*, literally, 'beautiful country'), Koreans were understood in its mirror image – weak, backwards and inferior. Such contrasts have their roots in US discourse during Korea's colonial and post-war period, which depicted Koreans as dirty, deceiving and ugly; and these Orientalist views of Koreans were internalized by Koreans themselves, through an acknowledgement of the inferiority of Korean aesthetics, ethics and social organization. 'South Koreans, then, have been made to feel inferior not just by virtue of their reliance on a superior US military, but by the *racial ideologies* of the military itself' (Kim, 2008: 54; emphasis in original).

This is not to say that Koreanness was a coherent, essential identity that collapsed into a schizophrenic condition only with contact with the West. Korea always had its own internal divisions of region and social class, and Koreans have always crossed borders, having existed as part of a cosmopolitan civilization centred in China for centuries (Seth, 2006). Thus, it is not the experience of the border that was new. However, Korea's late 19th century and early 20th century encounters with the West served as a crucible for modernist ideas of 'nationhood', as the country was 'forcibly incorporated into a nation-state system dominated by Western imperial powers' (Em, 1999: 339; Schmid, 2002). This period gave birth to a nationalist historiography that 'invented' the Korean tradition and origin, giving Koreans a new way of articulating their own identity in distinction to foreign Others, an intensified form of reflexivity and, thus, a means for engaging in anti-colonial struggle. But it also provided them with a framework for naturalizing the dualist image of the East and West and internalizing the Manichaean opposition of values that supports colonial and imperial discourses of power, in which the border – essential to the modern conception of the nation – denies forms of hybridity and interpenetration.

In this process, English served a key role. On the one hand, English was a powerful mechanism for instilling and internalizing a desire for the western Other (Pennycook, 1998). As Fanon said, 'to speak a language is to take on a world, a culture' (1967: 38). Particularly since the days of the US military occupation (1945–1948), English has been a language of power, and to speak English was to access all the positive things that the US represented in Korea. Intellectuals educated in the US, for example, secured important positions in the newly established South Korean government, leading many people to treat English as crucial for social advancement. But on the other hand, assimilation through English was also made impossible by dominant global ideologies of English, which define the 'native speaker' not purely in terms of linguistic abilities, but in terms of race and national origin (Widdowson, 1994; Brutt-Griffler & Samimy, 2001; Leung et al., 1997; Holliday, 2005; Park & Wee, 2009). Prevalent US media depictions of Asian Americans and Asian nationals as speakers of broken, accented, incomprehensible English were circulated in Korean society through the dissemination of media products and the movements of people between the two countries (Lo & Kim, 2012). This forced Koreans to accept that their English would only be a mimicry, never a legitimate language, and it would be forever subject to evaluation by the 'native speaker', despite the fact that significant amounts of hybridity and interpenetration between Korean and English have existed since Korea's independence and even more so today (Park, 2008). By reinforcing and naturalizing social, racial and national difference, English thus imposed impervious modern borders of identity, trapping Koreans under a veil of inferiority and anxiety.

Junuk

This anxiety is 'real' in a bodily sense. A striking example is the feeling of *junuk* that often characterizes Koreans' attitude towards English. The term *junuk* refers to a feeling of inadequacy, as in when one stands before a powerful figure and feels completely helpless and feeble, subsumed by a strong sense of inferiority. While any structure of power and hierarchy may subject a person to *junuk*, encounters with English, particularly interactions with native speakers of English, are commonly talked about as contexts that heighten this helpless sense of inadequacy. Koreans' talk about English is full of jokes, tales, complaints and assertions about how they become petrified upon encountering an English-speaking foreigner (Park, 2009), how they feel ashamed of their lack of English skills as they struggle to find words to express their thoughts and how they wish they would overcome their *yeongeo ulleongjeung* ('English nausea') – the debilitating fear and anxiety of speaking English. Indeed, it is this *junuk* that makes English a national obsession. It is the desperate want to escape from this inferiority that leads Koreans to pursue English at all costs. Even speakers who have reasonable competence in English are subject to this feeling. Literary critic and scholar of English literature, Yun Jigwan, speaks of this in the following way (translated from Korean):

> The fact that I am an expert in the English language does not mean that I am immune to this wave of mass hysteria [of the English frenzy]. I am not free to look at this commotion from a distance and click my tongue at it. If English is not one's mother tongue, mastering some English will neither let one escape from the domination of English nor make the internalized inferiority complex about English go away forever. ... Even so-called English language specialists undoubtedly suffer from *junuk* about English, though it may be manifest in a different form.

> Because of my job as an English literary scholar, I occasionally visit the US. Whenever I lecture at an American university or attend an academic conference, the problem of English constantly follows me and bothers me like an evil spirit, clinging to some part of my brain. In front of those who possess the marbles of English as their own and who can freely play with those marbles anyway they want, I feel the awkward self-consciousness of a country teacher who must reluctantly demonstrate his puny skills with the marbles. At the same time, this *junuk* sometimes turns into anger and lament, as I remember I have my own set of marbles that I can handle all too well. (Yun, 2001: 111–112)

Inferiority complex, awkwardness, anger and lament – Yun's account highlights the psychological reality and complexity of the anxiety Koreans feel towards English. It is instructive that Yun interprets this anxiety from a post-colonial perspective, locating his frustration within the relations of power in which the academic authority of the West demands knowledge to be represented and exchanged in its own terms, in the language of English. After all, the title of his essay translates as 'English, colonialism of my heart'.

Yun's essay was, in fact, written as part of a debate with novelist Bok Geoil, who argued that English should be made an official language of Korea, in order to boost Koreans' competence in English (Park, 2009). This extract is thus a call to problematize the hegemony of English by critiquing its process of internalization, which Yun seeks to expose by confessing his own anxiety about English. But his confession also reveals that the greatest source of his frustration seems to lie in his belief that English will never become his own language, that he will never be recognized as a native speaker. Pure linguistic competence, no matter how advanced, does not make the language one's 'mother tongue' (*mogukeo*). Elsewhere in the same essay, Yun also states, 'if English is not your mother tongue, your English language skills will always be limited, always inferior to those of a native speaker' (p. 121), criticizing the false hopes (of people such as Bok) that greater investments in English language learning will give Koreans equal status to native speakers.

From a sociolinguistic perspective, this statement may seem problematic, for it does not acknowledge the multiple ways in which the ownership of English may be defined or the local creativity that contests a centre-based model of linguistic legitimacy (Park & Wee, 2009). That is, rather than contesting notions such as 'mother tongue' or 'native speaker', Yun treats them as essential categories, proposing a resistance that works around them, instead. But here I am not interested in criticizing Yun's perspective. Instead, I want to show how his statement illustrates the importance of the border in the generation of anxiety about English. For Yun, his source of frustration is nothing other than the impenetrable boundaries of identity, according to which, Koreans are – by definition – illegitimate speakers of English who will always be subordinate to the authority of 'native speakers'. The sense of inferiority and inadequacy that oppresses the Korean emanates not from the English-speaking Western individual, but from the sheer monumentality of the border that separates the Korean from that Westerner, denying all possibility of Koreans' creative and transformative appropriation of English. The border makes any Korean attempt at using English unnatural and, thus, awkward, alien and anxious, even though Koreans live in a world where English is a common presence, where hybridity and border crossing are unavoidable. It is this contradiction that overwhelms the Korean with a feeling of *junuk*, as they are cast as inferior people who linger along the border hoping for a chance to cross over to the other side, to which (they are told) they do not belong.

The Future?

If anxiety about English leads to Korea's frantic quest for English, what effect does this pursuit have? The Korean English frenzy has been going on for more than a decade, coinciding with Korea's national project of globalization that started in the mid 1990s, and this has given rise to a generation of Koreans who have experienced a very different kind of exposure to English, compared to their parents' generation. For example, *jogi yuhak*, or early study abroad, in which pre-university students are sent to study in English-speaking countries, has emerged as an important strategy for inculcating 'native English' in the child (Park & Bae, 2009; Song, 2010). The popularity of *jogi yuhak* among middle class households has now resulted in a contingent of transnational youths who feel much more comfortable in interacting with English speakers in cross-cultural context than their parents' generation. They speak fluent English, if not in an accent indistinguishable from 'native speakers', and they are able to freely express their thoughts without being constrained by the anxiety that paralyzes older Koreans. If new forms of transnationalism have led to this change, does this mean that the feeling of *junuk* will someday no longer bother Korean speakers of English? As globalization makes border crossing increasingly mundane and trivial, will English cease to carry the meaning of a border that splits the Korean psyche and infuses the experience of speaking it with tension and anxiety? Will all Koreans, one day, finally be free from the burden of English?

Whether this will be the case will have to be seen. But the discussion above suggests that the question is not really about whether Koreans will be able to acquire 'native' accents or not. If imperfect mastery of accent were the primary issue, the anxiety of border crossing should be irrelevant to Korean migrants to the US, who, by the second generation, usually speak with little discernible deviation from mainstream American English. Yet, English means a tension between longing and belonging to Korean Americans as well. Under the racialized social order of the US, Korean Americans (along with other Asian Americans) are seen as 'forever foreigners' (Tuan, 1998). They are always invisible in the space of citizenship, never recognized as 'Americans' and denied their belongingness in mainstream US society, evidenced by the perennial question, 'Where are you from?' Linguistically, Korean Americans are also subject to stereotypes circulating in mainstream US society, which view them as speakers of English with a foreign accent – of 'Yellow English' (Lo & Reyes, 2009). In this sense, Korean Americans still live on the borderland, always working towards assimilation, but always seen as 'not quite'. The real issue, then, is not so much opportunities for acquiring the right kind of accent and competence, but the discourses of power – which impose boundaries upon the world – and the tension that this brings about in the subject caught in between.

The real challenge thus lies in how Koreans can contest the distinctions of identity that instill borders in their mind. Increased transnationalism may not necessarily trivialize border crossing, but, in fact, may reinforce the ideologies that support oppositions of identity, particularly if that transnationalism is exploited and commodified for the purpose of gaining greater material benefits. Through *jogi yuhak*, for example, the student is supposed to be better prepared for the neoliberal job market, securing better chances of success through the competence and fluency in English gained abroad, which is commonly understood as the acquisition of a 'native' accent of English. As such strategies of linguistic investment conform to the dominant order of the global linguistic market, in which 'native' English accents of the West are considered more valuable than 'non-native' ones, it does little to contest that order and, in fact, may be seen as reproducing it.

Of course, things do not always have to be this way. The border, after all, is not only a site of anxiety and pain, but it may also be a locus for contestation and resistance. Thus, in some contexts, *jogi yuhak* students, who often have greater transnational connections and international experience than local native speakers in their destinations of study, may look down upon them as 'backward' (Shin, 2012) and take pride in their own ability to move flexibly across different accents or norms of English, constructing themselves as true cosmopolitans (Kang, 2012). But it is also important to remember that *jogi yuhak* is a phenomenon constrained by class relations, in which accessibility is restricted to those who can afford it financially. This means the global hierarchy of power and legitimacy, which obtains between the native-English-speaking West and non-native Koreans, may be reproduced domestically in terms of class, as the wealthy come to be praised for the competence in English they have acquired through their study abroad. In this case, the potential of border crossing to contest dominant ideologies is lost, as an opposition based on racial, national boundaries is simply replaced with a class-based one.

Conclusion

While I acknowledge the subversive potential of border crossing, I feel skeptical that the oppressive ideologies of identity, which trigger anxieties about English, can be thrown off so easily. My reason for this is the sheer weight of the burden. This anxiety is simply too heavy to be lifted from our shoulders without serious reflexive work, strenuous critical analysis and commitment to combat all the forms of inequality that threaten to reintroduce the borders that objectify Koreans. Through this chapter, I have tried to illustrate the actuality of this anxiety and the extent to which it permeates Koreans' psyches. By speaking of that experience in terms of border crossing, I hope that we Koreans will be able to creatively rework the border and use it to emancipate ourselves from the neocolonial relations of power that give rise to such anxiety. But in order to do so, I believe it is important first to fully understand the nature of this anxiety by taking a more reflexive stance. It needs to be dwelled upon, relived and put into historical perspective so that we can truly come to a position where we can contest the borders of schizophrenic pain. The anxiety that goes with English is not something that we can just move away from easily.

References

Bhabha, H. (1994) *The Location of Culture*. New York, NY: Routledge.

Brutt-Griffler, J. and Samimy, K. (2001) Transcending the nativeness paradigm. *World Englishes* 20 (1), 99–106.

Demick, B. (2002) Some in S. Korea opt for a trim when English trips the tongue. *Los Angeles Times*, March 31, A3.

Em, H.H. (1999) Minjok as a modern and democratic construct: Sin Ch'aeho's historiography. In G. Shin and M. Robinson (eds) *Colonial Modernity in Korea* (pp. 336–361). Cambridge: Harvard University Press.

Fanon, F. (1965) *The Wretched of the Earth*. London: MacGibbon and Kee.

Gim, N. and Gim, J. (2007) Yeongeo mos haneun 'yeongeo gonghwaguk'. *Chosun Ilbo*, May 2. Online at http://news.chosun.com/site/data/html_dir/2007/05/02/2007050 200081.html

JanMohamed, A.R. (1985) The economy of Manichean allegory: The function of racial difference in colonialist literature. *Critical Inquiry* 12, 59–87.

Kang, Y. (2012) Singlish or Globish? Multiple language ideologies and global identities among Korean educational migrants in Singapore. *Journal of Sociolinguistics*, 16/2, April, 2012.

Kim, N.Y. (2008) *Imperial Citizens: Koreans and Race from Seoul to LA*. Stanford, CA: Stanford University Press.

Leung, C., Harris, R. and Rampton, B. (1997) The idealized native speaker, reified ethnicities, and classroom realities. *TESOL Quarterly* 31 (3), 543–560.

Lo, A. and Kim, J. (2012) Linguistic competency and citizenship: Contrasting portraits of multilingualism in the South Korean popular media. *Journal of Sociolinguistics*, 16/2, April, 2012.

Lo, A. and Reyes, A. (2009) Introduction: On yellow English and other perilous terms. In A. Reyes and A. Lo (eds) *Beyond Yellow English: Toward a Linguistic Anthropology of Asian Pacific America* (pp. 3–17). Oxford: Oxford University Press.

Park, J.S. (2008) Two ways of reproducing monolingualism in South Korea. *Sociolinguistic Studies* 2 (3), 331–346.

Park, J.S. (2009) *The Local Construction of a Global Language: Ideologies of English in South Korea*. Berlin: Mouton de Gruyter.

Park, J.S. and Bae, S. (2009) Language ideologies in educational migration: Korean *jogi yuhak* families in Singapore. *Linguistics and Education* 20, 366–377.

Park, J.S. and Wee, L. (2009) The three circles redux: A market-theoretic perspective on world Englishes. *Applied Linguistics* 30 (3), 389–406.

Pennycook, A. (1998) *English and the Discourses of Colonialism*. London: Routledge.

Phillipson, R. (1992) *Linguistic Imperialism*. Oxford: Oxford University Press.

Schmid, A. (2002) *Korea Between Empires, 1895–1919*. New York, NY: Columbia University Press.

Seth, M.J. (2006) *A Concise History of Korea: From the Neolithic Period Through the Nineteenth Century*. Lanham, MD: Rowman & Littlefield.

Shin, H. (2012) From FOB to cool: Transnational migrant students in Toronto and the styling of global linguistic capital. *Journal of Sociolinguistics*, 16/2, April, 2012.

Skutnabb-Kangas, T. (1988) Multilingualism and the education of minority children. In T. Skutnabb-Kangas and J. Cummins (eds) *Minority Education: From Shame to Struggle* (pp. 9–44). Clevedon: Multilingual Matters.

Song, J. (2010) Language ideology and identity in transnational space: Globalization, migration, and bilingualism among Korean families in the USA. *International Journal of Bilingual Education and Bilingualism* 13, 2–42.

Tuan, M. (1998) *Forever Foreigners or Honorary Whites? The Asian Ethnic Experience Today*. New Brunswick: Rutgers University Press.

Walkerdine, V. (2006) Workers in the new economy: Transformation as border crossing. *Ethnos* 34 (1), 10–41.

Widdowson, H.G. (1994) The ownership of English. *TESOL Quarterly* 28 (2), 377–389.

Yun, J. (2001) Yeongeo, nae maeumui sikminjuui (English, colonialism of my heart). *Sahoebipyeong* 28, 110–126.

13 English and Mandarin in Singapore: Partners in Crime?

Rani Rubdy

Introduction

The current consolidation and expansion of English as a global language and its potential for eliminating linguistic diversity have earned it, deservingly or not, the various negative appellations of a 'killer language' (Skutnabb-Kangas, 2003), a 'Tyrannosaurus Rex' (Swales, 1997), a 'lingua frankensteinia' and 'lingua diabolica' (Phillipson, 2008). These different avatars of English – suggestive of the deadly mythological serpent Hydra with its multiple heads, at once virulent and unassailable (as invoked by the title of this volume) – are all conjured up with the purpose of establishing a link between global Euro-American dominance and English language hegemony. But even as we call English a 'killer', we all know that it is not languages per se that kill, threaten, endanger or eliminate, but rather, the power of their speakers. We know that they do so by interventionist policy decisions about how languages may be acquired, used and accessed in particular communities. As Phillipson reminds us, any language can serve good or evil purposes; it is human agency that will ultimately determine which of these will prevail.

Singapore presents an especially pertinent case study when it comes to the dynamics of English language hegemony in a multilingual society. Firstly, because in contrast to other Asian countries, which at independence elected to make a major indigenous language the national language, Singapore chose to adopt the colonizer's language as its *de facto* working language and medium of education. Consequently, the speed with which English has achieved dominance in Singapore means that English is integrated into every aspect of its societal fabric. Second, in pursuit of its national globalizing goals, which has entailed the aggressive institutionalization of English (and, more recently, Mandarin), it actively denigrates and discourages the use of the real mother tongues, namely, the Chinese dialects brought by the original immigrants to this British colony and 'Singlish' – the local variety of English that has emerged as a result of language contact and restructuring. Thirdly, despite its commitment to a project of 'multiracialism' (Benjamin, 1976) and its espousal of a bilingual policy that accords equal status to all of its four official languages, the official discourse tends to privilege particular languages over others. This is driven primarily by an orientation towards an ideology of pragmatism, which emphasizes the *economic value* of a language as a central consideration in shaping Singapore's language policies.

Given its emphasis on pragmatism, the logic that guides the state's language policy is that languages which are perceived to be 'obstacles to economic development' can have no place in the Singaporean linguistic landscape and must, therefore, be eliminated. As a consequence, Singapore's language planning has no official use for either the various Chinese dialects (with the exception of Mandarin) or Singlish (the colloquial variety of Singapore English). These have been the targets of national campaigns that aim, as far as possible, to ensure that Singaporeans stop using them (Rappa & Wee, 2006). Singapore's approach to language policy is thus incompatible with the vibrant local practices of its multilingual ecology, creating an environment that reduces, rather than promotes, linguistic diversity.

Two main issues, relating to the reduction of Singapore's linguistic diversity, call for attention. Firstly, the considerable language shift towards English and Mandarin that has occurred over the last four decades since Singapore's independence in 1965, despite its avowed commitment to a bilingual education policy and, secondly, the intra-language discrimination exercised against the Chinese dialects and Singlish – stemming primarily from the government's emphasis on maintaining a single exonormative standard for each of the official mother tongues, as well as English, in conjunction with its orientation towards linguistic instrumentalism (Wee, 2003). Whereas the promotion of English as the language of Asian modernity and the universal medium of education since the 1980s, accompanied by an increasing trend among young Singaporeans to use it as their main home language, makes English language dominance the 'usual suspect' in the elimination of language diversity, it is by no means the sole culprit. Within the Chinese community, the promotion of English has worked in tandem with that of Mandarin to erode the status and use of the Chinese dialects as home languages. In the case of Singapore, therefore, it is not merely the impact of one, but of two major world languages – a double whammy – that is operative in marginalizing the indigenous languages. For this reason, although the chapter focuses mainly on English-language dominance in Singapore, issues relating to Mandarin, where relevant, will also be considered.

The Language Ecology of Singapore

Singapore has always had a rich, complex and dynamic multilingual ecology, which has evolved over the decades since the arrival of the original British immigrants in 1819. Even prior to the establishment of Singapore as a British trading post by Raffles, there was already a heterogeneous population of local Malays and 'Indonesians', Southern Chinese and Indian traders and some mixed ethnic groups, such as the Peranakans and Eurasians. The rapidly expanding economy generated by the establishment of the trading post resulted in an even more rapid influx of immigrants, the majority of whom came from southern China, the Malay peninsula, the Indonesian archipelago and South Asia. The population in this era exhibited considerable richness and diversity, in terms of origin and multilingual repertoire (Gupta, 2008; Lim, 2010).

The most important groups were the 'Malays' from Malaya, plus Javanese, Boyanese, Bataks and Buginese from Indonesia, the Tamils, Malayalees, Punjabis, Sikhs and other ethnic groups from the Indian subcontinent, including Ceylonese, and the Hokkiens, Teochews, Hakkas, Hainanese and other dialect groups from China. Additional minorities included Arabs and Filipinos and the Straits-born Chinese or Babas. By the turn of the 19th century, Singapore had become a cosmopolitan city, with small groups of Armenians, Jews and Japanese and Europeans. It also saw, at this time, the expansion of the population of Eurasians, most of whom spoke a variety of vernaculars to begin with, but soon adopted English as a mother tongue, giving rise to Eurasian English (Gupta, 1994; Wee, 2010).

Until the middle of the 20th century, most of these Asian communities spoke the vernacular languages their ancestors brought to Singapore and often several other languages as well. Beyond each community's vernacular, there was Bazaar Malay, which had been established for centuries as an interethnic *lingua franca* in the Malayan peninsula. Hokkien – the largest single Chinese dialect – also functioned as a *lingua franca*, especially among the Chinese community. Even after the growth of the Chinese population exceeded that of the Malays in the late 19th century, Bazaar Malay was still the second most understood language after Hokkien and the most important language for interethnic communication (Lim, 2010: 27).

There had already been in place a *capitan* (captain) system, which divided the community into three basic groups: the Malays, Chinese and Indians, plus a non-*capitan*-ed group of 'Others' (Bloom, 1986: 352). The British found it advantageous to preserve this ethnically-based division, and this came to constitute the cultural logic of Singapore's project of multiracialism, which forms the cornerstone of its current language policy. Before independence in 1965 – based on this categorization of ethnic groups – four more or less independent school systems had evolved in Singapore, each with a different language as the major medium of instruction. The Malay- and Chinese-medium schools did not teach English at all in the early years, although by the 1920s and 1930s, English began to be taught as a subject. English-medium schooling was provided by the British for the English-speaking elites among the local population, with about 32% of students enrolled in English-medium schools in 1947 (Tickoo, 1996). By the 1950s, education had become effectively universal, with the enrolment in English-medium education overtaking that of Chinese-medium education.

Because of the country's racial and linguistic diversity, 'multiracialism' was one of the first policies introduced by the newly independent government (1965). It stressed that equal treatment be accorded to each ethnic group and its associated mother tongue, as this was crucial to maintaining racial harmony in the management of ethnicity. However, because Singapore's version of 'multiracialism' assigns ethnic membership on the basis of one's father's race, the highly complex and heterogeneous linguistic/cultural/racial structure within each ethnic group has been drastically reduced and regional and sub-group differences suppressed. In practical terms, Singapore's multiracialism is thus limited to four official categories: Chinese, Malay, Indian and Others. While the category 'Malay' is relatively unproblematic, since the Malays form a fairly homogeneous group, the label 'Chinese' does not faithfully characterize the internal diversity inherent in the dialect-based identities among members of the Chinese community. A similar problem arises with the application of the category 'Indian', since the Indian community is relatively heterogeneous, comprising at least Malayalee, Sikh, Sindhi, Gujarati and Tamil communities (Rappa & Wee, 2006: 85). These regional differences have been completely glossed over in the strict categorization of Singaporeans into four ethnic groups.

This discrepancy likewise exists in the categorization of the four official languages in Singapore: Malay, Mandarin, Tamil and English. Of the four official languages/three mother tongues, only Malay and Tamil are 'true mother tongues', even though the fact that Tamil is spoken by 'a majority of Indians' means that there are a number of other Indians for whom Tamil is not their real mother tongue (Purushotam, 1998). Mandarin had few native speakers in Singapore until the 1980s, since many members of the Chinese community still spoke mutually unintelligible Chinese dialects. However, in 1979, the government began to strenuously promote Mandarin, and, as a result of this drive, the oral use of Mandarin in social interaction rocketed, making it the single largest native language of children under 10 (Gupta, 2008: 107). Together, English and Mandarin have almost completely supplanted Hokkien and Bazaar Malay, both of which had been in widespread use before Singapore's independence. But this state of affairs has come about at a price – the reduction of diversity and the official disinheritance of its true mother tongues.

English in Singapore: The Language of Asian Modernity

Singapore gained its independence in 1965 after being ejected from the Federation of Malaysia, due to political differences between Singapore's leaders and the central government in Kuala Lumpur. Separation from the Federation presented the first generation of Singapore's leaders with a real political challenge. Two key issues of immediate concern to the government were: the management of ethnic diversity and the need for rapid economic development in the face of a lack of natural resources. The city-state pinned its hope on export-oriented manufacturing and in attracting foreign investment on as large a scale as possible. The need for a skilled workforce became essential, in turn, requiring a reorganization of the educational system.

From an economic point of view, English – the language of science and technology and of international trade and commerce – was seen as a basic need. Political insecurity called for the creation of national unity and the forging of a national identity that transcended ethnic boundaries (Chiew, 1983: 45). English, being a non-native language and not associated with any of the ethnic groups, was considered neutral (Kuo, 1980: 59). English education became the lynchpin of Singapore's bilingual education policy and standards in its use began to receive attention at the highest levels of decision-making (Tickoo, 1996: 437). At the same time, since its nation-building ambitions were to be achieved while still maintaining an Asian identity, the government consistently encouraged Singaporeans to be bilingual in English, plus a mother tongue – a policy known as 'English-knowing bilingualism' (Pakir, 1992).

According to the 2010 Census of Population, Singapore has a population of 5 million. Its current racial composition is roughly 74% Chinese, 13.4% Malay and 9.2% Indian, while the remaining 3.3% are mainly Eurasians, Europeans and Others (Department of Statistics, 2010). Singapore's language policy broadly corresponds with this racial categorization. While Malay, Mandarin and Tamil are designated as 'mother tongues' (MT), there is no official MT for the 'Others' category. Even though English is recognized as an official language, it is excluded from the list of mother tongues, owing to the government's insistence on representing Singapore as a fundamentally Asian society (Wee, 2010).

Accordingly, the mother tongues and English are positioned such that there is a functional allocation between them. English functions as the language of modernity, while the three MTs are seen as cultural anchors that connect individuals to traditional values, as well as staving off the potentially negative effects of Western cultural influences that are associated with the use of English. By assigning English and the MTs to different domains, the language policy thus treats the relationship between them as one of complementarity.

Since the MT is officially assigned, it does not always reflect the languages spoken at home. This obscures the heterogeneity of the various ethnic communities. Table 13.1, based on the 2000 Census of Population of Singapore, shows that, except for the Malays, the officially assigned MT is quite often not the home language.

Table 13.1 Language most frequently spoken at home (in percentages)

Home Ethnicity	Frequency of Language Used at Home (percentage)				
	Chinese Dialects	English	Malay	Mandarin	Tamil
Chinese	30.7	23.9		45.1	
Malay		7.9	91.6		
Indian		35.6			42.9
Others		68.5			

Source: Rappa and Wee (2006)

One consequence of the bilingual policy, and its attendant ideology of pragmatism, is that, notwithstanding the equal status accorded to its four official languages, the functional polarization between the MTs and English, in fact, conceals a hegemonic dimension (Tan, 1996: 109) that clearly privileges English over the local languages. The fact that English has become so strongly associated with educational achievement and material wealth has made it a highly desirable and important language in the minds of Singaporeans. Many parents have switched to English as their home language to give their children a head start in school and to ensure their future career prospects, even at the risk of losing their ethnic identity (Chew, 1999: 41). As a result, although English is found to be emotionally unacceptable as a mother tongue for Singaporeans by the government, its status in education, government, administration and business has enabled it to emerge as a dominant *lingua franca* among Singaporeans. English is fast becoming the main language of some Singaporean households, as it penetrates deeper into more personal and intimate domains of use, displacing the mother tongues and rendering the concept of indigeneity meaningless in Singapore (Gupta, 2008: 99). An even more devastating outcome of the state's energetic promotion of English is that it has led to a massive language shift over the last 30 years. The rise of English is most pronounced in Chinese and Indian homes, with many Singaporeans describing themselves as literate only in English. Chinese homes citing English as the home language rose from 10.2% in 1980 to 23.9% in 2000. For Indian homes, the corresponding figures are 24.3% in 1980 and 35.6% in 2000. Even in Malay homes, where the shift to English is thought to be less pronounced, there is still a discernible movement towards English, from 2.3% in 1980 to 7.95% in 2000 (Stroud & Wee, 2010: 186).

The converse is true with regard to the mother tongues. Despite Singapore's commitment to bilingualism, it appears that the adoption of the ascribed MT has not occurred equally across all ethnic groups (Vaish et al., 2010). Table 13.2 shows that from 1990 until 2005, English increased as the language spoken at home in all three ethnic groups. At the same time,

Table 13.2 Language trends in Singapore

Language spoken at home	Ethnicity								
	Chinese			Malay			Indian		
	1900	2000	2005	1900	2000	2005	1900	2000	2005
English	19.3	23.9	28.7	6.1	7.9	13.0	32.3	35.6	39.0
Mandarin	30.1	45.1	47.2						
Malay				93.7	91.6	86.8	14.5	11.6	10.6
Tamil							43.2	42.9	38.8
Dialect	50.3	30.7	23.9						
Others	0.5	0.4	0.2	0.1	0.5	0.2	10.0	9.9	11.6
Total	100.0	100.0	100.0	100.0	100.0	100.0	100.0	100.0	100.0

Sources: Singapore Department of Statistics (2001); Census of Population and Singapore Department of Statistics (2006); General Household Survey 2005, Socio-Demographic and Economic Characteristics, Release I

the use of Malay, Tamil and the Chinese dialects has dropped significantly and this downward trend continues. Since 2001, less than 2% of Chinese students in each cohort have come from dialect-speaking homes, as parents prefer their children to learn both English and Mandarin well.

A recent report from the Chinese Review Committee states that 'the number of Chinese students entering Primary 1 (P1) who speak predominantly English at home has risen from 36% in 1994 to 50% in 2004' (Ministry of Education, 2004: 4). This figure was further projected to be 60% by 2009. According to the Chinese language newspaper, *Lianhe Zaobao*, the key challenge for the Speak Mandarin Campaign is no longer about Mandarin versus dialect, but on getting Chinese parents who use English at home to speak more Mandarin to their children (Channel News Asia, 2009.)

Similar trends are also seen in the Malay community (Abdullah & Ayub, 1998) and even more so among the Tamils (Saravanan, 1998). In a recent study involving 233 participants ranging from 12–72 years of age and intended to gauge the extent to which Malays are, indeed, still maintaining their community language, Cavallaro and Serwe (2010) found the results far from optimistic. While Malay is still unrivalled in interactions with senior members of the community, English is making inroads everywhere else, its influence being particularly strong for young adults (18–24 years), whose use of English as a home language has, in fact, doubled. Cavallaro and Serwe concluded that even domains that were once traditionally safe havens for Malay in Singapore are slowly being eroded.

The ascendance of English is even more pronounced among the Indian population which comprises speakers of at least a dozen different Indian languages, with Tamil being the home language of the majority (43%) of

Indians in Singapore (Saravanan, 1998: 158). A major factor for Tamil-speaking Indians shifting to English, is that they do not see Tamil as offering specific material or instrumental advantages, which English so eminently provides. Consequently, since English-medium education was introduced in Singapore, there has been a sharp increase in the use of English as the principal language in Indian households, from 24.3% in 1980 to 35.6% in 2000, and to 39% in 2005, and this has been at the expense of Tamil which has dropped from 52.2% to 42.9% to 38% during the same periods (Saravanan *et al.,* 2007: 61). This language shift from Tamil to English (as a result of 'subtractive bilingualism'), has created a lack of confidence among Tamil children, as well as their parents, and a strong parental preference for English (Saravanan *et al., ibid.*).

What complicates matters is, because Tamil is a language characterized by extreme diglossia, Spoken Tamil has little or no prestige amongst Tamil speakers themselves, who tend to treat Literary Tamil as the only 'correct' variety (Saravanan, 1994: 86) – a preference strongly endorsed by the education system. Schiffman considers this strong cultural bias on the part of the educational establishment as being, in some sense:

> anti-Tamil, because it denigrates the home variety, which is the actual "mother tongue" of the Tamil community, and attempts to replace it with a variety never used for authentic communication by Tamils anywhere. (Schiffman, 2007: 212)

Not surprisingly, Tamil is not being maintained as a home language by the the better-educated, younger Tamils, who have little sense of ownership of the Tamil language and, consequently, no stake in its future use.

As a result of government language-planning and policy-making in the early years, English has become firmly entrenched in Singapore – a nation well on its way to becoming 'English-dominant' (Schneider, 1999: 193). Paradoxically, for a majority of Singaporeans, the success of the bilingual education policy has meant moving away from their mother tongues, with the two dominant school languages – English and Mandarin – displacing the languages of the home.

The Speak Mandarin Campaign and the Making of a Mother Tongue

The government of Singapore has always considered linguistic diversity to be an obstacle to nation-building. The Chinese community posed a major language-policy challenge, not only as the largest ethnic community in Singapore (78%), but also the most heterogeneous, utilising a large number of Chinese languages – referred to in national discourse as 'Chinese dialects' (Rappa & Wee, 2006: 91). In the 1957 census, 11 Chinese dialects were identified as mother tongues: 39% claiming Hokkien, 22.6% Teochew, 20% Cantonese, 6.8% Hainanese, 6.1% Hakka and the remaining 4.7% other Chinese and Malay dialects (Bokhorst-Heng, 1998; 2008).

Ever since independence in 1965, the Peoples' Action Party (PAP) government (and, particularly, Lee Kuan Yew) has attempted to reduce linguistic diversity and to homogenize the Chinese community, fervently arguing that a divided Chinese community would be detrimental to the survival of the nation (Bokhorst-Heng, 1999: 237). Instead of using the populations' actual home languages in education, the government's solution to linguistic and ethnic diversity was to change the language used in Chinese homes. Mandarin was the most logical choice as an official mother tongue, mainly because of its status as the official standard language in China and its perceived association with ancient Chinese culture and traditions.

Consequently, in 1979, the Speak Mandarin Campaign (SMC) was launched. This is an on-going campaign, re-launched annually with undiminished zeal. The goal of the campaign was to encourage the greater use of Mandarin, while simultaneously discouraging the use of the other Chinese dialects. There was also a cultural argument that Chinese Singaporeans needed to be 're-ethnicized' through Mandarin as a way to counter the dominance of English and its potential threat of de-culturalization through decadent Western influences.

Essentially, and especially in the early years, the thrust of the campaign was to pit Mandarin against the other Chinese dialects, often playing on the layman's misconceptions of 'language' versus 'dialect'. This was made explicit in the discourse of the SMC's slogans over the years: 'Speak more Mandarin and less dialect' (1979, inaugural year), 'Mandarin's in, dialect's out' (1983), 'Start with Mandarin, not dialect' (1986), 'Better with more Mandarin, less dialect' (1988) (Lim, 2009: 54). In addition to claiming that Mandarin can be a unifying force in the Chinese community, the government also depicted the dialects as 'vulgar' and indicating a 'lack of education', as against Mandarin, which was 'refined' and associated with 'academic success' (Bokhorst-Heng, 1999: 250).

By positioning Mandarin and the dialects in direct contrast with each other in campaign speeches, the leaders simultaneously reinforced the validity of Mandarin and the inappropriateness of the dialects. Faced with the choice of Mandarin or dialects, the choice – Lee Kuan Yew said in his 1979 campaign speech – is 'obvious'. In a similar vein, Goh Chok Tong asserted, 'Indeed, wise parents will never let their children speak dialect at all' (*The Straits Times*, 26 October, 1981). Bokhorst-Heng comments that:

> in this dichotic structuring of language meanings, then, the government simultaneously created a void by banishing dialects from nation, community and home, leaving the Chinese community and individuals with no mother tongue, and then filled that void by prescribing Mandarin as their mother tongue. (Bokhorst-Heng, 1999: 252)

Several initiatives have been adopted, in conjunction with the SMC, to ensure that its objectives met with success. Passing Mandarin examinations became necessary for children to move up the educational ladder. When it was found that the language of the home did not reinforce the learning of Mandarin in school, the government encouraged parents to sacrifice their dialect for the sake of their children's education – to help 'reduce the burden' of learning two Chinese languages simultaneously. The government also exploited the ideology of pragmatism, by suggesting that parents who did not do so would be making it more difficult for their child to succeed in school.

Perhaps the most drastic measure taken was the banning of the dialects from the media. The use of dialects on television and radio programmes was officially forbidden, and the Media Development Authority (MDA) stopped authorizing dialect films and videos unless they were dubbed in Mandarin (Wee, 2010).

In recent years, the thrust of the SMC has changed, with the economic development of China being posited as a strong motivating factor. This is reflected in the way the 2006 SMC campaign objective was framed: 'Apart from promoting Mandarin as an avenue for understanding one's roots and Chinese culture, the campaign also highlights the importance of Mandarin for economic and business competitiveness'. An emphasis on Mandarin's economic value has made more parents pay attention to the learning of the language by their children. Secondly, a number of non-Chinese parents have petitioned the schools to allow their children to study Mandarin as MT, rather than the MT designated for their own ethnic group (Malay or Tamil) (Wee, 2003; Wee & Bokhorst-Heng, 2005).

Mandarin's associations with economic value, backed by the numerical dominance of the Chinese in the population (74% in 2010), has given it a higher position in relation to the other two official mother tongues. It is quite possible for business transactions in Malaysia and India to be conducted in English, so the economic imperative to learn Malay or Tamil is weakened (Wee, 2003: 217). Unfortunately, this means that there is an increasing dominance of English-Mandarin bilingualism, vis-à-vis English-Tamil and English-Malay bilingualism, raising the fear of an increase in Chinese chauvinism among the non-Chinese communities and leading them to question the government's commitment to multiracialism (Bokhorst-Heng, 1999).

Undeniably, the government has been largely successful in containing the use of dialects and in turning Mandarin into a mother tongue and the language of the private domain of the home. Census data clearly show how Mandarin has displaced Chinese dialects as the main home language among the Chinese community. In 1957, Mandarin had less than 0.1% native speakers in Singapore, Mandarin use in the home has grown from 10% in

1980 to 30% in 1990 and to 45% in 2000. The Chinese dialects decreased in use from 81% in 1980 to 50% in 1990 and to 31% in 2000 (Lim, 2010: 30). Mandarin has become the language of choice for intra-ethnic communication in all domains for many young Chinese Singaporeans (*ibid.*). One consequence of the replacement of the dialects with Mandarin is the inter-generational communication gap that has made it difficult for grandchildren to communicate with their grandparents – a cultural loss that is probably irreversible (Pakir, 1993: 83).

Changes in immigration policies have also affected the composition of Singapore's Chinese population. Singapore now finds itself needing to rely increasingly on 'foreign talent', in order to overcome the limits of local resources. For this, it has turned to China and India as favoured sources of 'foreign talent', while targeting mainland Chinese individuals as desired immigrants to Singapore, either for education or business. As a consequence of these new policies, there is now a significant mainland Chinese population in Singapore, with the number of new migrants from China estimated to be close to 100,000 (Chan, 2006: 9). These include approximately 36,000 students from mainland China, who are studying in Singapore's local schools and, as these students are often accompanied by their mothers, another estimated 5,000 *peidu mamas* or 'study mamas'. Based on the present flow of migrants and visitors from China, one can predict the continued dominance of Mandarin in the future (Lim, 2009).

At the same time, local multilingual practices seem to run counter to the official discourse. Contrary to the strong official stance that it is (only) Mandarin that is needed to engage in business with China, many of the younger generation of Singaporeans are finding that dialects have economic functionality in informal (local) markets in the region. The dialects are found to be of use in other contexts, too, for example, in facilitating work-place communication or in bridging social-class divisions in the army (Wee, 2010: 104). Consequently, in recent years, there has been a new surge of interest in the Chinese dialects. Lim (2009: 63) mentions that the Chinese clan associations that had, in the last 30 years, been offering only Mandarin lessons have lately started conducting dialect classes – for Hokkien, Teochew, Cantonese and Shanghainese – with people apparently clamouring for the sessions (*The Straits Times*, 9 September, 2002).

The various Chinese dialects/languages have also been used in local films, such as *I Not Stupid*, *Money Not Enough*, *Singapore Gaga* and *881 Getai*, which have seen great success and popularity, both locally and on the international scene. The film *881 Getai* has served to revitalise Hokkien among young Singaporeans by making it 'cool'. Such films have shown that dialects can still be appreciated 'for their expressiveness' and 'realness that locals enjoy' and that they are 'an important part of Singapore' (Lim, 2009: 64–65, citing Foo, 2008).

Interestingly, the government is well aware of the expressive/ indentification value of the dialects and it does not hesitate to use them in times of crisis, as has happened in the course of political campaigns, public health messages and other political events. The Chinese dialects have been commonly used by electoral candidates, from both the ruling and opposition parties, especially to communicate with the 'grassroots'. In addition to English and Mandarin, Hokkien, Teochew and Cantonese are used to reach out to older Chinese Singaporeans and to better connect with voters.

These examples indicate that despite its attack against the dialects, the government has not entirely succeeded in subduing them. People find the dialects resonate much more strongly in contrast with Mandarin – the mother tongue of none of the Chinese communities that made up the original immigrants to Singapore. Thus, in spite of the government's efforts to regulate and control the language choice of the targeted community, it would appear that Singaporeans still make choices in favour of the languages that express their identities, namely, the Chinese dialects and Singlish (see below).

Even though the thrust of the SMC has changed in recent years, the official discourse has not changed since the launch of the SMC three decades ago. This became obvious in 2008, when a local academic, speaking at a conference on language diversity, was quoted in the newspapers as making the observation that Singapore is not as multilingual as it used to be. This prompted a response from no less than the principal private secretary to Minister Mentor, Lee Kuan Yew, who reiterated that:

> It would be stupid for any Singapore agency or NTU (Nanyang Technological University) to advocate the learning of dialects, which must be at the expense of English and Mandarin. (*The Straits Times*, 18 March, 2009)

Wee (2010: 104–5) suggests that the government is tolerant of occasional instances of dialect use when they are of an innocuous *ad hoc* nature, but when a stronger attempt to champion the use of dialect is perceived, the government is quick to stridently reiterate its stance against them.

The top-down implementation of the SMC has improved the extent and standard of Mandarin among the Chinese and has made Mandarin the major native language in Singapore, but it has also reduced diversity and multilingualism. Indeed, Gupta (2008) predicts that in future generations, there are likely to be fewer Singaporeans with a knowledge of more than the two school languages – English and Mandarin – concurring with Bokhorst-Heng's (1999: 262) analysis that for all its commitment to 'multiculturalism' in the Singapore project, there is as much essentializing and homogenizing going on as in assimilative monocultural national projects, making Singapore, in effect, 'a patch work of internally homogenized communities'.

The Speak Good English Movement and the Official Disinheritance of Singlish

By the end of the 20th century, the use of English in Singapore was no longer restricted to the social elite. As Singapore has grown more modern, more prosperous and more networked globally, a critical mass of native speakers of English have emerged among the younger generation of Singaporeans. The variety of English they use is one that has evolved within a multilingual and multicultural ecology and it has undergone much linguistic restructuring, due to its contact with the local languages. However, while English in Singapore has been analyzed as having attained endonormative stabilization (according to Schneider's 2007 Dynamic model of post-colonial Englishes), the variety upheld by the Singapore government is Standard British English, leading it to maintain a strongly prescriptive stance toward the emergence of new varieties of English. To confound matters, there exists a wide range of variation among Singapore's English-speakers, which has been analysed by some scholars as located along a lectal continuum (Platt & Weber, 1980), while others – like Gupta (1989) – describe Singapore English as diglossic. Most of the proficient adult users of English in Singapore use two grammatically distinct varieties of English: a L (Low)-variety, also called Singapore Colloquial English (SCE) or 'Singlish', and a H (High)-variety or standard English. Most proficient users of English are able to switch from one variety to the other with great ease when the context demands. In recent years, the widespread popularity of Singlish has come under scrutiny from the government and has caused much alarm.

Singlish, the emergent home-grown colloquial variety of Singapore English, exhibits a high degree of influence – in terms of its phonology, syntax and vocabulary – from the local indigenous languages, particularly Malay, Hokkien and Cantonese (Platt & Weber, 1980: 18). It has been analyzed by some scholars as being more Asian in structure than English. Some of its characteristics are: a lack of inflectional morphology ('He eat here yesterday'), the productive use of reduplication ('I like hot-hot curries') and the use of discourse particles ('I won't get married, *lor* – I have no choice but to not get married'). Because of its immense popularity and its usefulness in maintaining solidarity and friendship, many young professionals, and even expatriates, think it is trendy to use Singlish in informal conversations with local colleagues and friends. As a result, it is this variety that has emerged as the single dominant *lingua franca* in modern-day Singapore.

At another level, however, Singlish represents ungrammatical English, which, not infrequently, stops well short of being understood by non-Singaporeans. Because of its association with the lower strata of society, Singlish is viewed as an uncouth and inferior variety by the Singapore government, and its speakers are described as 'less intelligent' and 'less competent' than those who can speak standard English (Tickoo, 1996: 447). By conflating 'colloquial' practices with 'ungrammatical' ones, the government fails to distinguish between the relatively playful and the linguistically self-assured uses of Singlish from those that indicate a genuine lack of competence in the standard variety (Wee, 2010: 112), stigmatizing both.

This is evident in this excerpt from then-Prime Minister, Goh Chok Tong's, 1999 National Day Rally Speech, stressing that Singaporeans should refrain from speaking Singlish:

> Singlish is broken, ungrammatical English sprinkled with words and phrases from local dialects and Malay which English speakers outside Singapore have difficulties in understanding... Let me emphasize that my message that we must speak Standard English is targeted primarily at the younger generation... We should ensure that the next generation does not speak Singlish. (*The Straits Times*, 19 August 1999)

In April 2000, sparked off by its concern at the accelerated use of Singlish among young Singaporeans, the Singapore Government launched the 'Speak Good English Movement' (SGEM) – an annual campaign following along the lines of the 'Speak Mandarin Campaign'. The catalyst for this was the success of the local situation comedy, *Phua Chu Kang*. The programme was named after the lead character, whose liberal use of Singlish humour made it the most widely watched show on local television. The fear is that if Singaporeans became more comfortable with Singlish, they would be unable to speak 'proper' English, making it impossible for them to be understood internationally. Hence, the slogan for the SGEM states, 'Speak well, be understood'.

The SGEM has spawned a variety of measures designed to promote standard English and to help Singaporeans move away from Singlish. The last 10 years have seen a myriad of texts, editorials, public speaking forums, cartoons, posters and skits, story-telling competitions, seminars, debates, lectures and lessons and the setting up of an official website to regulate public usage, offset by the formulation of a new English-language syllabus by the Ministry of Education and in-service training to prepare some 8000 teachers 'to help lead the way to better English standards in the country' (Nirmala, 1999).

The ostensible aim of the SGEM is 'to encourage Singaporeans to speak grammatically correct English that is universally understood' (SGEM, 2000). Its implicit agenda is to stem the spread of Singlish and eliminate it before it becomes an integral part of the cultural life of the present generation of school-goers in Singapore (Rubdy, 2001; Chng, 2003). In other words, the relationship between standard English and Singlish is viewed as one of displacement, rather than of co-existence or complementarity, in which standard English is employed for international communication, while allowing for the use of Singlish in informal, local and private domains (Rappa & Wee, 2006: 95). And just as a situation of crisis was created in 1978–79 – by attributing Singaporean students' poor examination results in Mandarin to the various other Chinese dialects which were still being used at home, in justifying the initiation of the Speak Mandarin Campaign – the current standard English-Singlish debate is premised on the construction of a 'crisis of falling standards' that needs to be resolved, inevitably paving the way for government intervention.

In 1999, the existence of Singlish was even construed by then-Prime Minister, Goh Chok Tong, as posing a threat to the nation's economic well-being:

> We cannot be a first-world economy or go global with Singlish…The fact that we use English gives us a big advantage over our competitors. If we carry on using Singlish, the logical final outcome is that we, too, will develop our own type of pidgin English, spoken only by three million Singaporeans, which the rest of the world will find quaint but incomprehensible. We are already half way there. Do we want to go all the way? (National Day Rally Speech, 1999)

Perhaps the clearest statement of how strongly the state views the oppositional relationship between Singlish and 'good English' came from then-Senior Minister, Lee Kuan Yew:

> Do not popularize Singlish. Do not use Singlish in our television sitcoms, except for humorous bits, and in a way that makes people want to speak standard English… Singlish is a handicap we must not wish on Singaporeans. (*The Sunday Times*, 15 August 1999)

The following excerpt from a speech by former PM Goh Chok Tong clearly attempts to link Singapore's ambitions of becoming a global player with the linguistic capital that standard English alone can offer:

> Speaking good English is crucial if the country is to achieve its goal of becoming a first-world economy and a world class home… We cannot be a first world economy or go global with Singlish. (National Day Rally Speech, 1999)

At the launch of the SGEM, Prime Minister Goh was at pains to brush off any desire to link Singlish with a Singaporean identity and specifically reminded well-educated Singaporeans of the responsibility they had towards the lesser-educated, mono-dialectal speakers of Singlish:

> They should not take the attitude that it is cool or feel that speaking Singlish makes them more "Singaporean"... If they speak Singlish when they can speak good English, they are doing a disservice to Singapore. (*The Straits Times*, 30 April 2000)

In castigating Singlish, he ignored the fact that for many Singaporeans who have grown up speaking English as their dominant language, it is the colloquial vernacular that is acquired before standard English, and it is the bearer of authenticity for most Singaporeans (Gupta, 1994: 128). Crucially, it is this variety that has identification and integrative functionality for Singaporeans; a situation that is usually associated with the unifying force of an L1 (a first language).

The notion that only one variety of English is acceptable in Singapore is clearly at odds with everyday multilingual reality, which often involves the switching and mixing of various codes. This process of erasing any complexity which hybridity and heteroglossia can pose, has, of course, been a hallmark of Singapore's national cultural policy, whether in matters related to ethnicity, religion or language, despite the fact that mixture and fusion in all cultural domains have been an integral component of everyday living in this multiracial society (Kramer-Dahl, 2003: 178). The Singaporean government appears to work on the premise that languages and cultures should be kept distinct, cutting against the very core of a multilingual ecology, in which individuals inhabit a complex and often overlapping cultural universe and where the pervasiveness of contact languages makes the permeability of group boundaries the norm and calls for relativist conceptions of group identification and inter-group relations (Lian, 1999: 46).

The official disinheritance of Singlish (similar to the Chinese dialects) is a clear case of intra-language discrimination (Wee, 2005). Contrary to the government's view, supporters of Singlish have suggested that the presence of Singlish does not jeopardize or compromise Singaporeans' ability to acquire 'standard' or 'good' English (Wee, 2005). Indeed, Singlish could be pedagogically useful as an educational resource in aiding the learning of standard English (Rubdy, 2007). Supporters of Singlish see no reason why the two varieties of English cannot co-exist or even be simultaneously used in certain contexts. Alsagoff (2010) demonstrates that from a globalization perspective, instances of code-switching between standard English and Singlish are actually a form of 'glocal' communication, i.e. the use of English as a global tool appropriated to local contexts for simultaneously expressing both global and local cultural orientations. From yet another perspective, one might argue that Singlish has emerged as a form of 'people's English', de-elitized by Singaporeans, very much in the spirit of Parakrama's (1995) claims for de-hegemonizing English.

It is ironic that, possibly driven by this very insight, the government has, in times of crisis, in contravention of its own proscriptions, resorted to using the very same linguistic resources that it denigrates, as happened in the course of dealing with the SARS (Severe Acute Respiratory Syndrome) epidemic in 2003. It commissioned a SARS Rap song (the 'SAR-VIVOR Rap'), which included a number of Singlish constructions, including a generous interspersing of the particles -*leh* and -*lah* and words derived from Malay and Hokkien. Their rationale was that, just as dialects were considered necessary to communicate the nature of the SARS crisis to the elderly, Singlish was also necessary in communicating with less-educated Singaporeans (Wee, 2010: 107).

A decade on, the Singlish-Standard English debate continues. The SGEM, which has had a number of prominent language specialists, including local linguists on its advisory board, still follows its prescriptive stance. Referring to the SGEM website's hardline approach to 'correctness', Gupta (2010: 76) notes that it has largely fostered a 'maven culture' for English in Singapore, breeding insecurity among its users, rather than genuinely helping to improve their English, while Bruthiaux (2010: 96) suggests that the main concern of the SGEM seems to be 'not intelligibility but respectability'.

The use of Singlish, particularly among younger Singaporeans, continues to be robust. In the last decade, websites such as *Talking Cock.com* (founded in 2000) and *The Dictionary of Singlish and Singapore English* have emerged, comprizing the layperson's documentation of the Singlish lexicon and the use of Singlish in texts. These have gained tremendous support and popularity among Singaporeans, as well as non-Singaporeans, and they bear testimony to the way Singlish has been recognized as a part of the Singaporean identity (Lim, 2009: 61). Although Rappa and Wee (2006) suggest that considering English in Singapore tends to be seen in instrumental terms, and Singlish is seen to be at odds with the project of modernity, Singaporeans are unlikely to resist official attempts to eliminate it. The liminality and vitality of Singlish is such that it seems under no peril of being killed off. Indeed, Bruthiaux (2010: 100) expresses serious doubts regarding the effectiveness of the SGEM, claiming that there is no demonstrable evidence of the project having succeeded since its establishment 10 years ago.

Concluding Thoughts

There are moral, hegemonic and ideological issues at play around the choice of medium of education and associated language shifts (Gupta, 2008). It is therefore important to reveal and demystify the processes of symbolic domination (Bourdieu, 1991), both historical and contemporary, whereby certain languages have come to be disenfranchised, thus providing local leaders with information that can help them to devise programmes of action that are maximally functional in defending and reclaiming marginalised languages (Garrett, 2006). In Singapore, there is some urgency to promote additive bilingualism and ensure that minority languages continue to be relevant in the speakers' environment. An important issue is making the environment more conducive to choices that enhance linguistic diversity (Cavallaro & Serwe, 2010: 164).

As Stroud and Wee (2010) suggest, a radically different approach to policy-making is required, that has greater reference to autonomy, choice and reflexivity. They contend that a sociolinguistic ordering around notions of ethnicity and nation do not fit easily with the multilingual dynamics of late modern societies, such as Singapore. They argue for the need to formulate new nation-state narratives constructed around an idea of 'linguistic cosmopolitanism'. Basically, they argue that with consumption increasingly becoming a key channel for the construction and communication of identity, societal development in late modernity is generating linguistic hierarchies of value that are reconfiguring issues of language and ethnicity into questions of language and class (Stroud & Wee, 2010: 188). As a result, Singaporeans are primarily making instrumental choices in matters of language, acquiring and using languages for a variety of reasons that have more to do with their perceived use-value than any inherent ownership or the performance of ethnic identities. They cite the development of widespread (unofficial) bilingualism that cuts across ethnic boundaries, resulting in speakers acquiring languages (other than English) that bear no designated (ethnolinguistic) identities, e.g. the Chinese learning Malay, the converse desire among Malay and Indian families to acquire Mandarin and the use of Chinese dialects as linguistic resources in social interactions across linguistic and ethnic groupings. Such sociolinguistic practices and ideologies no longer fit comfortably into existing policy frameworks.

More recently, Singapore has decided to reposition itself as 'a cosmopolitan global city', in order to attract talented foreigners as potential new citizens in its ambitions to stay ahead of its competitors. This means that it is likely to grow even more heterogeneous as it rapidly transforms itself into a cosmopolis that has all the characteristics of a society in late modernity (Chua, 2003). Crucial to this process is the recognition that the policies put in place for its survival in an era of earlier modernity can no longer be adequate or relevant in a late modern world. If Singapore's language policy is to be re-engineered, it must be based on a model that optimally reflects current practices and ideologies held within its multilingual ecology. In consideration of the very valid points raised by Stroud and Wee and other critiques, the following key issues need to be addressed in the near future:

(1) Singaporean language policy currently recognizes only 'English plus official mother tongue' bilingualism and expects Singaporeans to demonstrate equal proficiency in both English and their official mother tongue. Instead of this unrealistic ambition of full bilingualism, a more appropriate model to adopt would be one of *plurilingualism*, which recognizes that a person's functional proficiency in various languages

will inevitably involve a range of levels dependent upon different needs.

(2) 'Standard language' has to be treated as endonormatively evolving from within each community, according to its own histories and cultures of usage. The guiding principle should be *local standards for local contexts*. This entails eschewing a blind and uncritical espousal of standard UK-style English (or American-style English) as the only norm(s) worthy of being the medium of education and making locally 'available' Englishes, such as standard Singapore English, a legitimate alternative. This would not only enable the expression of local identities, but also be in harmony with the local multilingual ecology.

(3) In the case of English, at the practical level, the fallacy that a single variety of (standard) English is the only appropriate vehicle for communication for all Singaporeans should be challenged, exposed and abandoned. The government needs to adopt a more realistic and tolerant view of the sociolinguistic dynamics of English and *accept variation* as a fact of life, backed up by a rationale based on evidence of language in use (Bruthiaux, 2010: 105).

(4) There is a need for Singapore's language policy to become more reflexive and more open to granting individual autonomy, by acknowledging the need for Singlish, at least in the local context. For speakers who have no access to the standard variety, Singlish is a valuable linguistic resource that enables this sector of the population to negotiate their ways within the local economy. 'The call for the maintenance of Singlish is therefore a call for *the respect of the linguistic human rights* of this group of speakers' (Chng, 2006: 65).

(5) The *concept of mother tongue* itself will have to be broadened to include many more languages than the current three. This will mean that the state will need to abandon the essentialist opposition between a 'Western' language and Asian 'mother tongues' as an ideology that is no longer tenable.

(6) The Singapore government should give up its outdated, essentialist and highly prescriptive ideology of linguistic and cultural purism and the concomitant vision of a single fixed national/cultural identity for Singaporeans based on such ethno-linguistic considerations. In a world increasingly characterized by global cultural flows, language practices typically involve mixed codes and multiple communicative frames, and it is in the performance of these hybrid codes that identities are most often negotiated and refashioned (Pennycook, 2003). This means rethinking English as a resource for *glocalized communication*, where the global-and-local divides dissolve in the situated appropriation of a global means by local social actors for local purposes (Lin *et al.*, 2002) and as a tool for re-working local identity (Pakir, 2000; Alsagoff, 2010; Pennycook, 2010).

The adoption of such measures will enable the government to realign its language policy with current global, as well as local, developments to render it more relevant, more just and more inclusive for Singapore's citizens. Until then, however, it would seem that so-called 'standardized' English in Singapore will remain, alongside Mandarin, as ever-powerful partners in crime.

References

Abdullah, K. and Ayyub B.J. (1998) Malay language issues and trends. In A. Gopinathan, S. Gopinathan, A. Pakir, Ho W.K. and V. Saravanan (eds) *Language, Society and Education in Singapore* (2nd edn) (pp. 179–190). Singapore: Times Academic Press.

Alsagoff, L. (2010) Hybridity in ways of speaking: The glocalization of English in Singapore. In L. Lim, A. Pakir and L. Wee (eds) *English in Singapore: Modernity and Management* (pp. 109–130). Hong Kong: Hong Kong University Press.

Benjamin, G. (1976) The cultural logic of Singapore's "multiracialism". In R. Hassan (ed.) *Singapore: A Society in Transition* (pp. 115–133). Kuala Lumpur: Oxford University Press.

Bloom, D. (1986) The English language and Singapore: A critical survey. In B.K. Kapur (ed.) *Singapore Studies* (pp. 337–458). Singapore: Singapore University Press.

Bokhorst-Heng, W.D. (1999) Singapore's "Speak Mandarin" campaign: Language ideological debates and the imagining of the nation. In J. Blommaert (ed.) *Language Ideological Debates* (pp. 235–265). New York, NY: Mouton de Gruyter.

Bokhorst-Heng, W.D. (2005) Debating Singlish. *Multilingua* 24, 185–209.

Bourdieu, P. (1991) *Language and Symbolic Power*. Cambridge, MA: Harvard University Press.

Bruthiaux, P. (2010) The "Speak Good English" movement: A web user's perspective. In L. Lim, A. Pakir and L. Wee (eds) *English in Singapore: Modernity and Management* (pp. 91–108). Hong Kong: Hong Kong University Press.

Cavallaro, F. and Serwe, S.K. (2010) Language use and language shift among the Malays in Singapore. *Applied Linguistics Review* 1, 129–169.

Chan, B. (2006) Virtual communities and Chinese national identity. *Journal of Chinese Overseas* 2 (1), 1–32.

Channel News Asia (2009) Singapore News, 17 March. Website, accessed 18 March 2011. http://www.channelnewsasia.com/stories/singaporelocalnews/view/415920/1/.html

Chew, P.G.L. (1999) Linguistic imperialism, globalism and the English language *AILA Review* 13, 37–47.

Chiew, S.K. (1983) Ethnicity and national integration: The evolution of a multi-ethnic society. In P. Chen (ed.) *Singapore: Development and Trends* (pp. 29–64). Singapore: Oxford University Press.

Chng, H.H. (2003) "You see me no up": Is Singlish a problem? *Language Problems and Language Planning* 27 (1), 47–62.

Chng, H.H. (2006) Beyond linguistic instrumetalism. In P.K.W. Tan and R. Rubdy (eds) *Language as Commodity: Global Structures and Local Marketplaces* (pp. 57–69). London: Continuum.

Garrett, P.B. (2006) Contact languages as endangered languages. What is there to lose? *Journal of Pidgin and Creole Languages* 21 (1), 175–190.

Gopinathan, S., Pakir, A., Ho, W.K. and Saravavan, V. (1998) *Language, Society and Education in Singapore: Issues and Trends* (2nd edn). Singapore: Times Academic Press.

Gupta, A.F. (1989) Singapore colloquial English and standard English. *Singapore Journal of Education* 10, 33–39.

Gupta, A.F. (1994) *The Step Tongue: Children's English in Singapore*. Clevedon: Multilingual Matters.

Gupta, A.F. (1998) A framework for the analysis of Singapore English. In S. Gopinathan, A. Pakir, W.K. Ho and V. Saravanan (eds) *Language, Society and Education in Singapore* (2nd edn) (pp. 119–133). Singapore: Times Academic Press.

Gupta, A.F. (2008) The language ecology of Singapore. In A. Creese, P. Martin and N. Hornberger (eds) *Encyclopedia of Language and Education Vol. 9: Ecology of Language* (2nd edn) (pp. 99–111). New York, NY: Springer.

Gupta, A.F. (2010) Singapore standard English revisited. In L. Lim, A. Pakir and L. Wee (eds) *English in Singapore: Modernity and Management* (pp. 57–89). Hong Kong: Hong Kong University Press.

Kramer-Dahl, A. (2003) Reading the "Singlish debate": Construction of a crisis of language standards and language teaching in Singapore. *Journal of Language, Identity, and Education* 2 (3), 159–190.

Kuo, E.C.Y. (1980) The sociolinguistic situation in Singapore: Unity in diversity. In E.A. Afendras, and E.C.Y. Kuo (eds) *Language and Society in Singapore* (pp. 39–62). Singapore: Singapore University Press.

Kuo, E.C.Y. and Jernudd, B.H. (1994) Balancing macro- and micro-sociolinguistic perspectives in language management: The case of Singapore. In S. Gopinathan, A. Pakir, W.K. Ho and V. Saravanan (eds) *Language Society and Education in Singapore* (pp. 25–46). Singapore: Times Academic Press.

Li, W., Saravanan, V. and Ng, J.L.H. (1997) Language shift in the Teochew community in Singapore: A family domain analysis. *Journal of Multilingual and Multicultural Development* 18 (5), 364–384.

Lian, K.F. (1999) The nation-state and the sociology of Singapore. In A. Kramer-Dahl and P.G.L. Chew (eds) *Reading Culture: Textual Practices in Singapore* (pp. 37–54). Singapore: Times Academic Press.

Lim, L. (2009) Beyond fear and loathing in SG: The real mother tongues and language policies in multilingual Singapore. *AILA Review* 22, 52–71.

Lim, L. (2010) Migrants and 'mother tongues': Extralinguistic forces in the ecology of English in Singapore. In L. Lim, A. Pakir and L. Wee (eds) *English in Singapore: Management and Modernity* (pp. 19–54). Hong Kong: Hong Kong University Press.

Lim, L. and Foley, J.A. (2006) English in Singapore and Singapore English. In L. Lim (ed.) *Singapore English: A Grammatical Description* (pp. 1–18). Philadelphia, PA: John Benjamins.

Lin, A., Wang, W., Akamatsu, N. and Riazi, A.M. (2002) Appropriating English, expanding identities, and re-visioning the field: From TESOL to teaching English for glocalized communication (TEGCOM). *Journal of Language and Identity* 1 (4), 295–316.

Nirmala, M. (1999) Teachers to go for English upgrading. *The Straits Times* 25 July, p. 1.

Pakir, A. (1992) English-knowing bilinguals in Singapore. In K.C. Ban, A. Pakir and C.K. Tong (eds) *Imagining Singapore* (pp. 234–262). Singapore: Times Academic Press.

Pakir, A. (1993) Two tongue-tied: Bilingualism in Singapore. *Journal of Multilingual and Multicultural Development* 14 (1/2), 73–90.

Pakir, A. (1998) Language and society. In L. Alsagoff, Z. Bao, A. Pair and L. Wee (eds) *Society, Style and Structure in Language* (pp. 3–17). Singapore: Prentice Hall.

Pakir, A. (2000) The development of English as a "glocal" language: New concerns in the old sage of language teaching. In W.K. Ho and C. Ward (eds) *Language in the Global Context: Implications for the Language Classroom*, RELC Anthology Series 41 (pp. 14–31). Singapore: Southeast Asian Ministers of Education Organization Regional Language Centre.

Parakrama, A. (1995) *De-hegemonizing Language Standards*. London: Macmillan.

Pennycook, A. (2003) Global Englishes, rip slyme, and performativity. *Journal of Sociolingusitics* 7 (4), 513–533.

Pennycook, A. (2010) *English as a Local Practice*. Oxford: Routledge.

Phillipson, R. (2008) *Lingua franca* or lingua frankensteinia? English in European integration and globalization. *World Englishes* 27 (2), 250–267.

Platt, J. and Weber, H. (1980) *English in Singapore and Malaysia: Status, Functions, Features*. Kuala Lumpur: Oxford University Press.

Purushotam, N.S. (1998) *Negotiating Language, Constructing Race: Disciplining Differences in Singapore*. Berlin/New York: Mouton de Gruyter.

Rappa, A.L. and Wee, L. (2006) The republic of Singapore. In A.L. Rappa and L. Wee (eds) *Language Policy and Modernity in Southeast Asia: Malaysia, the Philippines, Singapore, and Thailand* (pp. 77–104). New York, NY: Springer.

Rubdy, R. (2001) Creative destruction: Singapore's 'Speak Good English' movement. *World Englishes* 20 (3), 341–355.

Rubdy, R. (2007) Singlish in the school: An impediment or a resource?. *Journal of Multilingual and Multicultural Development* 28 (4), 308–324.

Saravanan, V. (1994) Language and social identity amongst Tamil-English bilinguals in Singapore. In R. Khoo, U. Kreher and R. Wong (eds) *Languages in Contact in a Multilingual Society* (pp. 79–93). Clevedon: Multilingual Matters.

Saravanan, V. (1998) Language maintenance and language shift in the Tamil-English community. In S. Gopinathan, S. Gopinathan, A. Pakir, Ho W.K. and V. Saravanan (eds). *Language, Society and Education in Singapore* (2nd edn) (pp. 155–178). Singapore: Times Academic Press.

Saravanan, V., Seetha Lakshmi, S. and Caleon I. (2007) Attitudes towards literary Tamil and standard spoken Tamil in Singapore. *International Journal of Bilingual Education and Bilingualism* 10 (1), 58–79.

Schiffman, H.F. (2007) Tamil language policy in Singapore: The roles of implementation. In V. Vaish, S. Gopinathan and Y. Lui (eds) *Language, Culture, Capital: Critical Studies of Language in Education in Singapore* (pp. 209–226). Rotterdam: Sense Publications.

Schneider, E. (1999) Notes on Singaporean English. In U. Carls and P. Lucko (eds) *Form, Function and Variation in English: Studies in Honour of Klaus Hansen* (pp. 193–205). Frankfurt am Main: Peter Lang.

Schneider, E. (2007) *Postcolonial English: Varieties Around the World*. Cambridge: Cambridge University Press.

Singapore Department of Statistics (2006) *General Household Survey 2005: Socio-Demographic and Economic Characteristics, Release I*. Accessed 20 March, 2011. Available at http://www.singstat.gov.sg

Singapore Department of Statistics (2010) Census of Population. Online article, accessed 18 March 2011. http://www.singstat.gov.sg/pubn/census2010.html

Skutnaab-Kangas, T. (2003) Linguistic diversity and biodiversity: The threat from killer languages. In C. Mair (ed.) *The Politics of English as a World Language: New Horizons in Postcolonial Cultural Studies* (pp. 31–52). Amsterdam & New York: Association for the Study of the New Literatures in English.

Speak Good English Movement (SGEM) (2000) Accessed 22 March, 2011. http://www.goodenglish.org.sg/category/movement/about-us

Speak Mandarin Campaign (SMC) (2006) Accessed 25 March, 2011. http://en.wikipedia.org/wiki/speak_mandarin_campaign

Stroud, C. and Wee, L. (2010) Language policy and planning in Singaporean late modernity. In L. Lim, A. Pakir and L. Wee (eds) *English in Singapore: Modernity and Management* (pp. 181–204). Hong Kong: Hong Kong University Press.

Swales, J. (1997) English as Tyronnosaurus Rex. *World Englishes* 16 (3), 373–82.

Tan, S.H. (1996) A critical review of sociolinguistic engineering in Singapore. In J. Blommaert (ed.) *The Politics of Multilingualism and Language Planning* (pp. 107–141). Antwerp: Universiteit Antwerpen.

Tickoo, M.L. (1996) Fifty years of English in Singapore: All gains, (a) few losses? In J.A. Fishman, W.C. Andrew and A. Rubal-Lopez (eds) *Post-Imperial English: Status Change in Former British and American Colonies 1940–1990* (pp. 431–456). New York, NY: Mouton de Gruyter.

Vaish, V., Tan, T.K., Bokhorst-Heng, W.D., Hogan, D. and Kang, T. (2010) Language and social capital in Singapore. In L. Lim, A. Pakir and L. Wee (eds) *English in Singapore: Modernity and Management* (pp. 159–180). Hong Kong: Hong Kong University Press.

Wee, L. (2003) Linguistic instrumentalism in Singapore. *Journal of Multilingual and Multicultural Development* 24 (3), 211–224.

Wee, L. (2005) Intra-language discrimination and linguistic human rights: The case of Singlish. *Applied Linguistics* 26 (1), 48–69.

Wee, L. (2010) 'Burdens' and 'handicaps' in Singapore's language policy: On the limits of language management. *Language Policy* 9, 97–114.

Wee, L. and Bokhorst-Heng, W.D. (2005) Language policy and nationalist ideology: Statal narratives in Singapore. *Multilingua* 24, 159–183.

14 English Language as Intruder: The Effects of English Language Education in Colombia and South America – a Critical Perspective

Anne-Marie de Mejía

Introduction

Unlike many of the countries referred to in this book, the historical linguistic legacy left by colonialism in Latin America relates mainly to Spanish and Portuguese. Exceptions to this include countries such as Belize, Guyana and the Falkland Islands and specific regions where African slaves were brought over to work – for example, on sugar cane plantations (Colombia) and on the railway networks (Costa Rica) – who used English as a *lingua franca*. In Central and South America, out of a survey of 22 countries, 16 have Spanish as the official language (or one of the official languages), one (Brazil) has Portuguese, three have English, one has French (French Guiana) and one has Dutch (Suriname) (Baker & Prys Jones, 1998). Nevertheless, during the 20th and 21st centuries, the presence of English (mainly as a foreign language) has been increasingly evident in this part of the world. It has become, and is becoming, very much an Intruder.

The Use and Status of English in Latin America

In their introduction to a Special Issue of the journal *World Englishes* on the topic of the role of English in South America, the guest editors referred to this part of the world as 'the other forgotten continent' (Friedrich & Berns, 2003: 83). They alluded to what they considered a 'region often forgotten and neglected by scientific channels', akin to Africa, in this respect. Whether this analogy holds today, is a matter for debate, particularly in the present scenario, where Brazil is increasingly being seen as an emerging world power and Spanish as an important international language (Graddol, 2006). However, there is one point on which the authors would seem to be correct – the general characterisation of South America by much of the world, particularly Europe and the United States, as 'a uniform continental block... culturally and linguistically monolithic' (Friedrich & Berns, 2003: 85). This belies the intense heterogeneity and diversity of the 13 countries, represented in the estimated 100-plus language families found here (Crystal, 1997, cited in Friedrich & Berns, 2003). There are, however, certain pronounced similarities among many countries in the region, in relation to the role and status of English – a relatively late arrival on the linguistic stage, dating, in most cases, but not all, from the growing hegemony of the United States after the Second World War.

In Costa Rica, as in many countries in Central and South America, English is currently valued as an important international language for tourism and international investment, although, somewhat curiously, there is also a small percentage of the population (the Afro-Costa Ricans brought from other Caribbean islands in the 19th century to work on the railways) who are native English speakers (Aguilar-Sánchez, 2005). Since the arrival of numerous retirees from the USA during the late 1980s and early 1990s, the Costa Rican government has promoted the learning of English by the local population to cater for the increasing numbers of backpackers, surfers, ecotourists and conservationists who visit the country every year.

In addition to the thriving tourist industry, international business enterprises, such as assembling plants, require workers to be able to understand instructions and communications in English and, in some cases, to be able to have a command of English in all skill areas, in order to be hired. This, in turn, has led to major changes in the education system, in relation to the learning of this foreign language. Since 1997, English has been taught from Grade 1 in the Costa Rican public education system. From 2001 onwards, the Costa Rican Ministry of Education has introduced the National Syllabus for English, which positions the language as a means of helping students 'to participate actively in the global economy to the benefit of the country' (MEP, 2001, cited in Aguilar-Sánchez, 2005: 168).

In Ecuador, Mexico and Argentina, English has also made important inroads into business and commerce (Friedrich, 2003; Alm, 2003; Baumgardner, 2006). Ovesdotter Alm (2003) reports on a study carried out in Quito, *Ecuador*, which tapped into the perceptions of Ecuadorians on the use of English in advertising and commerce, as well as the distribution of this language in advertisements and in the names of business enterprises. She found that 'English in Ecuador has taken on a specific function as *commercial capital* and that its use, as well as the perceived associations with English, is sociolinguistically stratified and related to self esteem' (Ovesdotter Alm, 2003: 143). Furthermore, the researcher noted that English served as a gatekeeper, indicating social status, as well as a 'personal marketing strategy' (Ovesdotter Alm, 2003: 155).

In a similar study carried out in *Mexico*, Baumgardner (2006) concluded that the strong influence of English in the world of business, as seen in advertising and shop and product names, often symbolized 'prestige, exclusiveness and/or modernity' (Baumgardner, 2006: 263). In addition, its use as an international language was seen to be associated with 'the widespread appeal of a global ideology' (Baumgardner, 2006: 263).

The case of *Argentina* – as reported by Friedrich (2003) in a study which examined the attitudes of Masters in Business Administration (MBA) students towards the use of English – also showed a strong perception of the intrinsic relationship between this language and job opportunities, particularly in managerial and administrative spheres. The researcher associated the high status of English among many Argentine business students with a tendency towards the 'commodification' of language (Heller, 2002) in striving towards competitive advantages, particularly in a climate of economic uncertainty, which characterised the country at the time the research was carried out.

Rajagopalan (2003), for his part, refers to the ambivalent status of English in *Brazil*, being both hated and desired by different groups. On the one hand, it is desired as 'a much-sought-out commodity... and a passport to professional success' by much of the middle and upper sectors of society (Rajagopalan, 2003: 94), while, on the other, many view the rapid penetration of the favoured variety – US English – with 'deep distrust and growing apprehension' (Rajagopalan, 2003: 98).

The Case of English in Colombia

Gloria Vélez-Rendón (2003) notes a similar ambivalence in *Colombia* towards the English language in general and to the United States, in particular. In fact, she ascribes the growing influence of British English and the British Council in the country to increasing anti-American feeling. However, for most of its history, in fact, Colombia has been associated not with English, but with indigenous languages and then Spanish, from the 15th century onwards.

Like other countries in the region, during the period of the colonisation by Spain, particularly in the 17th and 18th centuries, Spanish was the principal language of education for the indigenous communities. Similarly, educational provision for the descendants of the Spanish settlers was in the hands of the Catholic missionaries, who followed in the wake of the *conquistadores* (conquerors). Most schools were private and the languages taught were mainly Latin, Greek and Spanish. The sons and daughters of the wealthy were sent to study abroad in France and England, and, on their return, they promoted the spread of these languages in the country, particularly French, which was considered the language of culture and society (Zuluaga, 1996).

Following independence in 1810, the *Escuelas de Primeras Letras* (First Letters Schools) were set up, based on the liberal principles derived from the French Revolution. These later became primary schools. Then the *Escuelas Superiores de Artes Liberales* (Higher Schools for the Liberal Arts) were established at secondary level.

It was after the Second World War that English became the most important foreign language in Colombia, due to economic expansion, social, political and economic influence and the technological development of the United States. It was taught at secondary school level, alternating with the use of French. In 1979, after a visit by the Colombian president to France, a decree was issued, making English compulsory for Grades 6 and 7 and French mandatory for Grades 10 and 11, with a free choice of either English or French in Grades 8 and 9. As a report compiled by the British Council (1989: 7) revealed:

> The Colombian Ministry of National Education has no firm foreign language policy for the secondary school curriculum… concerning the place of English and French, with decisions being made as a result of political pressures rather than educational considerations.

In practice, most schools chose to teach English for four years and French for two, with an intensity of three hours per week at all levels, except during the final two years, when foreign languages were taught for two hours per week.

More recently, with the General Education Law (1994), foreign languages were introduced at primary school level, usually in Third Grade Primary, and it was stated that, at this level, attention should be focused on 'the acquisition of elements of conversation and reading in at least one foreign language' (Article 21). Although no particular foreign language is specified by law, most institutions have adopted English.

The National Bilingual Programme was initiated by the Colombian Ministry of Education (MEN) in 2004, with the aim of offering all students in Colombia the possibility of becoming bilingual in English and Spanish. Hitherto, access to bilingualism had been the privilege of students in private schools catering for the higher socio-economic strata. According to the Ministry, 'to be bilingual means to have more knowledge and opportunities to be competent and competitive and to improve the quality of life of all Colombians'[1] (Al Tablero, 2005: 3).

The main objective of the National Bilingual Programme is:

> To have citizens who are capable of communicating in English, in order to be able to insert the country within processes of universal

communication, within the global economy and cultural openness, through [the adopting of] internationally comparable standards. (MEN, 2006: 6)

The case was made for all school leavers to reach an intermediate level of proficiency in English, as this would constitute a comparative advantage, increasing both individual and national competence and competitiveness.

As part of this policy, a document, entitled *Basic Standards of Foreign Language Competence: English,* based on the Common European Framework of Reference for Languages (CEFR), was drawn up in 2006. The idea was to adopt a common language in which to establish levels of language performance throughout the different stages of schooling. The Common European Framework was considered suitable as a model, because it was the result of 10 years of research and because it provided a common language to establish performance levels in the foreign language throughout the Colombian educational system, particularly in relation to international standards. The following quotation makes this clear: 'the adoption of a common referent with other countries will allow Colombia to examine advances in relation to other nations and introduce international parameters at local level' (MEN, 2006: 57).

As can be noted – and in line with what has been said about other countries in the region – English is seen mainly as a means of increased competitiveness and internationalisation in Colombia. Moreover, in spite of its title, *The National Bilingual Programme* only refers to one type of bilingualism – English-Spanish – and does not take into account the many other languages in the country. In fact, Silvia Valencia Giraldo (2005: 1) has observed that:

> As a result of globalisation and the widespread use of English worldwide, the term 'bilingüismo' (bilingualism) has acquired a different meaning in the Colombian context. It is used by many… to refer almost exclusively to Spanish/English bilingualism… This focus on Spanish/English biling-ualism now predominates and the other dimensions of multilingualism and cultural difference in Colombia are often ignored. The existence of other languages in different regions of the country is overlooked, particularly the languages of indigenous Colombian populations. The teaching of other modern languages (e.g. French) has also been undermined by the spread of English and by people's increasing desire to 'invest' in English.

This position has been supported by Guerrero (2008), who notes that the choice of English over other foreign languages is justified by the Ministry of Education, 'given its importance as a universal language' (MEN, 2006: 1, cited in Guerrero, 2008: 34). She also observes that restricting the *Standards* document to 'foreign languages' excludes, by definition, the 67 indigenous languages present in our country.

Furthermore, Carlos Patiño (2005: 1), an ethnolinguist working with Amerindian communities, questions the use of the term 'bilingual' – as it applies to the learning of English at primary- and secondary-school level in Colombia – from a different point of view. He considers bilingual programmes for *majority language speakers* as less 'authentic'. The strong emphasis on the teaching of foreign or international languages in bilingual education programmes, he sees as a 'fashion', which cannot truly be considered 'bilingual' education, as English has no social basis in the country – 'it is not the language of any section of Colombian society'.

In addition, there have been concerns expressed by members of the Colombian Language Academy, who are worried about the status of Spanish in the face of what many consider the rapid rise of English, particularly in the upper and middle echelons of society. The emphasis on the teaching of subjects such as Science and Maths through the medium of English in private bilingual schools is seen as reinforcing the idea that Spanish is a language which is not appropriate for scientific development.

In this respect, Enrique Hamel (2003) in Mexico has championed the role of Spanish as a language of science in the face of the globalisation of English within an intercultural, plurilingual framework, arguing that:

> the total imposition of English would reinforce even more the already existing asymmetries both in the conditions of access to international science, as well as to the production and circulation of science and technology itself. (Hamel, 2003: 4)

Hamel advocates the development of common language policies in the field of the sciences, noting that whereas the French-speaking nations have constituted a solid policy of *francofonía*, the equivalent term, *hispanifonía*, does not exist. Nevertheless, he shows how it is largely due to the French that alliances have been agreed with both Spanish- and Portuguese-speaking nations in the American continent, in order to face up to the dominance of English in the region.

Reactions from Colombian Academics to the National Bilingual Programme

Many Colombian applied linguists have been critical of the role of foreign agencies in the implementation of the official language and education policies relating to the teaching and learning of English. Traditionally, the universities in Colombia – particularly the influential state (public) universities in the large cities of Bogotá, Medellín and Cali – have been responsible for the training and educating of foreign language teachers. However, the adopting of the Common European Framework of Reference for Languages (CEFR) as the point of reference for policies relating to the National Bilingual Programme has meant that private agencies, such as the British Council, have assumed a dominant role in many of these processes. An example is the initial use of both the Teaching Knowledge Test, designed by the University of Cambridge, and the implementation of the ICELT (In-service Certificate in English Language Teaching) model of professional development, which has been criticized as inadequate, because of its context insensitivity and it being top-down in character (González Moncada, 2007). This researcher also maintains that local research knowledge produced by Colombian universities has not been sufficiently valued in the implementation of these international standards.

A similar position has been advanced by Usma Wilches (2009), who has condemned an increasing tendency towards the standardization of language teaching and learning in the country based on the introduction of international models, as a move in the direction of 'uniformity through stringent normalization and control' (Usma Wilches, 2009: 136). He sees the adoption of models such as the CEFR as evidence that *international organisations* are driving definition of local standards within the context of language and education reform in Colombia, at the expense of local expertise, generating, as a result, 'inequality, exclusion and stratification' (Usma, 2009: 137).

In a recent publication (Guerrero, 2010), the author strongly criticises the discourses surrounding the debate on the importance of English for Colombia, particularly the discourse of equality, which promises equal opportunities for all who are able to demonstrate a command of the language. Guerrero maintains that there is, in fact, great inequality in learning opportunities for those who attend 'public, underfunded and overcrowded schools' and those who go to 'elite private schools' (Guerrero, 2010: 302). In addition, the claim in the *Standards* document that English will allow access to knowledge to keep up with the latest research at international level is seen by Guerrero as false, because:

> the decision to impose English in Colombia stems from mere economic interests led by the logic that if Colombia wants to have [a] better economy, it needs to participate actively in the consumption of knowledge and that English is the currency that makes it possible. (Guerrero, 2010: 304–305)

However, as Guerrero notes, the discourse of the access provided by English has been almost universally accepted as self evident by different sectors of Colombian society. In other words, it has become 'naturalised' (Fairclough, 1989) and, thus, it acts almost as a self-fulfilling prophecy.

Discussion

So let us recap on some of the most important issues which have arisen, regarding the effects of English language education in Colombia. First of all, it can be seen that English has been promoted as an important source of symbolic capital, which will help students and school and university graduates gain access to 'greater and better work opportunities' (MEN, 2006: 9). This notion has been so much accepted that some of the indigenous communities, particularly the Nasa in the Cauca Department in the south-west of the country, have requested English language programmes in their community schools (Gomez-Kramer, 2008). Secondly, it is important to note that although Colombia now has a National Bilingual Programme, this, in fact, only officially sanctions bilingualism in English-Spanish, which is associated with a highly 'visible', socially-accepted form of bilingualism. Bilingualism (or multilingualism) in minority Amerindian or Creole languages, on the other hand, leads, in most cases, to an 'invisible' form of bilingualism in which the native language is undervalued and associated with underdevelopment, poverty and backwardness (de Mejía, 1996). Thirdly, the implementation of current language and education policy has had the effect of stimulating the role of foreign organisations, such as the British Council, both in the coordination of projects, such as the National Bilingual Programme, The Basic Standards of Competences in Foreign Languages: English and some of the professional development programmes offered to English language teachers.

On the other hand, there have also been some positive effects of this policy, which may be summarised as follows. One of the big differences between previous formulations of language and education policies by the Ministry of Education in Colombia and the National Bilingual Programme is that, for the first time, English language teaching and learning is now a state policy (*Política de Estado*). As one of the advisors in the Department of Bilingualism in MEN, Rosa María Cely (2007: paragraph 33), acknowledges:

> For the first time English is State policy. [Before,] there was not an established programme in the Ministry. There were only isolated strategies depending on who was there. Now, the programme will continue, independently of who will be the next government.

The initiative of the Ministry of Education has certainly also helped to make bilingualism a household word in Colombia. According to a recent Ministry of Education report, we have the following regional bilingual programmes: *Bogotá Bilingüe* [Bilingual Bogotá], *Quindío Bilingüe, Monteria Bilingüe*, as well as *Medellín City, Neiva speaks English* and *Duitama 'dialogando con el mundo'* [Duitama speaking to the world]. Although officially most interest has centred on English-Spanish bilingualism, there have also been initiatives which demonstrate increased sensitivity towards other types of bilingualism, particularly involving indigenous languages. Furthermore, the department in the Ministry which deals with these groups (*Sección de Poblaciones*) is now in constant touch with their colleagues in the Bilingualism department.

The 'commodification' of English, which seems to characterize the role of this language in much of the region, has, in many cases, been accepted as a necessary part of economic progress. As Phillipson (2008: 21) succinctly notes in his critique of English as a neo-imperial language, 'the individuals concerned opt for the neoimperial language because it is felt that this linguistic capital will serve their personal interests best'. However, as Valencia Giraldo (2005: 17) points out, 'the current discourse on investment in English must be analyzed critically to determine who, in reality, benefits from the promotion of "bilingualism"'. This resonates with Guerrero's criticism of the apparent promotion of equality through access to English. Valencia Giraldo, along with Vélez-Rendón (2003), is concerned that instead of contributing towards more equal provision, the discourse of bilingualism with English may well widen the gap between public (state) and private education even further.

Conclusion

In light of the focus of this book, we may perhaps characterise the role of English among the Spanish- and Portuguese-speaking countries of Latin America as an 'intruder', albeit a rather fashionable gate-crasher, in the sense that English is a relatively late arrival on the linguistic stage here and not always warmly invited by all. Its ambivalent, or 'Janus-faced role', involving both 'fascination... as well as deep distrust' (Rajagopalan, 2003: 99) reflects the essential contradictions that this world language embodies in many parts of the world. The political implications are obvious. The very geographical location of Central and South America means that the United States has a powerful influence on the type of English considered worth investing in by many, particularly in the light of what Phillipson (2008: 2) has referred to as 'US dominance of the two American continents'. It seems very likely that 'acceptance of the status of English, and its assumed neutrality' (Phillipson, 2008: 24) in this part of the world will continue to lead to a generally uncritical uptake, particularly by upwardly mobile individuals who wish to become part of the economic 'imagined global community'(Ryan, 2006, cited in Phillipson, 2008: 3).

It is also interesting to note that there is some resistance to US influence, particularly to the effects of Plan Colombia – a US military aid package destined for the 'war on drugs' (Vélez-Rendón, 2003). Rather than dissuading individuals from pursuing the goal of English language learning, this aid package has led, in some cases, to the high profile of British English among young, upper class professionals in Colombia.

The expressed desire of the Ministry of Education in Bogotá (2006: 9) to help students learning English to 'open their minds and accept and understand new cultures and promote interchange between different societies' is a worthy aim and a little at odds with the rest of the discourse on competitivity. The discourse does not seem to be aimed particularly at the minority languages and cultures present in the country, which – as we have noted above – are not considered particularly valuable or useful by many in the mainstream. In this respect, it must be said that while additive English may constitute an asset for indigenous communities, subtractive English – which involves replacing native languages, instead of adding to a multilingual repertoire – would definitely have negative effects on language and identity construction. As Jim Cummins (2011: 7) notes, with regard to the dangers of devaluing minoritized cultures and languages within the school, 'benign neglect of minoritized languages and cultures is not sufficient – it simply renders the school complicit with the power relations operating in the society at large'.

If, however, Colombian students can be helped to recognize and positively accept alterity, and if the *National Bilingual Programme* can contribute to the enhancing of the value of linguistic and cultural diversity in Colombia, then the intrusion may well have been worthwhile. As Abadio Green Stocel – a linguist from the Nasa indigenous community – observes:

> It is not enough to recognise 'the other' in that dimension which interests us, or which seems correct, urgent or similar. In this case, we are looking at and projecting ourselves in the other, but we are not looking at the other as different. (Green Stocel, 1998: 7)

References

Aguilar-Sánchez, J. (2005) English in Costa Rica. *World Englishes* 24 (2), 161–172.

Alm, C.O. (2003) English in the Ecuadorian commercial context. *World Englishes* 22 (2), 143–158.

Baker, C. and Prys Jones, S. (1998) *Encyclopedia of Bilingualism and Bilingual Education*. Clevedon: Multilingual Matters.

Baumgardner, R.J. (2006) The appeal of English in Mexican commerce. *World Englishes* 25 (2), 251–266.

British Council (1989) *A Survey of English Language Teaching and Learning in Colombia: A Guide to the Market*. London: English Language Promotion Unit.

Cárdenas, M. (2006) Bilingual Colombia: Are we ready for it? What is needed? Paper presented at the 19th Annual English Australia Education Conference, Perth, Western Australia, 14–16 September, 2006.

Cely, R.M. (2007) Una Colombia bilingüe: Entrevista con Rosa María Cely (A bilingual Colombia: An interview with Rosa María Cely). *El Educador*. Online article, accessed 8 June 2009. http://www.eleducador.com/col/contenido/contenido.aspx?catID=107&conID=205

Colombia Ministerio de Educación Nacional (1994) *Ley General de Educación*. Online article, accessed 15 April 2011. http://www.mineducacion.gov.co/1621/articles-85906_archivo_pdf.pdf

Cummins, J. (2011) Preface. In A.M. de Mejía and C. Hélot (eds) *Empowering Teachers Across Cultures: Perspectives Croisées*, Enfoques Críticos. Frankfurt am Main: Peter Lang.

de Mejía, A.M. (1996) *Educación bilingüe: Consideraciones para programas bilingües en Colombia*. El Bilingüismo de los Sordos 1(2), 21–25.

de Mejía, A.M. (2006) Bilingual education in Colombia: Towards a recognition of languages, cultures and identities. *Colombian Applied Linguistics Journal* 8, 152–168.

Fairclough, N. (1989) *Language and Power*. London: Longman.

Friedrich, P. (2003) English in Argentina: Attitudes of MBA students. *World Englishes* 22 (2), 173–184.

Friedrich, P. and Berns, M. (2003) Introduction: English in South America, the other forgotten continent. *World Englishes* 22 (3), 83–90.

Gomez-Kramer, C. (2008) *Intercultural Bilingual Education*. Unpublished manuscript, Lesley University, Boston.

González-Moncada, A. (2007) Professional development of EFL teachers in Colombia: Between colonial and local practices. Íkala, Revista de Lenguaje y Cultura 12 (22), 309–332.

Graddol, D. (2006) *English Next*. London: British Council.

Guerrero, C.H. (2008) Bilingual Colombia: What does it mean to be bilingual within the framework of the National Plan of Bilingualism? *Profile* 10, 27–45.

Guerrero, C.H. (2010) Is English the key to access the wonders of the modern world?: A critical discourse analysis. *Signo y Pensamiento* 57, 294–313.

Hamel, R.E. (2003) *El Español Como Lengua de las Ciencias frente a la Globalización del Inglés: Diagnóstico y Propuesta de Acción para una Política Iberoamericana del Lenguaje en las Ciencias*. Unpublished manuscript, Universidad Nacional Autónoma de México (UNAM).

Heller, M. (2002) Identity and commodity in bilingual education. Paper presented at the Second International Symposium on Bilingualism, 23–26 October, Vigo, Spain.

Minsterio de Educacion Nacional (Colombia) (2005) *Al Tablero* 37(October–December).

Minsterio de Educación Nacional (Colombia) (2006) *Estándares Básicos de Competencias en Lenguas Extranjeras: Inglés*. Bogotá: Ministerio de Educación Nacional.

Patiño, C. (2005) La enseñanza del español. *Vigía del Idioma*, 6 July.

Phillipson, R. (2008) The linguistic imperialism of neoliberal empire. *Critical Inquiry in Language Studies* 5 (1), 1–43.

Rajagopalan, K. (2003) The ambivalent role of English in Brazilian politics. *World Englishes* 22 (2), 91–101.

Stockel, A.G. (1998) El otro soy yo. *Su Defensor* 5(49), 4–7.

Usma, J. (2009) Globalization and language and education reform in Colombia: A critical outlook. *Íkala, Revista de Lenguaje y Cultura* 14(22), 19–44.

Valencia Giraldo, S. (2005) Bilingualism and English language teaching in Colombia: A critical outlook. Paper presented at the Conference on English Language Teaching in Colombia, October, *Universidad del Quindío*.

Velez-Rendon, G. (2003) English in Colombia: A sociolinguistic profile. *World Englishes* 22 (3), 185–198.

Zuluaga, O. (1996) *La Enseñanza de Lenguas Extranjeras en Colombia en 500 Años*. Popayan: Taller Editorial.

Afterword: Could Heracles Have Gone About Things Differently?

Alastair Pennycook

It is never hard to find the latest news of the progress of this many-headed and foul-breathed monster English. No longer in its aquatic cave awaiting the arrival of Heracles, it now strides across the earth, devouring school systems, reorganizing social relations and polluting minds. The newest country on the planet, the Republic of South Sudan, for example, has announced that the sole language of secondary education will be the official language – English. And from there, as is all too often the case, the gradual downward creep of English may start, so that elementary schools will have to introduce English, in order to prepare students for secondary education. The increasing pressure to provide better access to English language resources broadens the base of English education.

In Korea, which has perhaps been gripped by 'English frenzy' (*yeongeo yeolpung*) more than any other country (see Park, this volume), this downward pressure now means that the average age of children starting to study English in and around Seoul is 3.7 years (Bai, 2011). This average figure accounts both for the 7.3% of children between the ages of three and five that have not yet started studying English, the 6.6% who begin learning English even before they reach two years of age, as well as the 1.3% of mothers who have been opting for so-called antenatal English education. Along with such early learning, Korea is now home to 'English villages', replete with castles, post offices and native speakers (or, at least, blond Caucasians, who look, in this racialized concept, like native speakers should). And if Koreans aren't importing English, they are exporting themselves: more than 40,000 school-aged Korean children – known as *jogiyuhaksaeng* (early overseas students) – are studying in the US, Canada, the UK, Australia, New Zealand, Singapore, the Philippines, Malaysia and elsewhere. Typically, the young Korean children go to live overseas with their mothers and 'this particular form of separated family is referred to as a *"wild geese"* family, who live apart so that they can educate their children in English-speaking countries' (Jeon, 2010: 59). For some students, this works; for others, they struggle to achieve adequate academic English in school, fall behind in their knowledge of Korean and end up somewhere inbetween.

Meanwhile, in Singapore, the former Prime Minister Lee Kuan Yew has announced that he feels the American version of English will probably prevail over other forms, and teachers may have to eventually accept this as inevitable. So while there may be no room for 'Singlish' in the Singapore school system, there may well be more acceptance of American English (Leow, 2011).

From Arizona in the USA, there has been some relatively good news for a change: 'State education officials will no longer force schools to retrain – or reassign – English immersion teachers because they speak with an accent.' (Fischer, 2011). Until recently, state officials had been documenting instances where teachers pronounced 'the' as 'da', for example, or 'another' as 'anudder' and on this basis, obliged such teachers 'with an accent' to retrain or be reassigned. Meanwhile, in Utah, USA, 'Utah's driver license law continues to force most refugees to take the exam in English, despite efforts to make the process easier for new arrivals. The language requirement has apparently led hundreds of refugees living in Utah to illegally drive with licenses from Arizona and Colorado, where translation is allowed' (Lyon, 2011). In the UK, Prime Minister David Cameron announced that 'unemployed people who cannot speak English will be forced to learn the language or risk losing their benefits' (Porter, 2011). And in Sri Lanka, the major initiative to increase English learning as part of President Mahinda Rajapaksa's 'English as a Life Skill' project has received a boost through a new agreement with India to help develop English teaching there (Radhakrishnan, 2011). This is a snapshot of just one week in the life of the foul-breathed, many-headed Hydra of English.

Such examples link to a number of the Hydra heads described in this book. In a class I teach on 'Global Englishes', one exercise we often do is to discuss the metaphors used to describe English, including several presented in this book – the Trojan Horse, for example – as well as some others, such as English as a 'Lingua Frankensteinia' (Phillipson, 2009), English as a 'killer language' (Skutnabb-Kangas, 2003) or as 'Tyrannosaurus Rex' (Swales, 1997) or English as a guilty language (and questions as to whether languages have agency and responsibility). We are also careful to emphasize that all the terms used to describe English – English as an International Language, English as a Lingua Franca, English as a Second Language, English as a Foreign Language, and so on – are equally metaphors (less colourful, perhaps, but equally parallel terms or phrases applied to language contexts to connect to a resemblance to known worlds).

As the different chapters in this book suggest, the heads of the Hydra give us many different ways of understanding the often pernicious roles English plays in the world. We see English as the playground bully in small island schools; a destructive juggernaut among Aboriginal Australian communities, as well as in Ethiopia and other regions of Africa; it appears as the nemesis, the arch-enemy, even a 'clobbering machine' of Māori in New Zealand; we see its 'malchemical' role as a standardized language that subjugates other language possibilities in Sri Lanka; English is a stern and intractable governess who just never seems to leave Hong Kong, and a well-intentioned auntie who, like the governess, rather overstays her welcome, meddling in family affairs and messing up the education in the Philippines and Brunei Darussalam; English works as a Trojan Horse, smuggling in cultural and ideological enemies unseen; a Siren who summons the innocent to their deaths on the rocks of broken educational promises and dismantled communities; a border, the crossing of which is an experience fraught with anxiety, tension and inadequacy; a chameleon, described in many different ways, depending on the circumstances; a partner in crime (along with Mandarin Chinese and the Singaporean government) in subjugating language variety and a reluctant partner alongside Bahasa Malaysia in Malaysian language education policy; and an intruder (though, at times, a rather fashionable gate-crasher) into the linguistic landscape of South America.

All of this gives us many thoughtful and troubling accounts of the roles English now plays around the world. This plurality of images of English is not, thankfully, yet another attempt to describe varieties of English, but has to do with its role as a divisive language (see Ramanathan, 2005; another metaphor that might have been picked up), a language bound up with economic and political relations, a language of threat, hope, desire, resistance and destruction. By contrast with the politically bland and moribund 'world Englishes' framework, with its catalogue of exoticized variety from putative norms, its celebration of 'new Englishes' emerging alchemically as a good thing for the world, the many-headed Hydra presents us only with malchemical concerns (Parakrama, this volume). Of course, the picture here is not all negative, but, generally, this is a space of critical engagement with the problems posed by English. And the metaphor itself does not present positive images: the Hydra did not have a mixture of heads, some threatening, some empowering. There were no nice heads. Thus, this book helpfully undermines most of those rosy myths about English as a language of opportunity, a language the world has chosen, a language needed for international communication, a language whose wondrous spread we should celebrate.

Beyond this, however, we need to consider some further complexities. As we look across these different accounts of English, it is clear that English is not the only player here: there are duelling aunties and partners in crime, including Bahasa Malay(sia), Chinese, Arabic, even Bislama and other local languages. The decision by South Sudan to make English the language of secondary education, for example, was also a decision to replace the former language of education, Arabic (Suleiman, 2011). It was, therefore, in this context, a decolonial move to signal freedom from what had been seen as the imposition of the former government of Sudan. We see similar politics in the move in former French colonies to move towards English. Nevertheless, the move to adopt English is a particular one. This policy for English in this fragile new nation is also one of nation building. All new secondary schools will be national boarding institutions, designed, in part, to foster national unity by mixing students from different states. There is some talk of introducing that other *lingua franca* of the region, Kiswahili, which, as Ngũgĩ wa Thiong'o (this volume) points out, is the only African language that is an active global player. This might link South Sudan more securely with its East African neighbours (especially Kenya and Tanzania), though, of course, English does this in other ways too. English is also, in another sense, a local language (Higgins, 2009), and given that the Ministry of Education is currently reviewing 240 English book titles from Kenya, these textbooks may at least have a local content.

Of course, we might hope that education beyond the primary level could continue in the indigenous languages of the country, rather than the official language – English. All indigenous languages are acknowledged as national languages, though counting and accounting for these complex language chains is difficult (Makoni & Mashiri, 2007). When we bring the project of nation building, schooling, literacy and language education into the context of local language ecologies, we all too often fall into the trap of also having to adopt those linguistic categorizations that emerged from the context of linguistic colonialism (Errington, 2008). We might indeed wish that the 60 or so languages of the Nilo-Saharan language family (Eastern and Central Sudanic) or the Ubangi languages of the Niger-Congo family, including those, such as Zande, spoken across the fragile and Europe-constructed borders, could play a more prominent role in education and the nation. But, as Mufwene (2010) reminds us, linguists are all too often insufficiently clear:

> about how countries that are rich in ecological, cultural, and linguistic diversity but are economically poor can, with their limited financial means, satisfy both the human rights of their populations to evolve out of poverty and the alleged rights of their languages to each be used in the education system and/or other cultural domains. (2010: 914)

Another complication emerges when we observe the ways in which English means different things to different Hydra heads. Indeed, what is discussed under the label of English is not always the same thing: one Hydra head, for example, is standard English – an assumed norm that may overlook the role of Aboriginal English, of Singlish; another Hydra head may be precisely these descriptions of English that do not account adequately for the political economy of English (Tupas, 2006); a different Hydra head may be the introduction of English into primary education, to the probable detriment of first-language education for many of the students; and a different Hydra head may be the role English plays in relation to neoliberal corporatization of economies and institutions. I have myself, on occasion, used the story of the blind monks and the elephant to illustrate the problem with understanding this many-faceted role of English. Just as each encountered a different part of the elephant and assumed the rest was made in this image (a foot leading to an image of a pillar-like being, a trunk to a flexible serpentine animal, a tail to a thin and rapid-moving creature), so we might argue that the many faces of English, or the many partial encounters with English, lead to many different images of English. For a primary student in Korea, a secondary student in South Sudan, an immigrant driver in Utah, a teacher in Arizona, an unemployed immigrant in the UK, an English teacher in Sri Lanka, English means something very different.

Ultimately, however, the elephant story is unsatisfying here. Although I have found it useful to speak of the elephantine myth of English, this story presents us with the problem that we, in fact, know what English is (an elephant), but that others fail to grasp this reality. Ultimately, this is both politically and epistemologically suspect. An image of English as hard to grasp, but ultimately elephantine, may be appealing, but fails to attend to the diversity of what English is. English is not the elephant in the room. The collective monks are, in a sense, right: English is all these things and more.

The Hydra myth gives us a different way of thinking about this, since it is not only many-headed, but also a piece of mythology. Mythologies may serve as useful metaphors, but, as Barthes (1972) reminds us, they are also complex. When we consider the myth of English (Pennycook, 2007), we need to consider not only those many myths about English that this book usefully addresses – that English automatically confers educational and economic benefit, that English is needed for international communication, that English is a language better suited to a globalized world than any other – but also that English itself is also a myth. It is the relentless repetition of the stories about this thing called English that perpetuate this mythological creature.

When we talk of English today, we mean many things and not many of them have to do with some core notion of language. The presence of English shifts not just the language ecologies of different contexts, but, more importantly, the discursive ecologies; English is not just a language, but a discursive field: English *is* neoliberalism, English *is* globalization, English *is* human capital. The question then becomes not whether some monolithic thing called English is imperialistic or an escape from poverty, nor how many varieties there may be of this thing called English, but rather, what kind of mobilizations underlie acts of English use or learning? Something called English is mobilized by English language industries with particular language effects. But something called English is also part of complex language chains, mobilized as part of multiple acts of identity; it is caught in a constant process of semiotic reconstruction.

So what can we do about it? We might argue that the Hydra only exists as part of a legend in which it is overcome by Heracles. The story, ultimately, is about the strength and bravery of Heracles. So is the notion of English as Hydra, we might ask, useful in the main, in order to turn those that oppose it into crusading heroes? The Heraclean/ Herculean (Phillipsonian?)[1] task of cutting off its heads, cauterizing the wounds before they grow back and, finally, decapitating the immortal head of English with a golden sword is, indeed, one of the great labours of this world. But might Heracles have gone about this differently? Is decapitation the best way forward? The point that we need to try to get at is this: it is not English – if by that, we mean a certain grammar and lexicon – that is the problem. It is the discourses of English that are the problem, it is the way that an idea of English is caught up in all that we do so badly in the name of education, all the exacerbations of inequality that go under the label of globalization, all the linguistic calumnies that denigrate other ways of speaking, all the shamefully racist institutional interactions that occur in schools, hospitals, law courts, police stations, social security offices and unemployment centres.

We can, by all means, as Ngũgĩ wa Thiong'o and Muhammad Haji Salleh (this book) both do and advocate, give more support to other languages, writing our poems, plays and prose in languages other than English, while also reminding ourselves that those other languages are never innocent players either in the politics of unequal semiotic resources. We need to improve our understanding of strategies of language revival and recognition and continue our battles for bilingual education (and, yes, the idea of teaching in English for the first four hours of school in the Northern Territory of Australia is disgraceful and should be discarded – see Robyn Ober and Jeanie Bell, this volume). We need to increase our battles against pernicious ideas about the benefits of standard English, to point to the negative alchemy (malchemy) of standardized English and to seize the possibilities in the radical differences of unstandardized, resistant language to help others to stand up to the playground bully, to find ways to block the wheels of the juggernaut, to tell the aunts and governesses that have overstayed their welcome that it really is time to go home.

But we also need to confront the problem of the myth, of the language ideologies that continue to construct the terms of the debate. We need to understand not only that monolingual mindsets deny the value of first language and bilingual education, but also that the idea that monolingualism is possible is part of the picture. That is to say, it is not only that so-called monolingual mindsets diminish educational and linguistic diversity, but also that the discourses that allow for the possibility of monolingualism as a concept are also complicit with this problem. The monological and enumerative strategies that link languages to worldviews, that construct languages as entities to be counted, battled over or beheaded does not ultimately help us in the struggle for a more equitable semiotic world. As Moore *et al.* (2010: 2) explain, this approach to languages 'privileges a conception of "languages" as neatly-bounded, abstract, autonomous grammatical systems (each of which corresponds to a neatly-bounded "worldview")'. Such an account, they argue, distracts attention from the complexities of speech communities and the dynamics of language contact. As Mufwene explains:

> the ideal world in which (rich) linguistic diversity can be sustained is far from being ours. There are really no language rights. Many people who are struggling to improve their living conditions in the current ever-changing socioeconomic ecologies are not concerned with maintaining languages and heritages, which are more properly archived in libraries and museums. The archiving is (to be) done by experts or some nonprofessional "glossophiles" (if I may suggest the term). (2010: 927)

So could Heracles have done things differently? Not if he is stuck only in his own mythological struggle with the many-headed Hydra – the Hydra and Heracles are mutually constitutive. But if he were given a chance to step outside this myth, to rethink the terms of the battle, to reconsider what we mean by the Hydra or by language, things might start to look a bit different. We need to move away from the reification and exoticization of languages, suggesting that to maintain one's L1 is somehow a guarantor of self-esteem, a consistent worldview, a useful education and economic advancement. As Mufwene (2010) makes very clear, all of this depends on the particular language under discussion, the nature of local ecologies and economic opportunities, the value accorded to different languages, the movement of people in search of livelihoods and so on:

> Linguistics must address issues arising from the real world of socioeconomic inequality more globally and not just from the point of view of languages as maps of world views and illustrations of mental/cognitive variation. The rest of the world happens to see languages as tools at the service of mankind, and this perspective is an equally legitimate one, just as is the view that a language can be an asset or a liability to a person or a population. (2010: 927)

The focus needs to move away from 'languages' and to focus instead on language practices (Pennycook, 2010), on the intersections between discursive practices (orders of meaning), generic practices (iterative forms) and stylistic practices (making new possibilities), in relation to economics, employment, migration and education. We need careful research that explores this and which separates the romantic glorification of language diversity from the harder questions about knowledge, existence and expression.

Note

(1) Robert Phillipson and I are really not so very far apart in much of what we argue and advocate. Indeed, far more people are content to align us with each other, than to separate our positions. Little asides such as this should not be taken too seriously.

References

Bai, J. (2011) Children start learning English by age 4. *The Korea Herald*, August 30, 2011.

Barthes, R. (1972) *Mythologies* (Annette Lavers, trans.). New York, NY: Hill and Wang (original work published 1957).

Errington, J. (2008) *Linguistics in a Colonial World: A Story of Language, Meaning and Power*. Oxford: Blackwell.

Fischer H. (2011) State halts practice of forcing action on 'accented' teachers. *Arizona Daily Star*, 31 August, 2011. Online at: http://92starnet.com/news/local/education/precollegiate/article_c8aa52c2-e844-5f2a-8264-4ad180a003ea.html.

Higgins, C. (2009) *English as a Local Language: Post-colonial Identities and Multilingual Practices*. Bristol: Multilingual Matters.

Jeon, J. (2010) Issues for English tests and assessments: A view from Korea. In Y. I. Moon and B. Spolsky (eds) *Language Assessment in Asia: Local, Regional or Global?* (pp. 55–82). Seoul: Asia TEFL.

Leow, S.W. (2011) American English 'likely to prevail': Lee Kuan Yew. *Straits Times*, Sept 7, 2011. Online at http://www.straitstimes.com/BreakingNews/Singapore/Story/STIStory_710302.html

Lyon, J. (2011) English-only thwarts Utah refugees seeking driver licenses. *The Salt Lake Tribune*, Sept 7, 2011. Online at http://www.sltrib.com/sltrib/home2/52501715-183/english-refugee-test utah.html.csp

Makoni, S. and Meshiri, P. (2007) Critical historiography: Does language planning in Africa need a construct of language as part of its theoretical apparatus? In S. Makoni and A. Pennycook (eds) *Disinventing and Reconstituting Languages* (pp. 62–89). Clevedon: Multilingual Matters.

Moore, R., Pietikäinen, S. and Blommaert, J. (2010) Counting the losses: Numbers as the language of language endangerment. *Sociolinguistic Studies* 4 (1), 1–26.

Mufwene, S. (2010) The role of mother-tongue schooling in eradicating poverty: A response to Language and poverty. *Language* 86 (4), 910–932.

Pennycook, A. (2007) The myth of English as an international language. In S. Makoni and A. Pennycook (eds) *Disinventing and Reconstituting Languages* (pp. 90–115). Clevedon: Multilingual Matters.

Pennycook, A. (2010) *Language as a Local Practice*. London: Routledge.

Phillipson, R. (2009) *Linguistic Imperialism Continued*. London: Routledge

Porter, A. (2011) Learn English to get a job or lose benefits, says Cameron. *The Telegraph*, 15 September 2011. Online at http://www.telegraph.co.uk/news/politics/david-cameron/8761311/Learn-English-to-get-a-job-or-lose-benefits-says-Cameron.html

Radhakrishnan, R. K. (2011) Sri Lanka, India join hands to teach English in schools. *The Hindu*, September 13, 2011. Online at http://www.thehindu.com/news/international/article2450642.ece

Ramanathan, V. (2005) *The English-Vernacular Divide: Postcolonial Language Politics and Practice*. Clevedon: Multilingual Matters.

Skutnabb-Kangas, T. (2003) Linguistic diversity and biodiversity. The threat from killer languages. In C. Mair (ed.) *The Politics of English as a World Language: New Horizons in Postcolonial Cultural Studies* (pp. 31–52). Amsterdam: Rodopi.

Suleiman, G.S. (2011) South Sudan: Arabic to Be Phased Out From Secondary Schools in Three Years. Website, accessed 23 August 2011. http://allafrica.com/stories/201108231678.html

Swales, J. (1997) English as Tyrannosaurus Rex. *World Englishes* 16 (3), 373–82.

Tupas, R. (2006) Standard Englishes, pedagogical paradigms and conditions of (im)possibility. In R. Rubdy and M. Saraceni (eds) *English in the World: Global Rules, Global Roles* (pp. 169–185). London: Continuum.

Coda: One Colonial Language: One Great Tragic Epic. English in Malaysia and Beyond

Muhammad Haji Salleh
Sasterawan Negara (Malaysian National Laureate)

The long journey of colonization by the English language – through aggressive and hegemonic colonialism – has brought about the epic tragedy of hundreds of languages, on five continents. This journey has been relentless in its aggression, up until this very moment. Even great languages, like Arabic, Mandarin, French, German and Japanese, are feeling its encroachment. As it strengthens, it influences not only the choice of languages, but it also radically changes their minds, their perceptions of the world, their ideas of what is right and wrong, what is good and proper and the very meanings of success and personal identity. As it wears down the ability of other languages to fight back, English continues to destroy them, no matter how dynamic, popular or close to the heart of the people they may be.

Over the centuries, many people have been moulded and, subsequently, conditioned to believe in what they perceived to be their 'predicament' as an inferior people with an inferior language, vis-a-vis English. Thus, it comes as no surprise that they surrendered quite easily to the invader. On the other hand, however, they have overlooked the huge achievements of Japan, France, Germany and the Nordic countries, which do not use English as their national or main language, but manage very well to prosper and contribute to the world. They have also forgotten that there are several countries which have chosen to use English, but have neither found, nor enjoyed the economic wealth and societal development that they thought would naturally come with it. This is truly a double tragedy and it has affected so many people in the world's former colonies.

The colonized mind and the colonized society have been conditioned to think that they have no history. History only began with the British and, therefore, for many of them, there must have existed a huge and silent vacuum before the arrival of the colonizers. Some countries intentionally blotted out their indigenous past, for various reasons, and only highlighted those events that transpired after the coming of the white man.

With such an overwhelming linguistic and cultural steamroller at work, surrender to the colonized predicament came quite effortlessly. When English was chosen as the main language or the teaching medium in the schools, there was an almost automatic loss of local knowledge and wisdom, which had been embedded in their languages and by which people had survived for thousands of years. More precious still was the loss of a wealth of practical solutions to very real social and cultural problems.

In the meantime, many have not gained new knowledge through English. As a Malay proverb says, *Yang dikejar tak dapat, yang digendung berciciran* (That which is sought is not found, that which is being held falls away, scattered). Thus, the colonized have been condemned to being quite uneducated, lacking in real knowledge, grace or polish, which their own cultures would have taught them.

Indeed, language is power. It has power over one's mind, one's economic welfare and life itself. The official and national language that is used in schools and universities, in administration and business, soon becomes the main medium of thought and communication and, therefore, it *stays* in the mind, to remind one of one's roots and identity. A national language can develop through practice, necessity and creativity. However, when it is subverted by English, it becomes stunted and gnarled and follows the history of others that have been destroyed by English. It ends up handicapped, lame and left behind by the times.

For writers, the choice of language is of paramount importance and significance. It defines the culture of their novels and poems and gives them a certain character. Whenever they choose a *colonial* language, they are immediately confronted by several questions. Among them is their prolonged loyalty to English – a language by which their country was subjugated. Ngũgĩ wa Thiong'o, the famous Kenyan novelist, unhappy with his colleagues' choice of English, once asked (1986: 9): 'When did we, as African writers, come to be so feeble towards the claim of our languages on us, and so aggressive in our claims on other languages, particularly the languages of our colonisers?' If our writers, the intellectuals and the inheritors of a linguistic and literary tradition, cannot be true to the claims of their heritage – their past – how can one expect a shopkeeper or a clerk to be so?

There are more things to be found in a language than merely profit and continuing economic power. Many writers, and along with them, the captured minds of millions of Anglophiles – the businessmen and contractors – are now holding us to ransom. For them, the solution to the choice of language is easy enough. If we retain English, we will soon be a developed and prosperous nation. This, of course, is not the real logic of the solution. These Anglophiles hurtle forward, heavily blinkered with English, seeing only from its perspective. However, if the blinkers were taken away, they might see a clearer horizon and in it, other alternatives, for example, dynamic countries, with ideas of innovation, with economic success, but minus the

English language. For example, my friends, who struggle for Malay as the national language of the country, have counted that there are more Nobel Prize winners in literature who write in languages other than English, than those who write in English (Nobel prize).

The reasons for championing English can be found in the politics of power. The colonized native-elite, which was earlier groomed by its colonial masters, has now taken over the administration of the country. This administration came not only in the form of senior officials in the civil service, but also in the government and in the banks, in the plantations and the mines. They have been able to control the pulse of the nation's economy and dictate the future of the country.

Perceiving that their status, their economic standing and power were all dependent on English, they have fought hard to extend the old (colonial) system that has generously bestowed them with privileges. This choice is made, however, without the consent of the majority, who – more often than not – studied in the national-language schools and are, no doubt, seen by the elite as second-class citizens. Along with them, those immigrants or expatriates and their children who chose English were automatically welcomed into their fold. Prior to Independence, we would have found them assisting the British to rule and profit from the country. Today, we see their continued efforts to hold onto English – their very weapon of power and superiority. Tragically, many of the post-Independence politicians were English-educated men and women, who turned finally into mere economic planners, without much real understanding of how cultures and national identities are formed and what they might mean in a new country.

Often 'culture' is a word that has no real meaning if it cannot be sold to tourists. But, one asks, if the aim is to attract tourists, what does one show them? These grand buildings, sky-scrapers and high-speed trains, under which once lay traditional villages, rubber plantations, *padi* fields and *dusuns* (villages)? Tourists do not come to see buildings; they might have grander ones at home. Many of them come to see unique cultures, musical and theatrical performances, not to forget the beauty of the land.

The rush to compete, to manufacture products within the shortest possible time, has created another sad phenomenon – in education. As I see children trudging to school and endless tuition classes, working their way through countless past question papers, I may be forgiven, I hope, for concluding that education is often reduced to 'mugging' for the most number of As. Ethics and aesthetics, history and culture, if introduced at all, are quite rare and insufficient in their discussion of the meaning, values and shape of a 'desirable' Malaysian citizen. Is the future of the country now being left to these unfinished graduates who mostly know how to memorize their chemistry and physics answers, but have forgotten how to be proud of their own language, culture and history or to feel like a human being, to relate to their parents or forebears across time?

And for many with colonized minds sitting on their Asian shoulders, education is only 'education' if it is in English. The reason given is that their children will later be able to communicate with others around the world in English and to study in British or Australian universities. But I have to ask: 'What about communicating with other Malaysians, with our past and our heritage?'

It is sad to observe that the profit motive and other quite selfish interests play a huge part in the reasoning of the debate for English. Often, it is also the status quo that discounts all other considerations. Of course, these are not the words used. Rather, other euphemisms that distract from the real meaning are employed. Words like 'development' and 'prosperity' are strategically situated in sentences, so that they will connote that, via English-language proficiency, the country and the economic condition of the people will be improved. This equation sees nothing in the proposition that a country must have a sense of national pride, a sense of history and a unique identity – all these may be found in its language and culture. Again, the practical argument has chosen to disregard the cases of Japan or China, Germany or France, Sweden or Switzerland. It has turned its eyes only to the old colonial country (which, we should remind ourselves, became prosperous partly because it has profited from the resources of its colonies and by using cheap labour all around the world to squeeze as much profit out of them as it can).

Success is not achieved because a country uses the language of its colonial power. It is its perception or philosophy of nature, how it uses its natural and human resources, its work ethic and, in fact, the whole world-view of its people that determines its present and future. And perhaps we should not forget that success has different meanings for different people. In a tropical country that does not push its inhabitants to gather food for winter and where nature is extremely generous, its work philosophy is different from those of the temperate regions. Here, in tropical Malaysia, relationships between people are extremely important. Mutually preserving values and traditions becomes a measurement of a successful society. Respect for others and interpersonal courtesy are significant goals. Happiness and spiritual satisfaction are paramount. These are not the end-products of a development targeting merely profit and material development. Are we now, after an English education, happier than the villager who has a patch of land and has the sea and nature as his village and city? Or are we further sucked into capitalism and a concept of success that is borrowed from *other* peoples or *other* environments?

A Language Subjugated

If a country does not use its own languages, but instead borrows one from the colonial power that earlier subjugated it, then it is almost certainly ensuring the death of these languages. I do not know of any country that has adopted the colonial language, while shunting aside the native ones, that has been able to return their own languages to the people as relevant, dynamic and able to handle the many changes that it must confront. Hawaiian and Māori are trying their best, but still, education in their lands is almost all in English. This predicament robs them of the opportunity to replace English, which forges ahead, it seems, whatever the hurdles. But when there is a strong national will, languages like Indonesian, Japanese and Vietnamese seem able to go forth into the future, even after colonialism.

A Poet Chooses His Language

While I have tried to sketch a terrifying worldwide scenario of what happens to a language subjugated, colonized and replaced, I also have a personal history of what has happened to me as a Malaysian and as a writer.

I went to a Malay school in a village called Sungai Aceh in Pulau Pinang (Penang, in the north-west of the Malaysian peninsula). The headmaster, my father's friend, persuaded him to send me to the Anglo-Chinese School in a town about seven miles away, perhaps because my marks were good, and he wanted me to keep his daughter company on the long bus trip to Nibong Tebal. As my father was very close to him, he relented, though his initial plan for me was to be a teacher of religious studies (an education that is traditional and non-Western), especially in times when it was believed that the mission schools' aim was to convert the locals. One wonders why so many mission schools were built in Malaya by a group of people from Europe and America. Not out of generosity, surely, because there were many in their own countries who were quite poor and needed education, like the children of the manual workers in London or the coal miners of the Midlands, during the periods after the two World Wars.

In my primary school in Sungai Aceh, all subjects were taught in Malay, except for a lesson of English (in the third year). So I used the language of my mother and father, grandmother and my neighbours in the school. As I entered the English-medium school for my upper primary, I had to leave Malay behind. I began to learn English – this strange language with an impossible spelling system and a pronunciation that was out-of-the-world, difficult and unnatural to my Malaysian lips. It sounded funny, too. It was an alien language. Why should one speak a funny language when there is one that is natural to one's breath, sound box and intonation?

But our teachers were patient. Their task was to draw us out from ourselves and lead us to this language and master it. It was perceived by them to be a better language than our own. So slowly we memorised as much as we could, helped along by British comics like *Beano* and American cowboy ones like *Roy Rogers* and *Tom Mix*. Of course, when one studied Malay, one was not helped by the likes of these comics, which, in this language (Malay) during the 1950s and 1960s, were mostly political in nature and sketched for adults. They appeared as comic strips in newspapers which I did not read, because they were essentially published for adult readers.

I remember little from these years, but on the other hand, I can clearly recall that our English lessons used the *Oxford English Course Books for Malayans*. However, when my whole family moved to Bukit Mertajam – a bigger town to the north – I left the mission school and entered high school at Standard 6. This was a colonial government school. English was, of course, the only language. We were punished if we ever spoke Malay or Chinese or Tamil, which reflected the mindset of our teachers and the government at that time. There was no space for any other language, and for the system and the teachers who grew up in that language, it was the only one the country 'needed'.

So I was further introduced to English, encouraged to discover the *Famous Five* and *Secret Seven*, *The Three Musketeers* (the names of whose characters I only later realized were comically mispronounced, according to how they would spell out in English). But my English teacher was a conscientious guide, training us to enjoy these well-known texts. I read and read (all in English, of course) and eventually became quite proud of the booklist that I would show to the class every week. Mine was among the longest, so my progress into English was quite rapid. To humour our native curiosity and our love of entertainment of any sort, we were shown English-language movies once a week, mostly made in Hollywood. Among them, in my crowded English past, were *Treasure Island*, *Captain Hook*, *Peter Pan* and supporting them were our favourites, *Mickey Mouse*, *Donald Duck*, *Woody Woodpecker* and also *The Three Stooges*.

Back in class, the *Golden Hind Geography* series, the history of Britain and how the British subjugated their colonies (none of the deception and the broken treaties were mentioned, of course) were our main staple. During the four years I was there, not a word of Malay was taught. Thus, the offerings that the Malay language provided for its people were quickly dismantled and discarded by the long years of a prejudiced, and even racist, system of education and administration.

However, when Malaysia was about to gain its independence in 1957, there was a weak attempt to teach Malay – the national language – as a subject for the Lower Certificate of Education. But as the language had been forgotten and designated for the bin, no one suitable could be found to teach the subject in my school. Finally, they had to choose someone who had some knowledge of Malay. But, ironically, he spoke mostly English and came to school wearing a 'cork hat' (a pith helmet) – the easily recognisable symbol of the British colonial administration or of a British hunter in the wilds of the colonies.

Together with some of my friends, I registered for the Malay language as a subject for the Lower Certificate of Education examinations. We proceeded to study on our own and, to our delight, we passed. I did well, too. This I consider to be one of my first post-colonial rebellions. I had made a subconscious move to include my mother tongue, albeit at a higher literary level, in my curriculum. I was also, subconsciously, making a statement for my language and my people.

English came to us in a package, complete with a British government, an English education for the humble peoples of the colony (so that they would be able to become clerks, supervisors of workers in the plantations and railways and peons in the offices), plus a troupe of teachers (who were completely convinced that no other language was good enough), comics, cartoons, movies and a dearth of children's literature. But Malay had no such package. There were only simple stories for children to help them read, a few *hikayats* (traditional narratives) that were quite difficult to obtain, as we could not find them in the libraries. Magazines were mostly for adults. However, there was one exception, *Utusan Kanak-kanak* – a newspaper published in Malay for children. My second step of returning to Malay was, at the age of 14, to publish in this newspaper and win a RM 5.00 prize.

In the meantime, my Malay practically remained at the village level, sometimes deteriorating into a rough and unpolished lingo. It was stunted, because it was meant to only be taught in the schools up to Standard 3 – the highest level was for those destined to be trained as teachers, i.e. Standard 6.

So I marched on into English, hearing subconsciously, from time to time, a faint call from Malay. I entered Form 4 at Malay College – a school claiming to be an 'Eton of the East' (again, a British model), once reserved for the nobility. In 1958, it partly opened its doors to the humbler classes, from which I hailed. Ironically, here some subjects *were* taught in Malay – Malay language, Malay Literature and Islamic Religion. There, after a steady staple diet of books and magazines and my continued interest in Malay and English, I happened to win a Wise and Butler Scholarship for essays in Malay and English and a translation from the former to the latter. From now on, there appeared a clear split in my linguistic life – I studied English, but felt, within myself, that there was also an older language that was closer to the heart of my existence, my village and country.

Later, in England, while following my teacher-training courses, I began to write my first poems in English, in 1963, in a damp spring in Wolverhampton. But again, almost subconsciously, I also began to write poems in Malay, a few weeks after that. Two languages and a sense of guilt gave me parallel poetic expressions. So I continued on 'rowing down two rivers'.

After my time in England, such parallel writing was quite rare. I would swing from one language to the other, depending on which country I was living in at the time. When I was in countries where English was predominant,

I tended to write more in that language. However, when I returned home to Malaysia or embarked on research for an extended period of time in Indonesia, I naturally returned to Malay.

To cut the story short, it was in the USA in 1972 that I felt the sharpest pangs of my own betrayal. I was still writing poetry in English and giving Malay a distant and secondary place. As I read through the different works of well known poets, I came to realize that Americans did not write in French, neither did the British write in other languages. Even though they were originally Scots or Welsh, British writers wrote in English – the national language of the country.

After a long period suffering from the guilt of choosing some other people's tongue, I made a conscious effort to write my poetry – the genre closest to my heart and my own medium of expression (besides academic literary criticism) – in the Malaysian national language.

English, with its thousands of poets, does not need another amateur writer imitating the British or American poets. Shouldn't I, as a Malaysian, be writing in Malay/Malaysian? But I honestly felt that my special predicament as a wandering student, living and travelling in many countries, was, indeed, a special and somewhat rare privilege. I was standing on a heap of fertile experience of the world, and I had a whole world of themes to write about. If I wrote in Malay, I would be able to transfer my experiences into that language as a whole new world, as had never been done before. Perhaps it would help to define the new Malaysian in a new century.

There was no doubt that English, while being a colonial language, was, for me, a borrowed language. Its roots were somewhere else. It grew from the rains and snows of Yorkshire and the winds of the White Cliffs. Its shoots grew from the ways and world-view of the British. All these define its character. As I wrote in two languages, I quickly came to notice that each language has its intricate and almost undefinable separate identity, and it was clear that this identity was related to the history and character of its people. The English I was using was an artificial language for me and for Malaysians in general, created by the British in Malaya. It is religious in its foundation, but it was later chosen to become a medium in the schools. It has no deep roots in the country and no mature local literature to speak of. Poetry and literature, for me, must come from genuine sounds, from the soul of the writer himself/herself.

Though English is a language I thought I knew quite well, I could not relate to Spenser or Chaucer or even Wordsworth or Browning. Neither could I relate to Cockney or the Scots dialect of English. But I could naturally delve into and enjoy the old *pantun* (traditional verses), *ceritera* (stories) and *hikayat* (epic tales) of the Malaysians, Bruneians, Singaporeans and Indonesians, who also used Malay. This showed me a path into the future, with a literature of deep roots and the pride of history. This language is now quite possibly in the top 10 languages of the world, going by its number of speakers. The Indonesians, who threw out the Dutch and their language, developed an old *lingua franca* to make it into a dynamic modern one, which they use in almost all sectors of their daily life. I now take my modern stance from them and, along with it, I find a pride and ease in using it.

As a language, Malay is gentler than English; it is awash with vowels. The seas of the Malay Archipelago and the Pacific Ocean break on its beaches. The sound of water enters its words and the ways in which they are pronounced. Each consonant is neutralized by adjacent vowels, thus eroding their sharp edges and giving it a gentler and nature-friendly music. In Malay literature, one is taught to use this graceful and smoother language, for it is considered that beauty is to be found in this harmonious flow of assonantal music. English is entirely different. More consonantal in quality, it also likes to cluster consonants that can become very awkward in sound and spelling – not my idea of a beautiful language. *Psychiatry, psoriasis, yonks, chromosome, xylophone* and *writhe* – all writhe within my mouth and, without doubt, belong to an alien spelling concept. Like many others, I have also concluded that English has one of the most illogical spelling systems of any language.

While the sounds are very different, Malay is marked by its extremely rich emotional content. Shades of meaning for the different emotions are carried by a series of subtle terms. This is especially true when they involve a relationship between close friends or relatives, where most of the time it is a play of feelings, expectations and performance. Taught to be refined in their interpersonal relationships, Malays listen to the sounds of words, in order to read the quieter nuances and the status of that relationship. As they catch on to them, they react accordingly. Thus, there are words in Malay which deal with emotions that are difficult to translate. One of them is *merajuk* – to sulk after feeling that one has been slighted by a friend, relative or lover. Another is *amuk/amok*, which describes a situation in which one goes on a violent spree, after a series of bouts of pent-up frustration. Interestingly, this word has also been taken into at least five European languages, including English.

Then there is also a huge local vocabulary that describes the tropical environment – from the different species of trees, bushes, grasses and epiphytes to animals, insects, birds, coral forms and fishes. Another special vocabulary contains words that sketch tropical storms, winds, rains and floods. As these are products of the tropics and its characteristic climate, they are not present in English.

For a culturally proud Malaysian, how does one correctly describe the heavenly fragrance of the famous *durian* if its very connotation in English is merely 'spiked' with a prejudiced 'stink'? The cultural meaning for this fruit is, indeed, complex, involving quite violent emotions and reactions. It sinks deep into not only the food of the Malaysians, but also into their metaphors, rituals, legends and oral stories.

Another cultural icon for Malaysia is the *kancil*, often translated into English as the mousedeer. This English term covers only the animal's physical shape, while all of its other traits of intelligence, such as being a wily trickster, are forgotten. In Malay, *kancil* has even become a metaphor, a cultural icon, and it has appeared in a series of popular tales. On the other hand, in English, a mousedeer is a mere description of a small, forest-dwelling deer – quite fragile and timid-looking.

If we venture further into the area of indigenous rituals, our predicament is, in fact, even more problematic. How does one bring out the ritual significance of the *sirih*, often translated as betel leaf? In Malay, this word resounds with, on the one hand, the meaning of an intricate performance of hospitality or as a symbol of giving and accepting in a marriage ceremony, but on the other hand, also of traditional cures used by folkhealers. In *Sulalat al-Salatin*, a sultan bestows *sirih* as a symbol of his authority and command. And to complicate matters, in the *pantuns* and *syair* – two popular indigenous poetic forms – *sirih* rhymes with *kasih*, love. In these poems, each time the word *sirih* is spoken, *kasih* (love) looms onto the horizon of its meaning.

There is yet another problematic word (for English translators, especially) – *bomoh*. Colonial translators use the term 'witch doctor' or 'medicine man' as its equivalent. In Malay, he is a wise elder who cures with herbs and by traditional methods. Often he is in contact with supernatural powers and he is frequently consulted when rituals are to be performed, a piece of forest is to be cleared or a house built. He is a wise, traditional doctor in Malay, but merely a primitive magician in English.

The list of untranslatable words and emotions grows longer as we contrast the languages. From experience and actual practice, I have come to realize that, in general, English captures its own universe of meanings, for the most part, quite separate from that of the Malay. As a poet, I cannot merely be satisfied to catch only the skin of their significance or a pimple or two of their sense, while I seek a more complete representation of reality, a more inclusive picture of the human condition. When writing in Malay, I do not have to struggle to awkwardly tag unfamiliar connotations or shades of significance onto English terms. They are already embedded in the words and the language, ready for use.

Different sounds also produce a different music and, consequently, different verbal aesthetics. The terrain of their sounds maps certain emotions in one's subconscious, where they are embedded. These sounds connect with a bundle of meanings found in the great lake of the language. This, too, is the lake of heritage. As I write in Malay, I connect the reader to this lake, quite effortlessly, as we drink from the same source. Writing in English, I would effectively disconnect my channel to this body of water and tradition. I would have to laboriously dig other, newer wells, which may merely unearth mud and brackish water.

Choice of Language and its Future

Ngũgĩ wa Thiong'o (1986: 26) once posed this dramatic question to his fellow-writers:

> We as African writers have always complained about the neo-colonial economic and political relationship to Europe-America. Right. But by our continuing to write in foreign languages, paying homage to them, are we not on the cultural level of continuing that neo-colonial slavish and cringing spirit?

Writers, he seems to say, are snared in their choice of language. The colonial ones are snared more cruelly. The African writer who continues to write in English (after Independence) is, in fact, an instrument in the continuation of its colonial tradition. Sadly, very few have heeded his words and very few have returned to their native languages. Ngũgĩ is the most well known of those who have done so. He has returned to his mother tongue, Gĩkũyũ, and is now still writing in it and continuing to help in the development of that language.

When one writes in one's own mother tongue, one is also assisting it to merge with the changes and new times. The writer, through his/her need to make sense of the world and to communicate his/her ideas, will help his/her language to adjust to change, to recreate itself in new needs and metaphors. If he or she abandons this language, it will most probably survive for a few more decades, but merely as a language of the traditional market, *pasar*, and it would not be able to develop on the scientific, epistemological and technological fronts. These are important horizons for real development.

Poets offer a language through their memorable lines and extraordinary metaphors. In Malay, for instance, the similes of the great proverbs are still with us. So are the lines of the famous works, like *Sulalat al-Salatin* and *Hikayat Hang Tuah*. They crystallize brilliant ideas and insights into neat musical compositions for us to take back into our lives. Eventually, the reader/listener measures the robustness of a tongue by these quotable thoughts, their depth and universe, that have been cast in beautiful lines to echo through time.

For me, no language is either superior or inferior to another. Each is a product of an environment, a civilization. For that environment and civilization, its *own* language is the most appropriate and efficient, because it has grown from a special earth and has collected a vocabulary to describe and negotiate its environment, its special situations and people. It is my belief that in Malaysia, all the local languages should be preserved and developed, for they are the wafts and wefts of the texture of our people and their identity. And Malay, the national language, should never be allowed to behave like English.

For a poet or a novelist, there can be no real resistance towards English (if one hopes to bring a transformation from a state of colonisation to real freedom) if he/she does not rebel against the colonial medium and return to the language of the land and the people. However much one is able to include local elements in that borrowed language, it is still a borrowed language. Many have suggested a new kind of English for a new situation in a country. But one has to ask, 'how come our writers are able to master and write in a colonial language, but are not able to understand and write in the national language of their country, when it has been around at least a thousand years before the coming of the colonial one?'

I think, in Malaysia, I am the only one to fully return home to my mother tongue after English. When I began to write more fully in Malay, my colleagues who wrote in that language welcomed me, albeit with some suspicion and doubt. My English poet-colleagues, who had been using me as a reason not to write in the national language, saw me as a threat to their own logic and argument and often accused me of being a deserter to their cause. They called me a 'chauvinist' for using my mother tongue – the national language. And the attacks have been continuing to this day. Of course, I had names for them, too. However, I must say that they have the right to English, but not to the point of demanding that it be the national language or the language of educational instruction and official communication.

I could have been an international poet in English; but now, I am, I think, an international poet, too, but in Malay. I also translate Malaysian poems into English and, from time to time, some of my own. Many publishers and anthologists recognize that not all poets write in English. There are many other languages that are as poetic as English, if not more so. Arabic, Bengali, Japanese, Mandarin and Persian are wonderfully melodious in their expressions, as are also Javanese, Hawaiian, Samoan and Māori. These are the languages of Mahmoud Darwish, Rabindranth Tagore, Po Chu-i and Jalaluddin Rumi and the many significant, but anonymous works of Southeast Asia and Polynesia.

Because they are beautiful, because they are unique and because they contribute to the intellectual treasury of humankind, we must protect them, use them and develop them or they will be run over by English. After some years, there would not be much to resuscitate or even to remember. We must fight so that we do not forget, fight so that we do not betray.

I must say that I sleep easier for not being a betrayer of the language of my forebears and of the heritage that they have bequeathed me and which it is my responsibility to prolong, especially in this millennium, when commercial and cultural globalisation engulfs everything and leaves everybody as a poor factory copy of another, without enough real identity and uniqueness. During these 40 years, my poetic language has matured, I think, and it has found its sounds for the new millennium. I have possibly helped put some good lines into the language. I have added some metaphors and brought them along with me throughout the world on my travels, to conferences and also during my various acts of writing or readings to Malaysian and international audiences.

I am always aware that English has plundered and destroyed many languages in its long history and that ours may be the next. As English rampages throughout the world, through the vocabularies and the media of many nations, I will continue to write my poems in my own wonderful mother tongue and national language and contribute my little bit to develop it and refine it so that it can stand tall in the world of great languages.

References

Canagarajah, A.S. (1999) *Resisting Linguistic Imperialism in English Teaching*. Oxford: Oxford University Press.

Nobel Prize. Facts on the Nobel Prize in Literature. Online webpage, accessed 15 July 2011. http://nobelprize.org/nobel_prizes/literature/shortfacts.html

Salleh, M.H. (2006) *Romance and Laughter in the Archipelago*. Penang: Universiti Sains Malaysia Press.

Thiong'o, Ngũgĩ wa (1986) *Decolonising the Mind: The Politics of Language in African Literature*. London: James Currey; Nairobi: Heinemann Kenya.

For Product Safety Concerns and Information please contact our EU Authorised Representative:

Easy Access System Europe

Mustamäe tee 50

10621 Tallinn

Estonia

gpsr.requests@easproject.com